HARDWARE
GROCERY

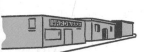

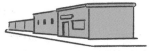

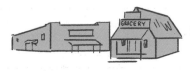

PUBLISHED BY KOYAMA PRESS
koyamapress.com
FIRST EDITION: SEPTEMBER 2018
ISBN: 978-1-927668-62-7
PRINTED IN CHINA

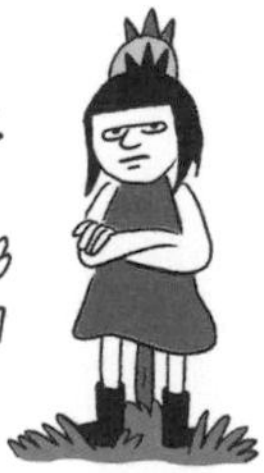

A HOUSE IN THE JUNGLE

NATHAN GELGUD

KOYAMA PRESS

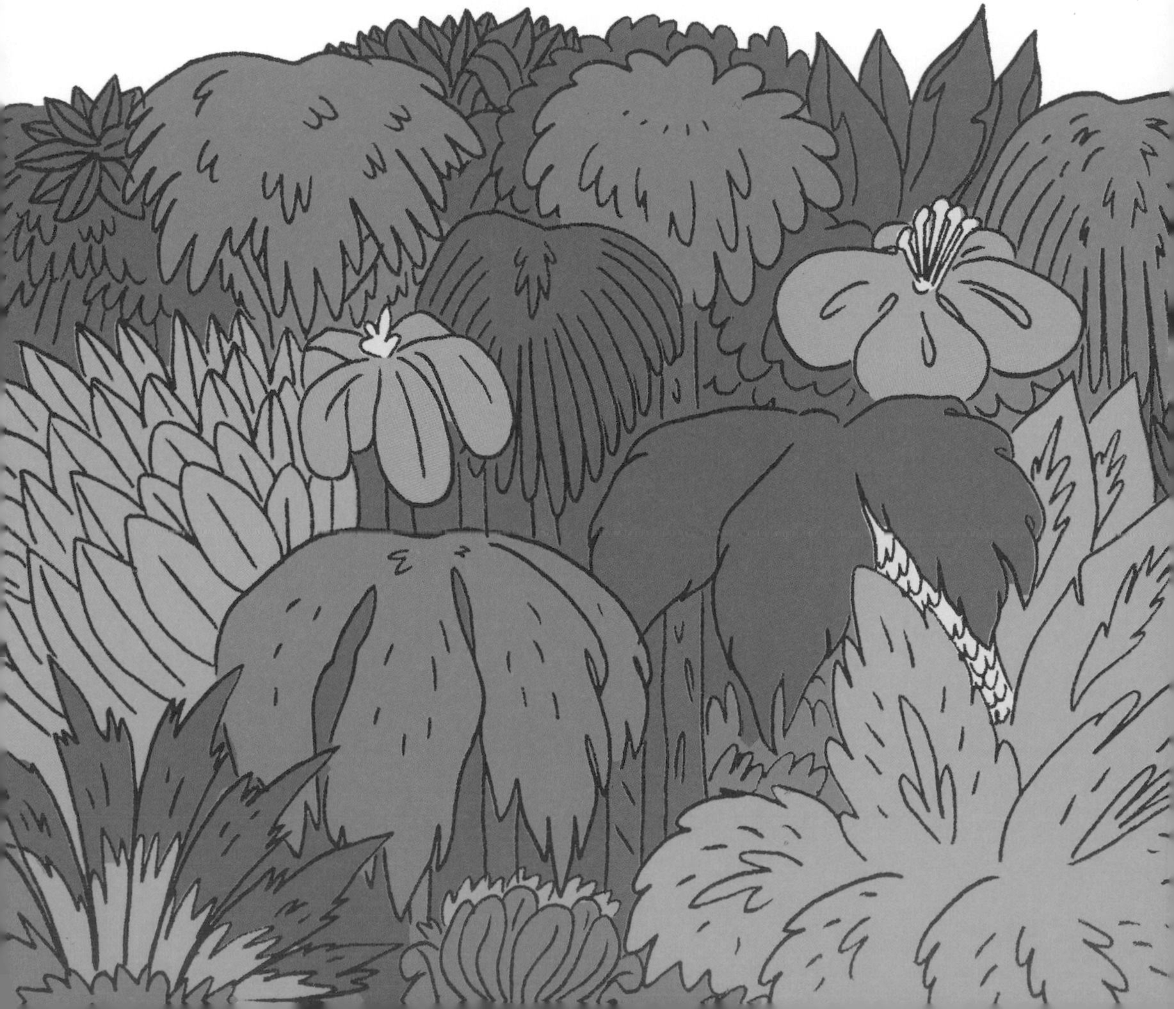

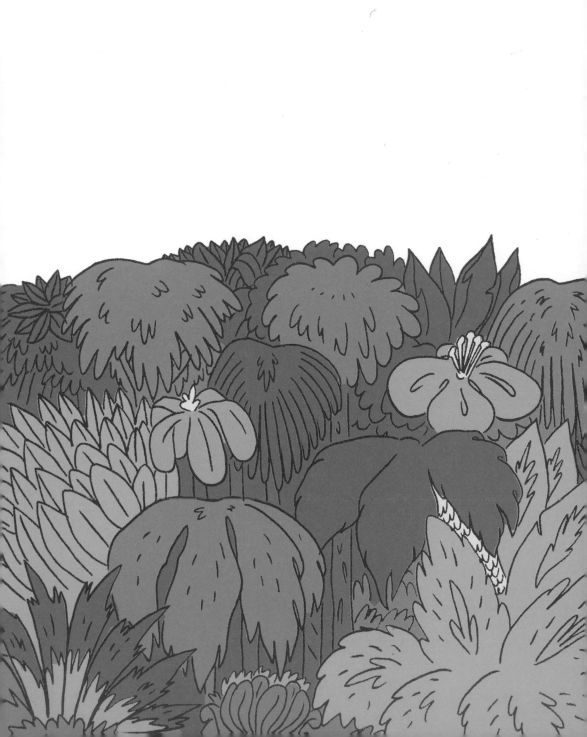

DEDICATED TO JOLIE

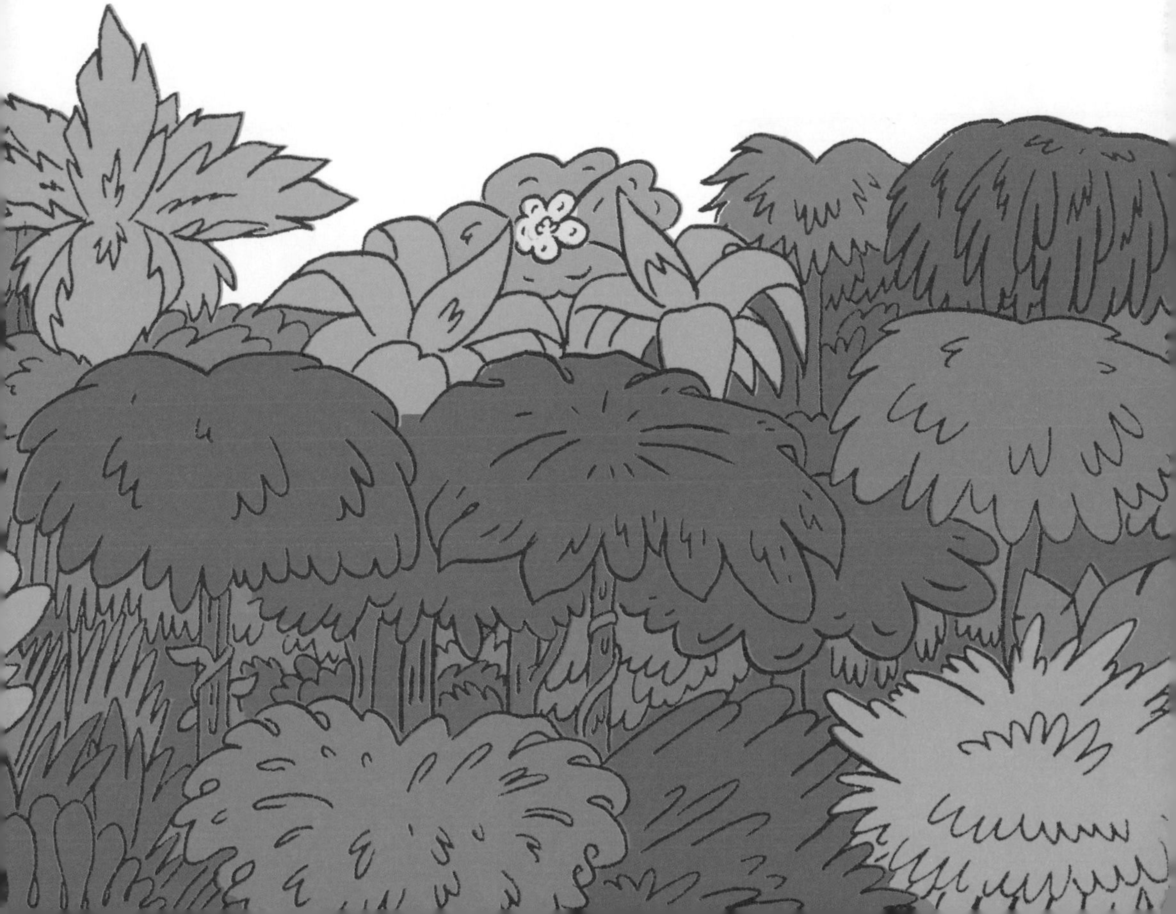

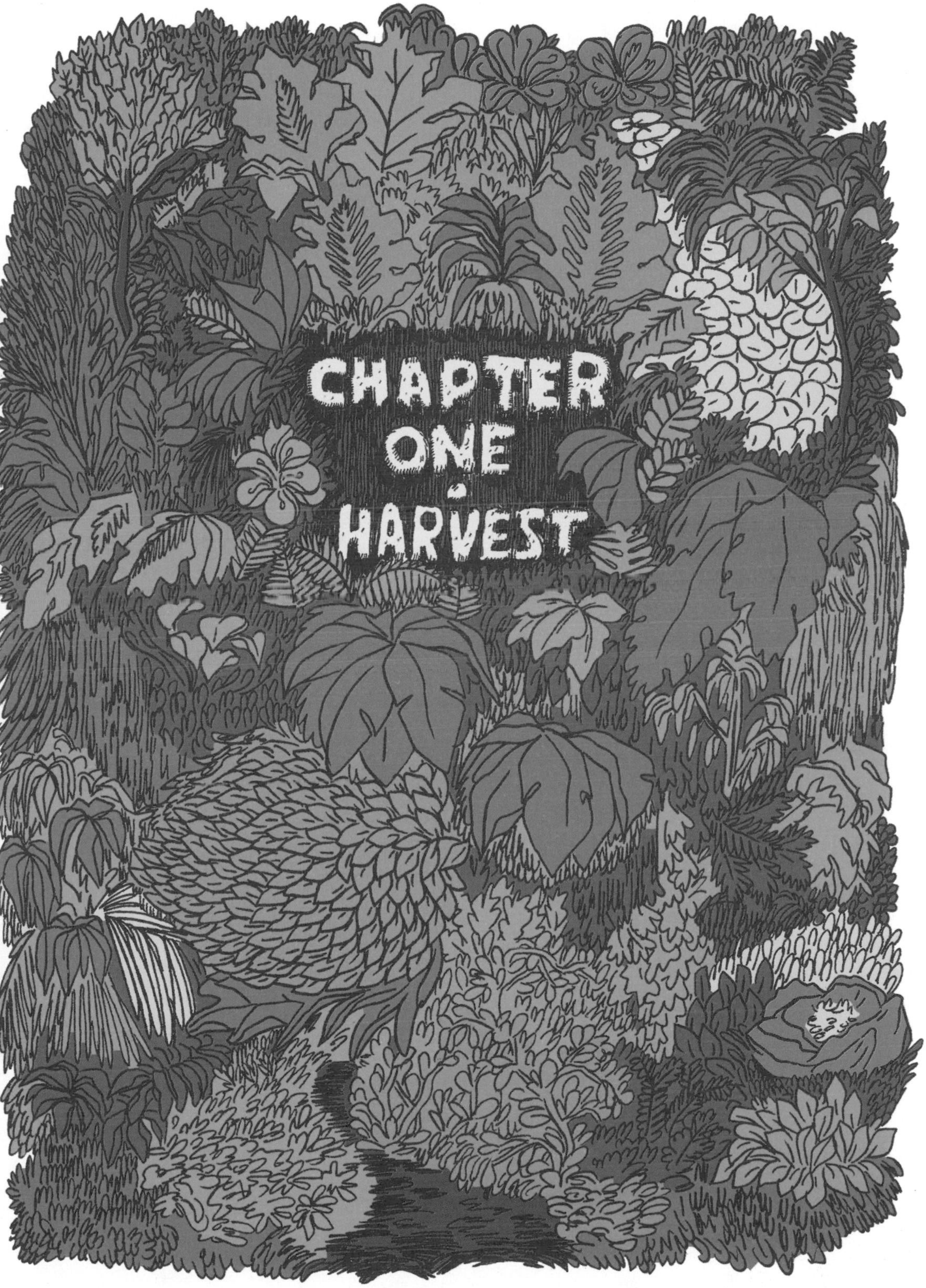
CHAPTER
ONE
HARVEST

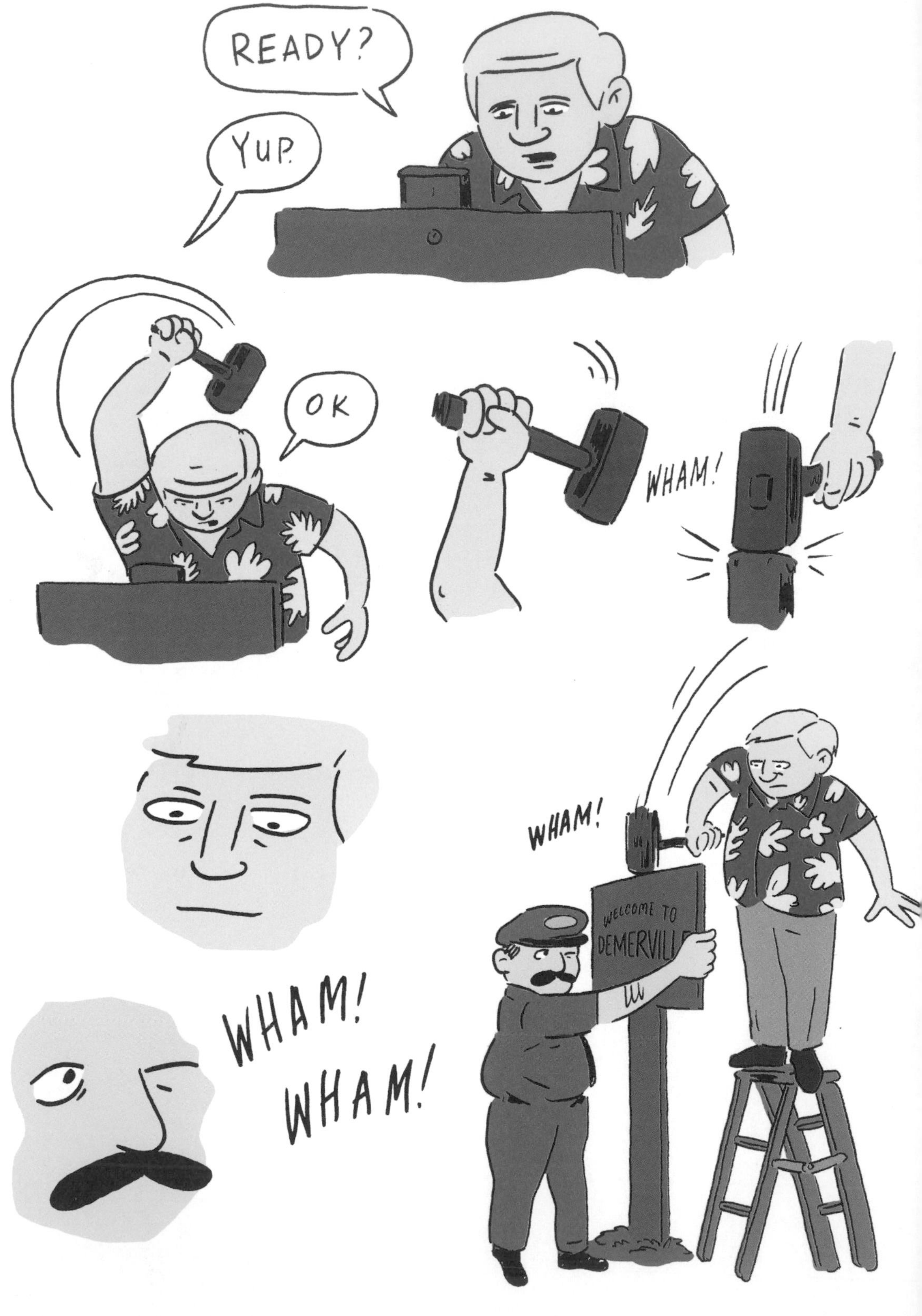
READY?
YUP.
OK
WHAM!
WHAM!
WELCOME TO
DEMERVILL
WHAM!
WHAM!

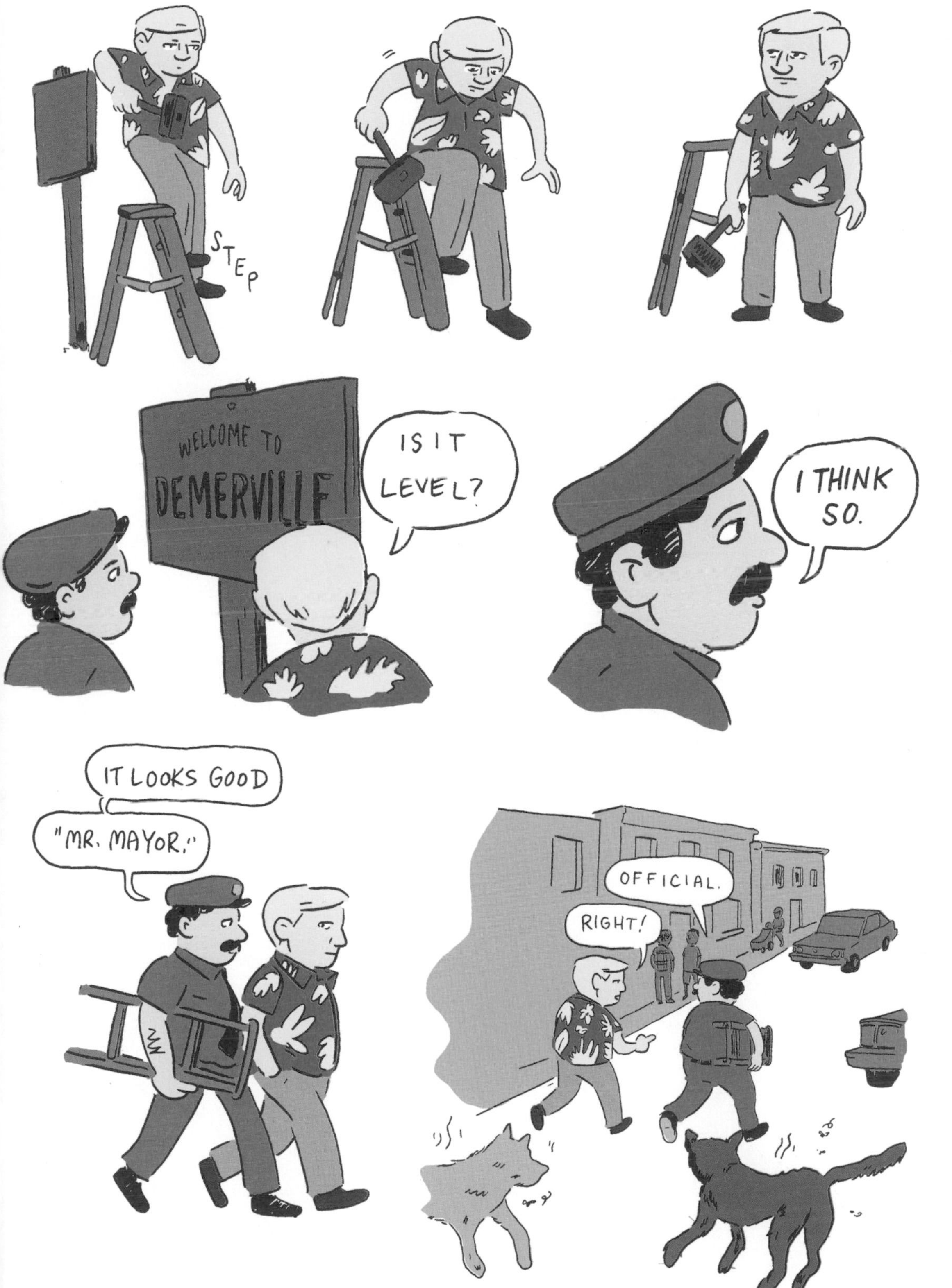
STEP
WELCOME TO
DEMERVILLE
IS IT LEVEL?
I THINK SO.
IT LOOKS GOOD
"MR. MAYOR."
RIGHT!
OFFICIAL.

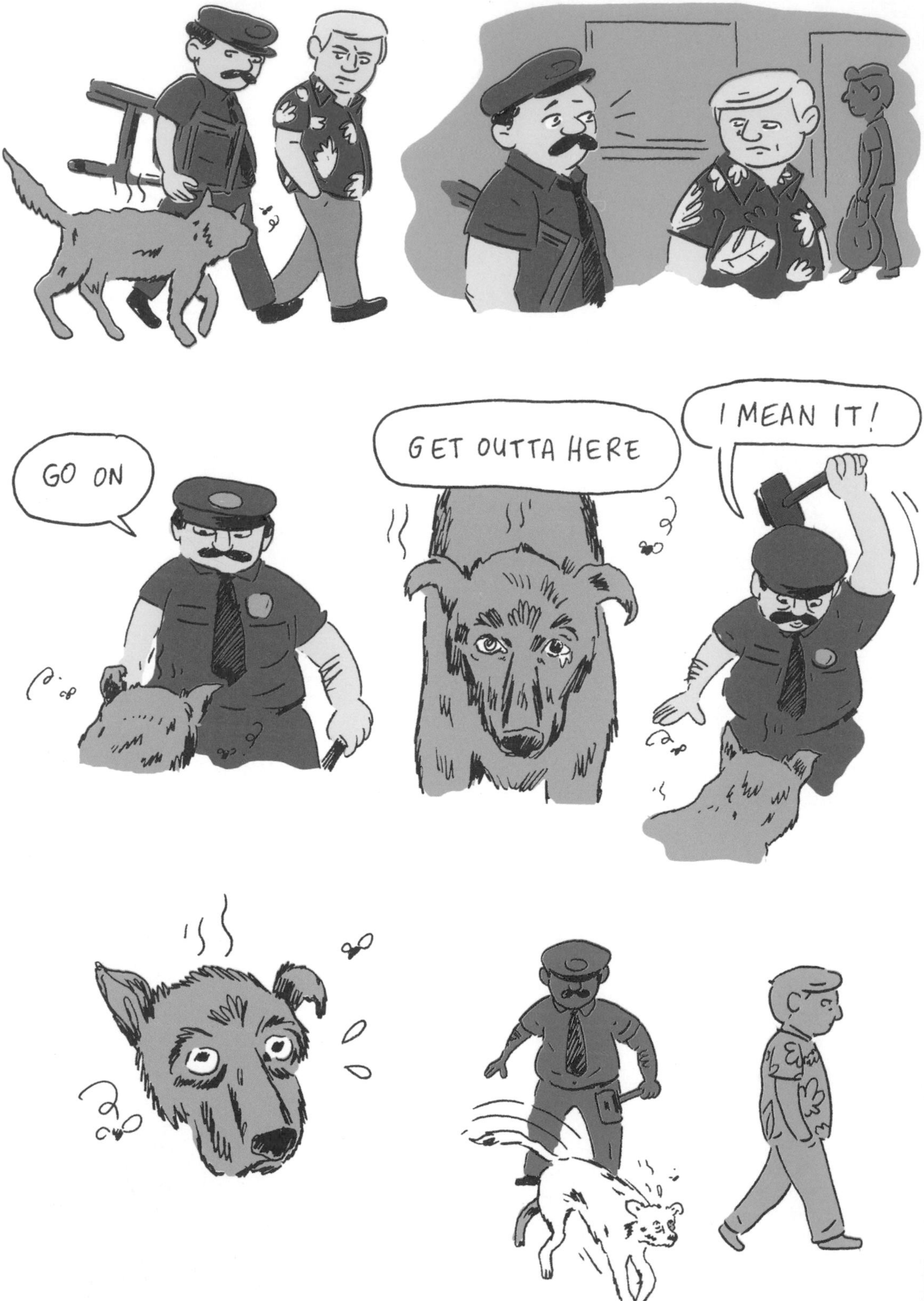
GO ON
GET OUTTA HERE
I MEAN IT!

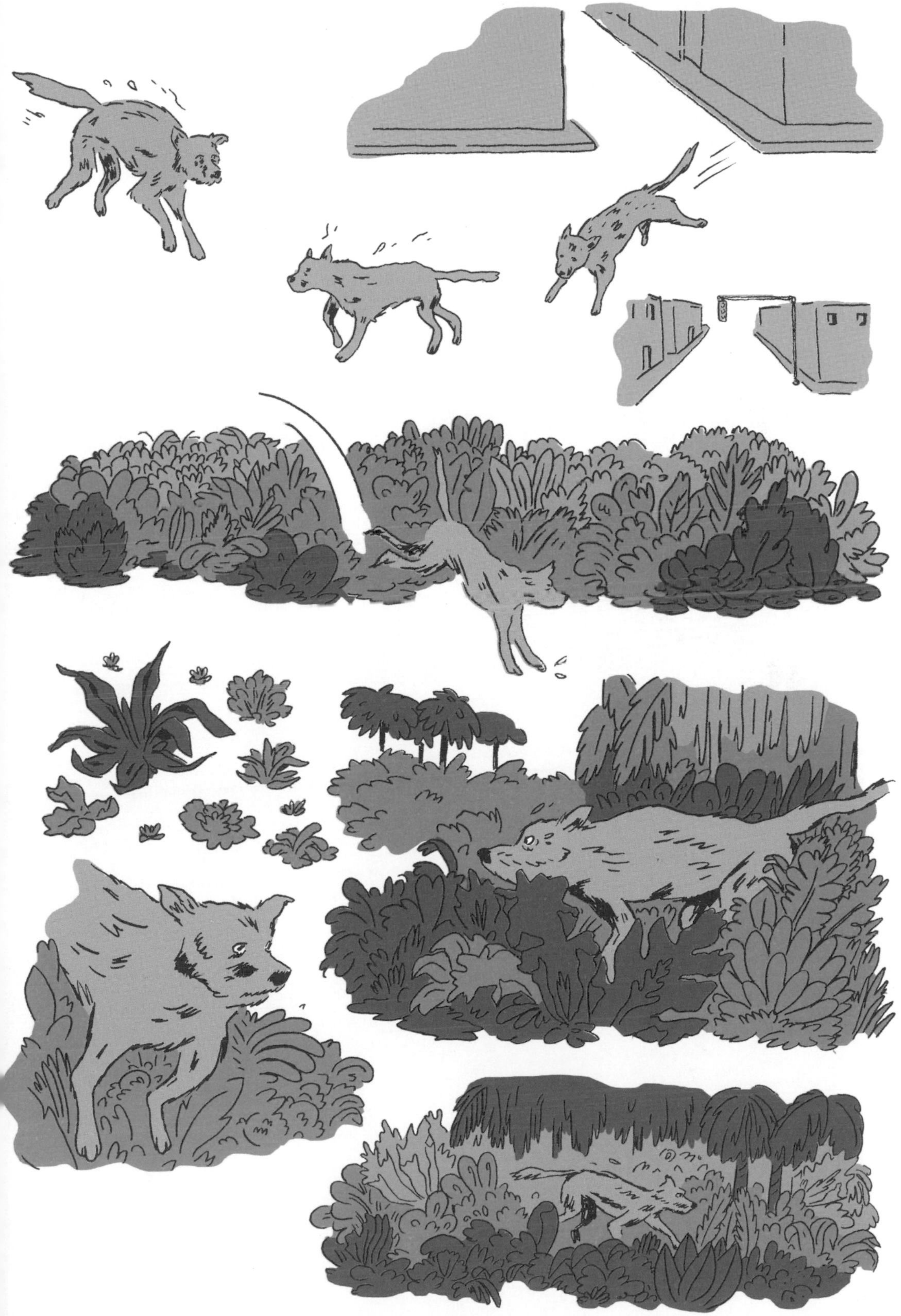

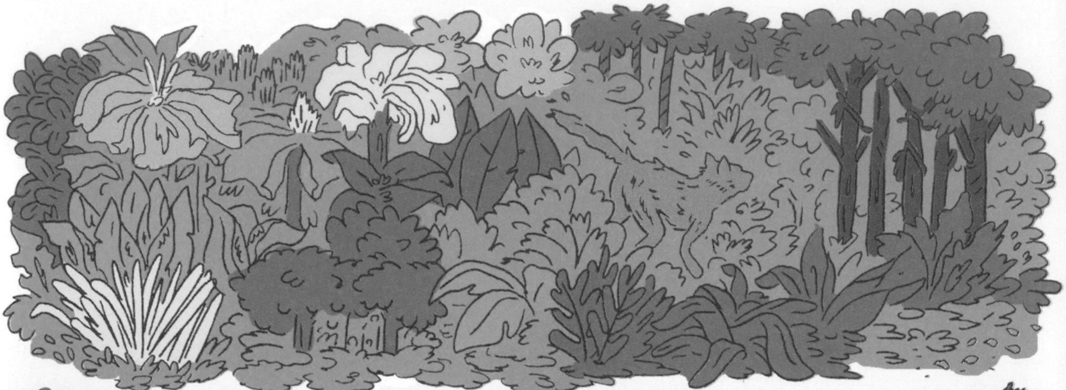
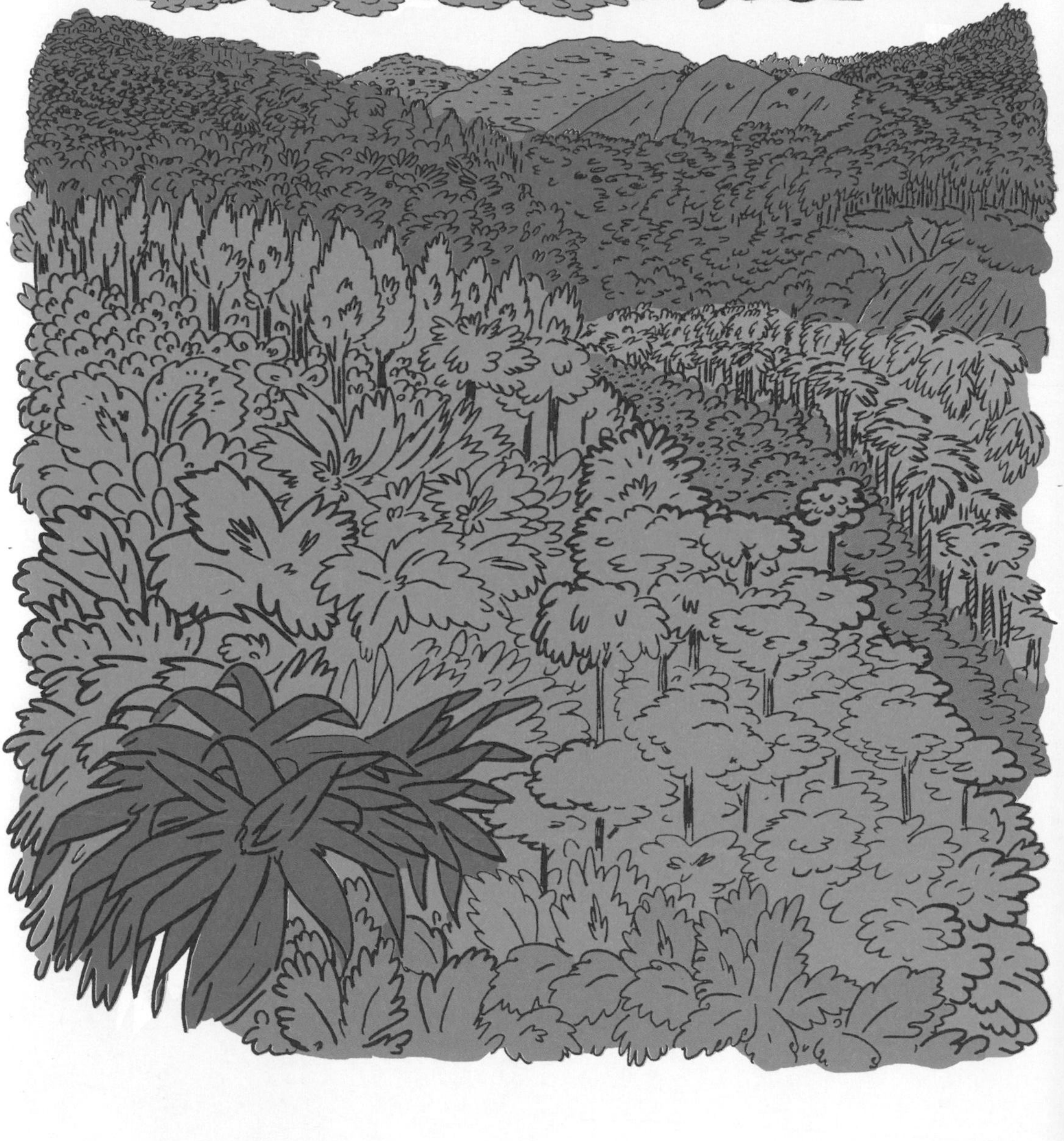

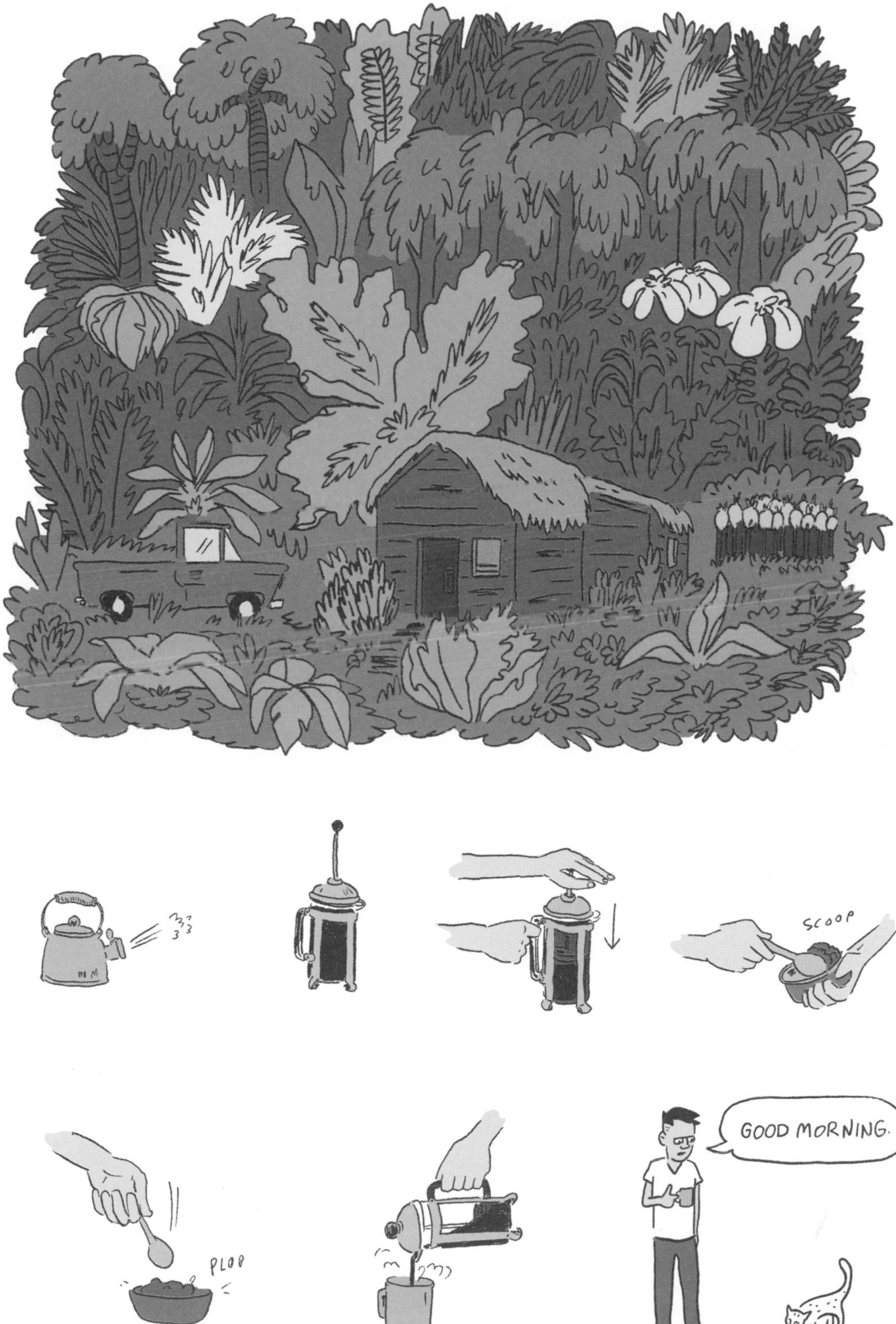
SCOOP
PLOP
GOOD MORNING.

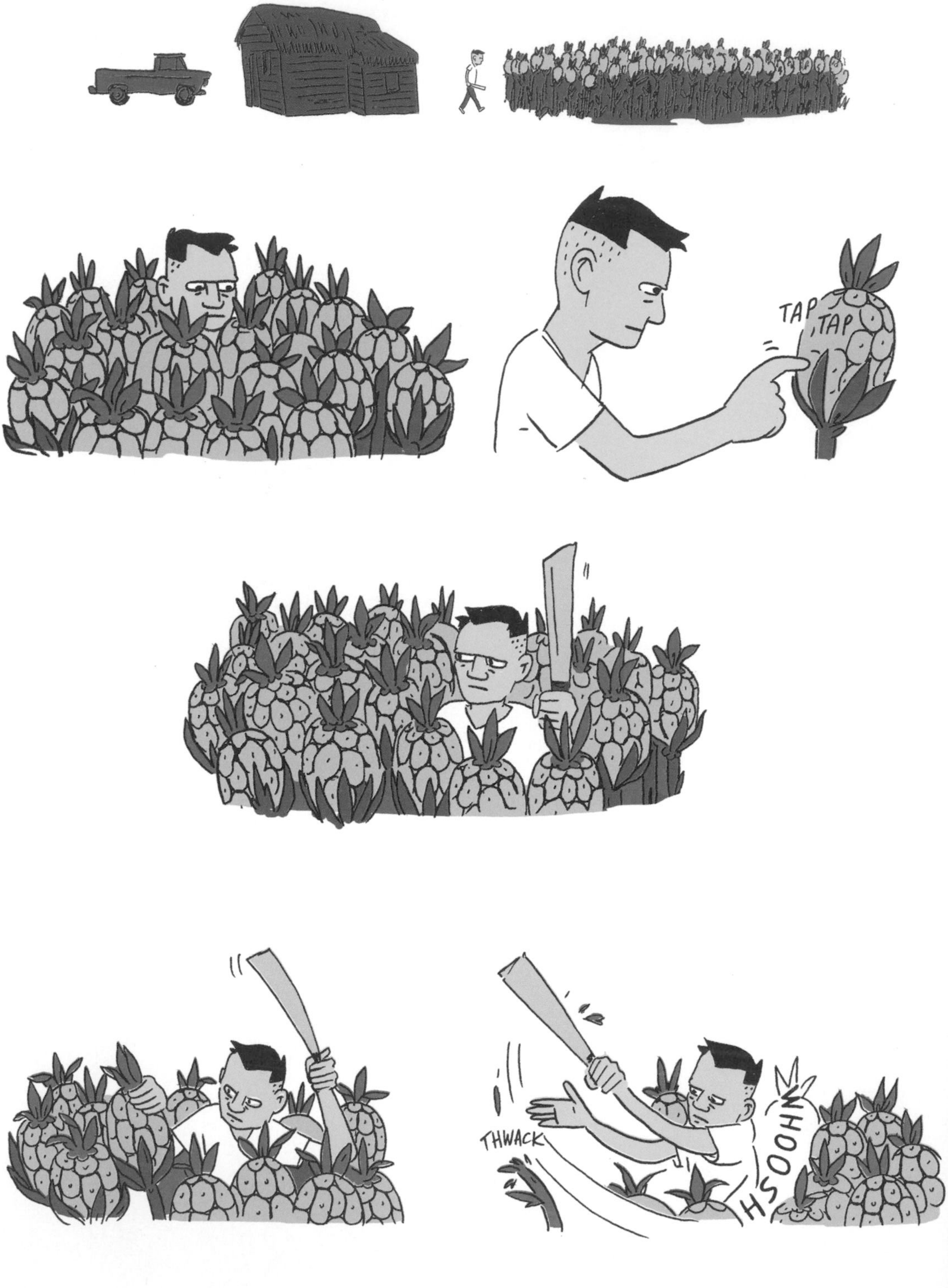
TAP
TAP
THWACK
WHOOSH

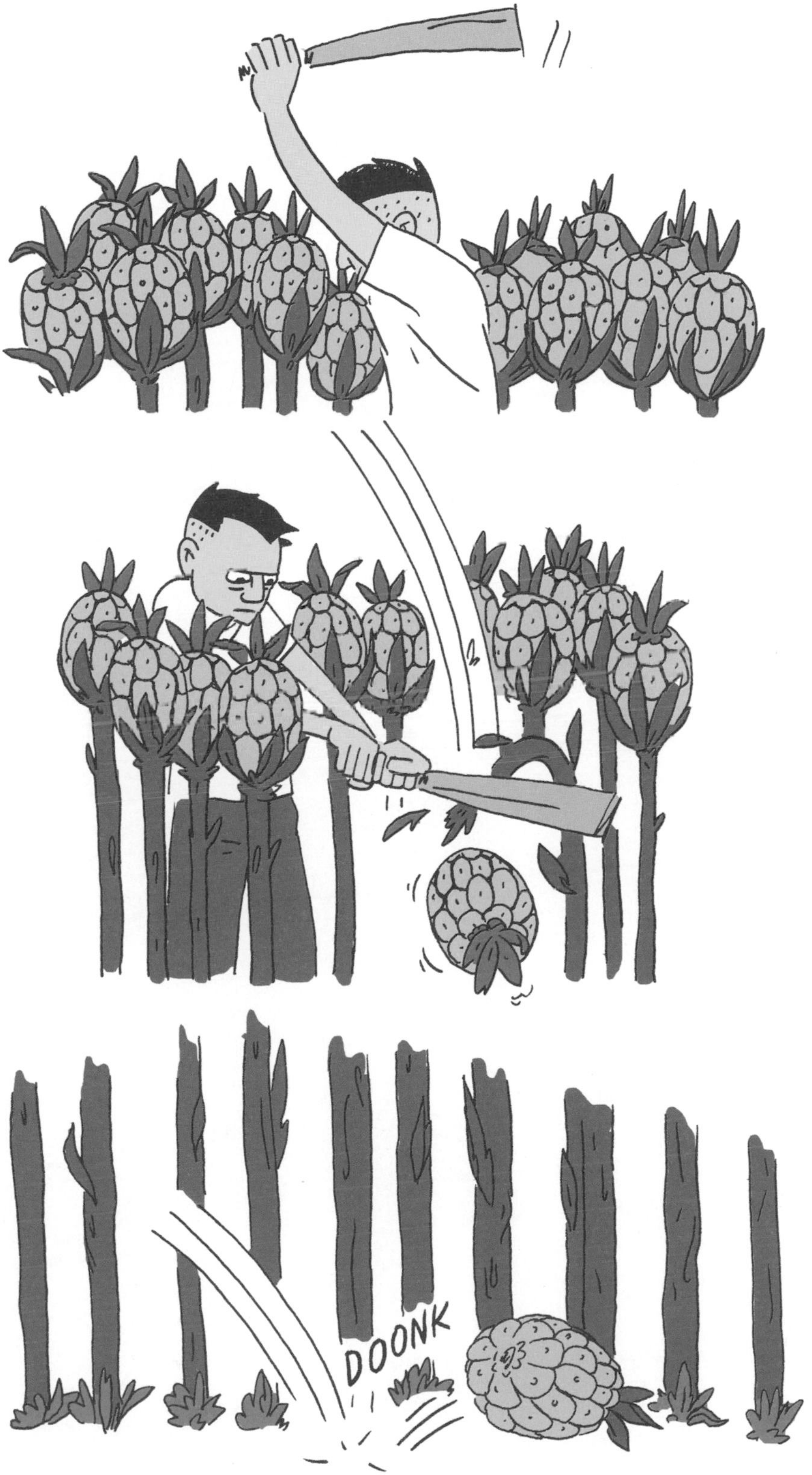
DOONK

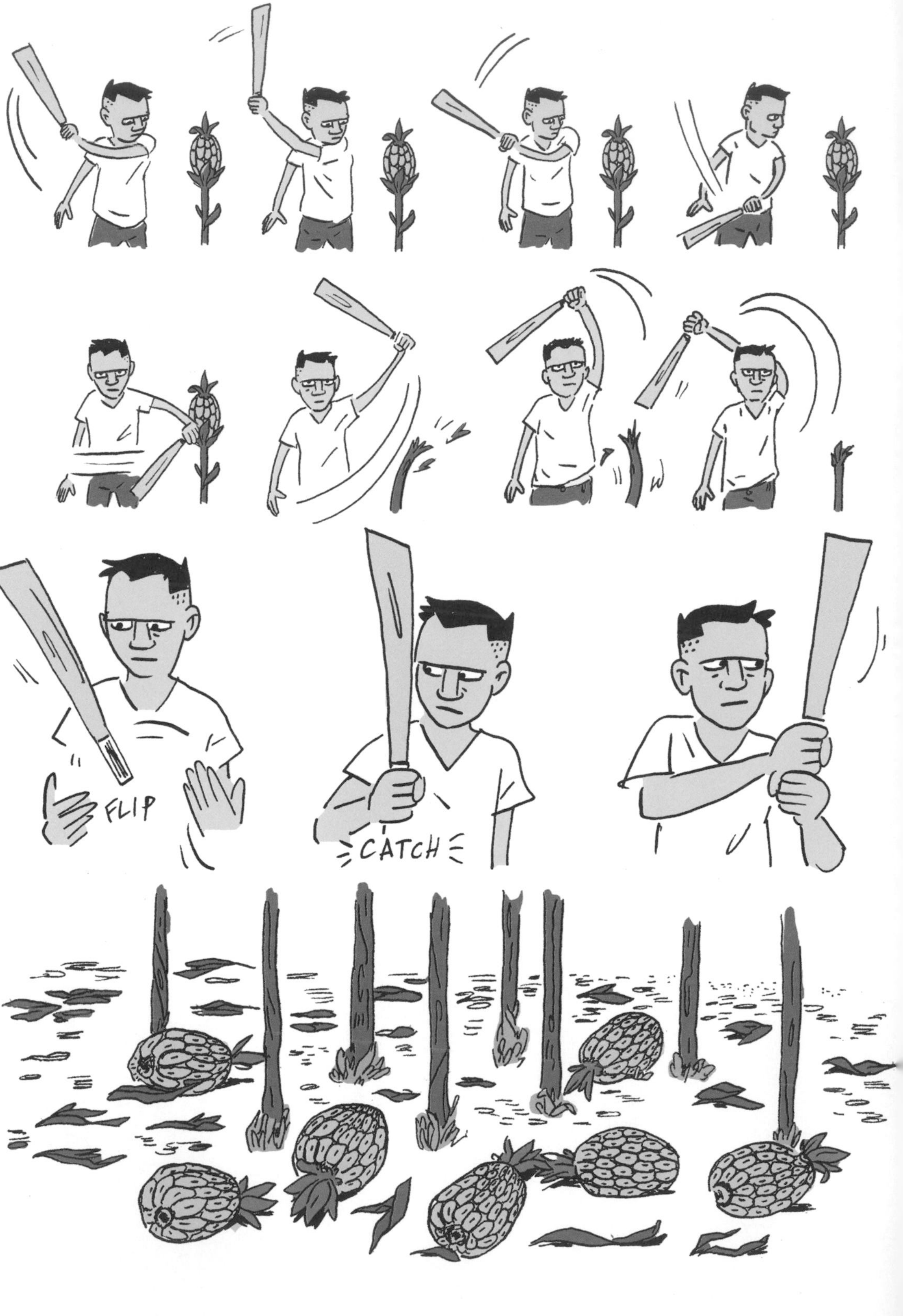
FLIP
CATCH

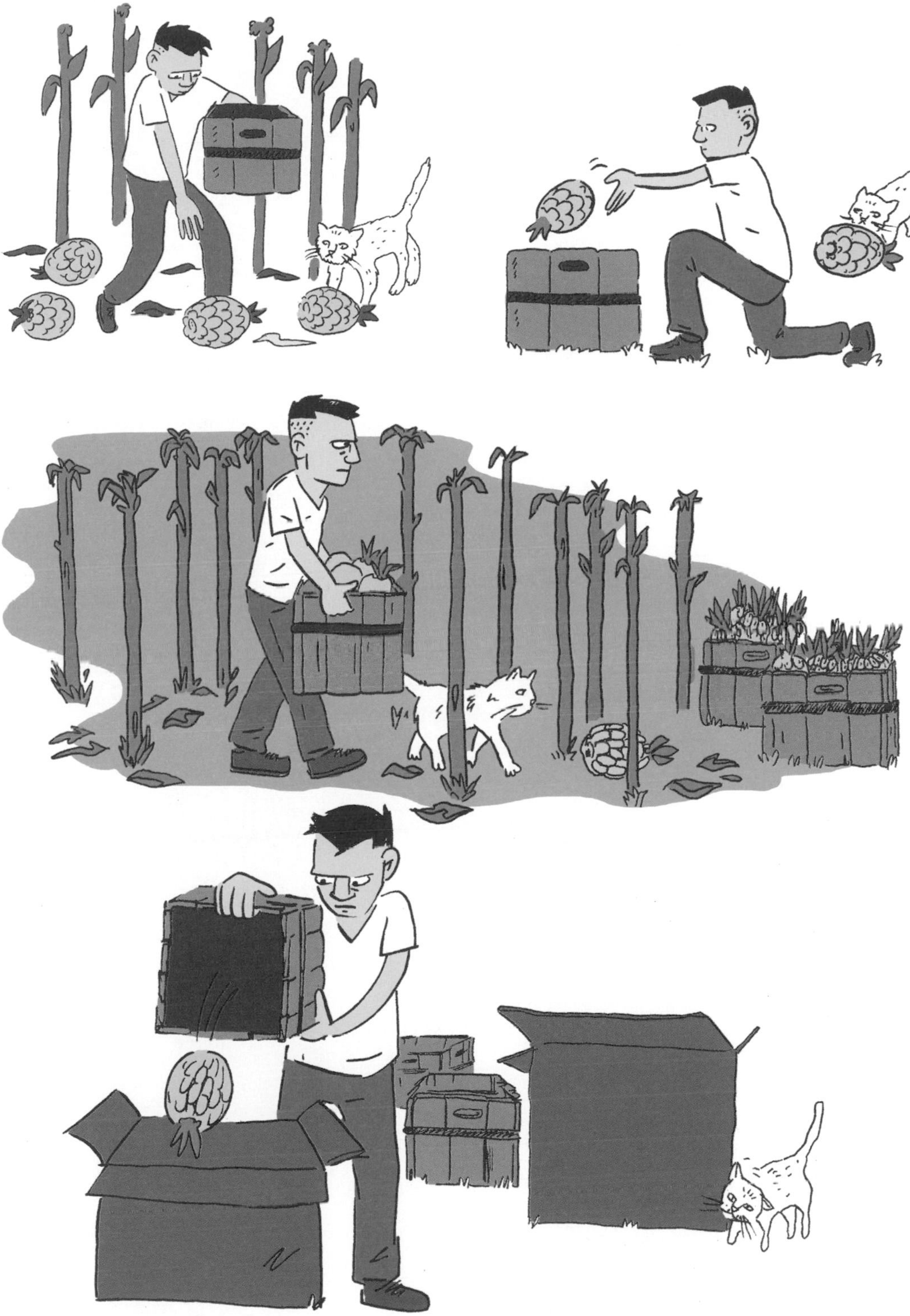

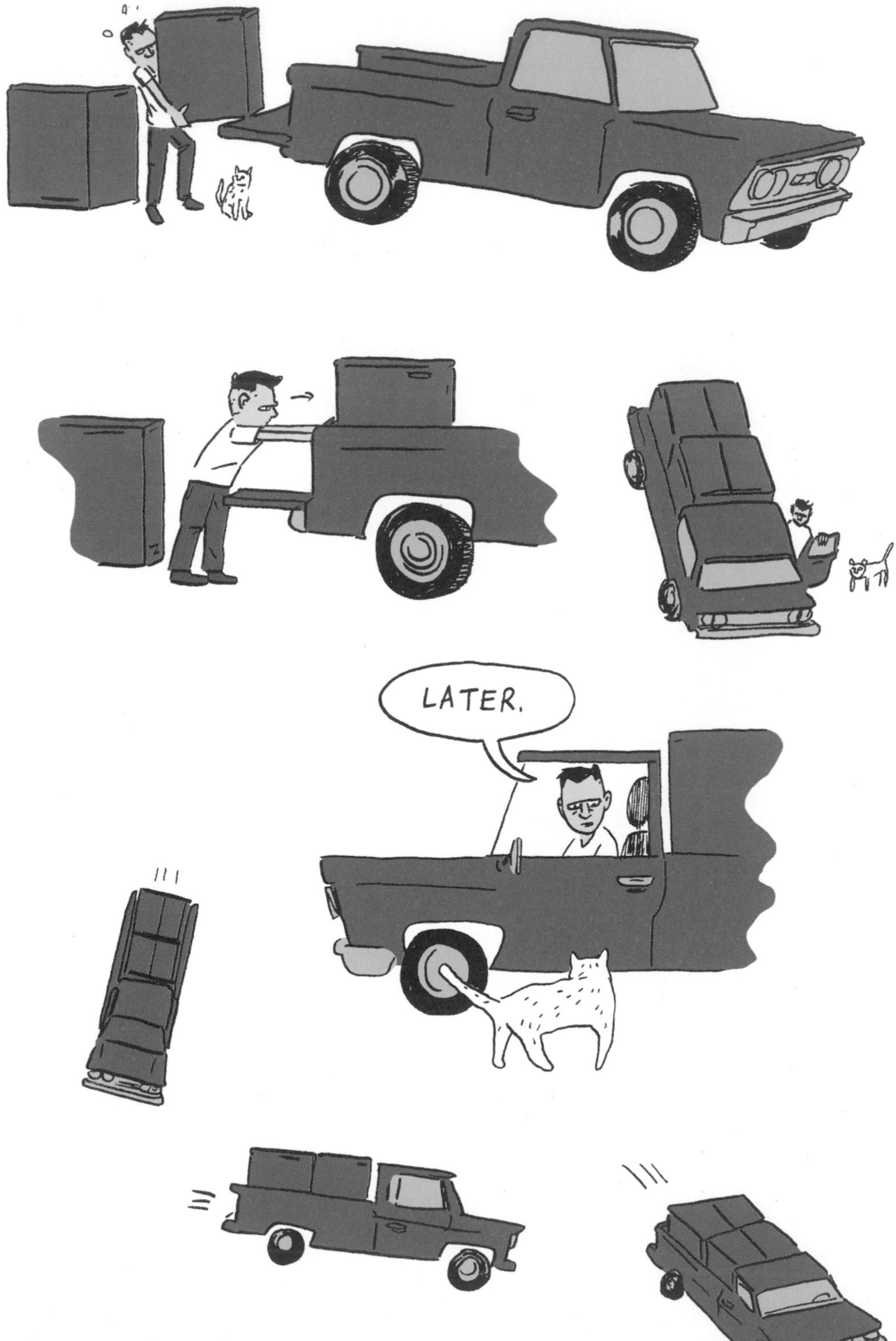
LATER.

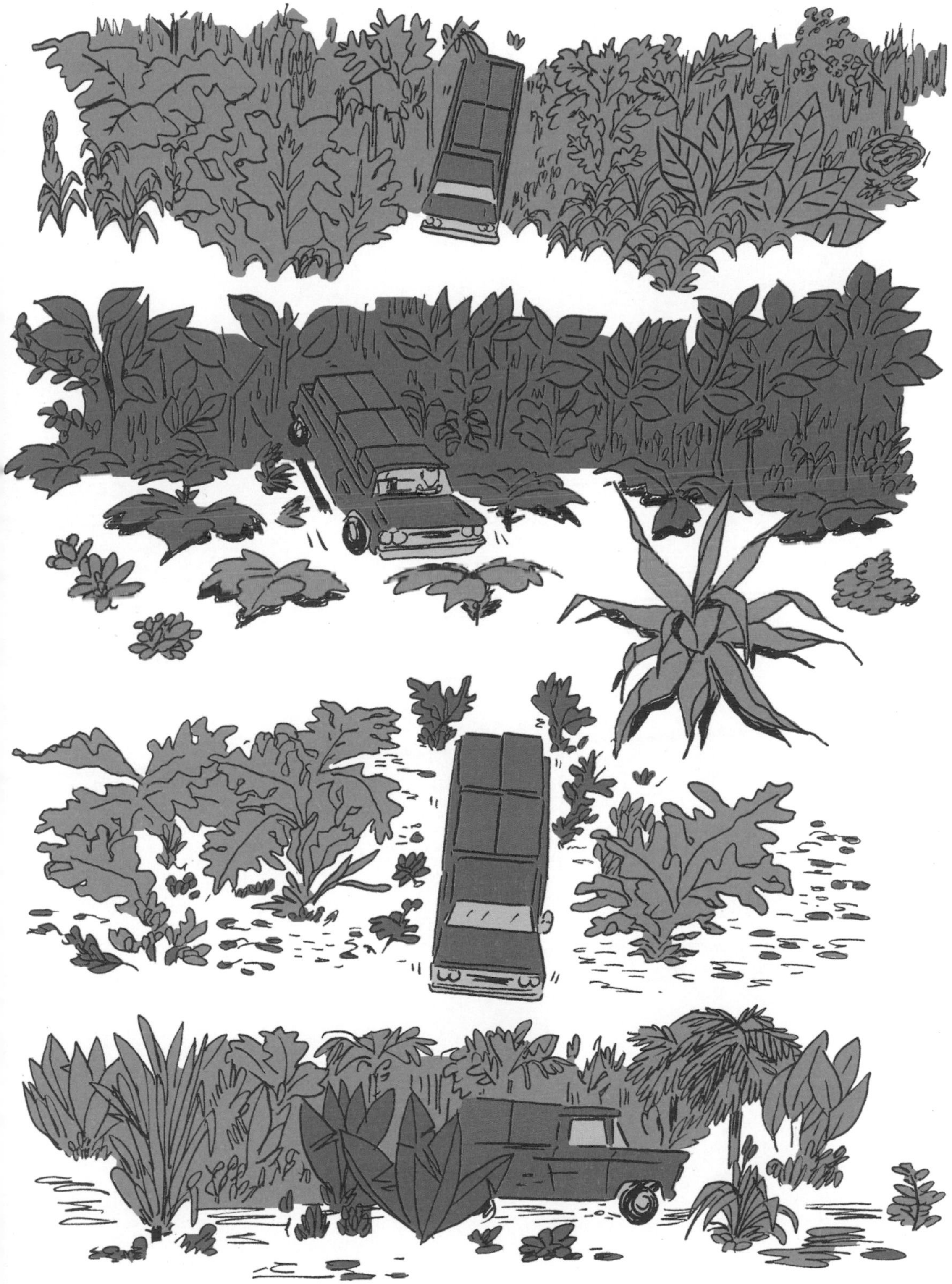

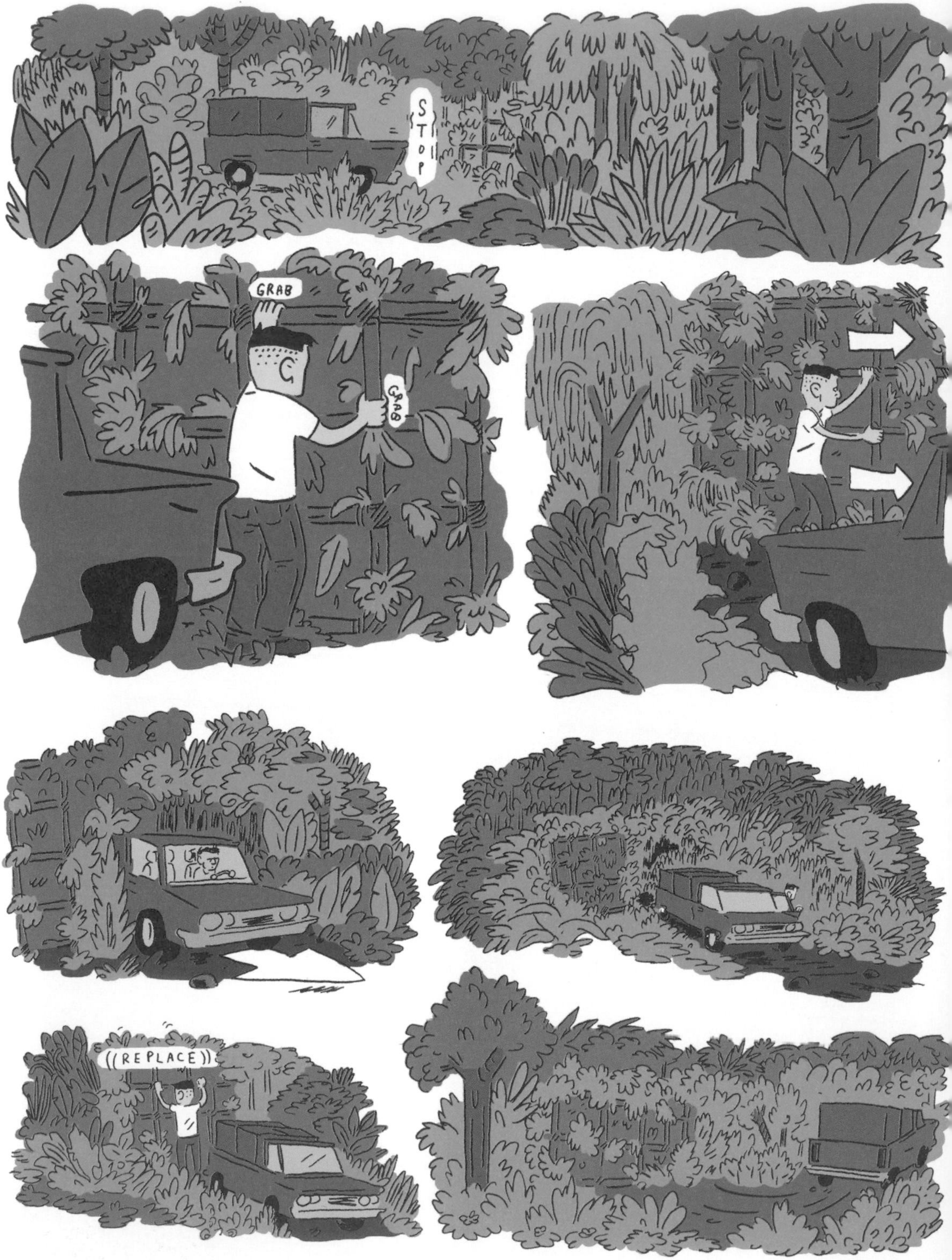
STOP
GRAB
GRAB
((REPLACE))

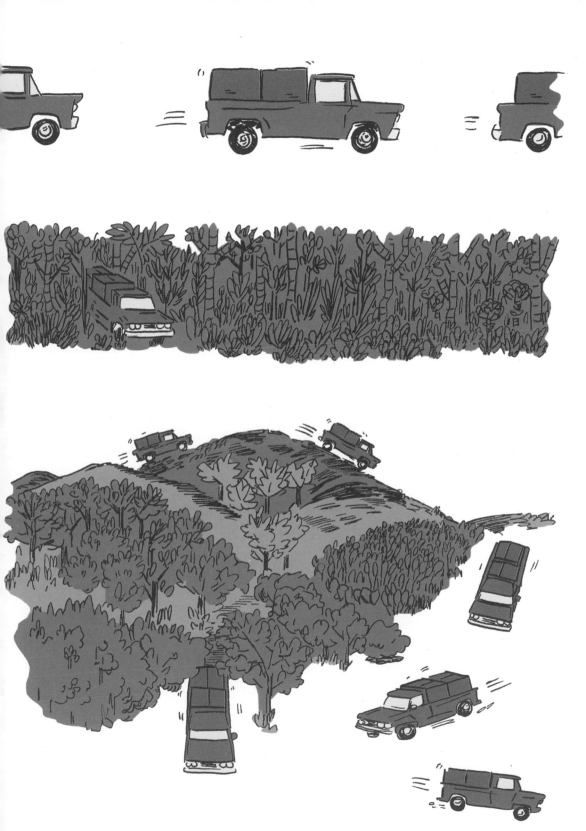

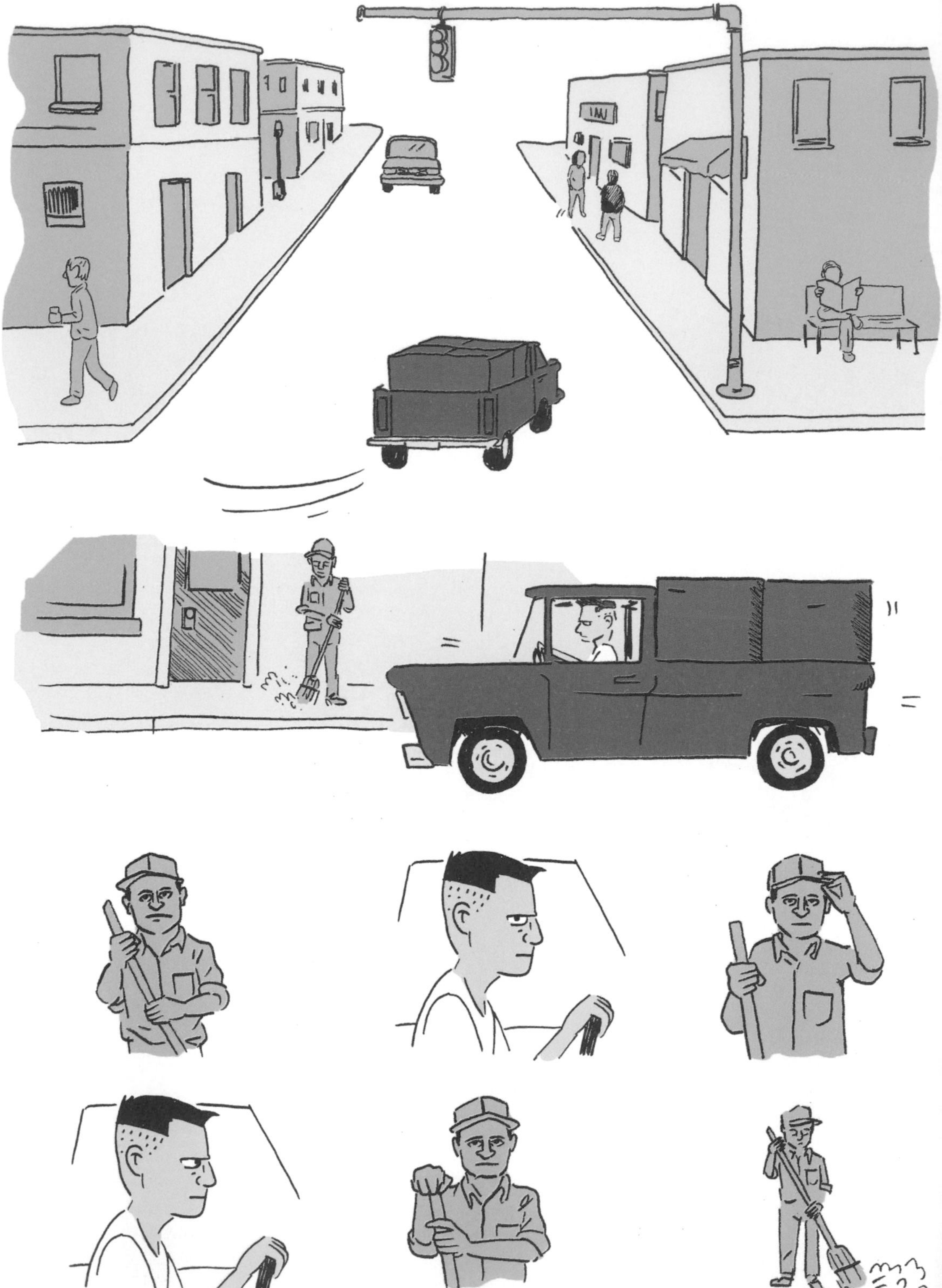

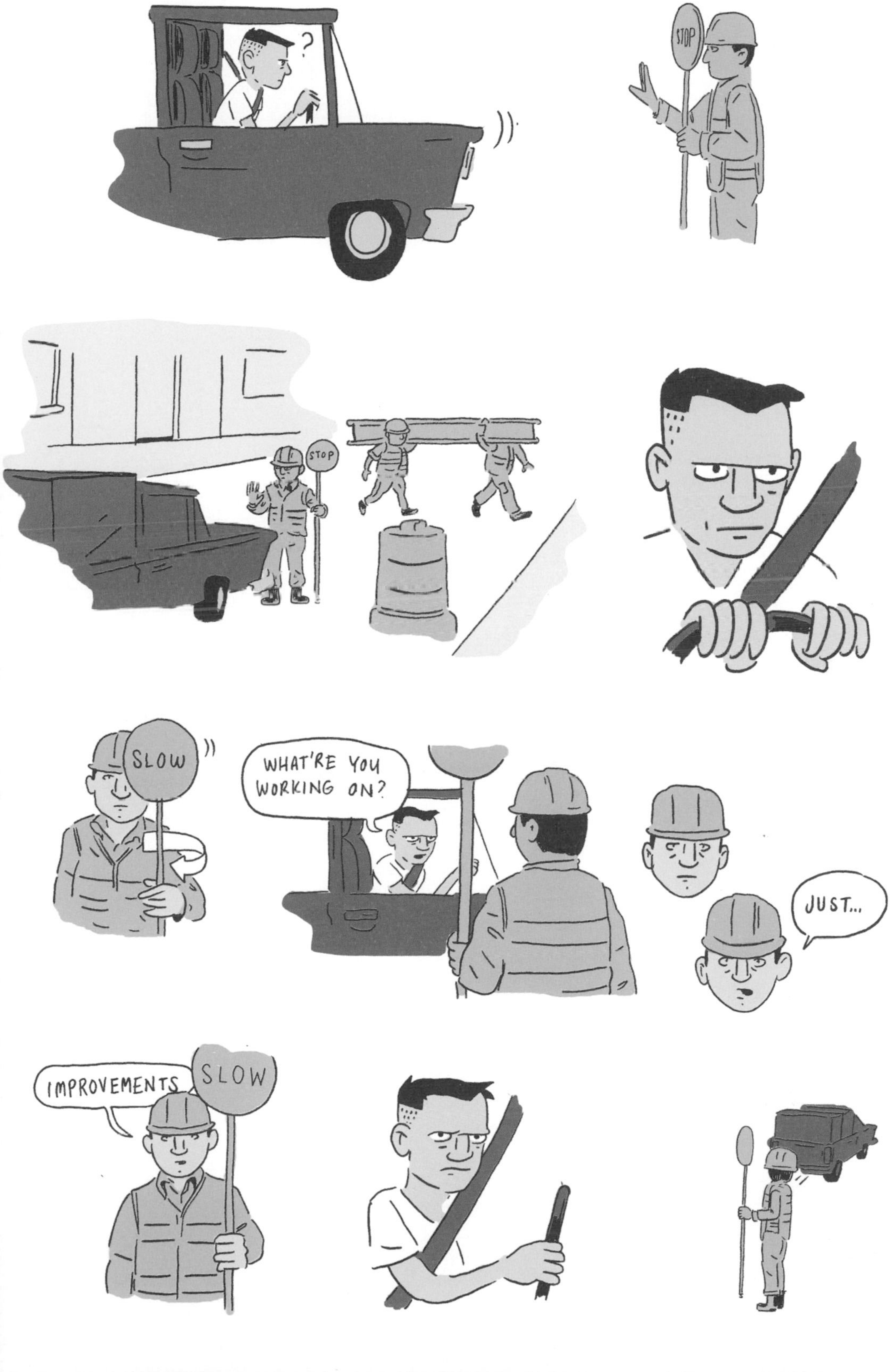
?
STOP
STOP
SLOW
WHAT'RE YOU WORKING ON?
JUST...
IMPROVEMENTS
SLOW

WHAT'S IN THE BOXES?

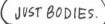

JUST BODIES.

HM. MUST BE CHILDREN TO FIT IN THERE.

NO. THEY'RE ADULTS.

JUST CUT IN HALF.

RIGHT. GUESS YOU COULD FIT A BODY IN THERE IF IT WAS CUT IN HALF.

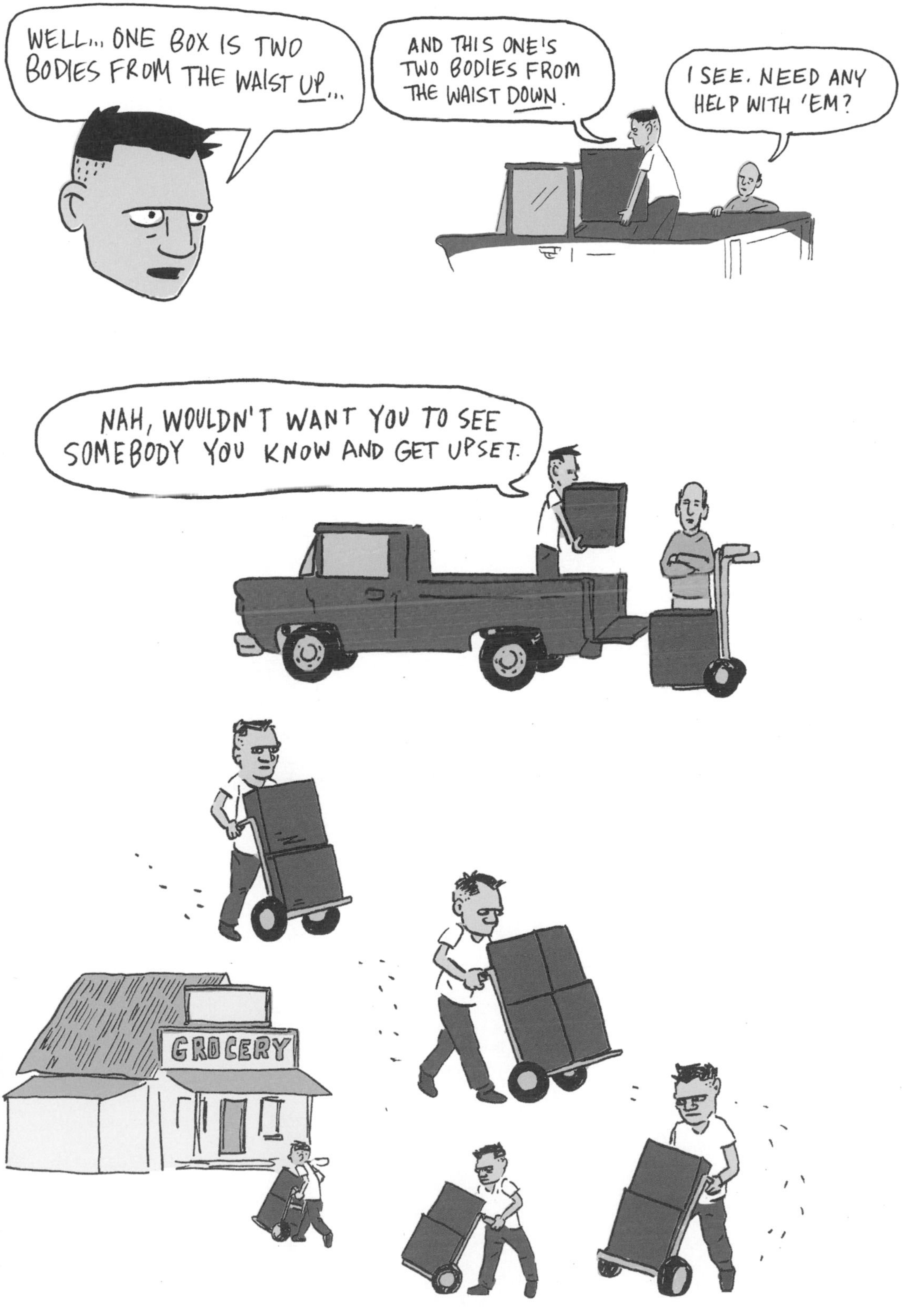
WELL... ONE BOX IS TWO BODIES FROM THE WAIST UP...
AND THIS ONE'S TWO BODIES FROM THE WAIST DOWN.
I SEE. NEED ANY HELP WITH 'EM?
NAH, WOULDN'T WANT YOU TO SEE SOMEBODY YOU KNOW AND GET UPSET.
GROCERY

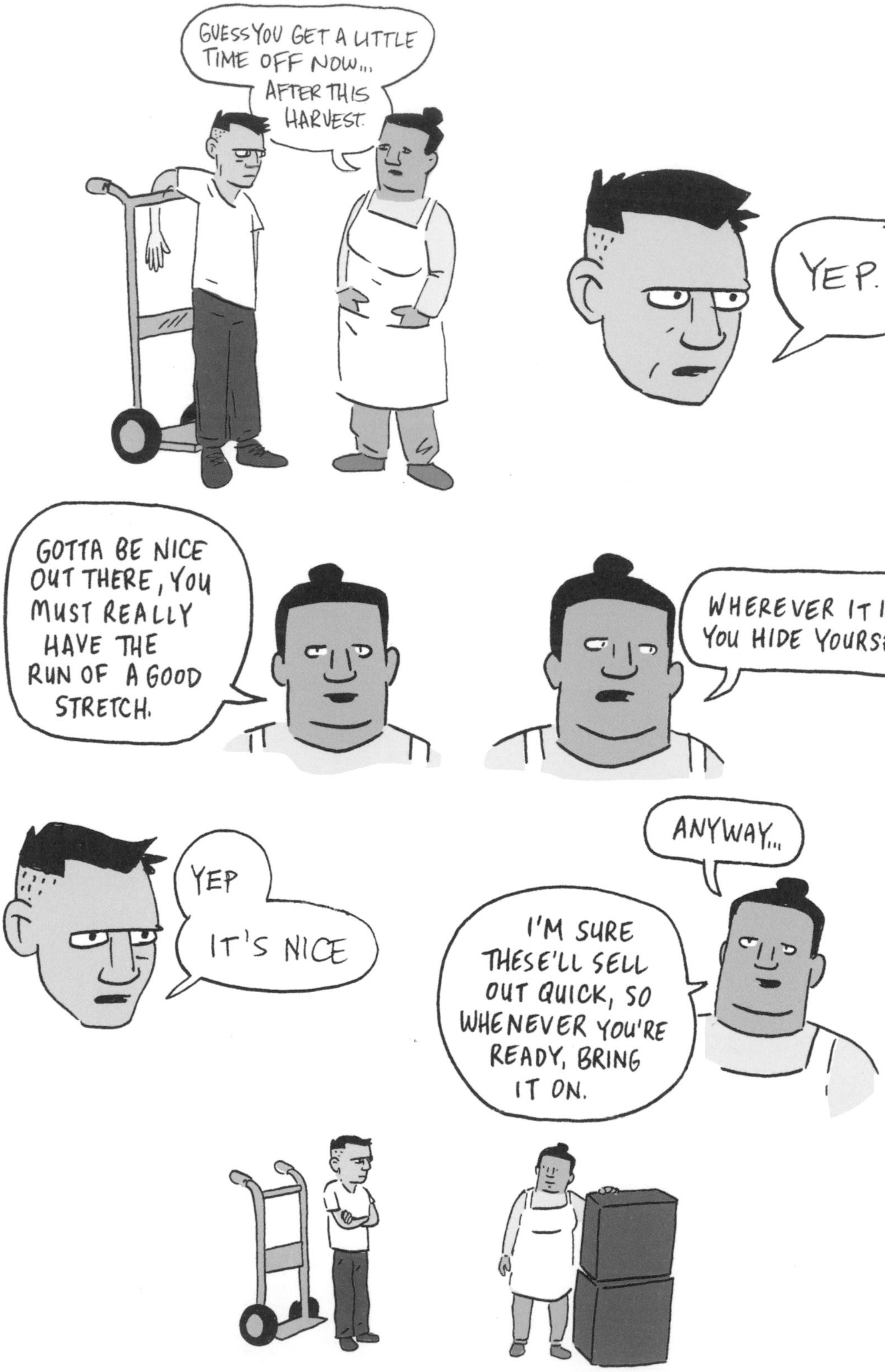
GUESS YOU GET A LITTLE TIME OFF NOW... AFTER THIS HARVEST.
YEP.
GOTTA BE NICE OUT THERE, YOU MUST REALLY HAVE THE RUN OF A GOOD STRETCH.
WHEREVER IT IS YOU HIDE YOURSELF.
YEP
IT'S NICE
ANYWAY...
I'M SURE THESE'LL SELL OUT QUICK, SO WHENEVER YOU'RE READY, BRING IT ON.

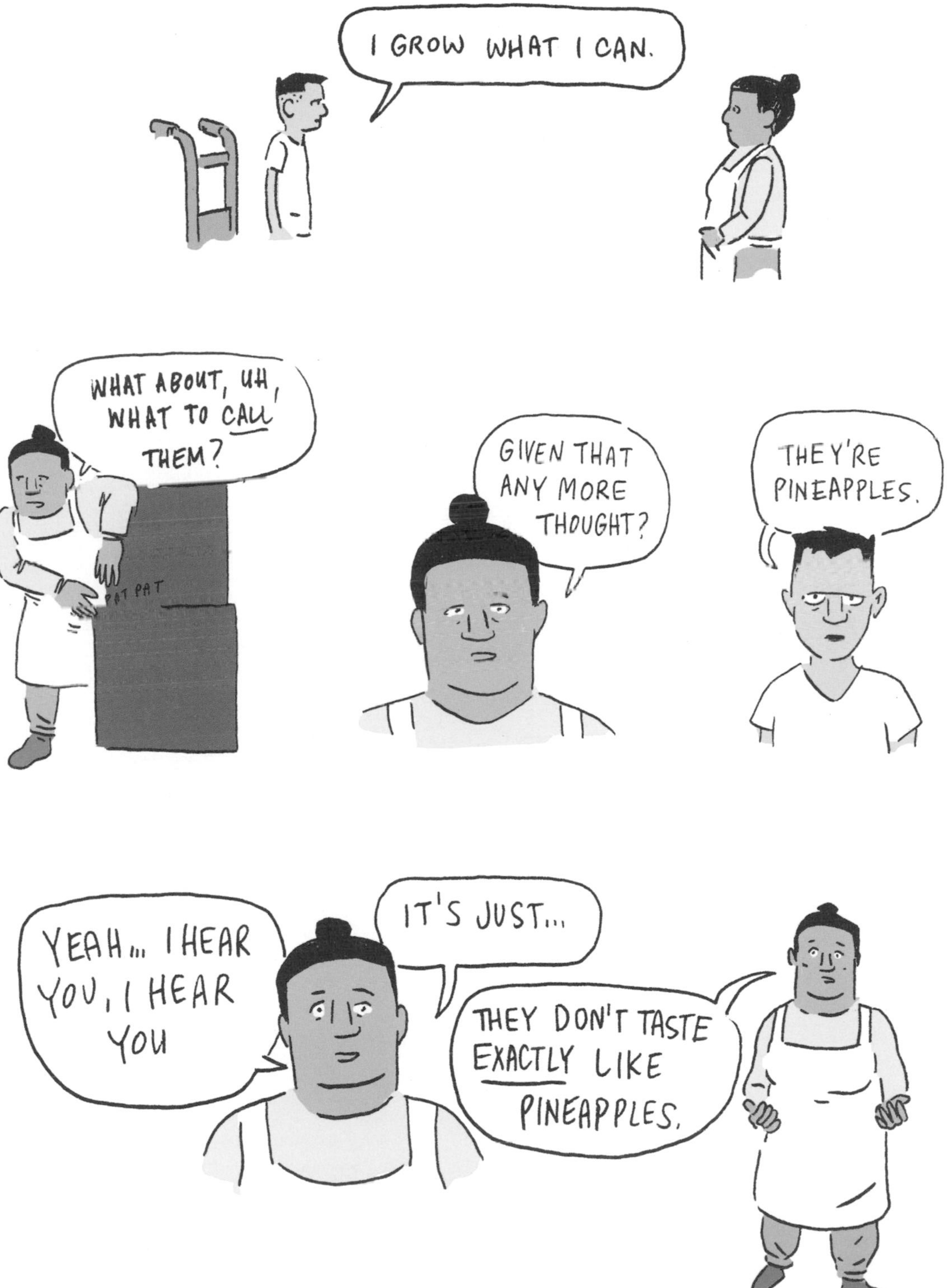
I GROW WHAT I CAN.
WHAT ABOUT, UH, WHAT TO CALL THEM?
PAT PAT
GIVEN THAT ANY MORE THOUGHT?
THEY'RE PINEAPPLES.
YEAH... I HEAR YOU, I HEAR YOU
IT'S JUST...
THEY DON'T TASTE EXACTLY LIKE PINEAPPLES.

AND IF I WERE TO STOCK REGULAR PINEAPPLES, PEOPLE WOULD NOTICE

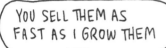

YOU SELL THEM AS FAST AS I GROW THEM

RIGHT?

RIGHT, RIGHT

SO WHY DO THEY NEED SOME CUTE NAME?

NO, NO

IT WOULDN'T HAVE TO BE CUTE

JUST...

I DON'T KNOW...

SOMETHING WE COULD SAY ABOUT THEM, AND WHY THEY'RE A LITTLE BETTER THAN PINEAPPLES.

IT MIGHT BE ... FUN?

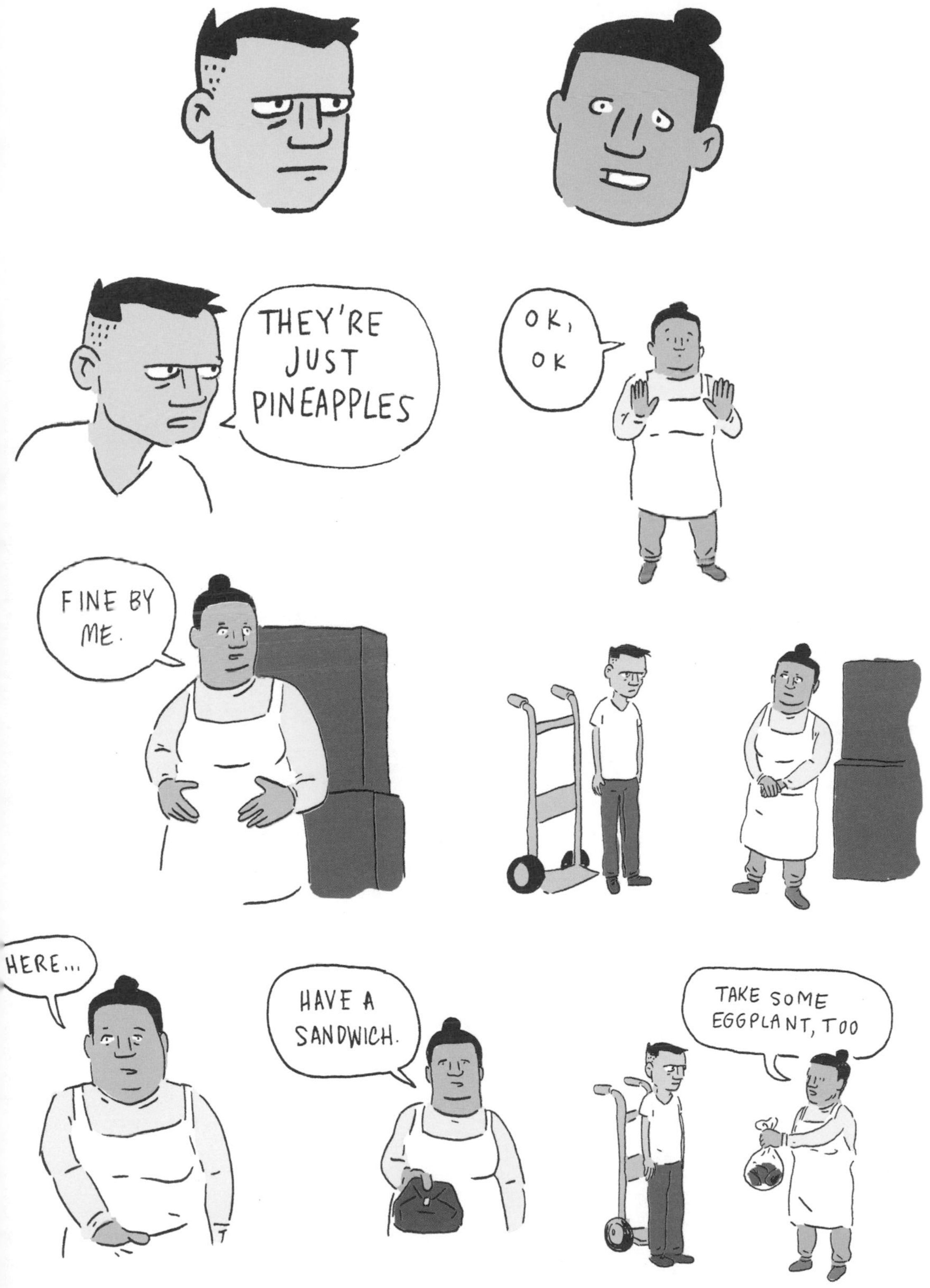
THEY'RE JUST PINEAPPLES
OK, OK
FINE BY ME.
HERE...
HAVE A SANDWICH.
TAKE SOME EGGPLANT, TOO

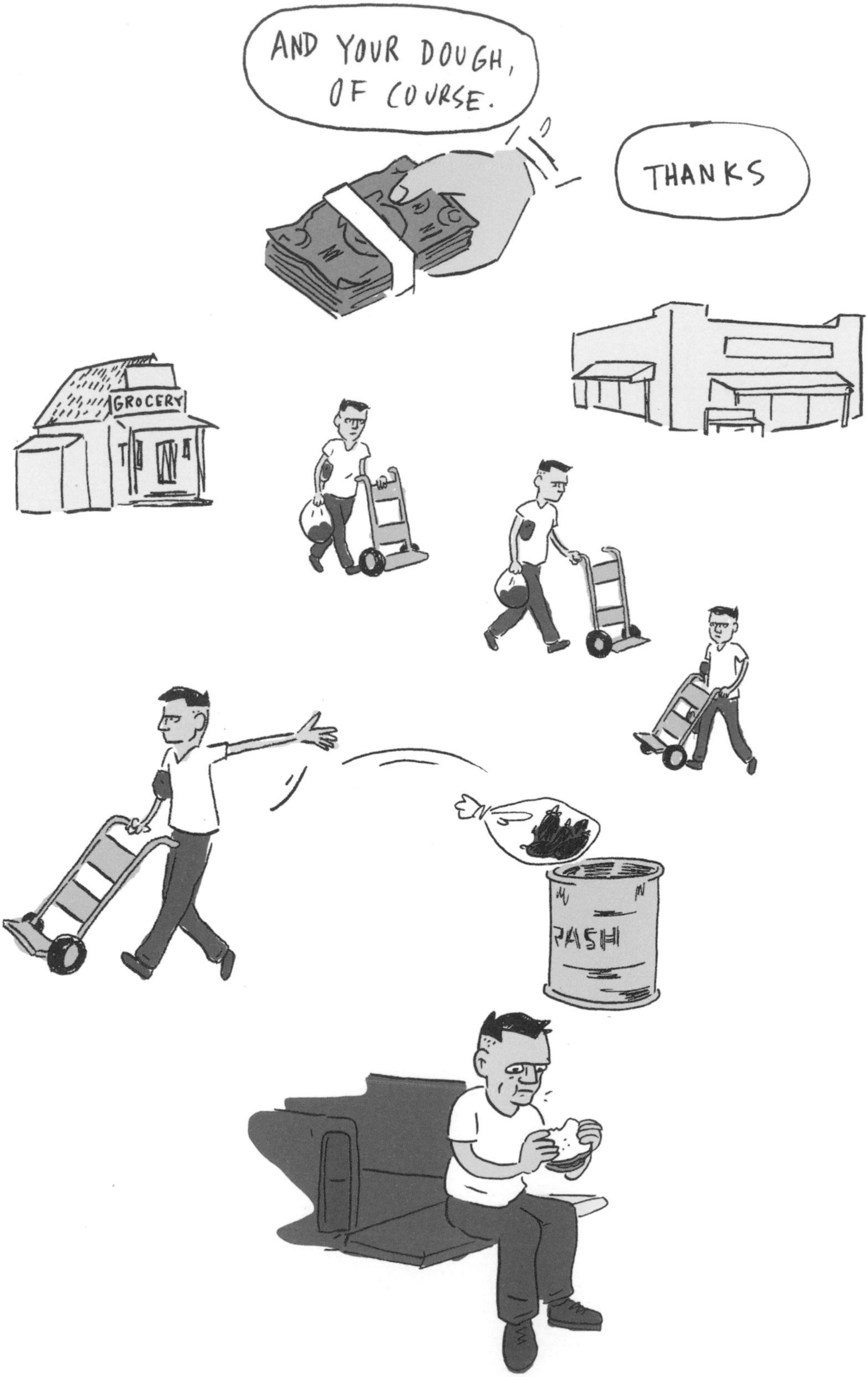
AND YOUR DOUGH, OF COURSE.
THANKS
GROCERY
TRASH

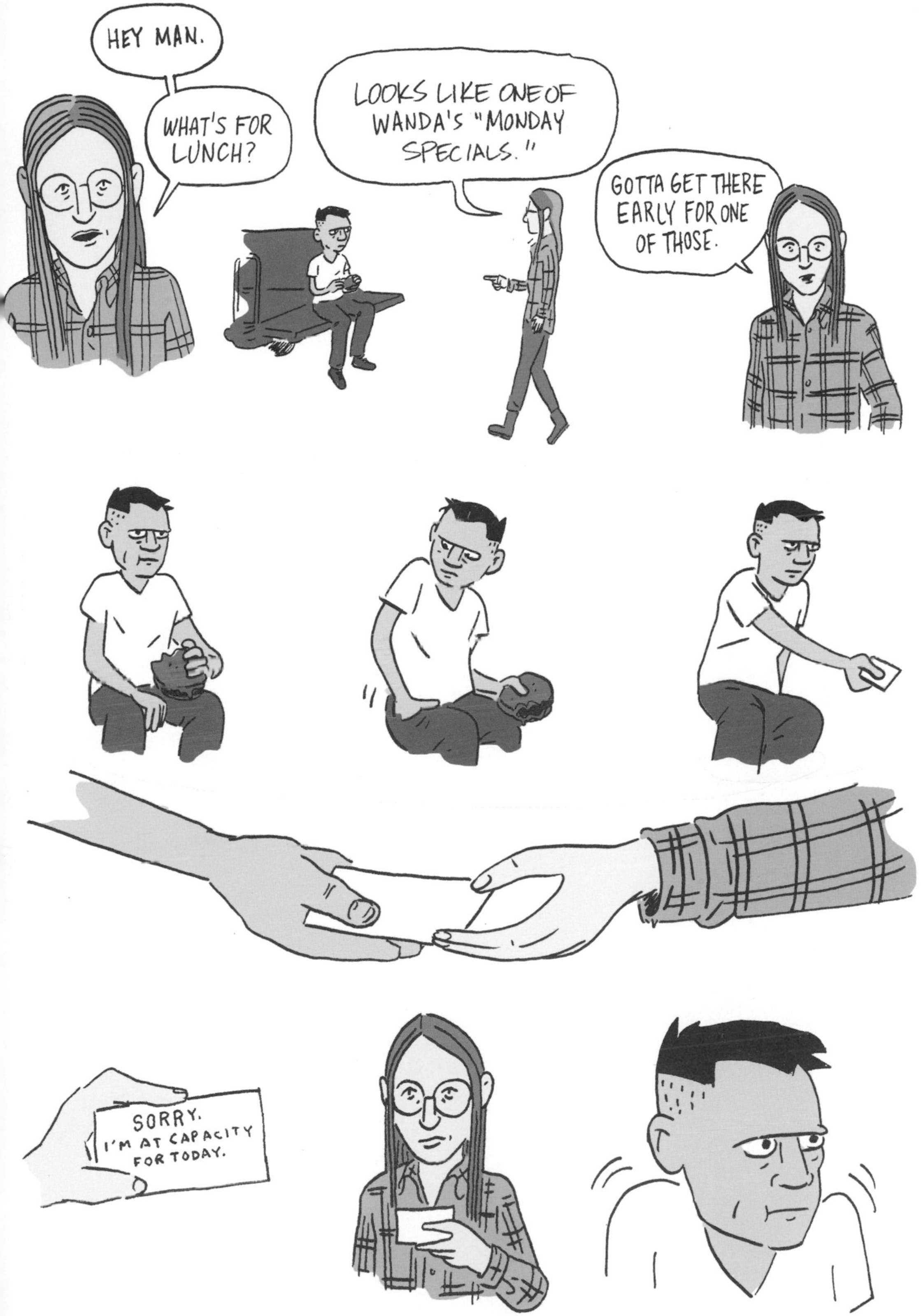
HEY MAN.
WHAT'S FOR LUNCH?
LOOKS LIKE ONE OF WANDA'S "MONDAY SPECIALS."
GOTTA GET THERE EARLY FOR ONE OF THOSE.
SORRY. I'M AT CAPACITY FOR TODAY.

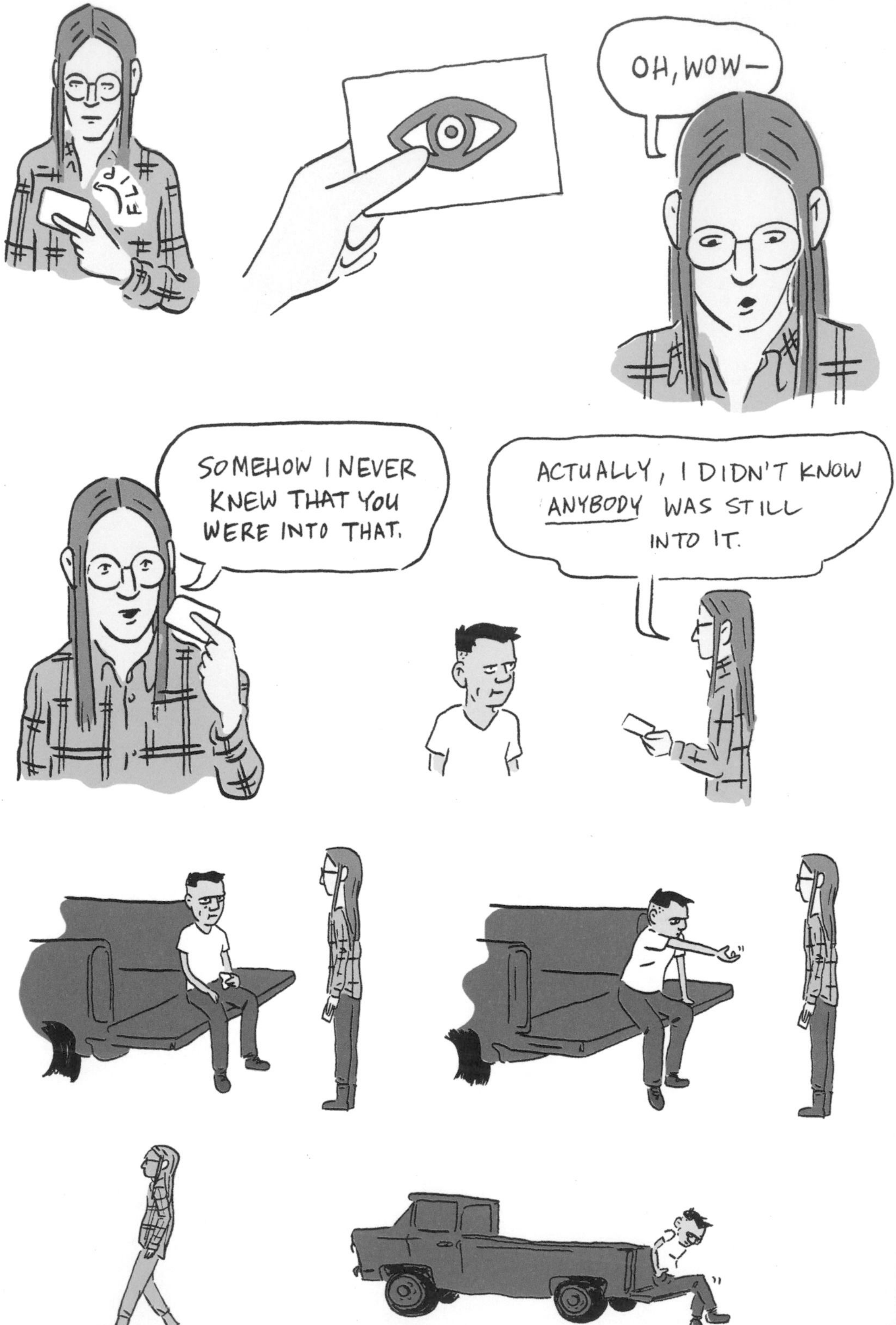
FLIP
OH, WOW—
SOMEHOW I NEVER KNEW THAT YOU WERE INTO THAT.
ACTUALLY, I DIDN'T KNOW ANYBODY WAS STILL INTO IT.

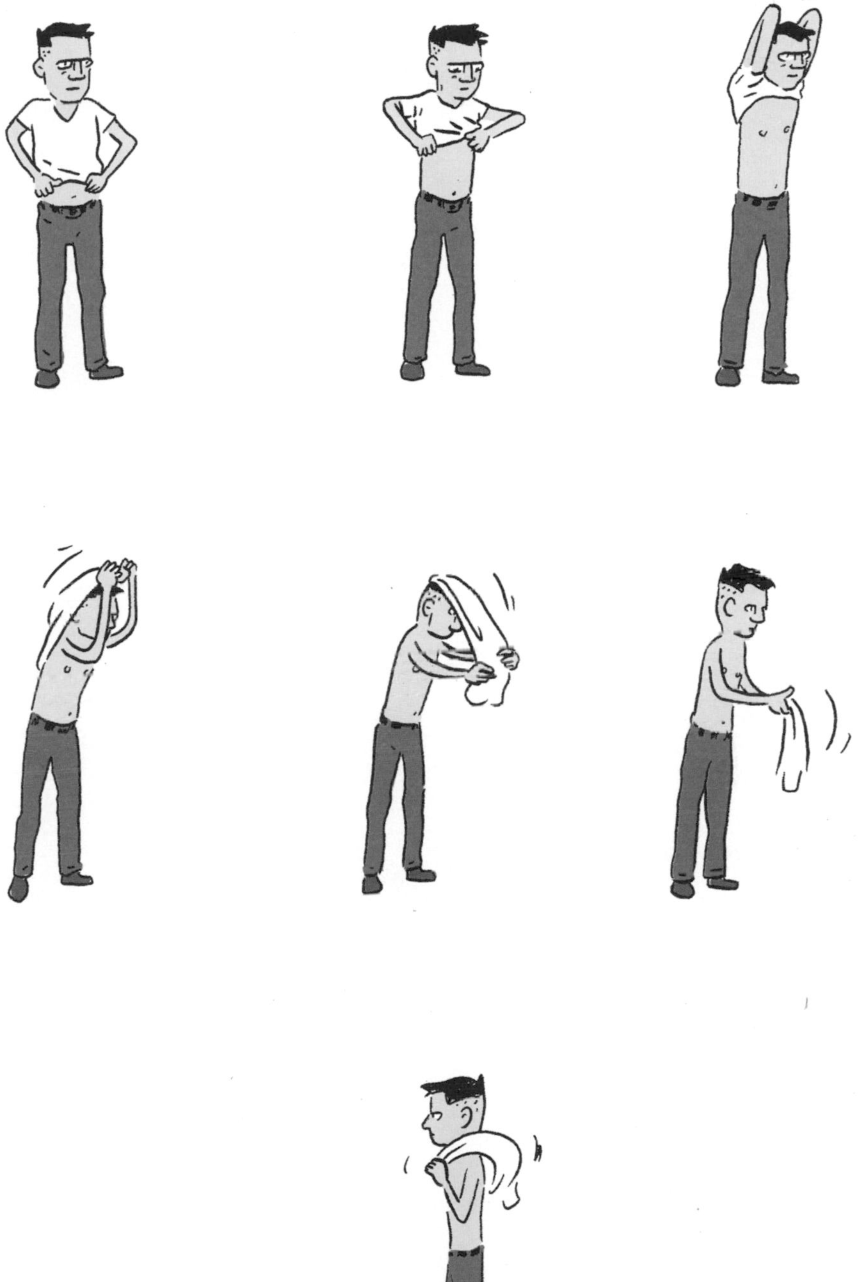

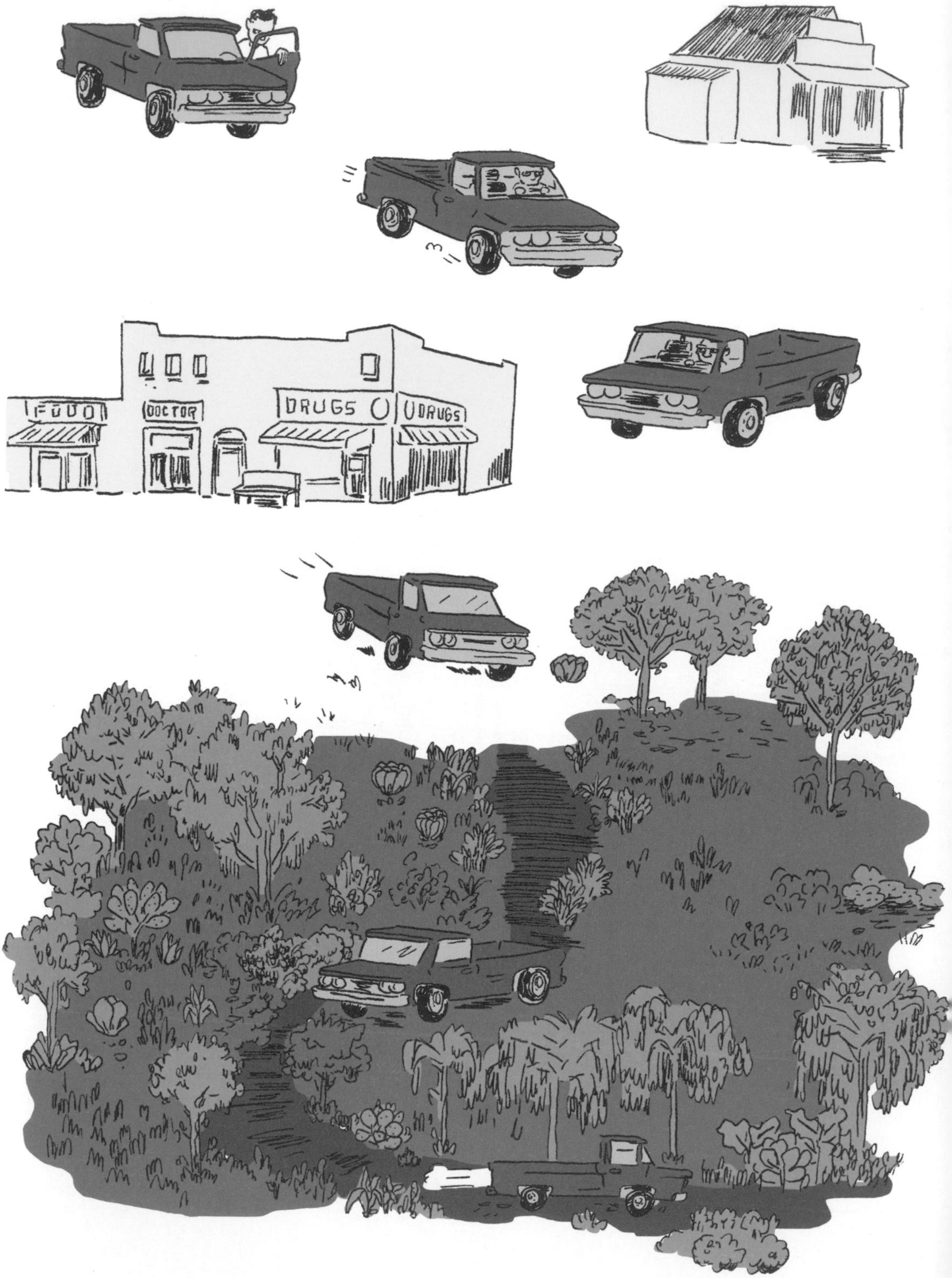
FOOD
DOCTOR
DRUGS
DRUGS

BACK IN
STOCK

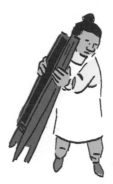

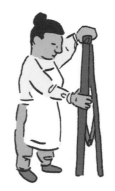

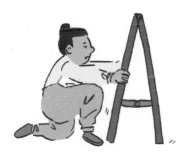

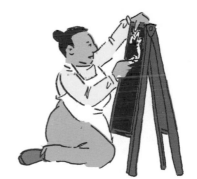

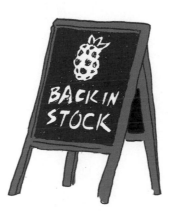

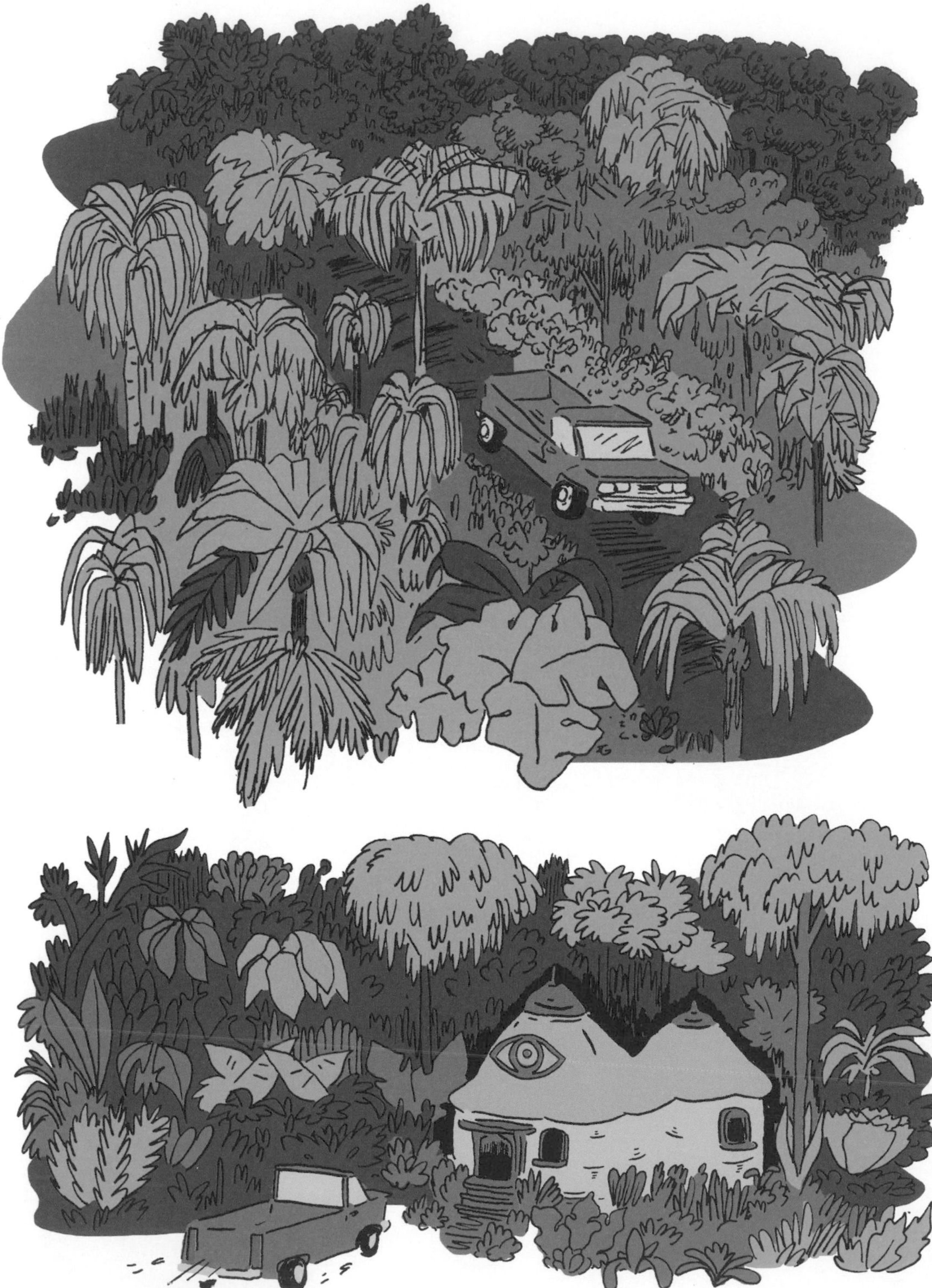

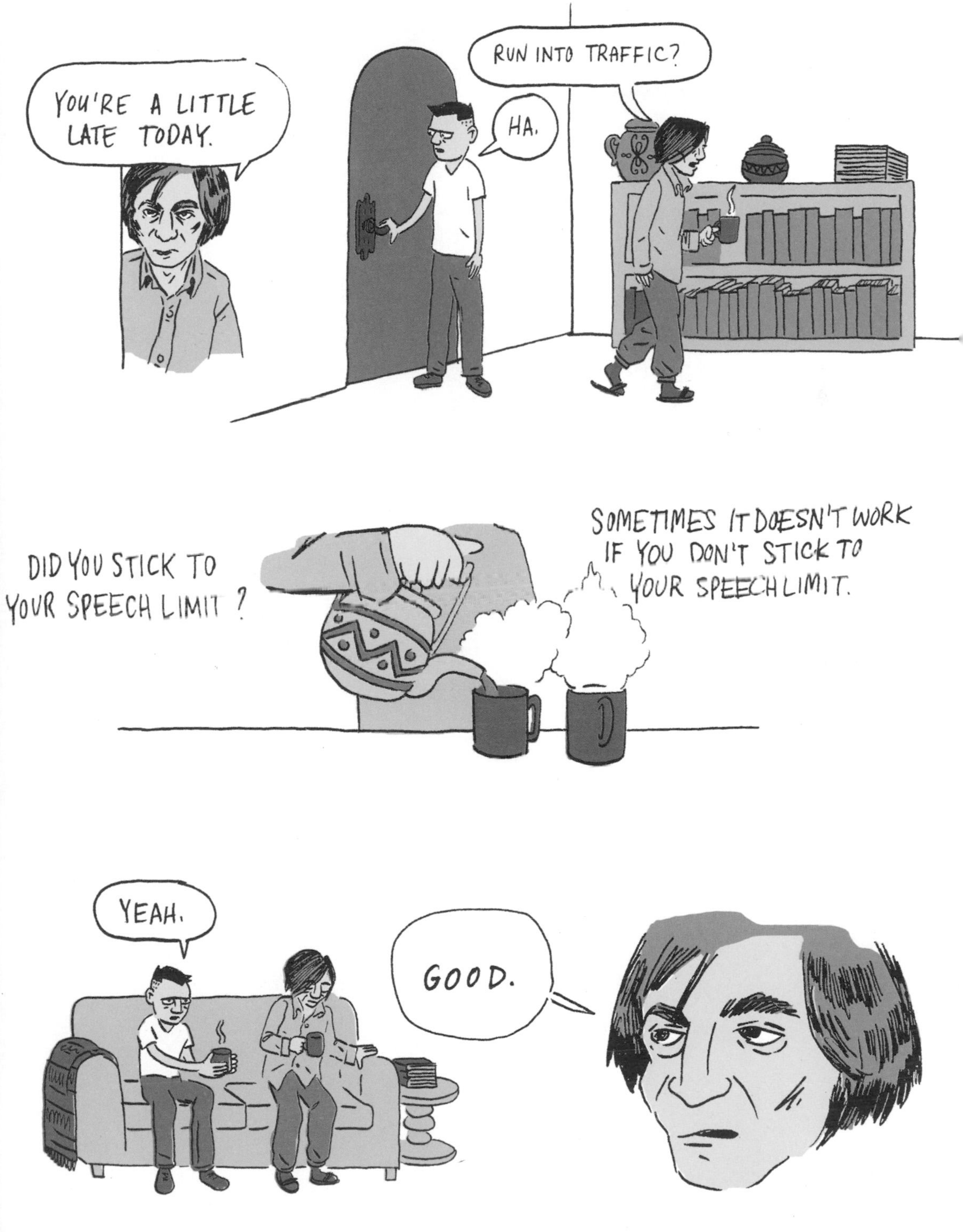
YOU'RE A LITTLE LATE TODAY.
HA.
RUN INTO TRAFFIC?
DID YOU STICK TO YOUR SPEECH LIMIT?
SOMETIMES IT DOESN'T WORK IF YOU DON'T STICK TO YOUR SPEECH LIMIT.
YEAH.
GOOD.

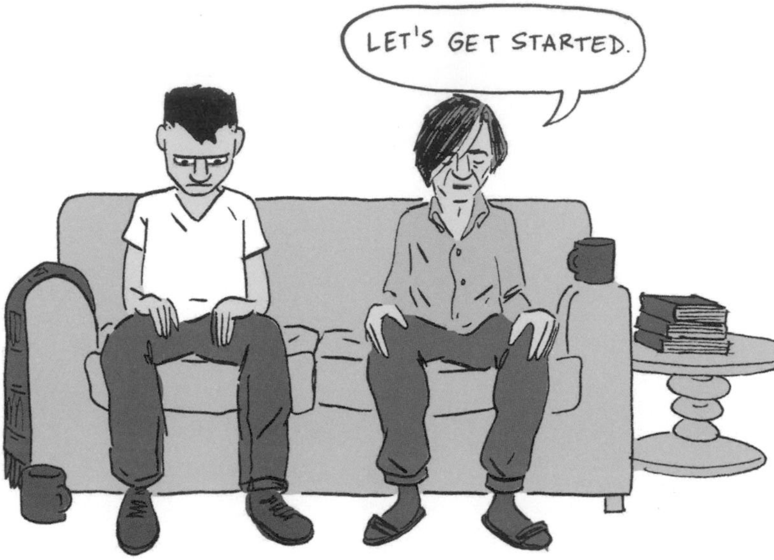
LET'S GET STARTED.

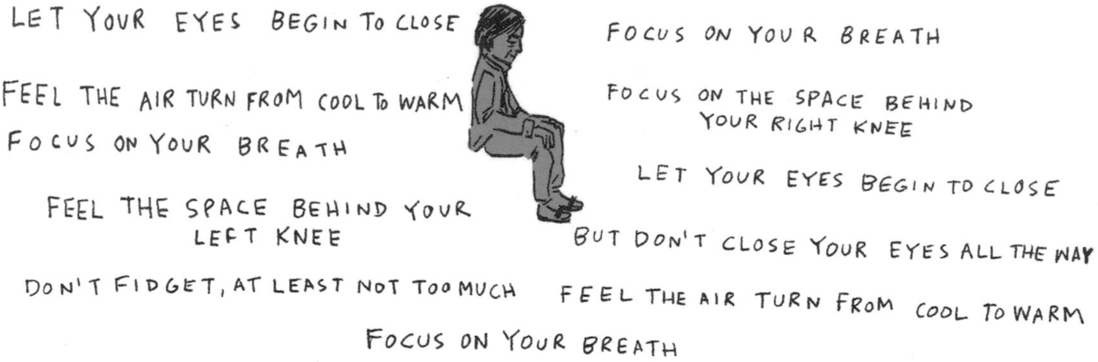
LET YOUR EYES BEGIN TO CLOSE
FEEL THE AIR TURN FROM COOL TO WARM
FOCUS ON YOUR BREATH
FEEL THE SPACE BEHIND YOUR LEFT KNEE
DON'T FIDGET, AT LEAST NOT TOO MUCH
FOCUS ON YOUR BREATH
FOCUS ON THE SPACE BEHIND YOUR RIGHT KNEE
LET YOUR EYES BEGIN TO CLOSE
BUT DON'T CLOSE YOUR EYES ALL THE WAY
FEEL THE AIR TURN FROM COOL TO WARM
FOCUS ON YOUR BREATH

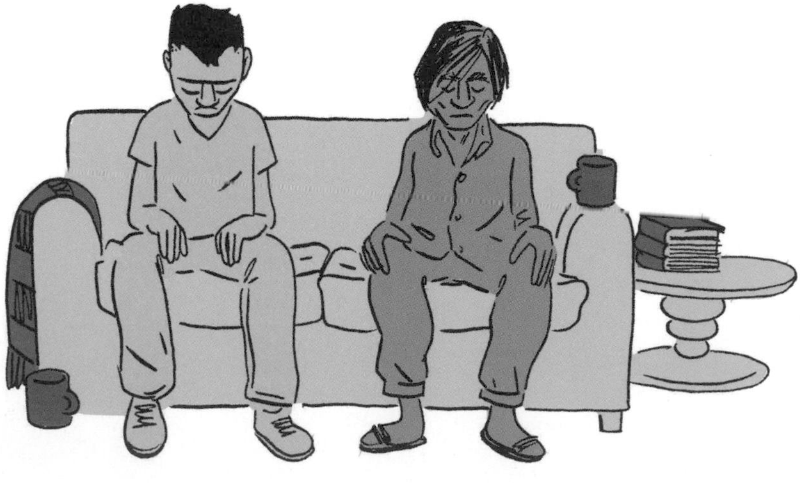

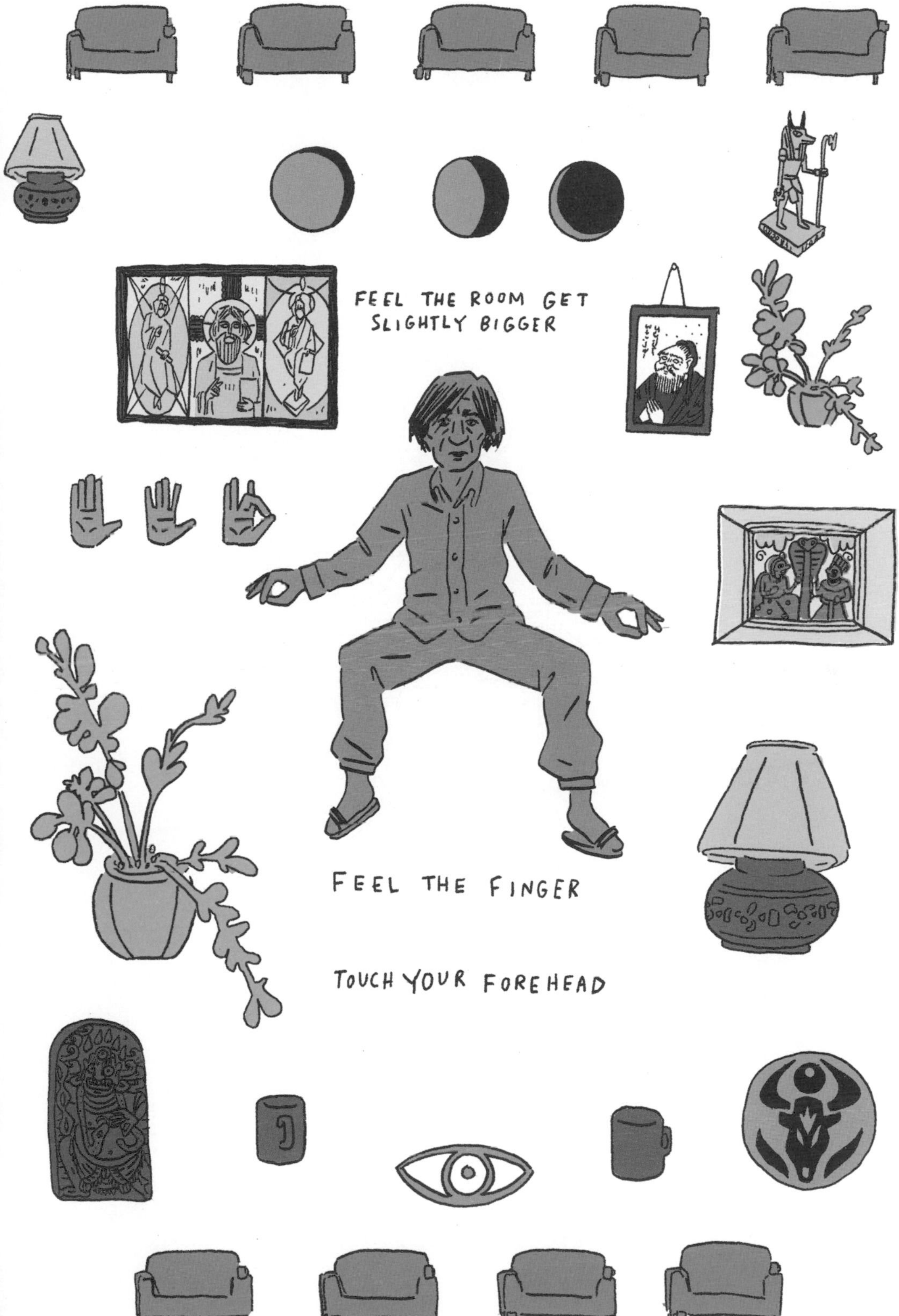
FEEL THE ROOM GET SLIGHTLY BIGGER
FEEL THE FINGER
TOUCH YOUR FOREHEAD

FOCUS ON YOUR BREATH

FEEL THE AIR TURN FROM COOL TO WARM

FEEL THE ROOM GET
SLIGHTLY BIGGER

FEEL THE FINGER

TOUCH YOUR FOREHEAD

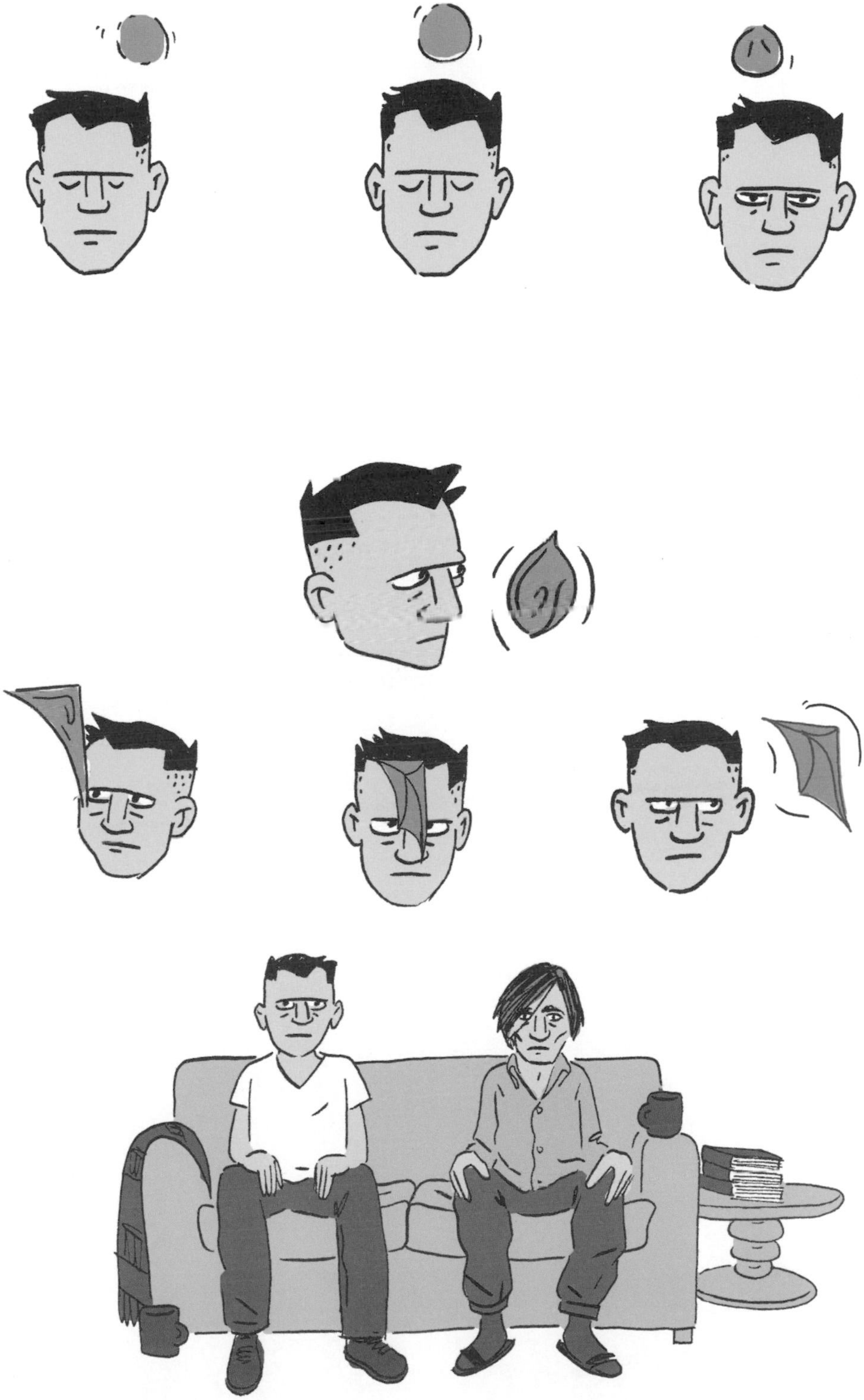

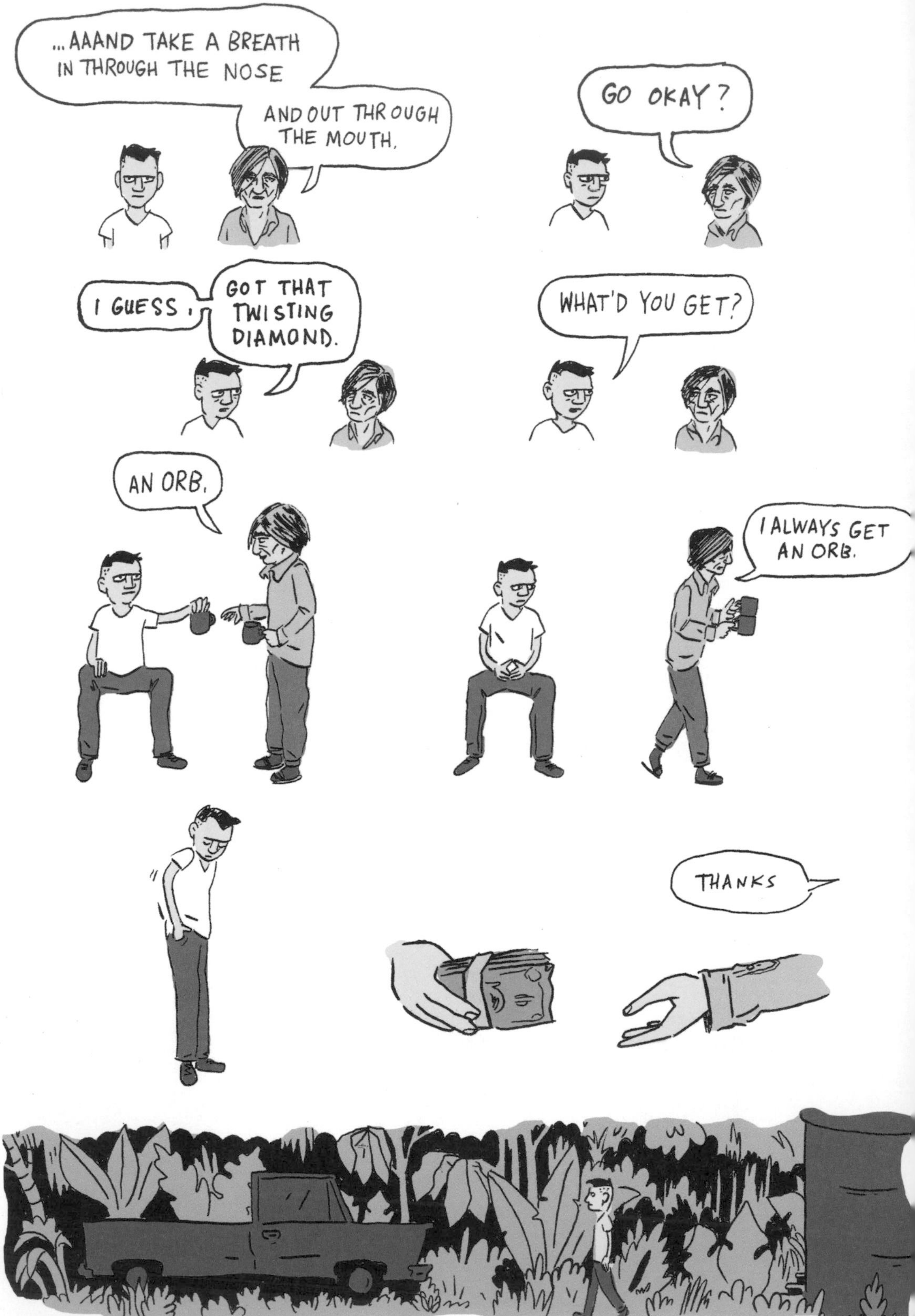
...AAAND TAKE A BREATH IN THROUGH THE NOSE
AND OUT THROUGH THE MOUTH.
GO OKAY?
I GUESS.
GOT THAT TWISTING DIAMOND.
WHAT'D YOU GET?
AN ORB.
I ALWAYS GET AN ORB.
THANKS

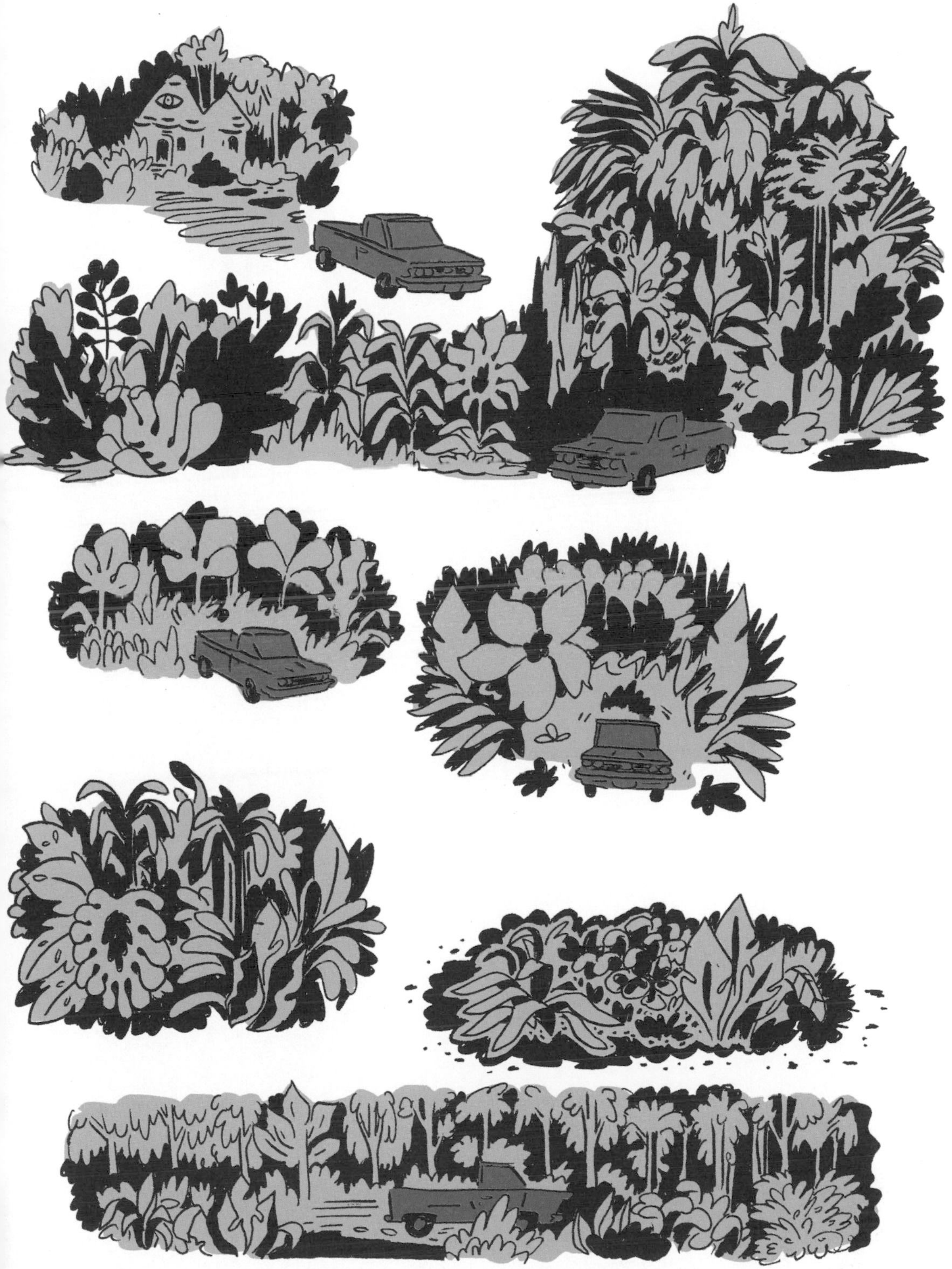

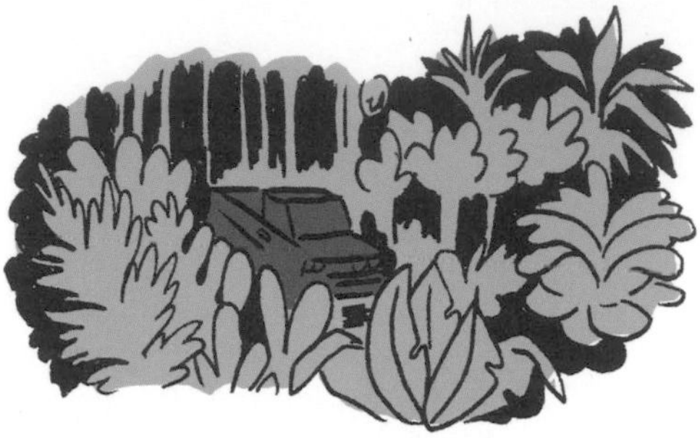
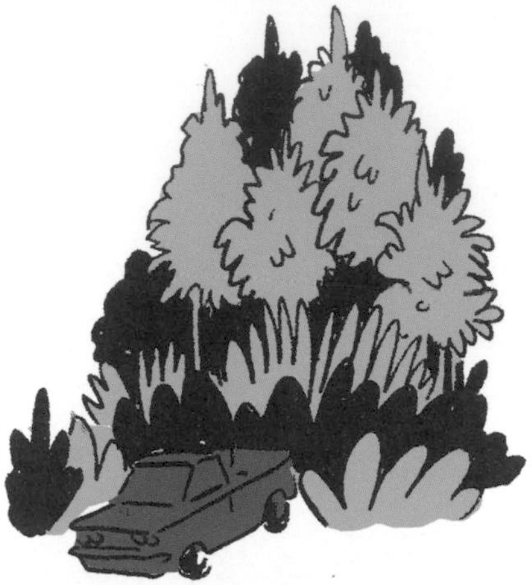
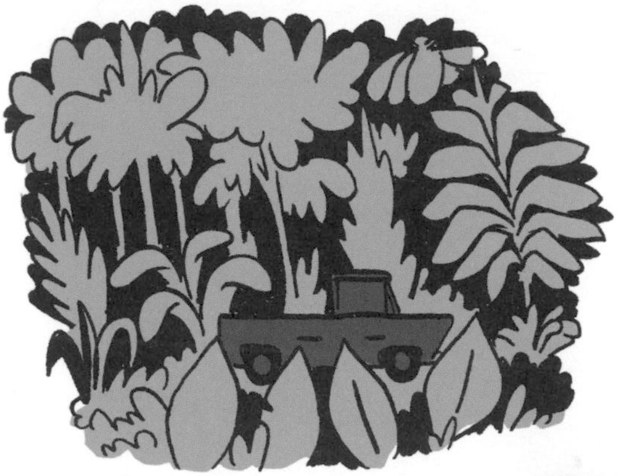
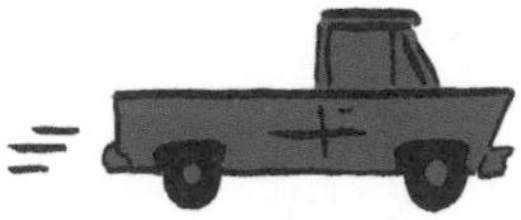
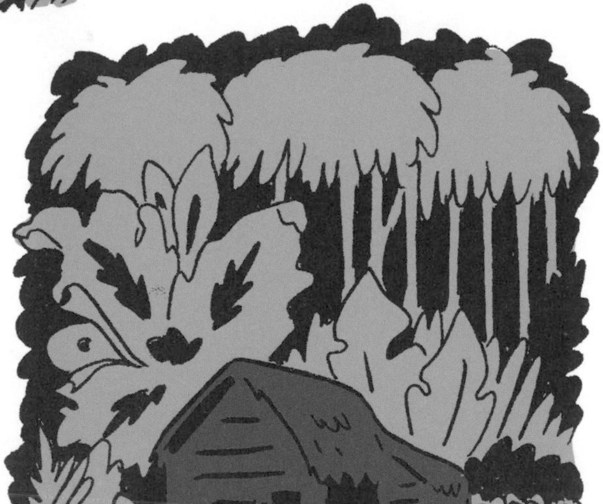
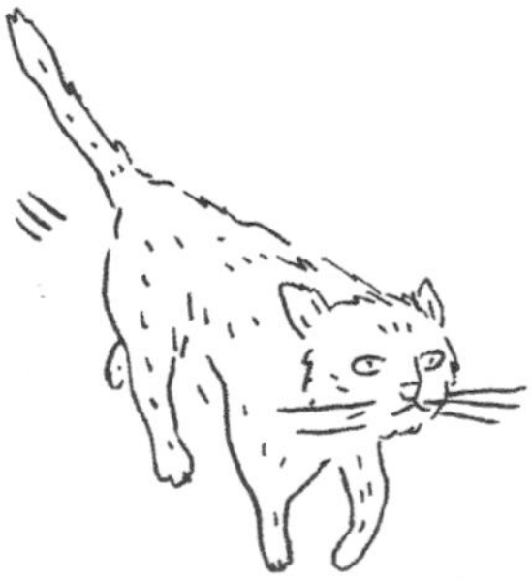
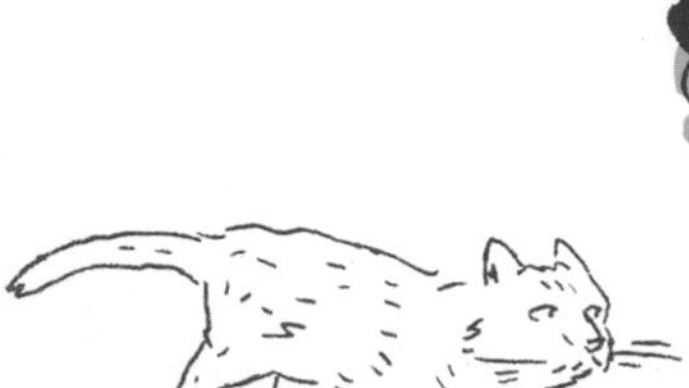
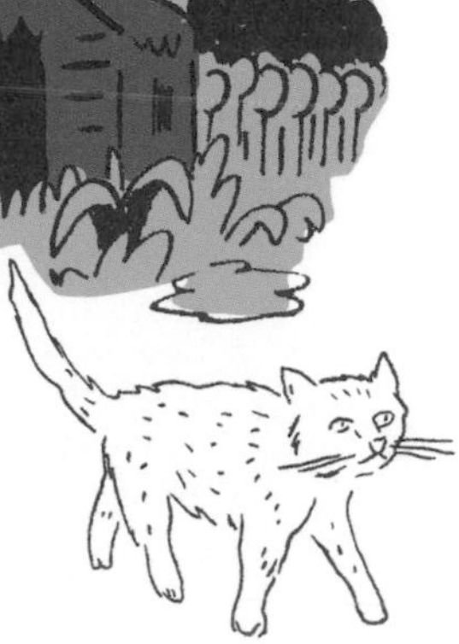

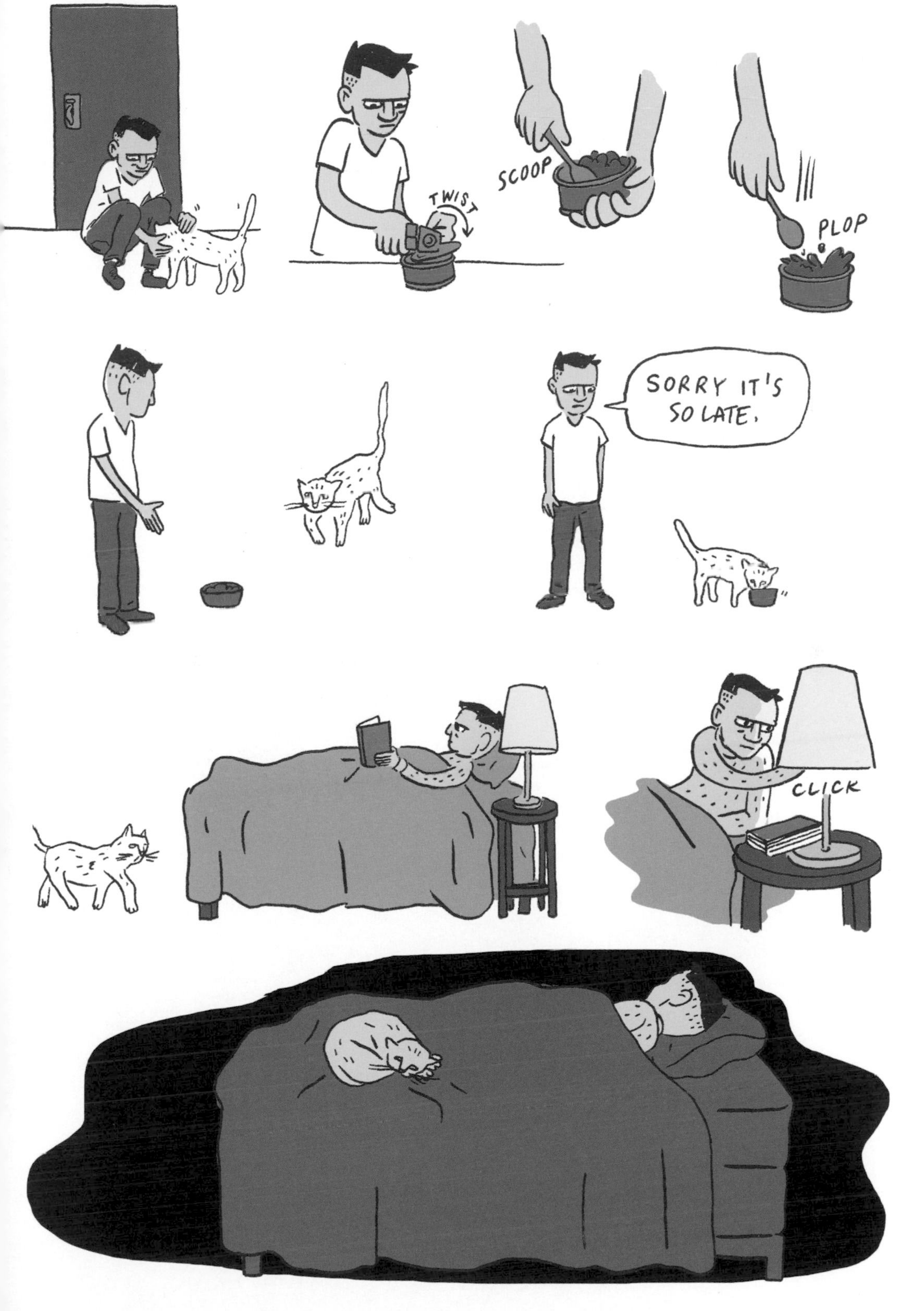
TWIST
SCOOP
PLOP
SORRY IT'S SO LATE.
CLICK

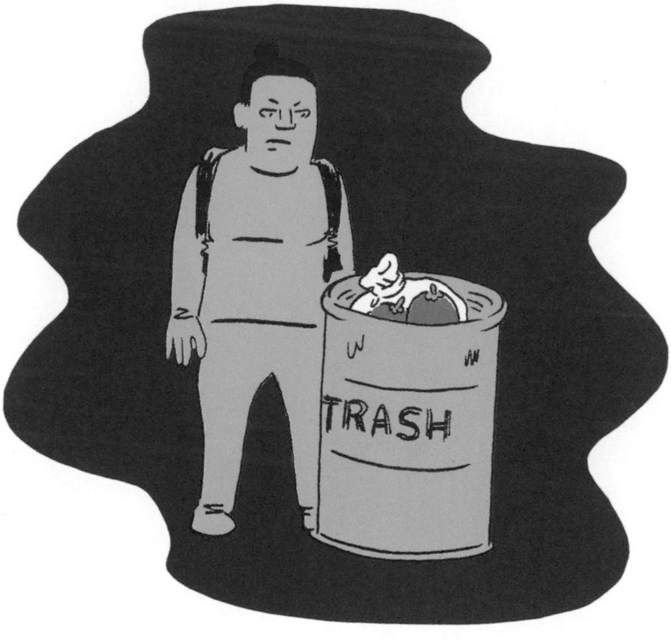
TRASH

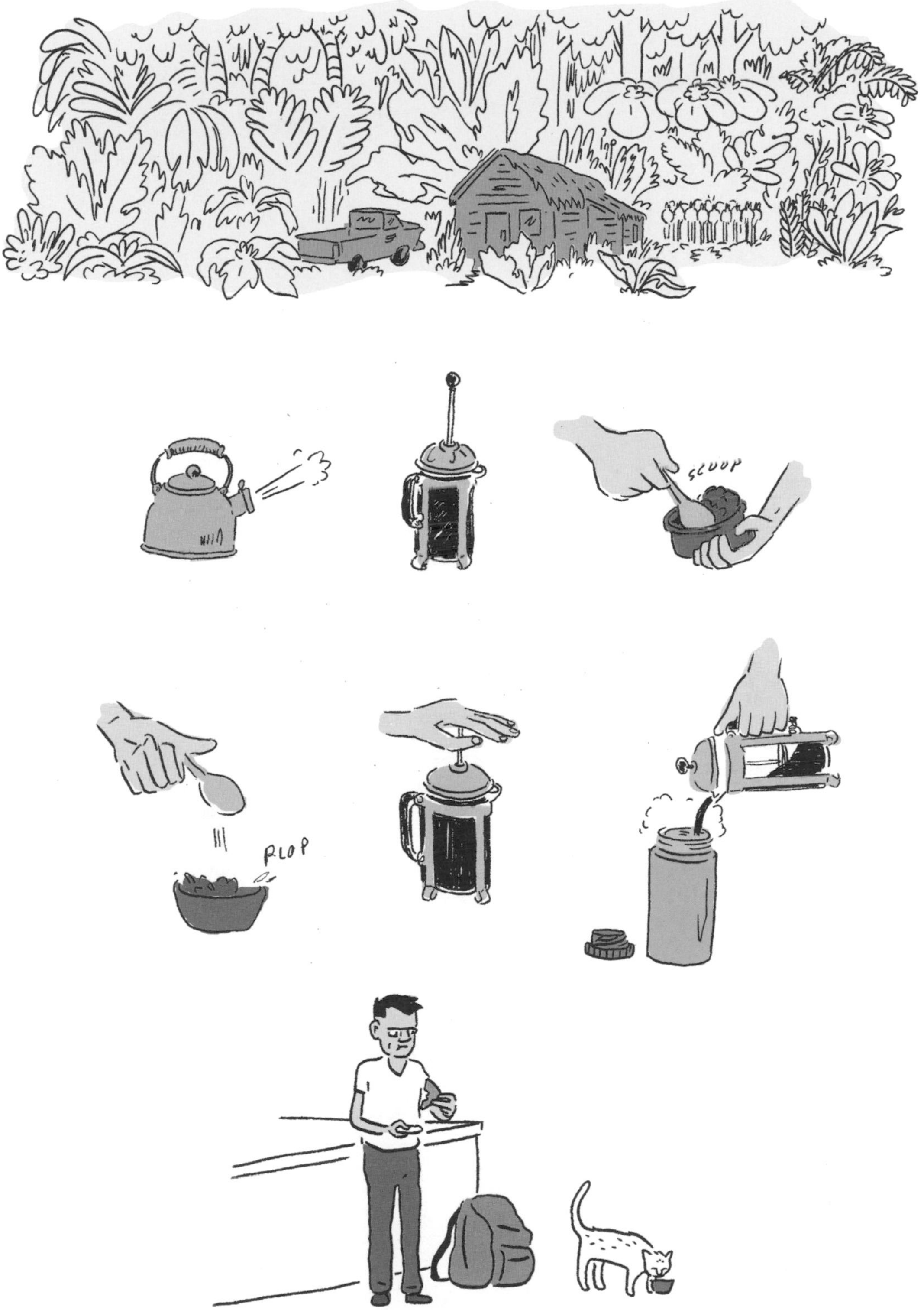
SCOOP
PLOP

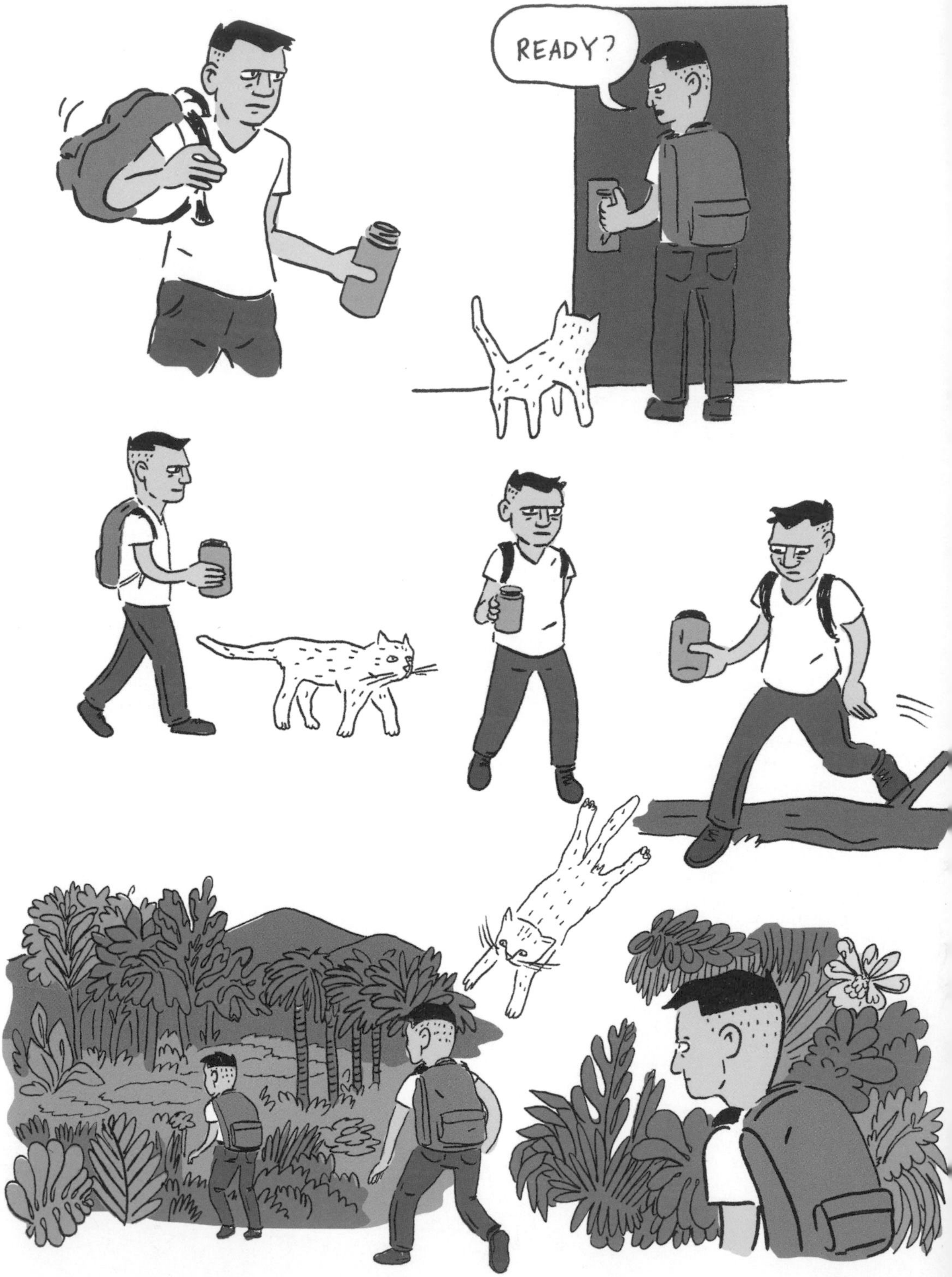
READY?

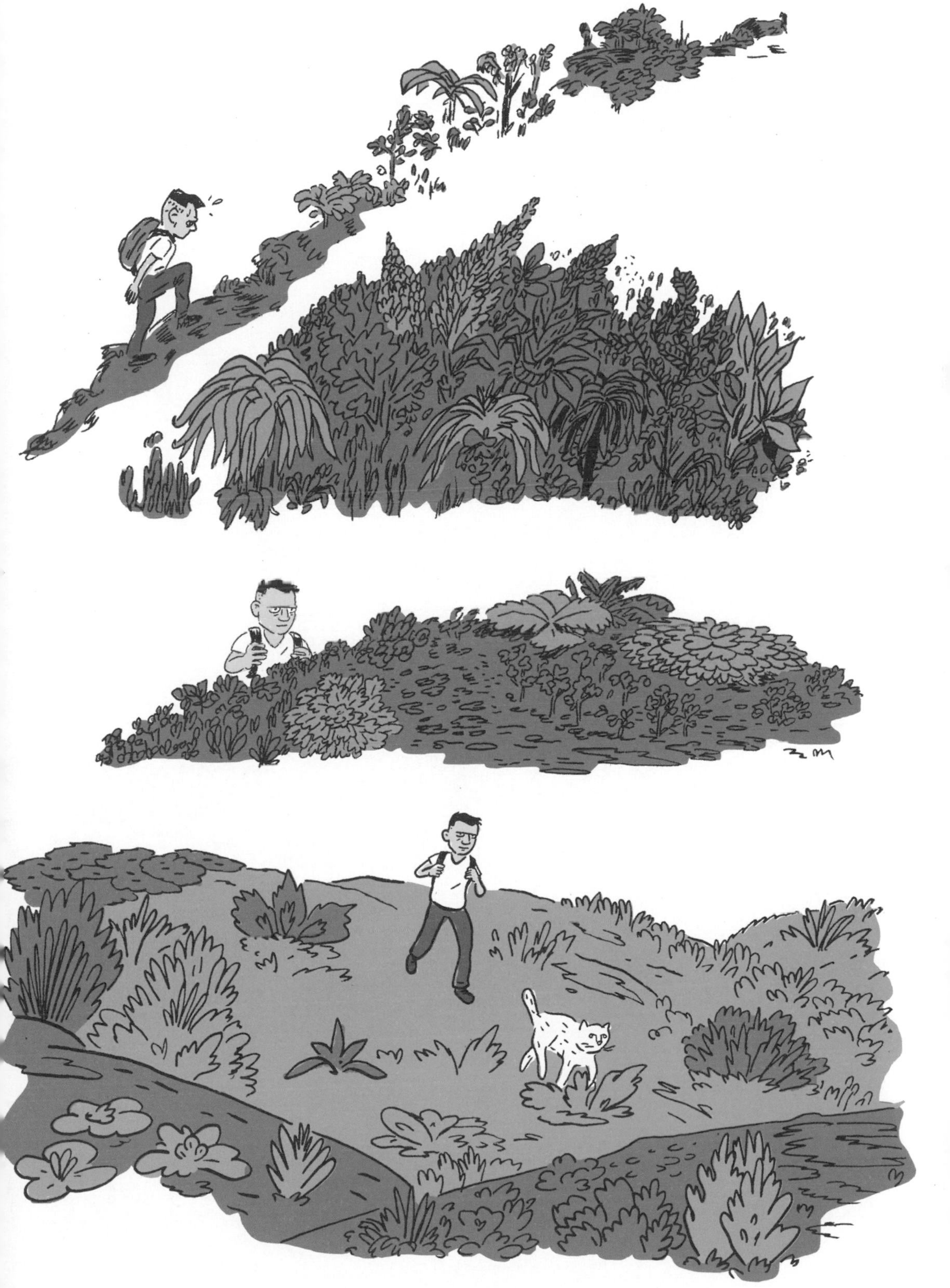

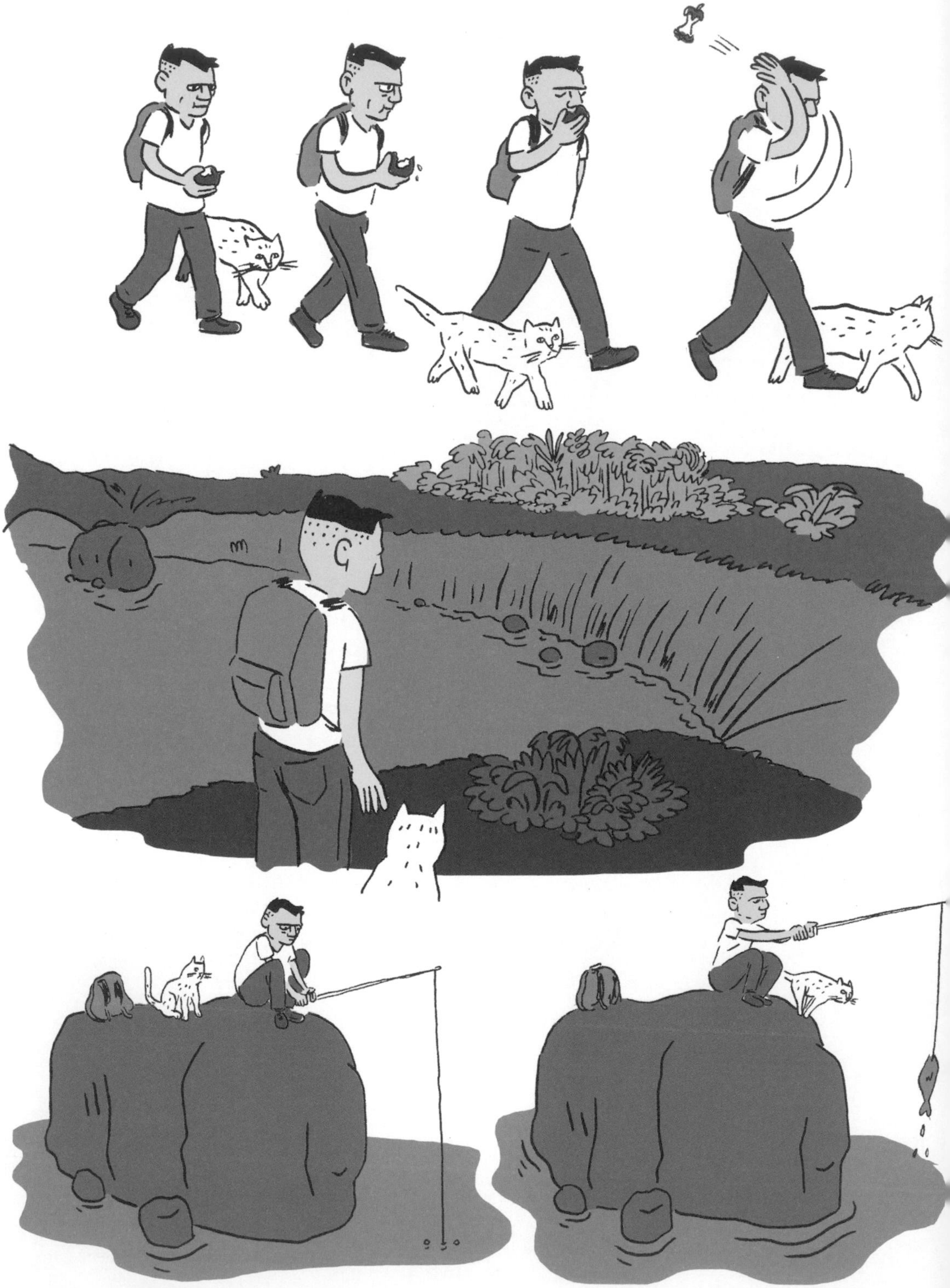

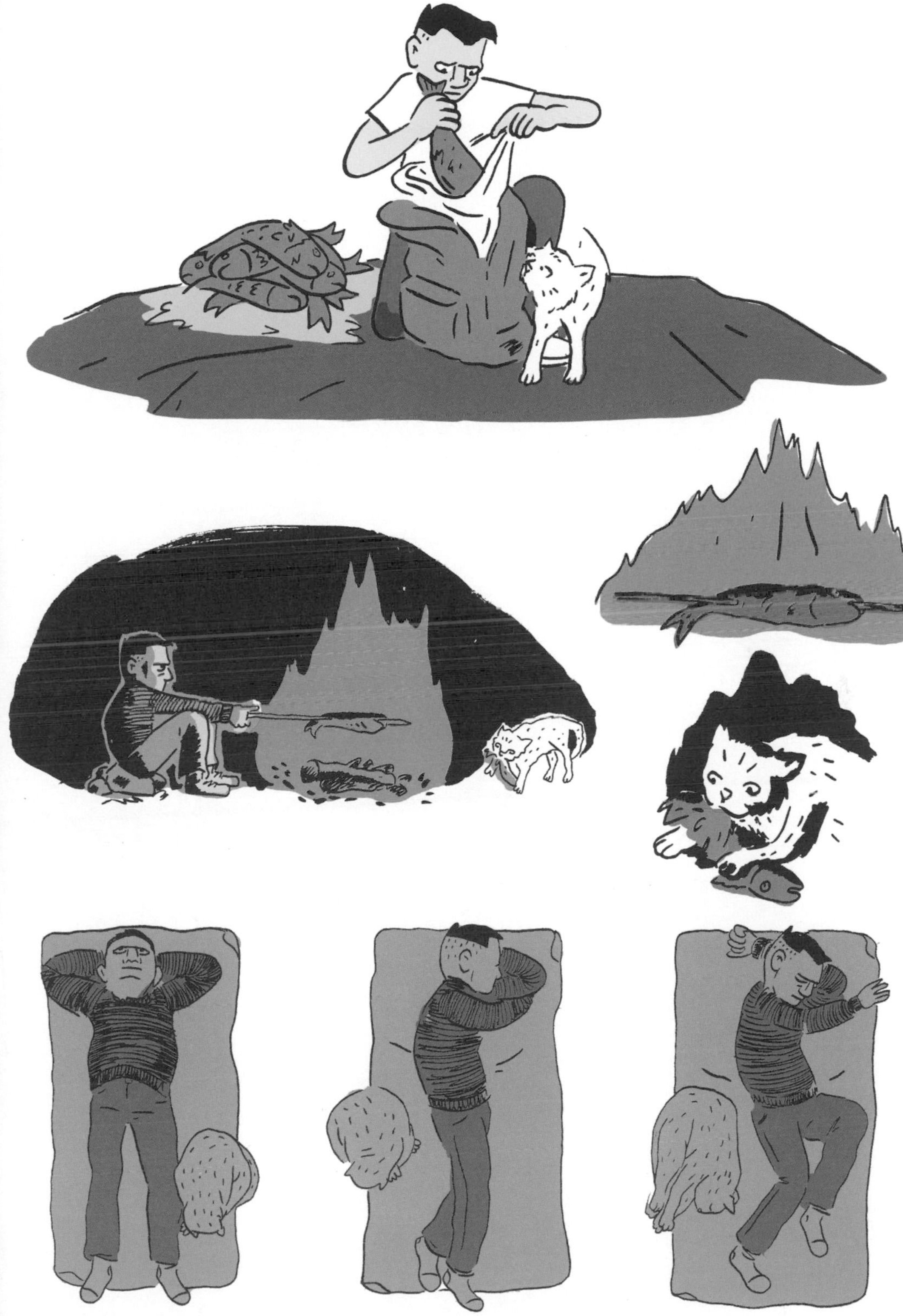

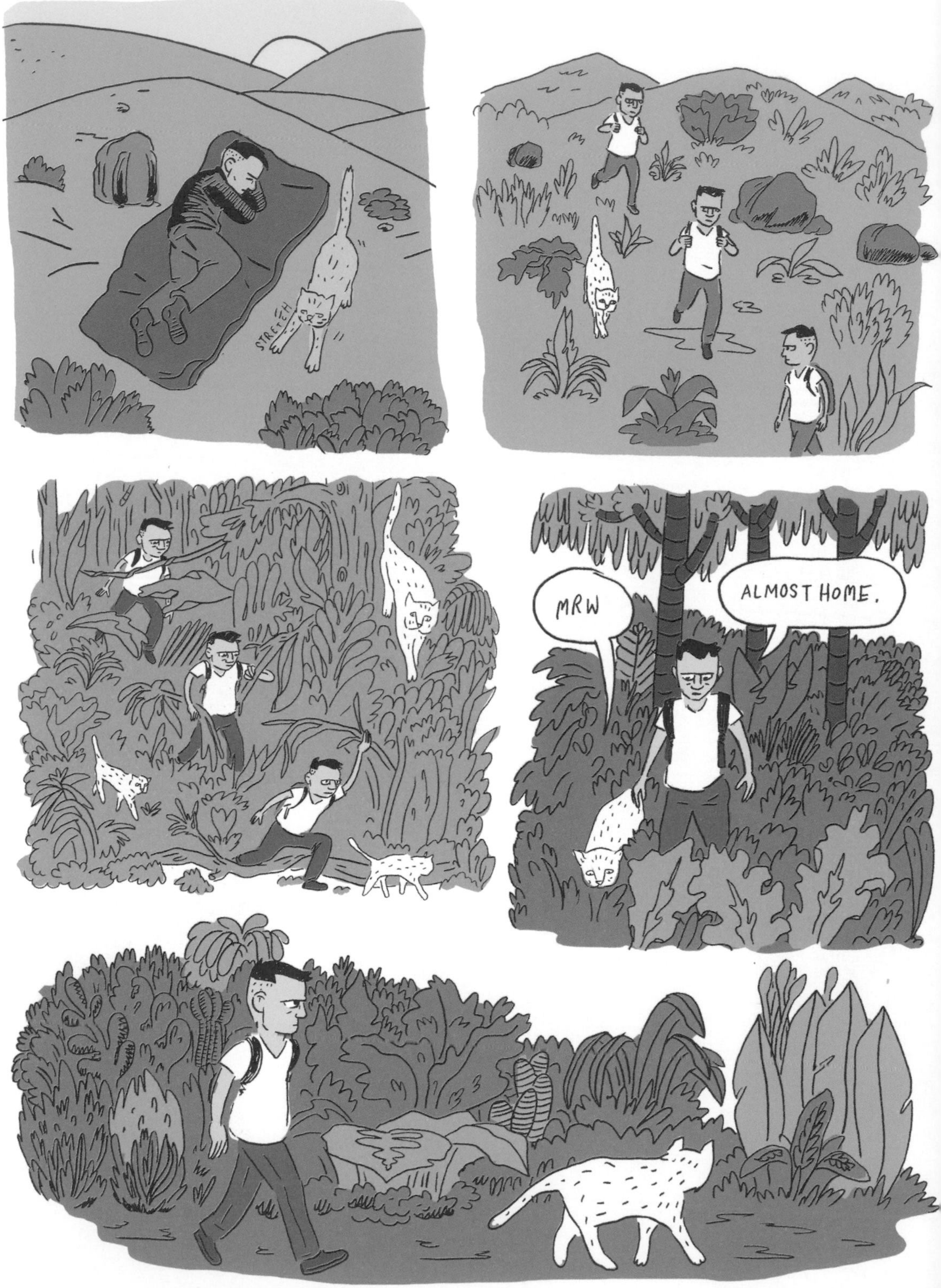
STRETCH
MRW
ALMOST HOME.

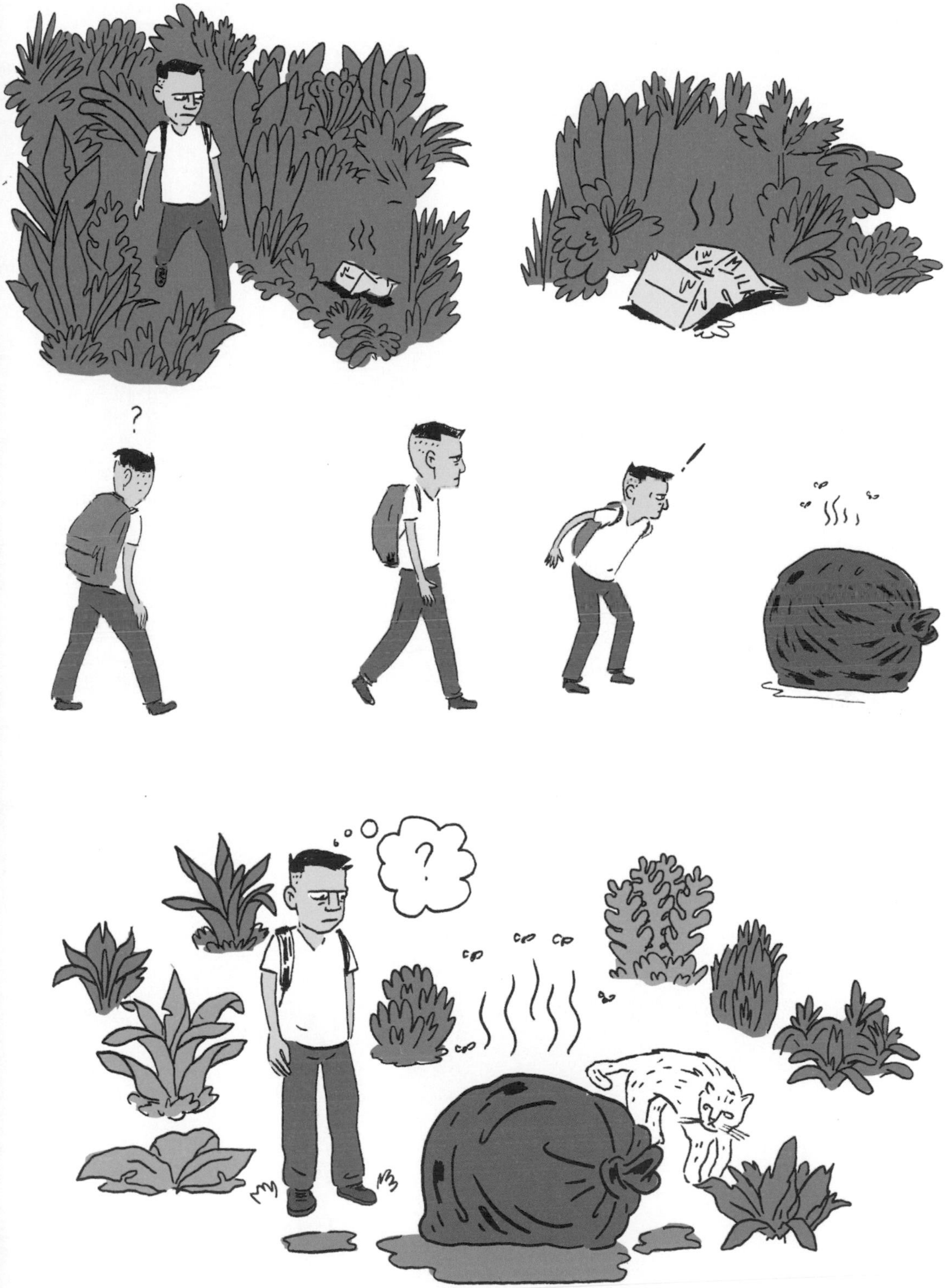

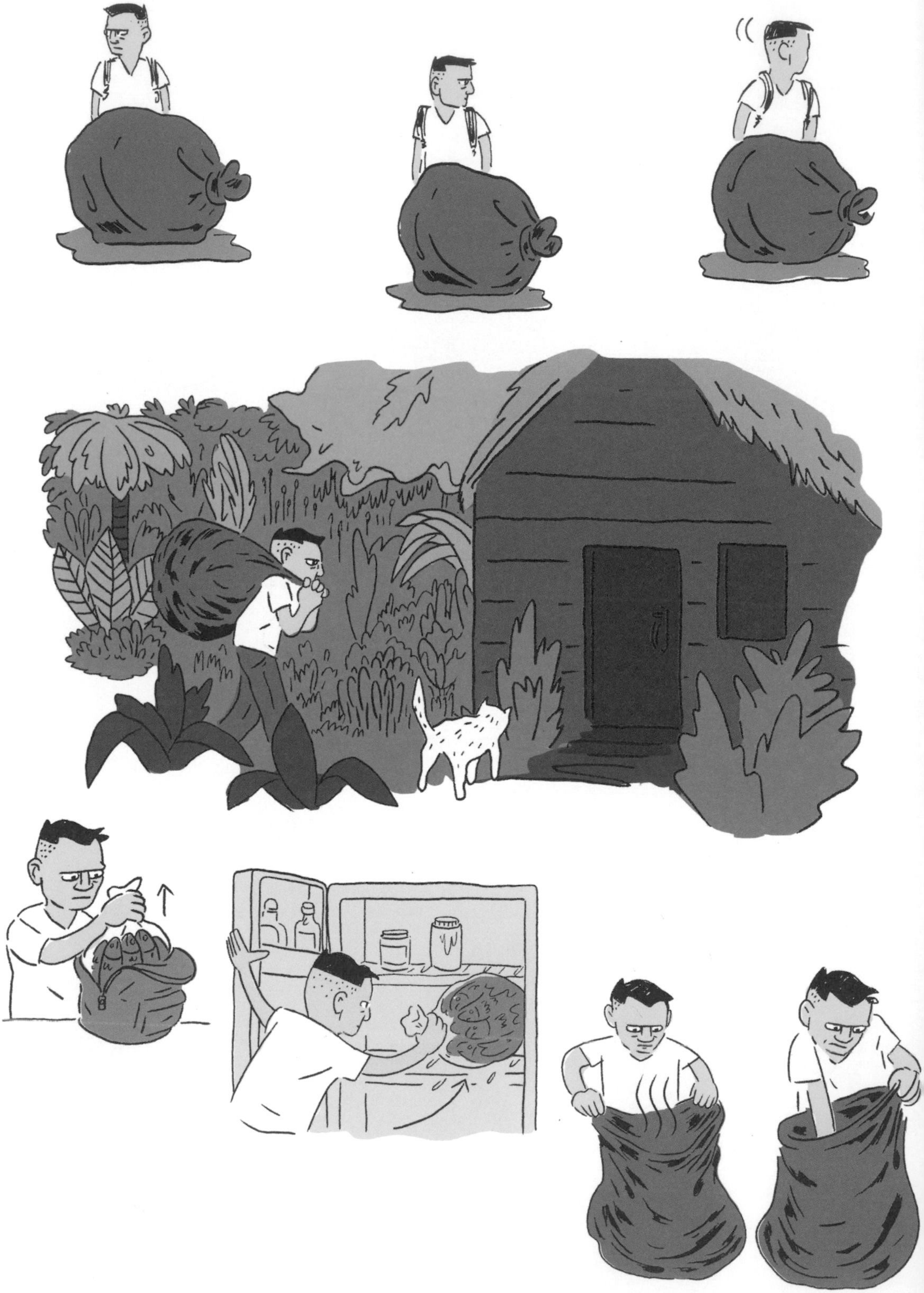

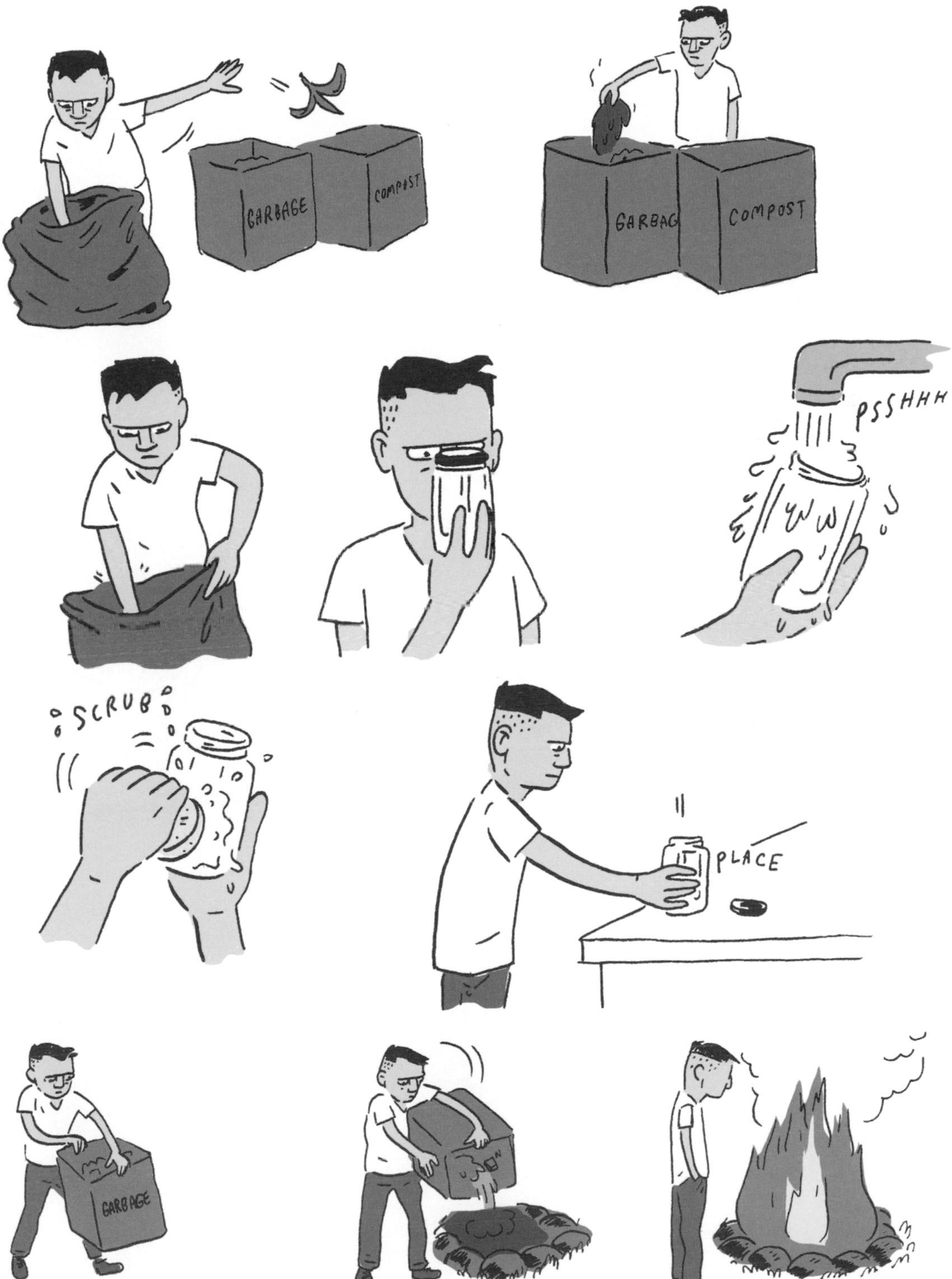
GARBAGE
COMPOST
GARBAG
COMPOST
PSSHHH
SCRUB
PLACE
GARBAGE

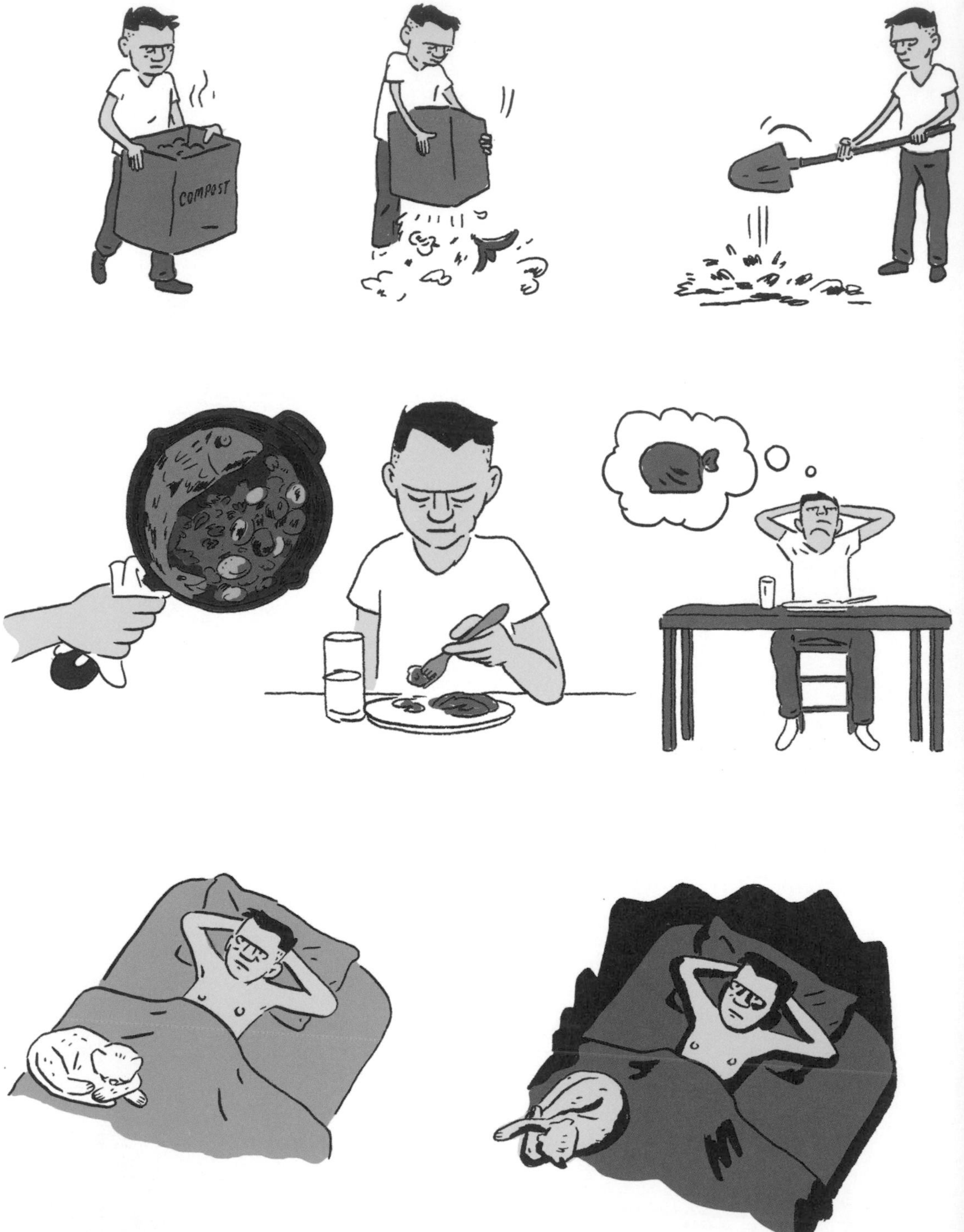
COMPOST

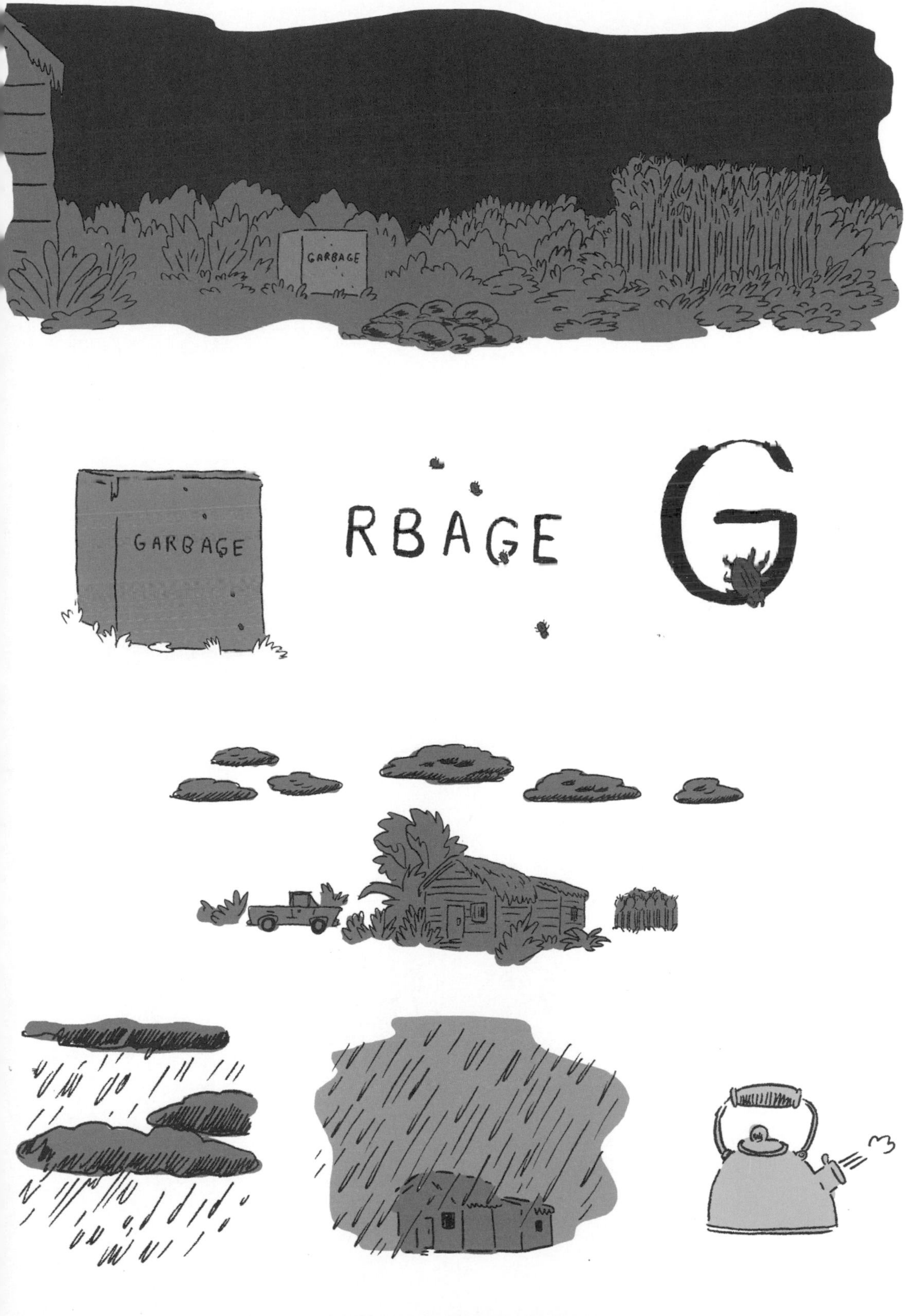
GARBAGE
GARBAGE
RBAGE
G

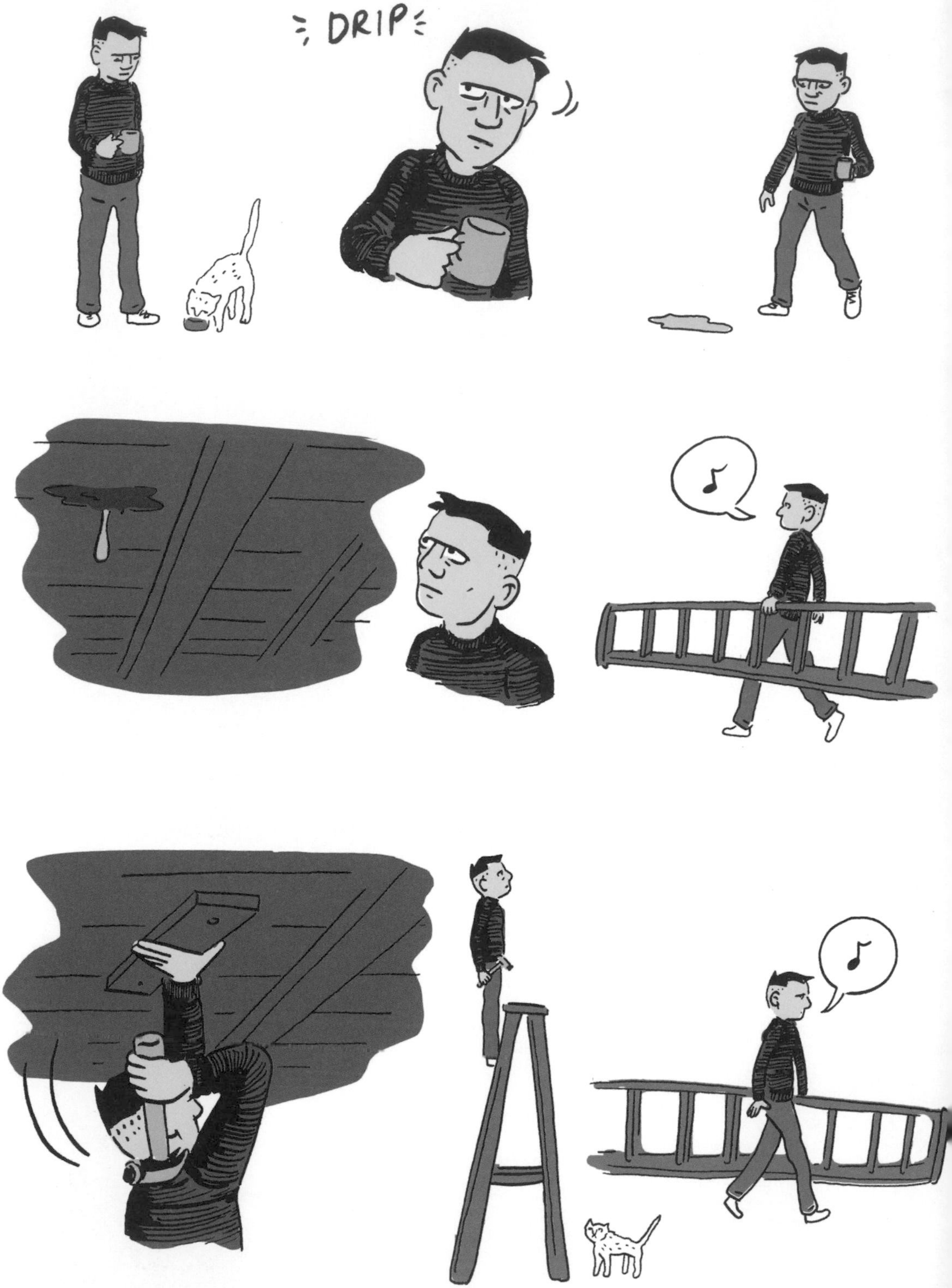
DRIP
♪
♪

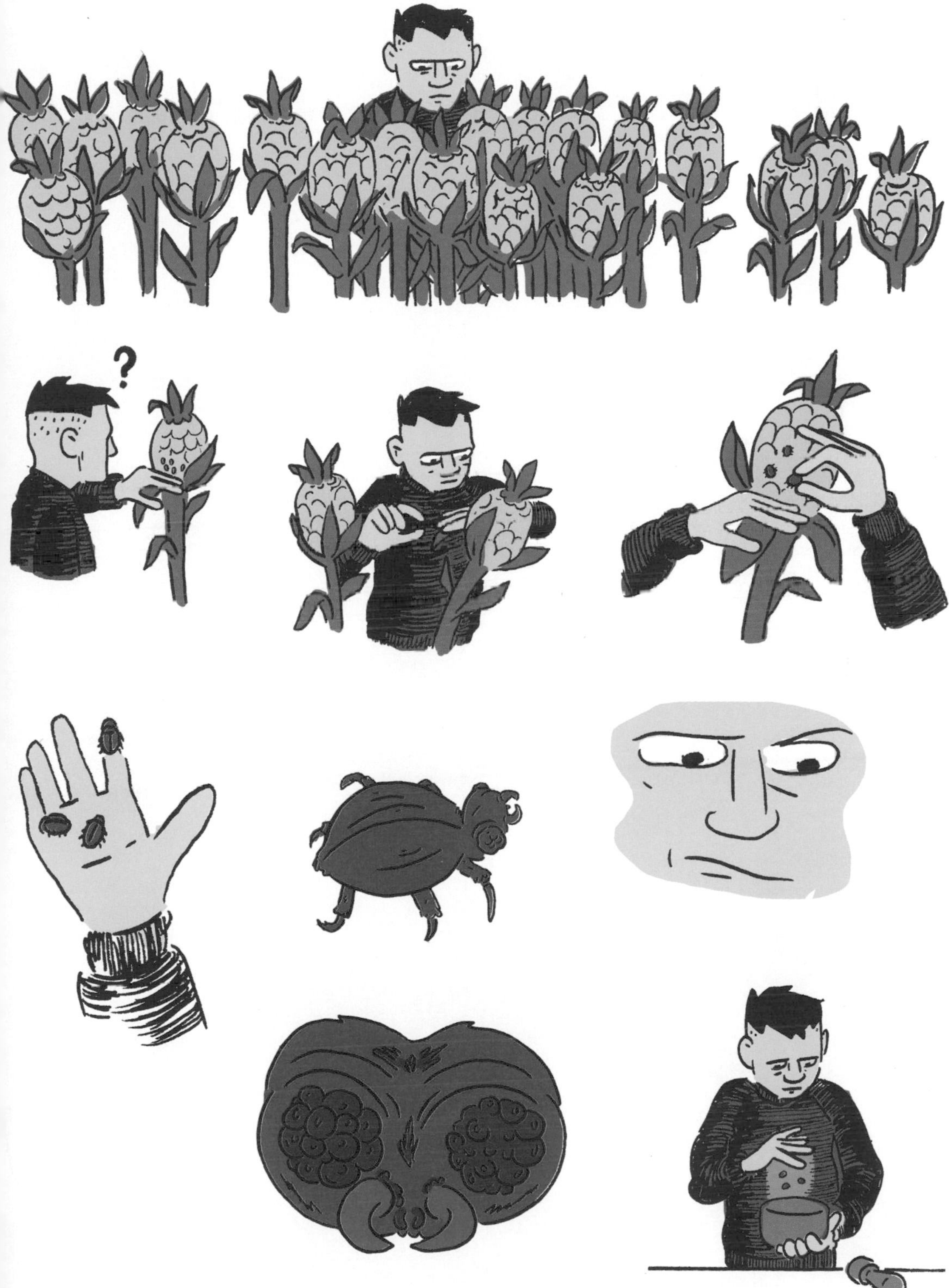
?

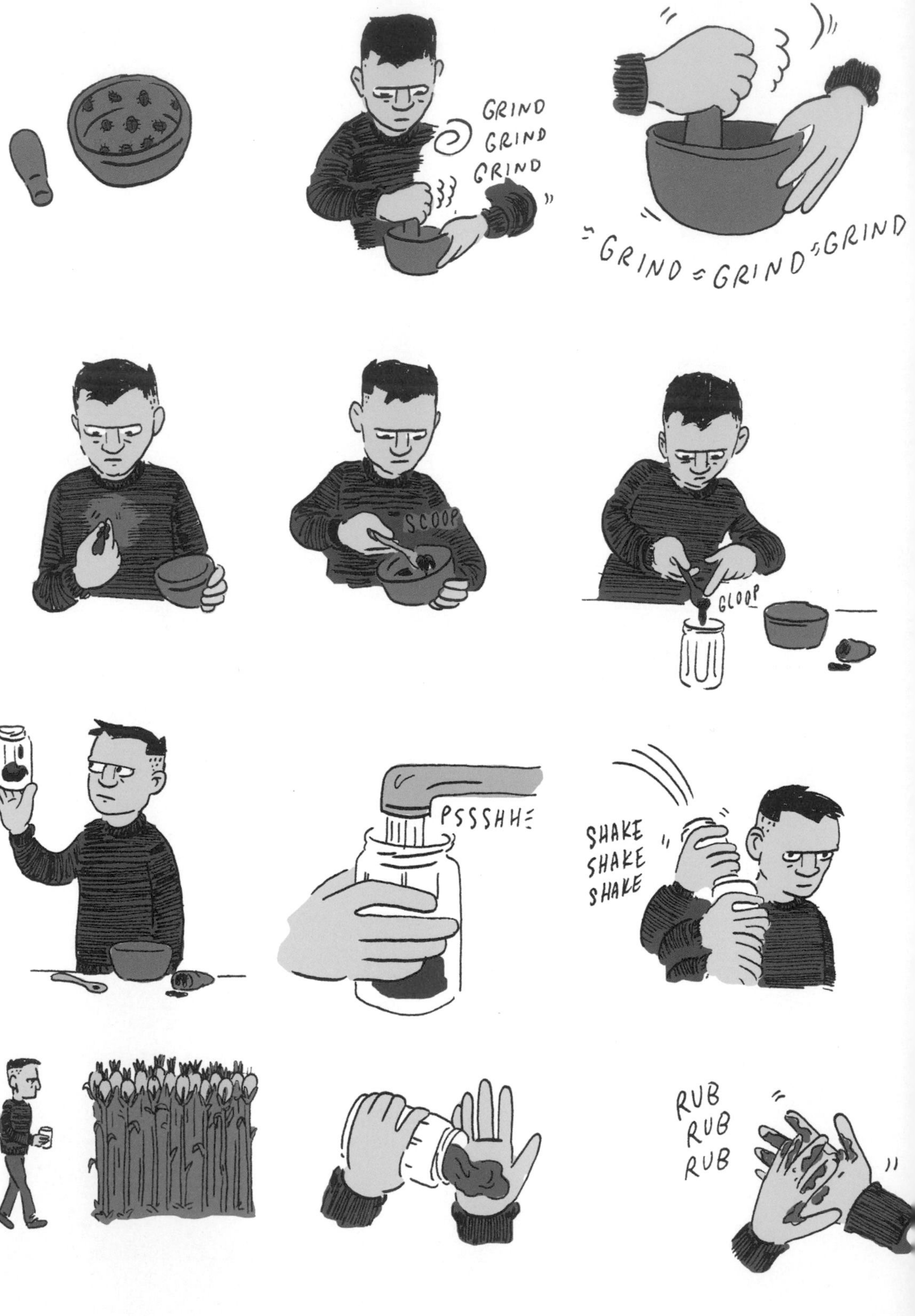
GRIND
GRIND
GRIND
GRIND GRIND GRIND
SCOOP
GLOOP
PSSSHH
SHAKE
SHAKE
SHAKE
RUB
RUB
RUB

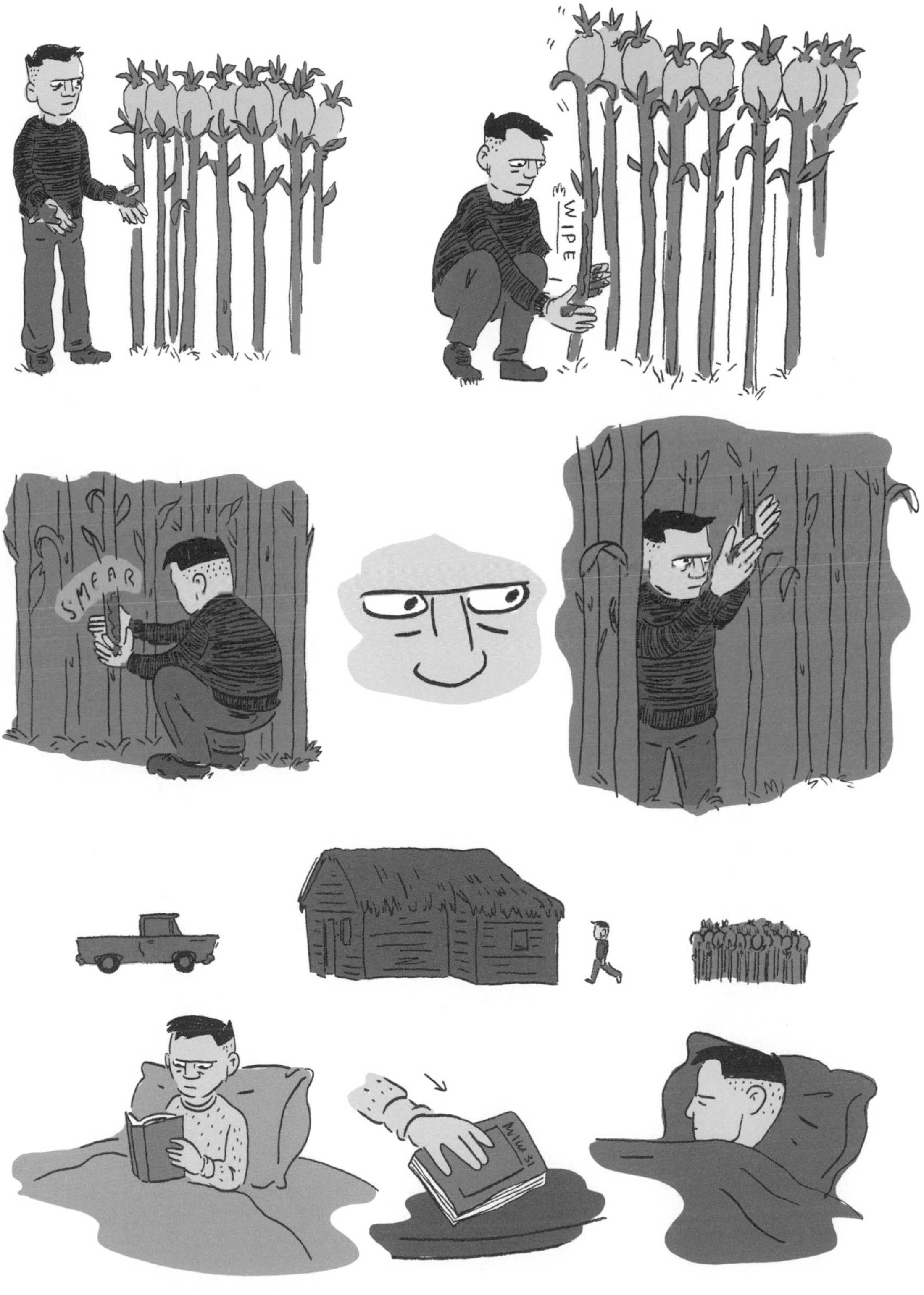
WIPE
SMEAR

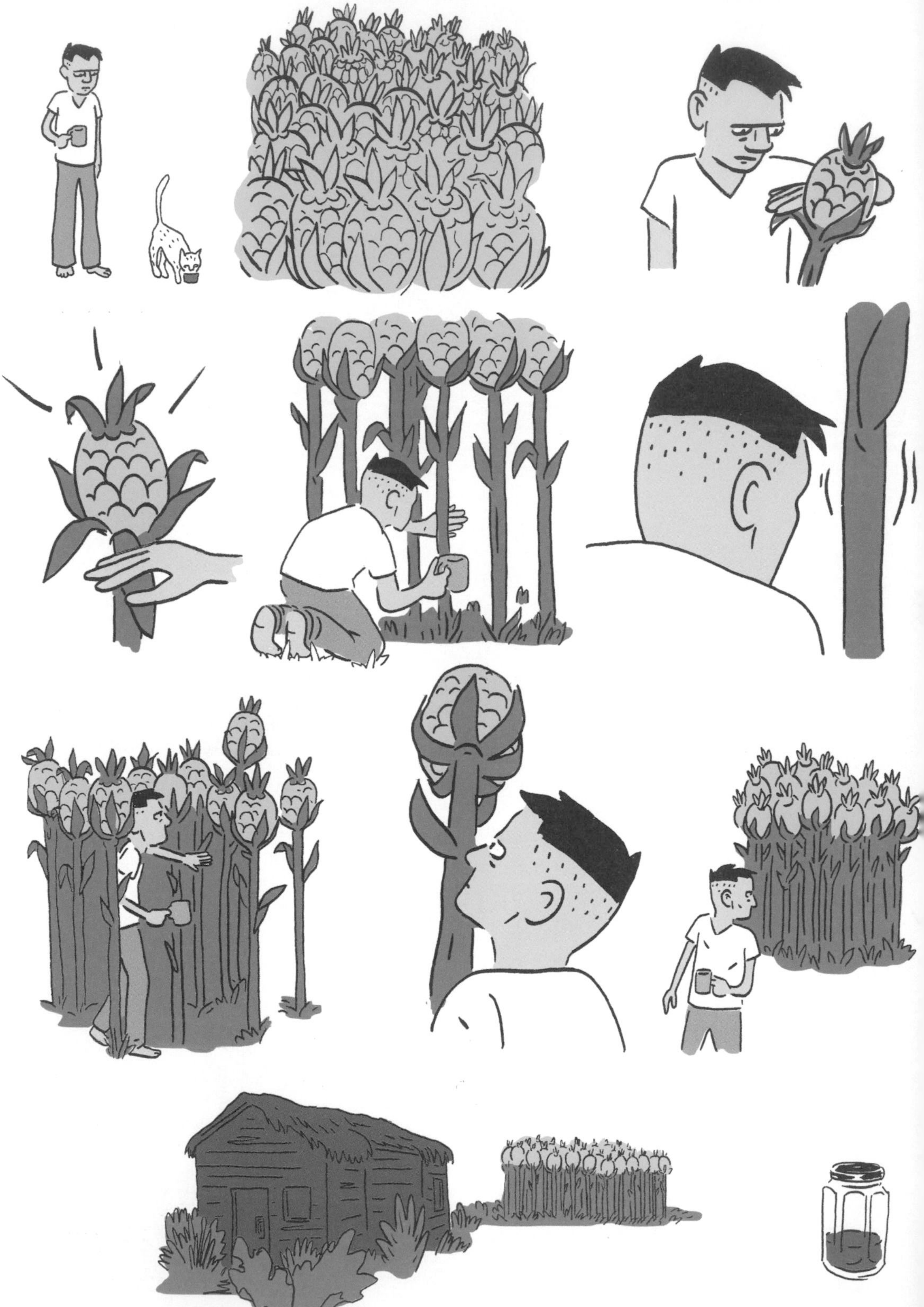

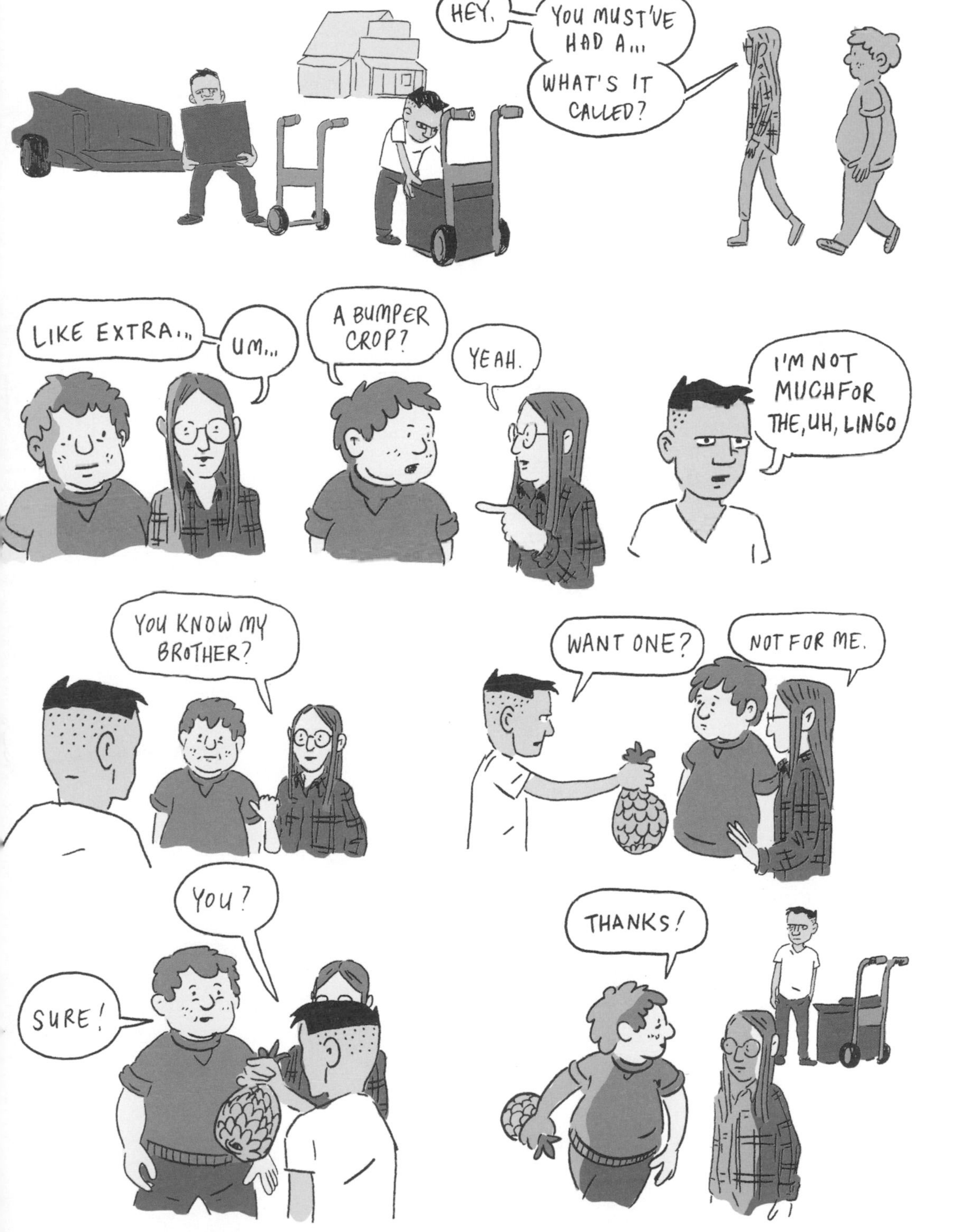
HEY.
YOU MUST'VE HAD A...
WHAT'S IT CALLED?
LIKE EXTRA...
UM...
A BUMPER CROP?
YEAH.
I'M NOT MUCHFOR THE, UH, LINGO
YOU KNOW MY BROTHER?
WANT ONE?
NOT FOR ME.
YOU?
SURE!
THANKS!

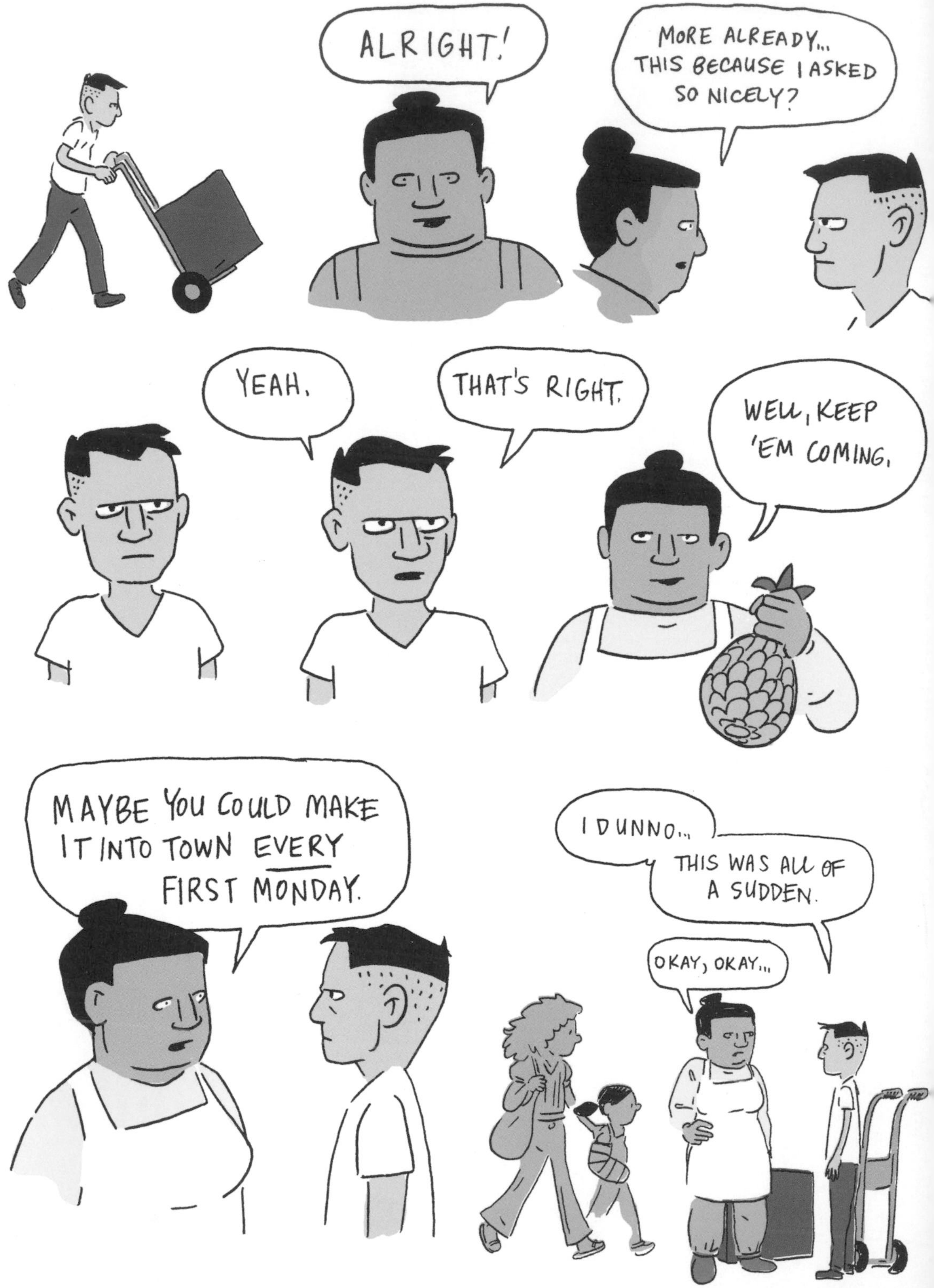
ALRIGHT!
MORE ALREADY... THIS BECAUSE I ASKED SO NICELY?
YEAH.
THAT'S RIGHT.
WELL, KEEP 'EM COMING.
MAYBE YOU COULD MAKE IT INTO TOWN EVERY FIRST MONDAY.
I DUNNO...
THIS WAS ALL OF A SUDDEN.
OKAY, OKAY...

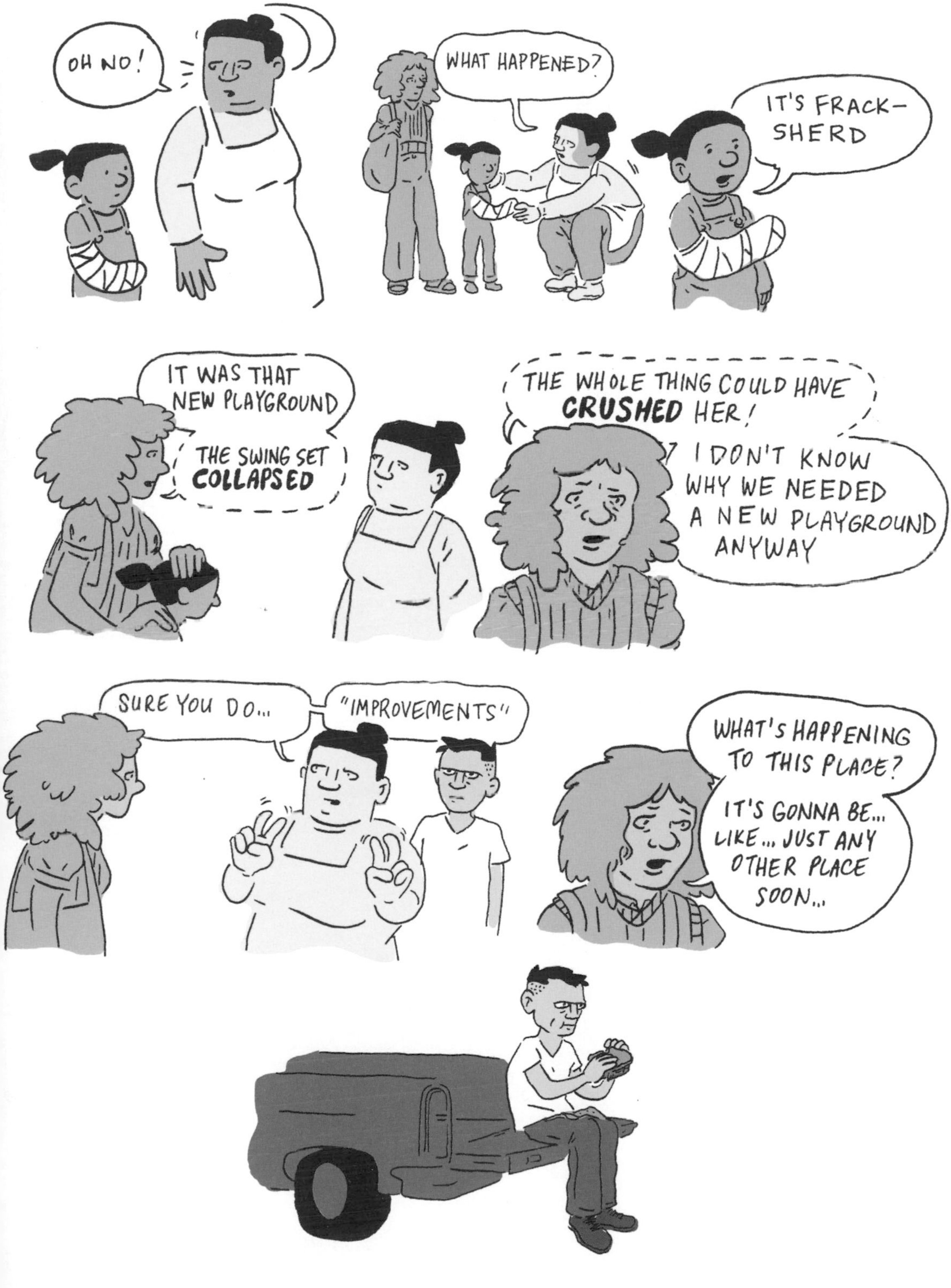
OH NO!
WHAT HAPPENED?
IT'S FRACK-SHERD
IT WAS THAT NEW PLAYGROUND
THE SWING SET COLLAPSED
THE WHOLE THING COULD HAVE CRUSHED HER!
I DON'T KNOW WHY WE NEEDED A NEW PLAYGROUND ANYWAY
SURE YOU DO...
"IMPROVEMENTS"
WHAT'S HAPPENING TO THIS PLACE?
IT'S GONNA BE... LIKE... JUST ANY OTHER PLACE SOON...

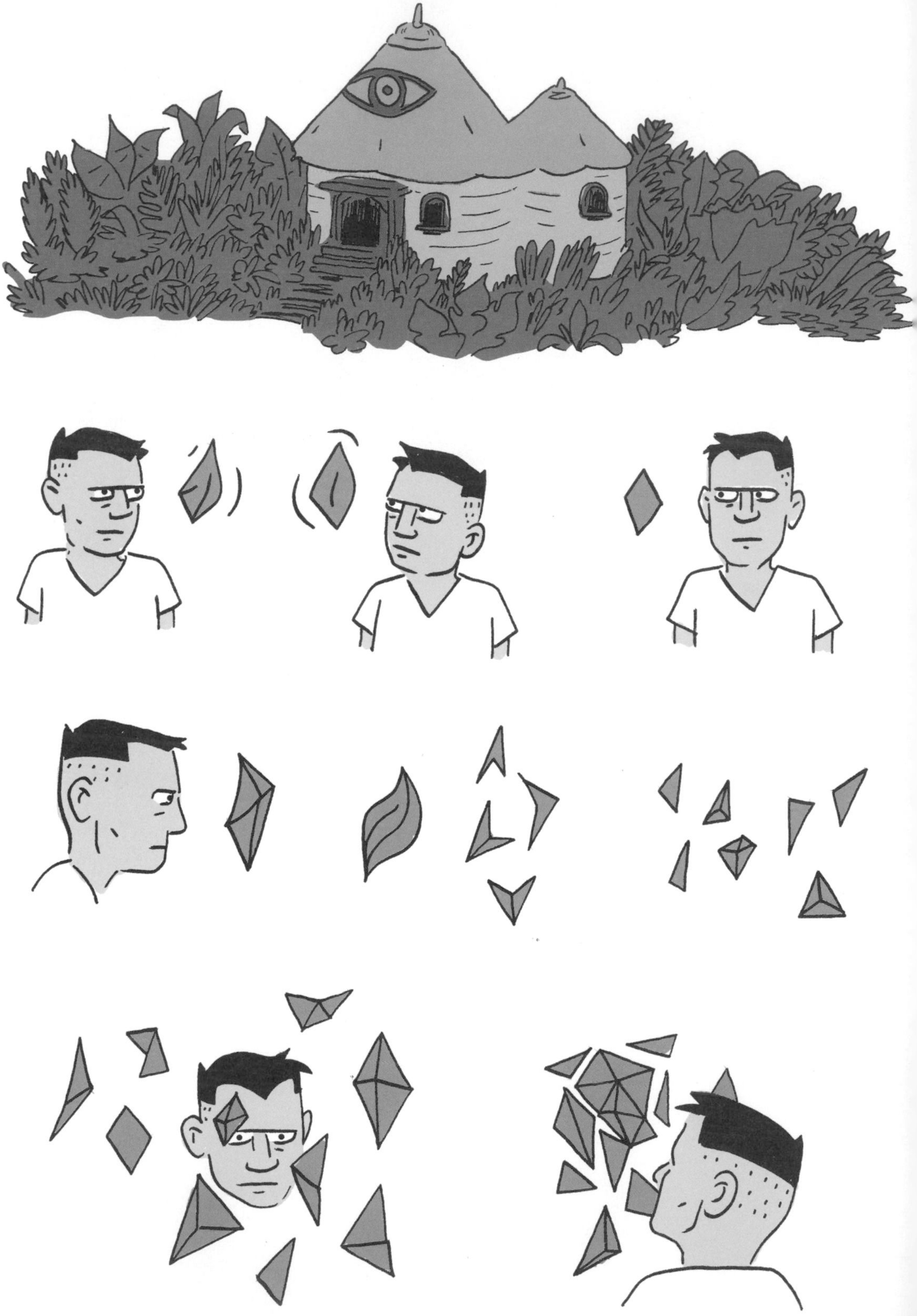

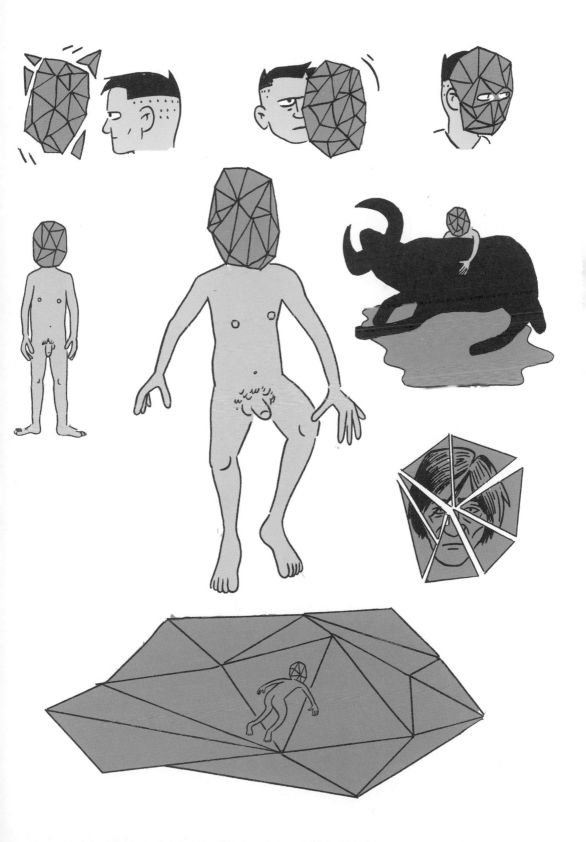

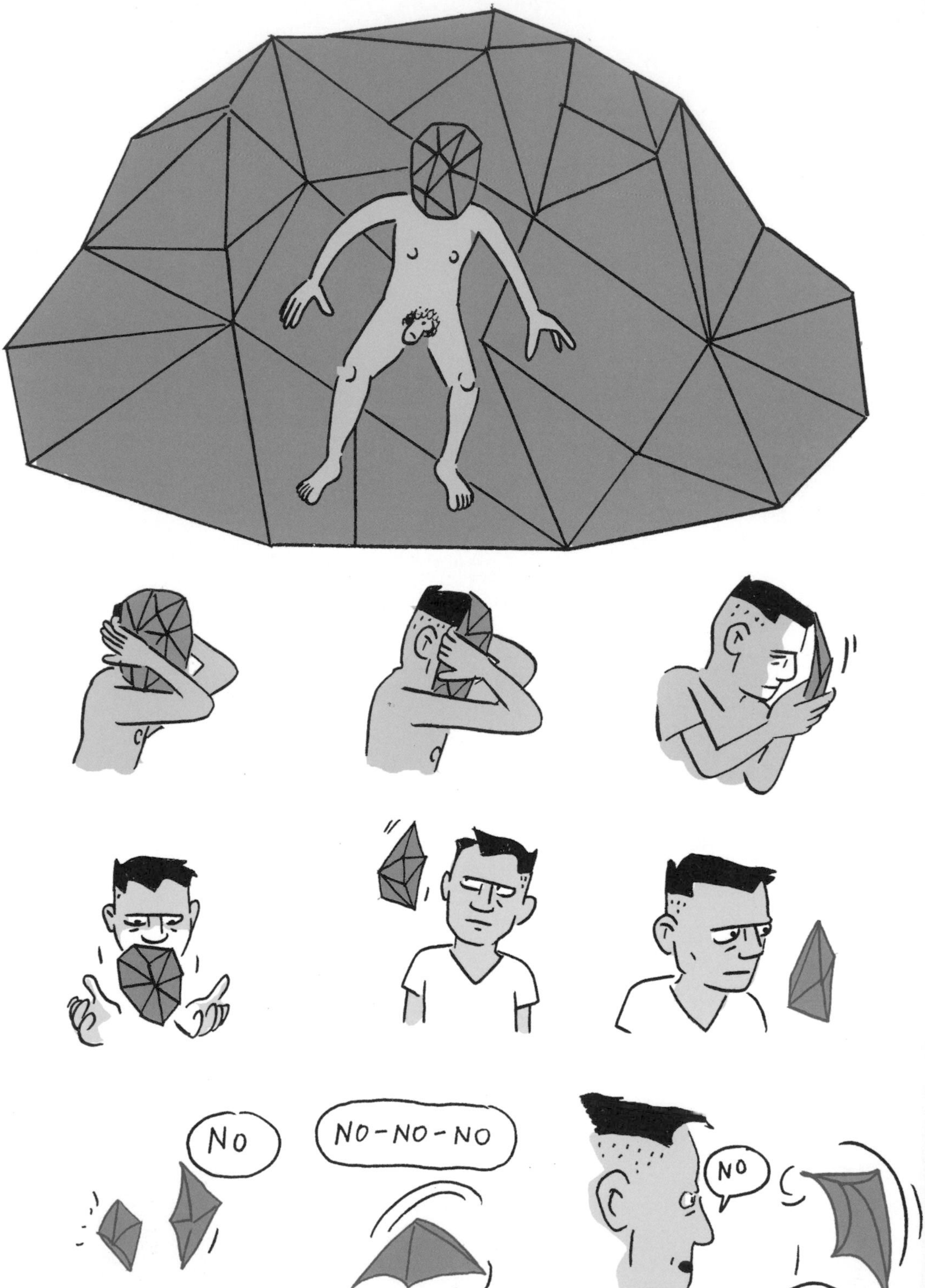
NO
NO-NO-NO
NO

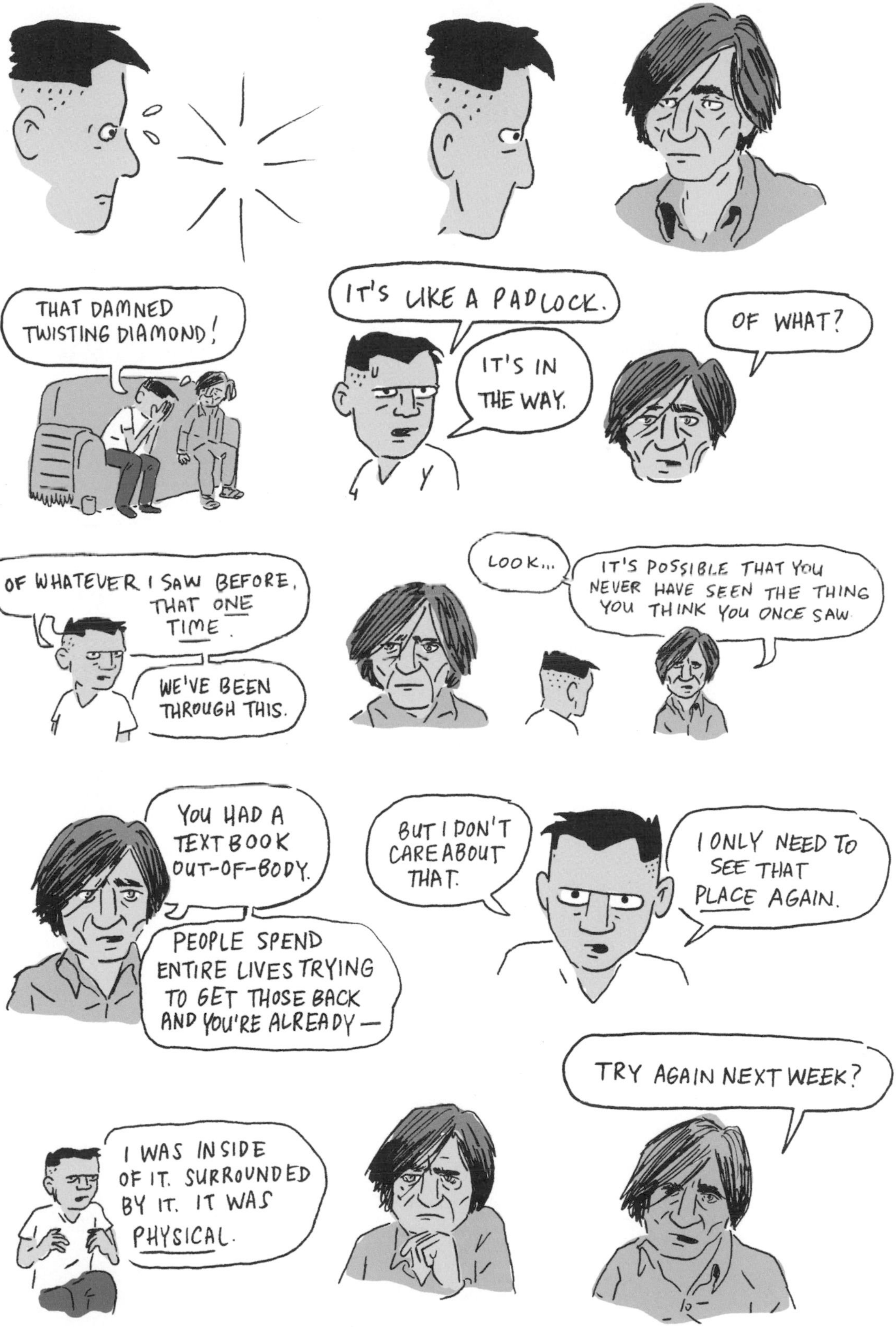
THAT DAMNED TWISTING DIAMOND!
IT'S LIKE A PADLOCK.
IT'S IN THE WAY.
OF WHAT?
OF WHATEVER I SAW BEFORE. THAT ONE TIME.
WE'VE BEEN THROUGH THIS.
LOOK...
IT'S POSSIBLE THAT YOU NEVER HAVE SEEN THE THING YOU THINK YOU ONCE SAW.
YOU HAD A TEXTBOOK OUT-OF-BODY.
PEOPLE SPEND ENTIRE LIVES TRYING TO GET THOSE BACK AND YOU'RE ALREADY—
BUT I DON'T CARE ABOUT THAT.
I ONLY NEED TO SEE THAT PLACE AGAIN.
I WAS INSIDE OF IT. SURROUNDED BY IT. IT WAS PHYSICAL.
TRY AGAIN NEXT WEEK?

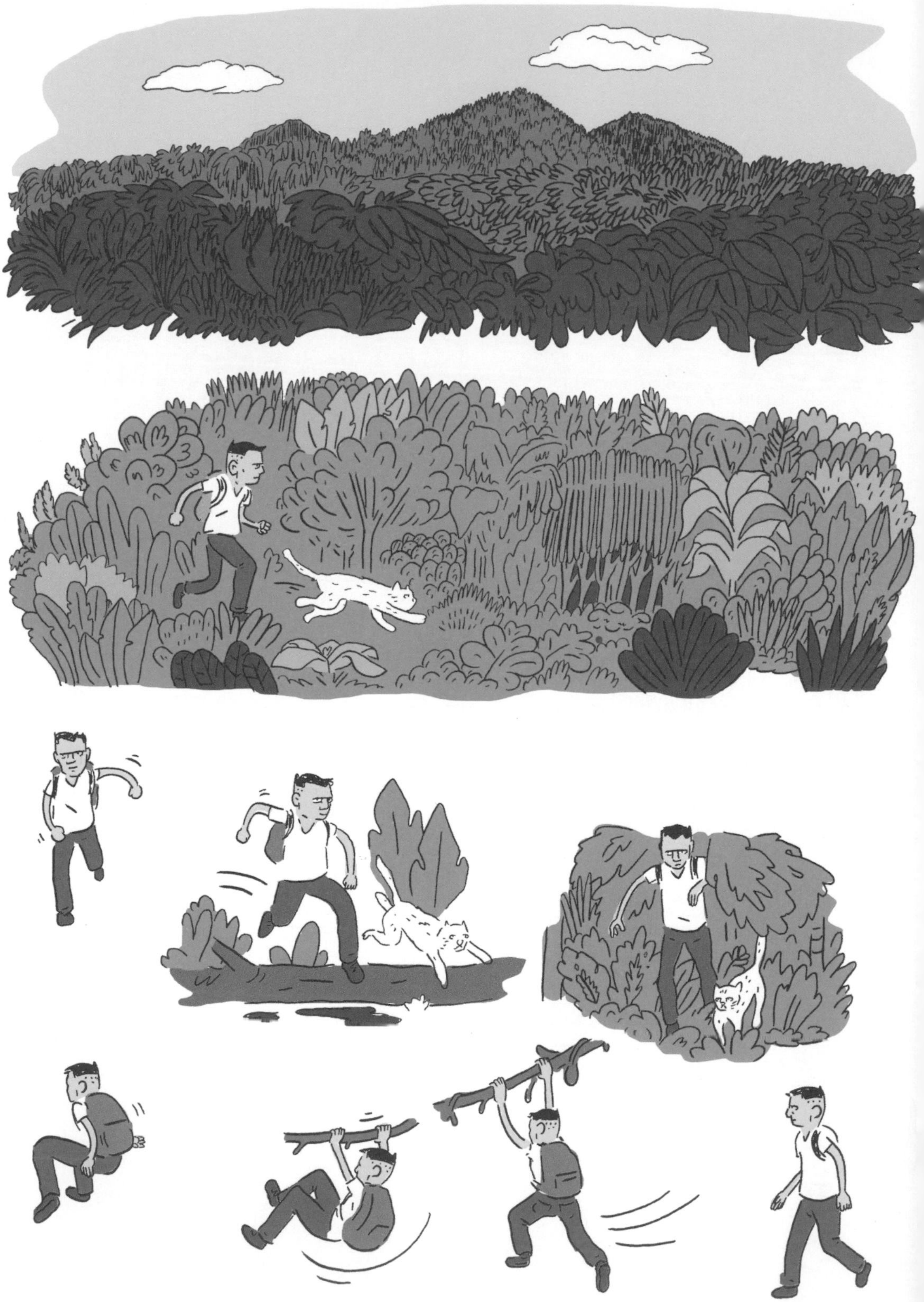

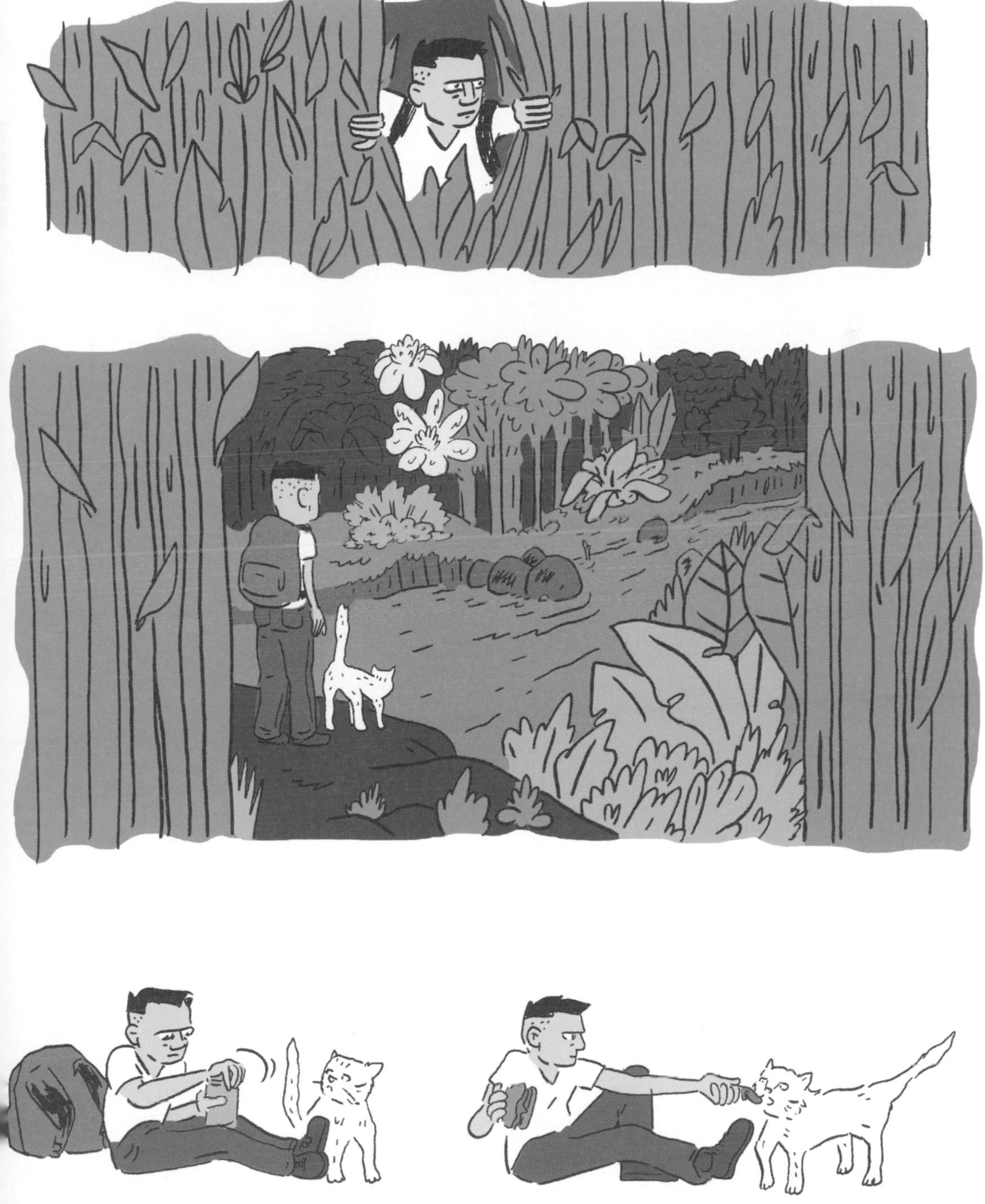

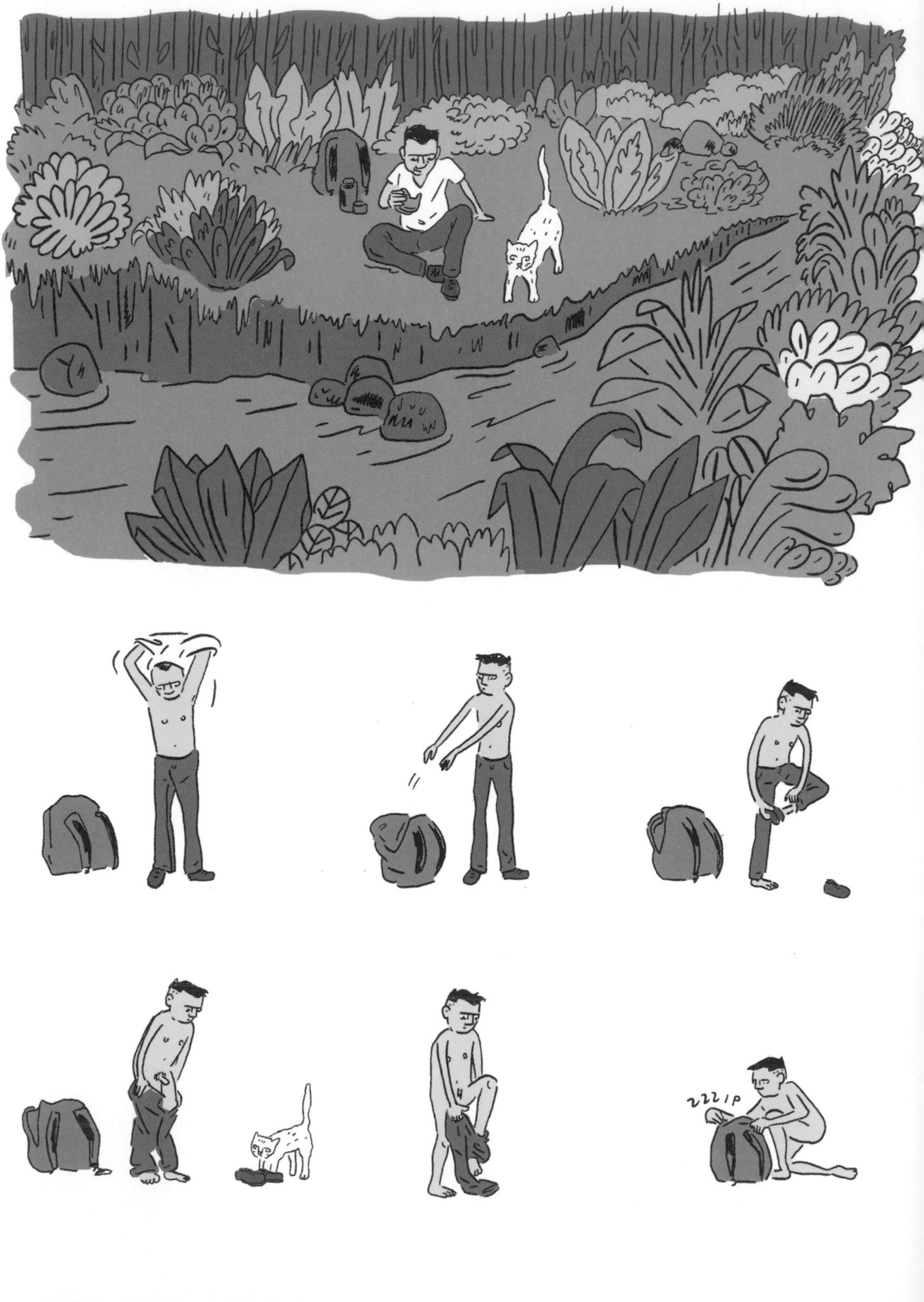
ZZZIP

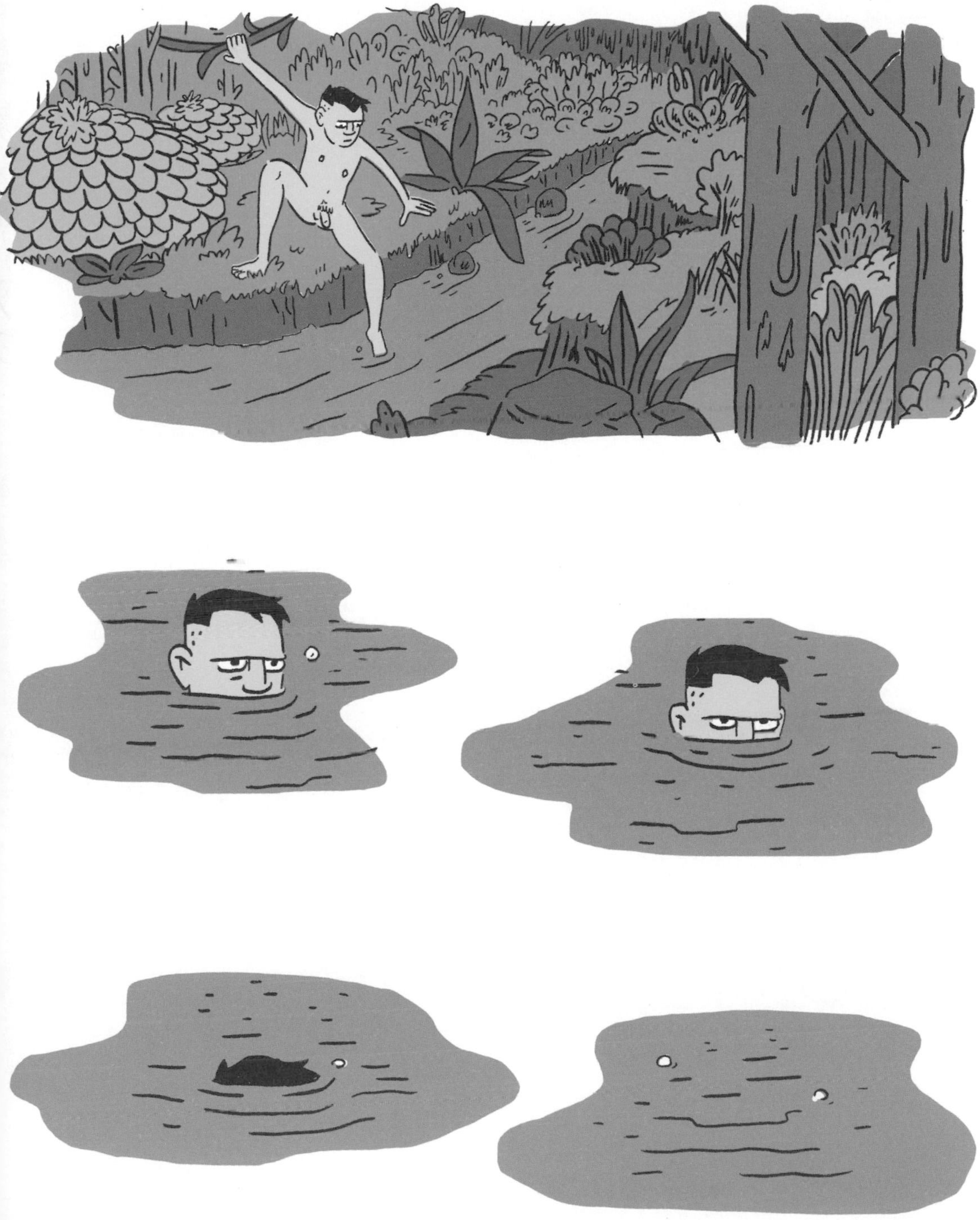

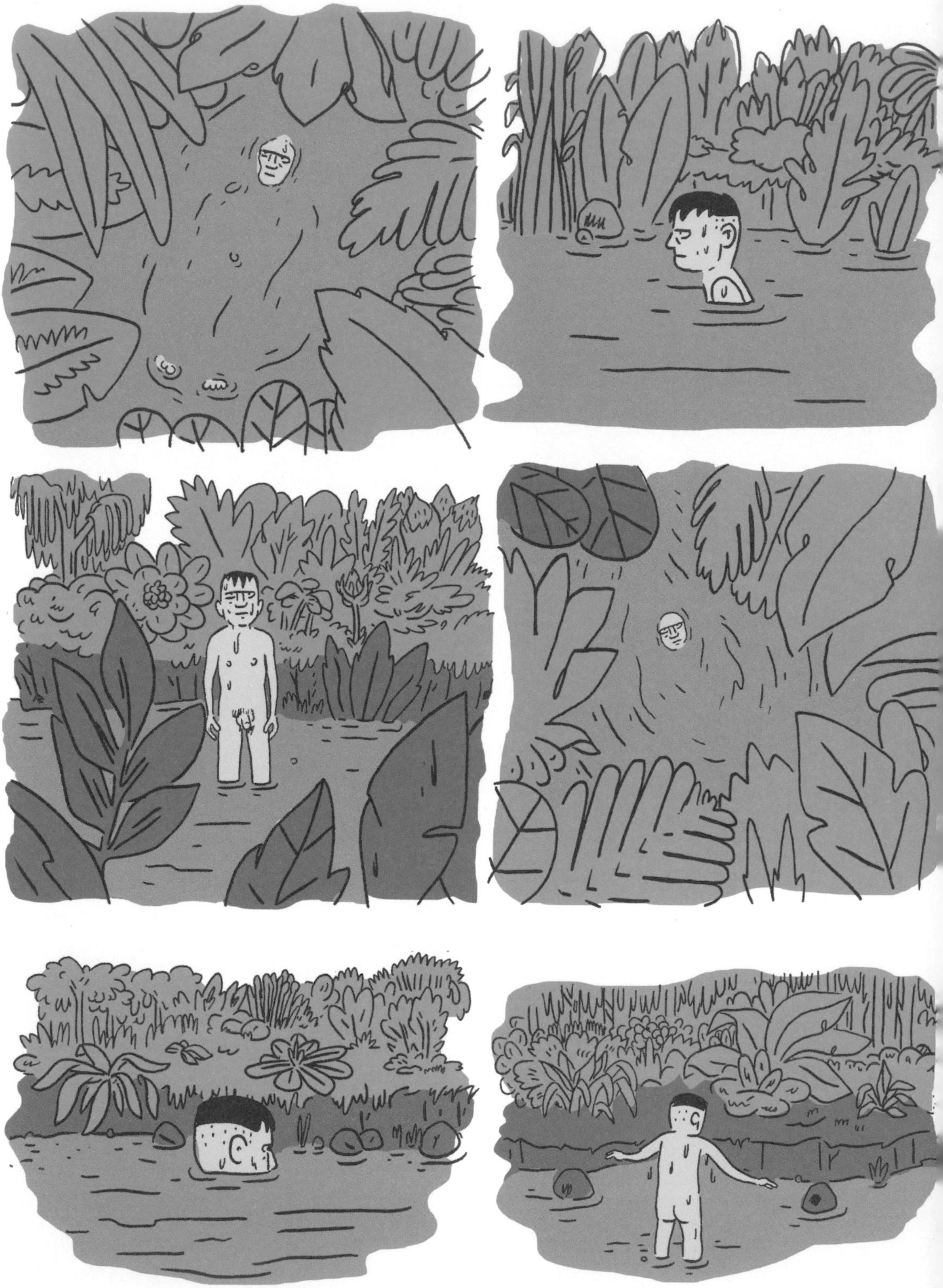

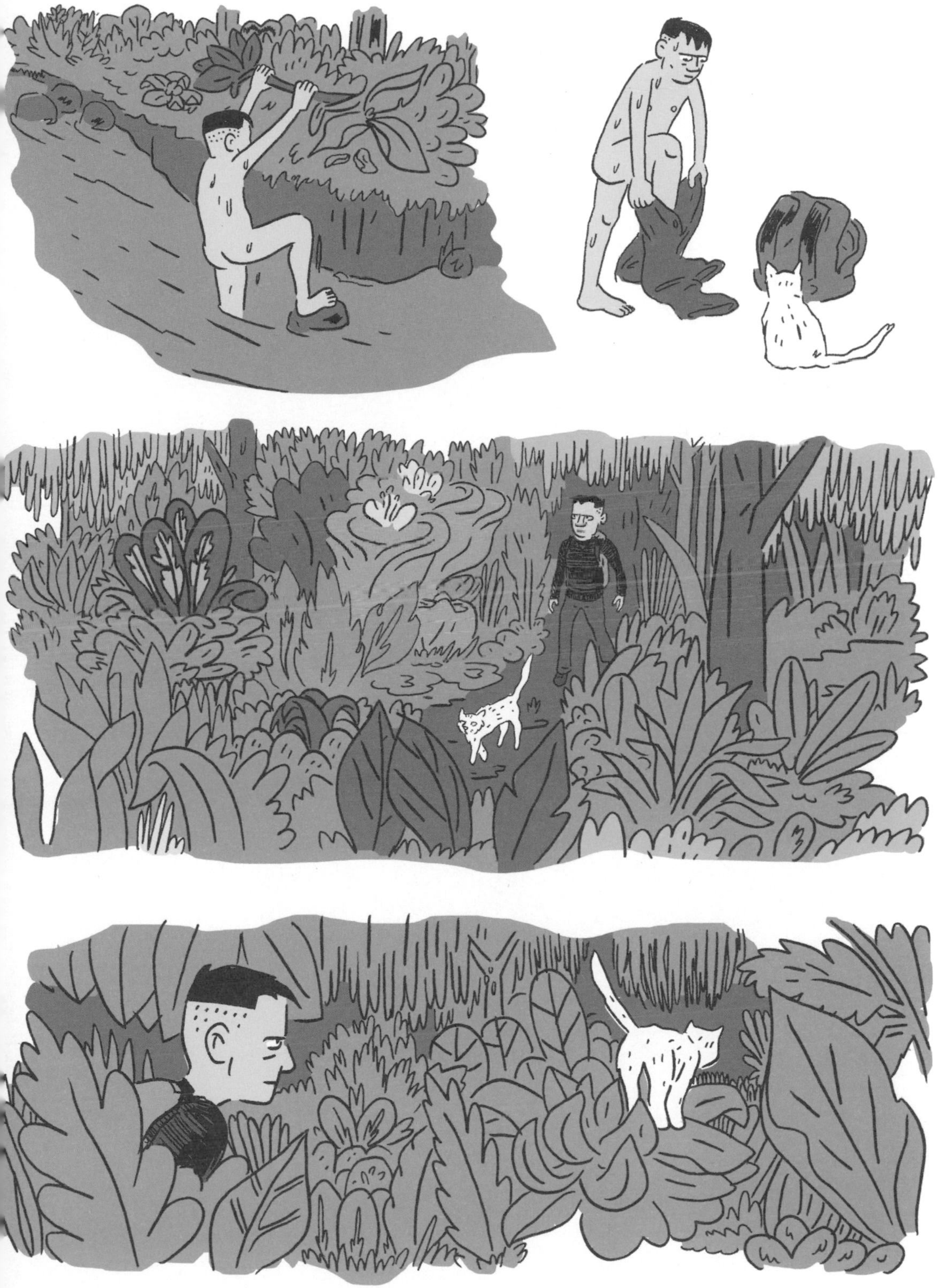

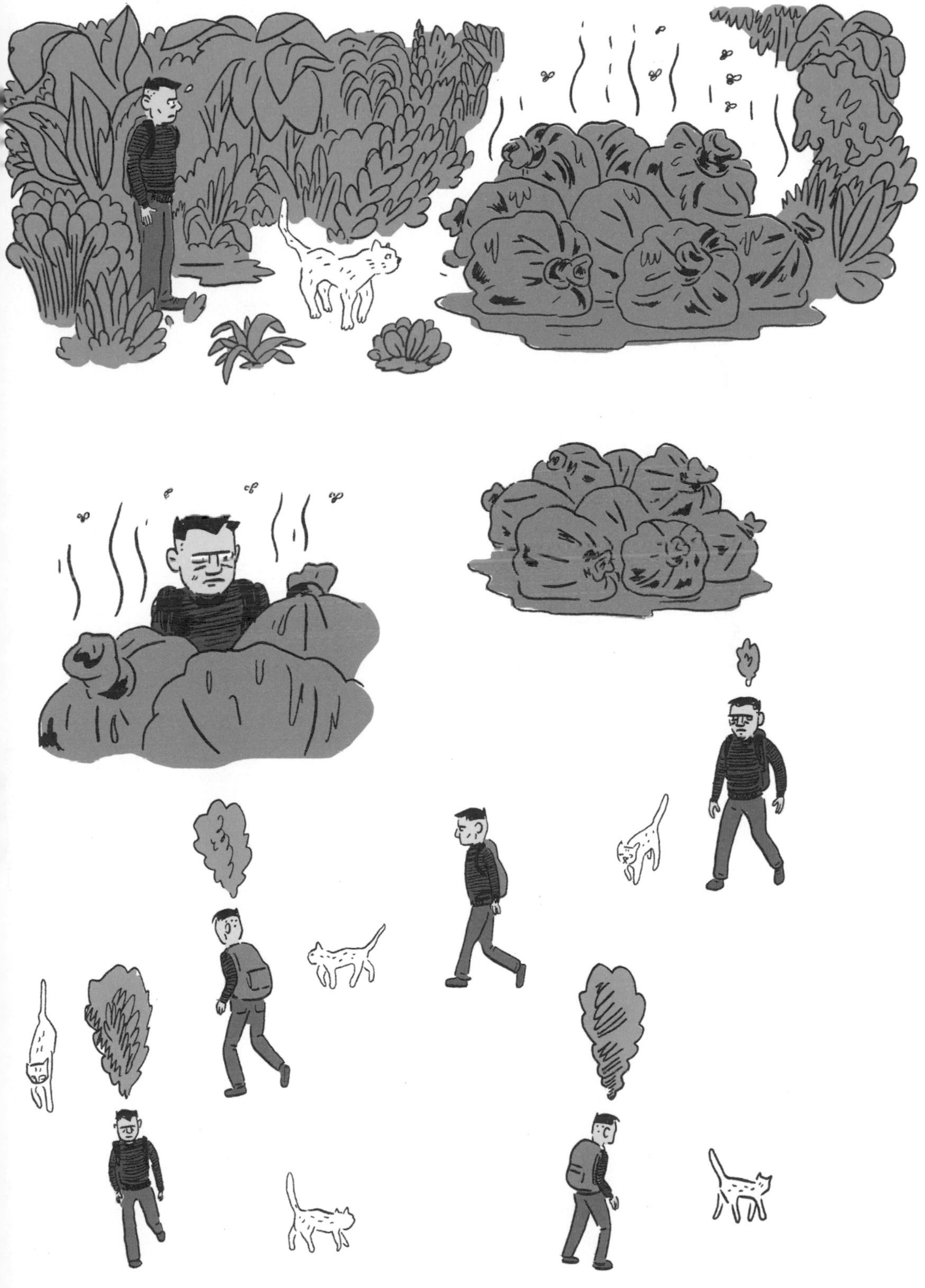

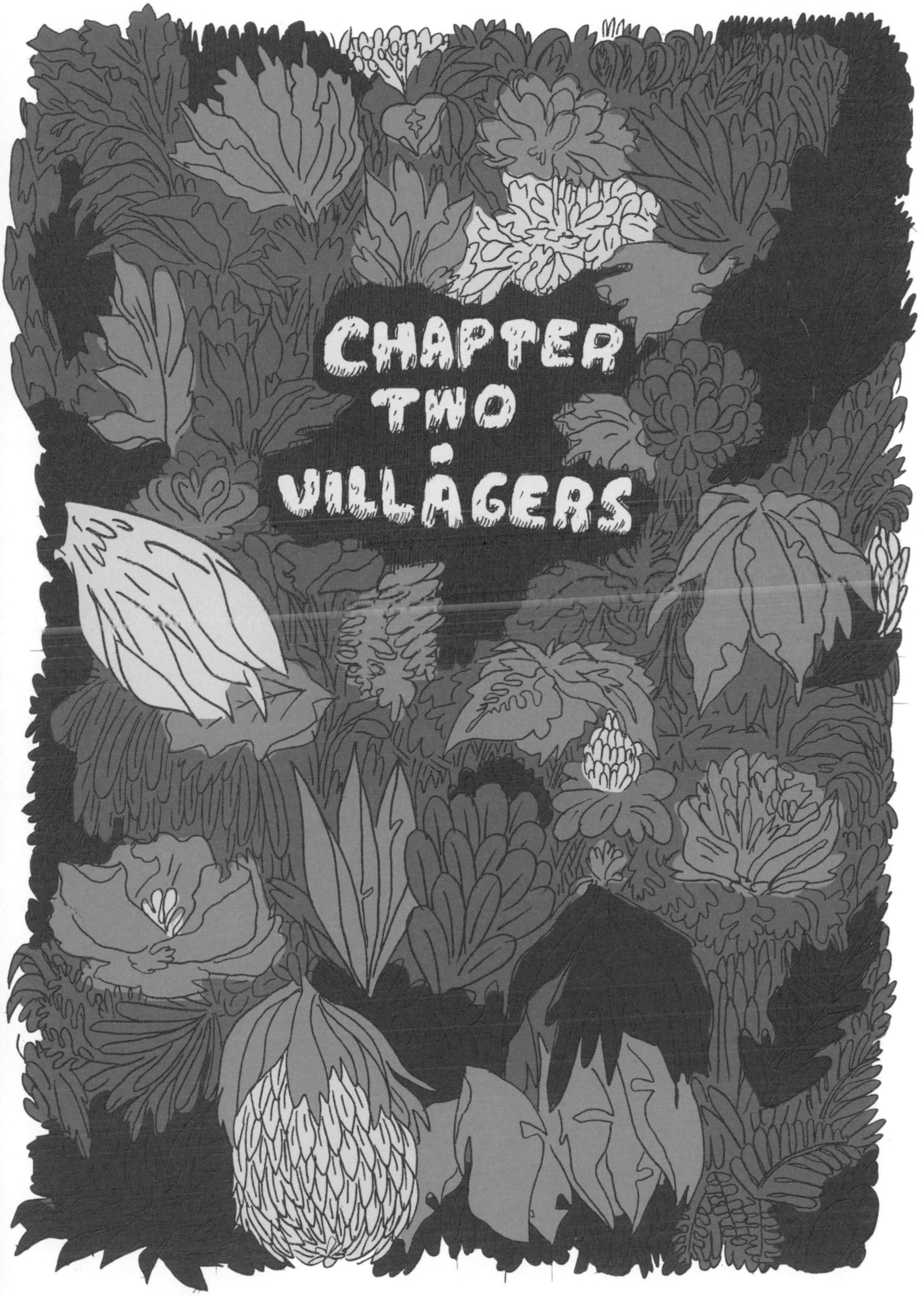
CHAPTER
TWO
VILLAGERS

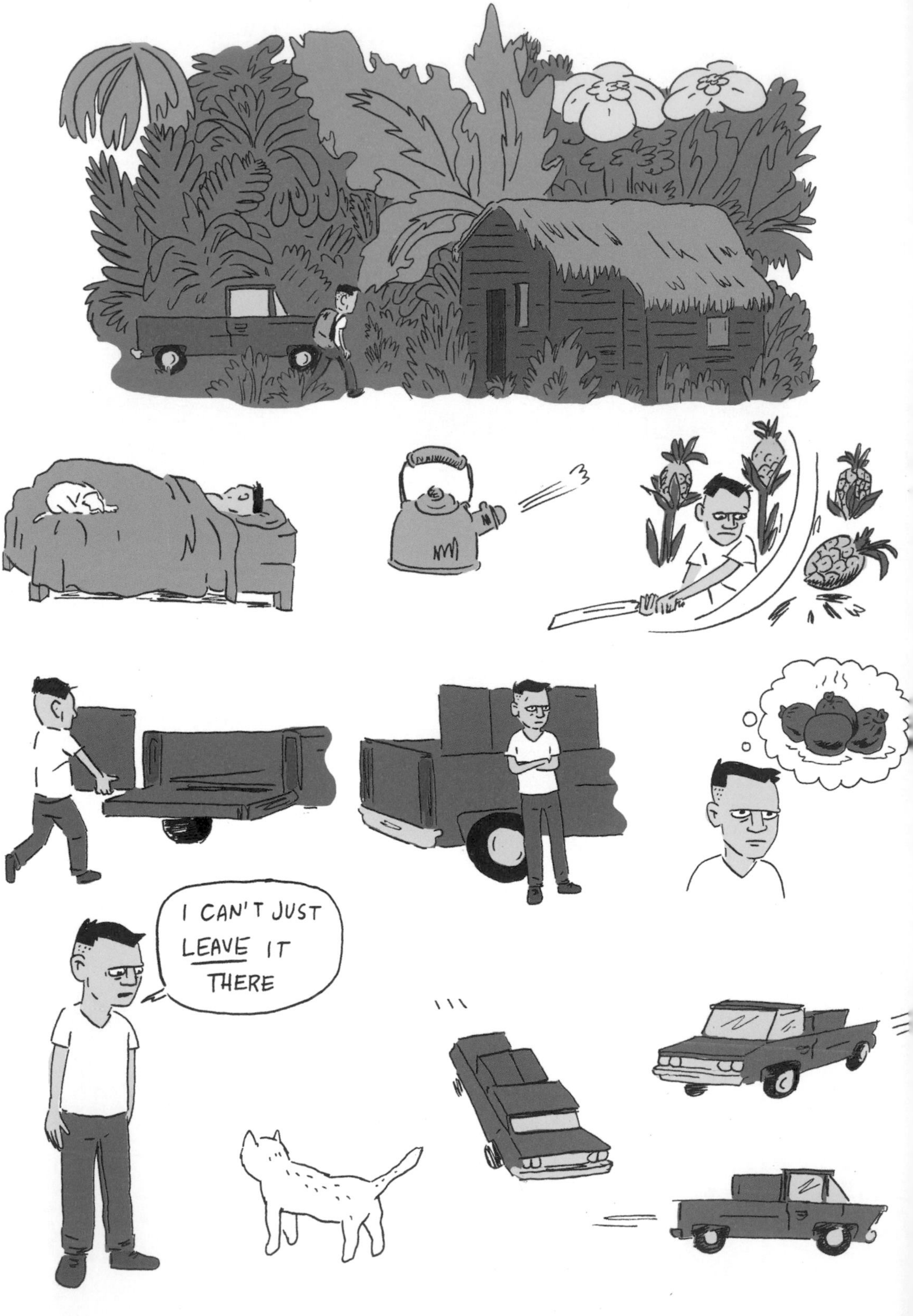
I CAN'T JUST LEAVE IT THERE

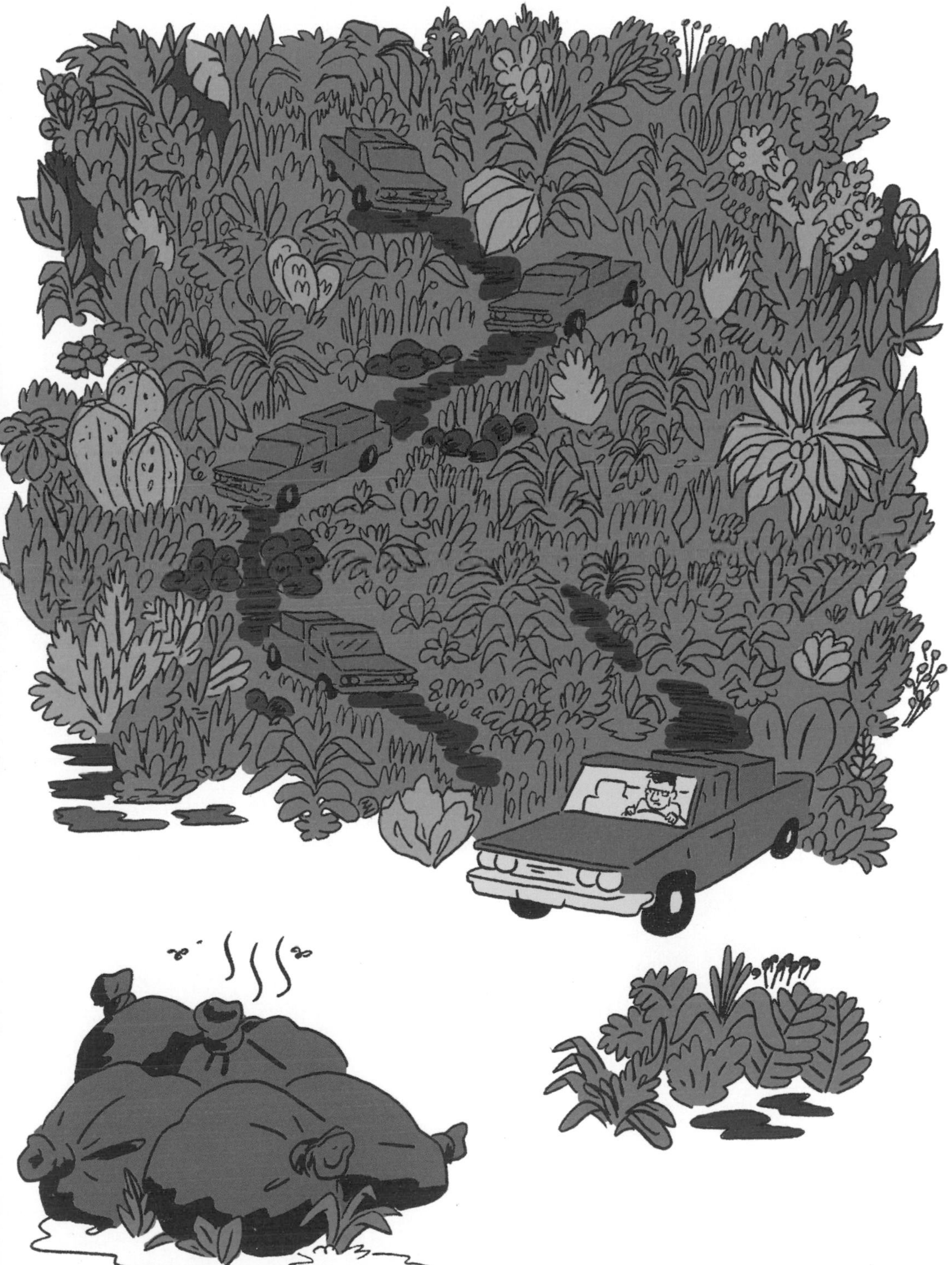

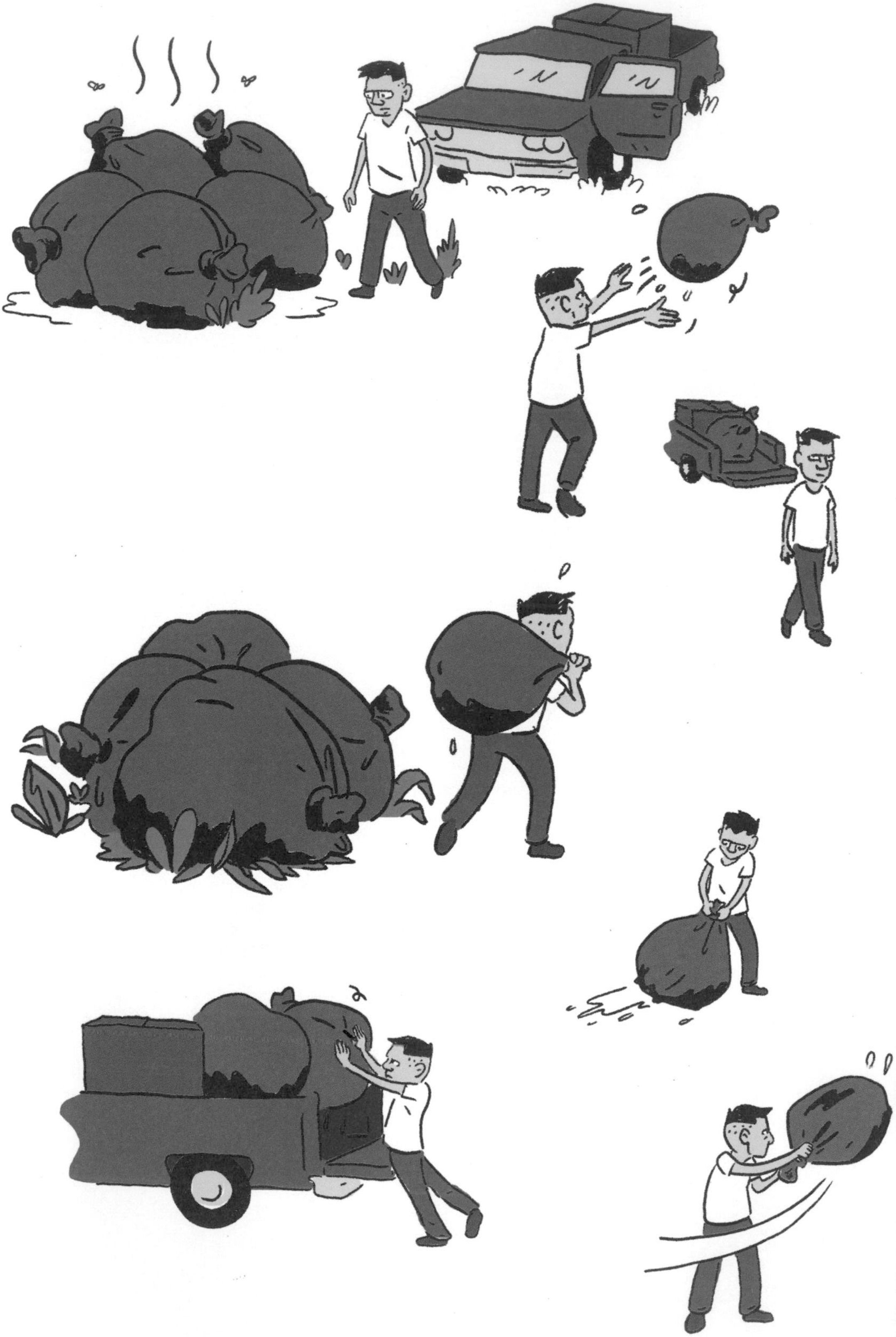

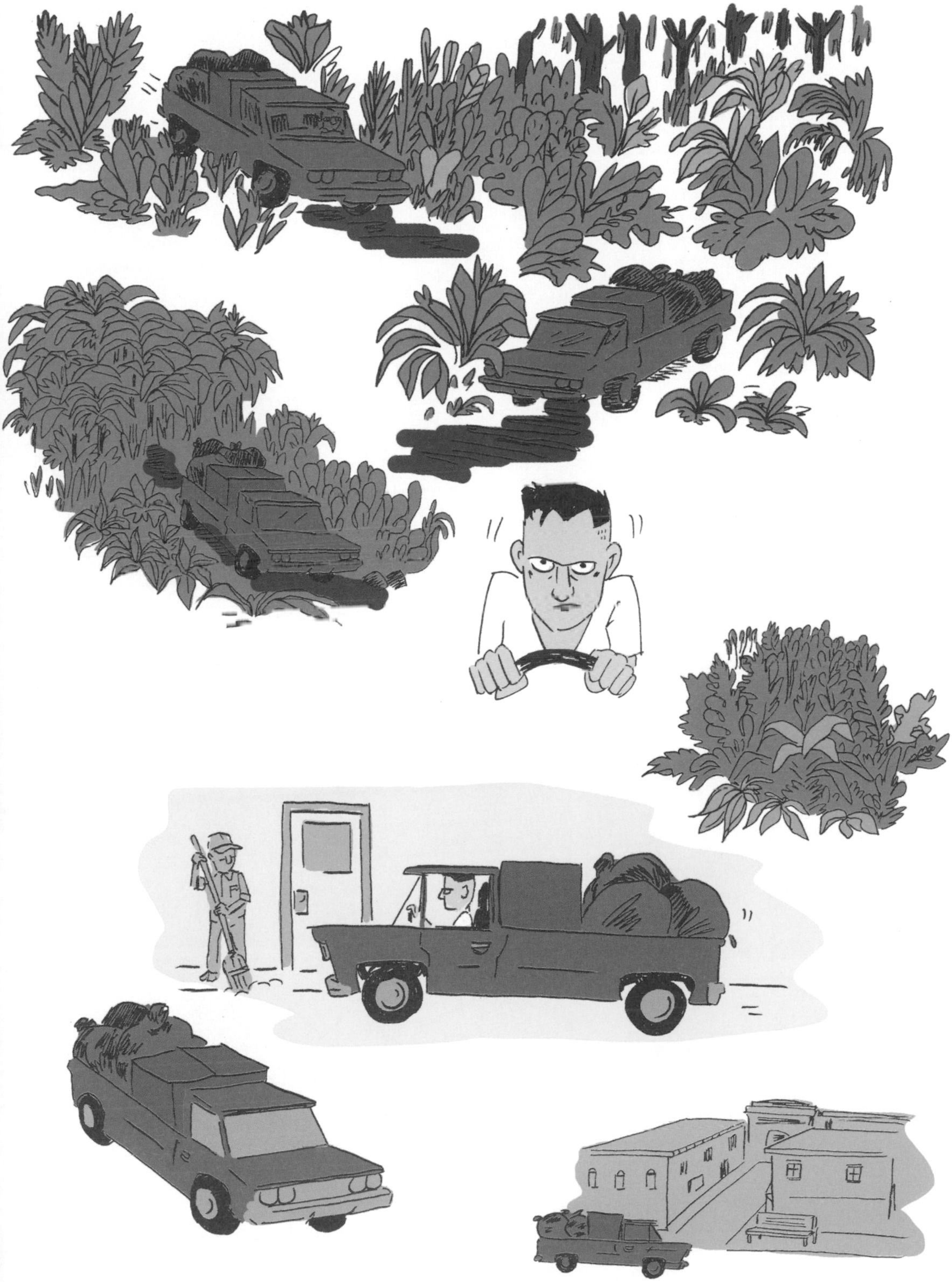

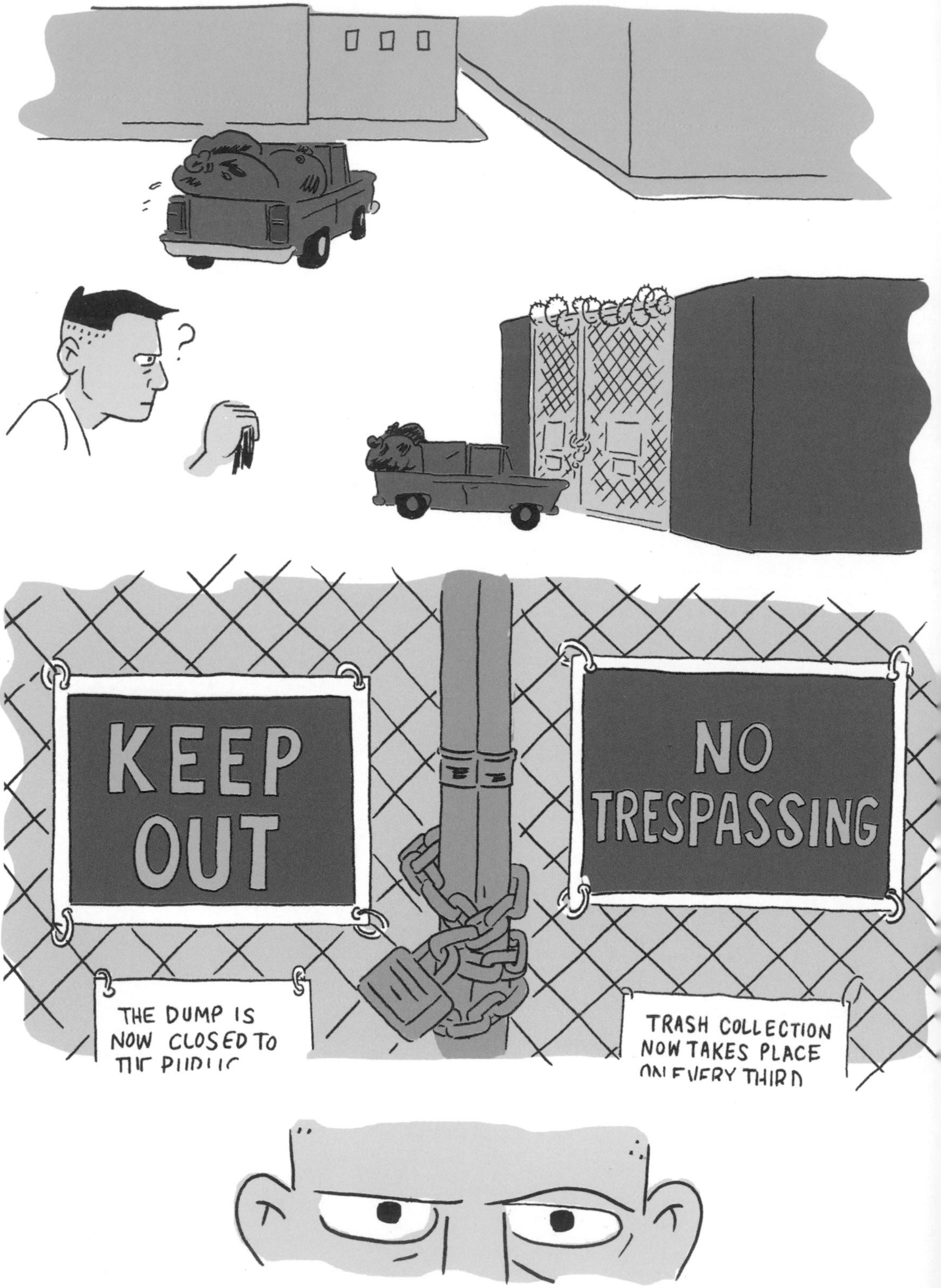
?
KEEP OUT
NO TRESPASSING
THE DUMP IS
NOW CLOSED TO
TRASH COLLECTION
NOW TAKES PLACE

 GOOD MORNING.

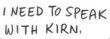 I NEED TO SPEAK WITH KIRN.

 CONCERNING?

 WASTE DISPOSAL

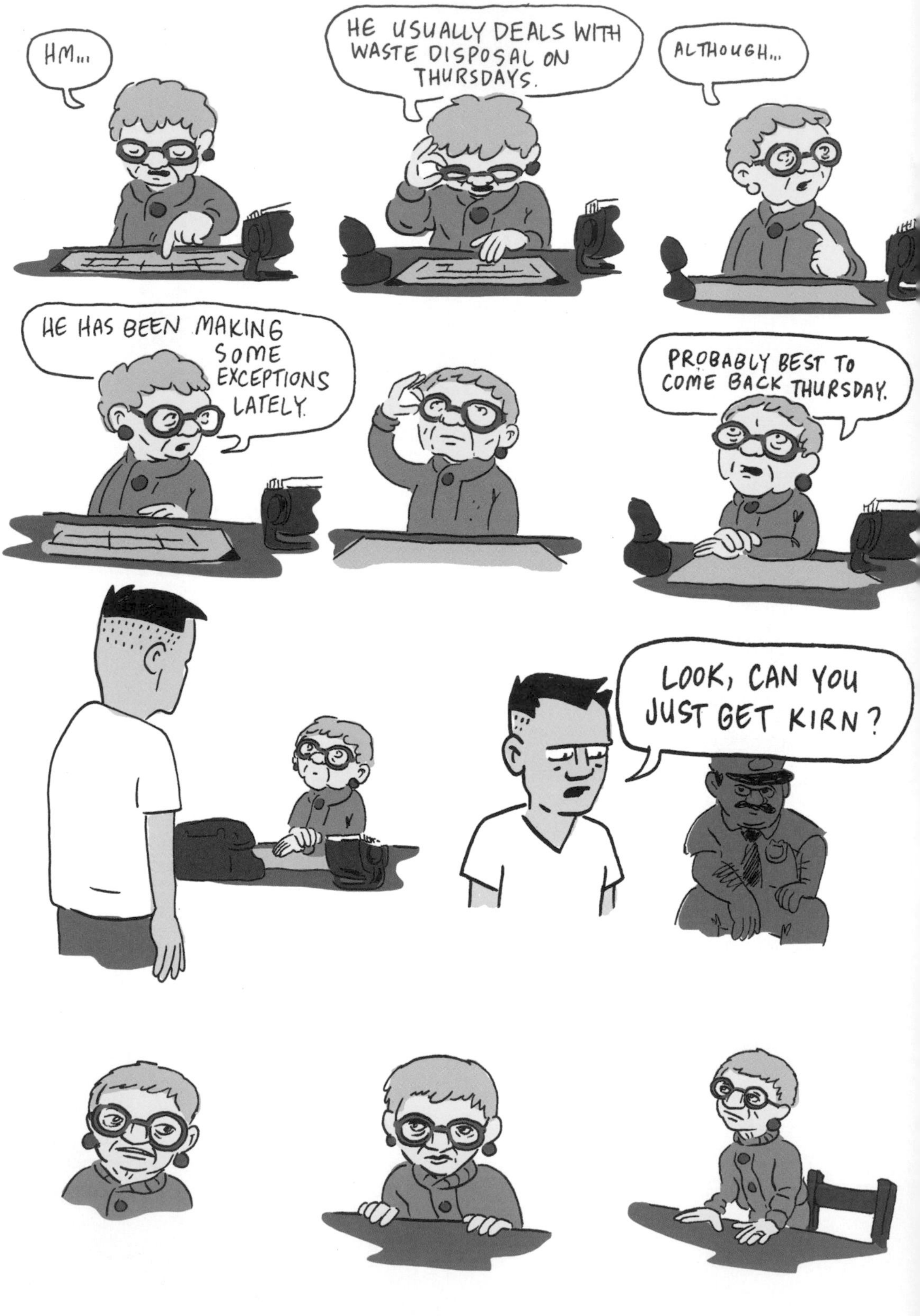
HM...
HE USUALLY DEALS WITH WASTE DISPOSAL ON THURSDAYS.
ALTHOUGH...
HE HAS BEEN MAKING SOME EXCEPTIONS LATELY.
PROBABLY BEST TO COME BACK THURSDAY.
LOOK, CAN YOU JUST GET KIRN?

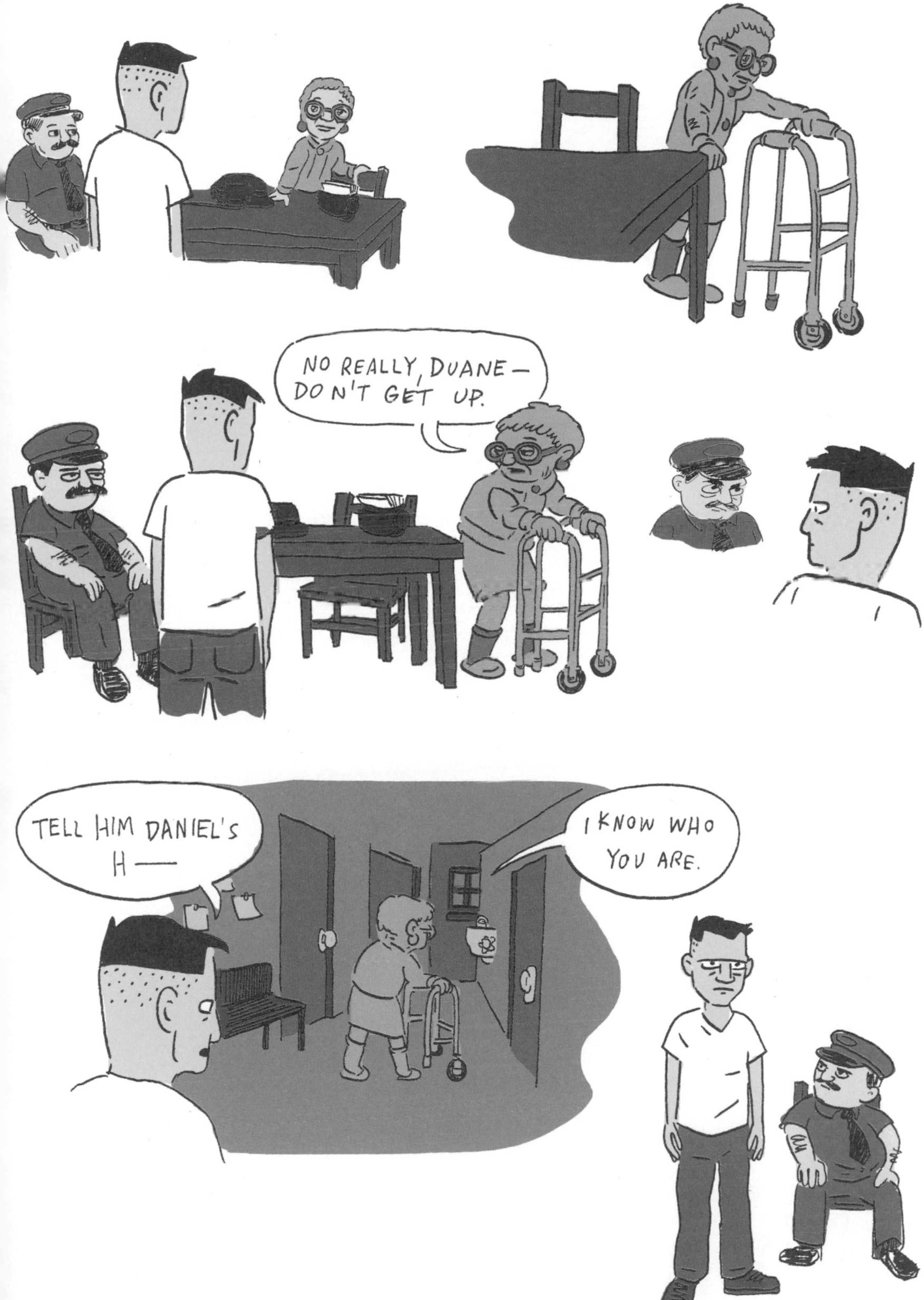
NO REALLY, DUANE—
DON'T GET UP.
TELL HIM DANIEL'S
H—
I KNOW WHO
YOU ARE.

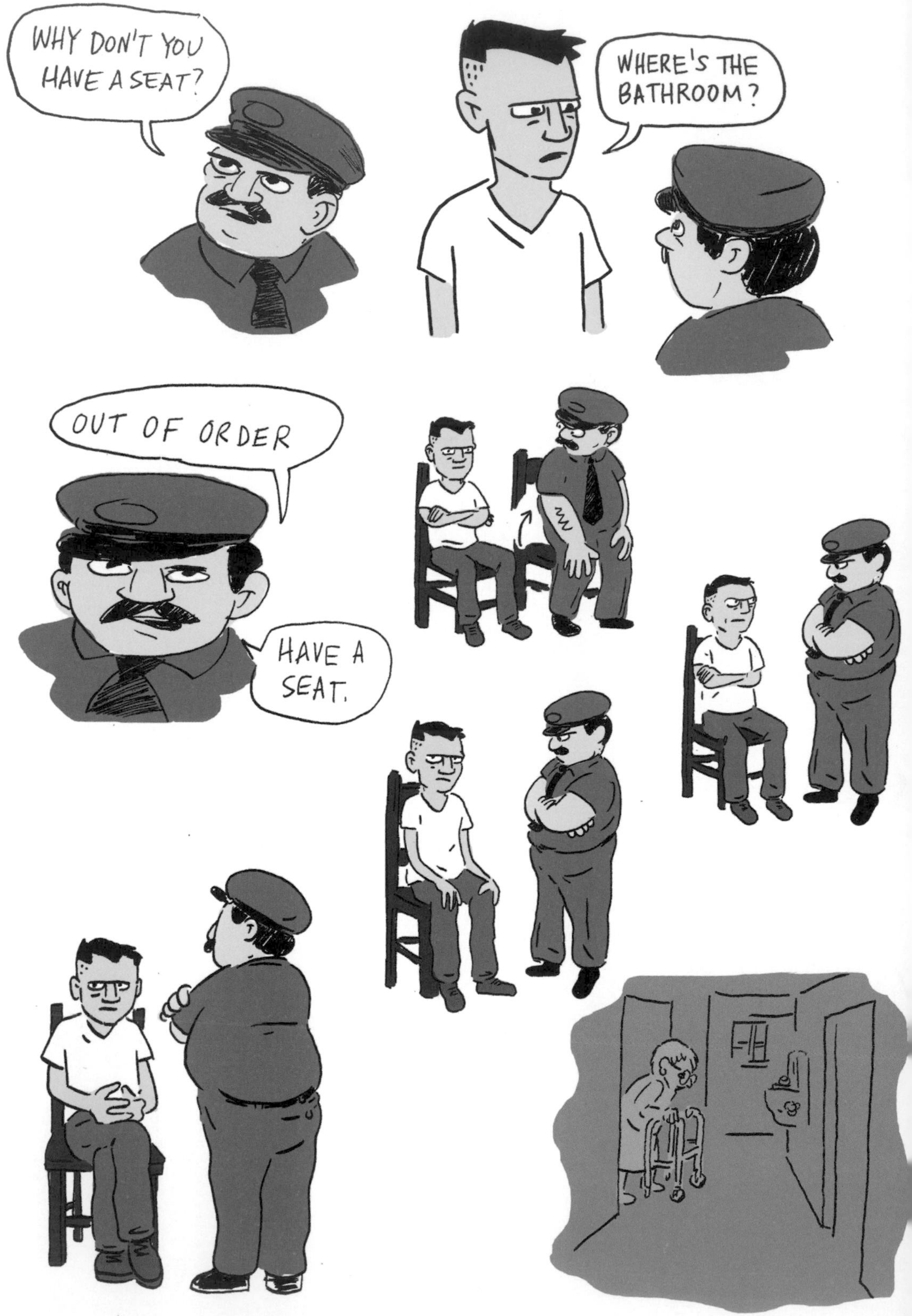
WHY DON'T YOU HAVE A SEAT?
WHERE'S THE BATHROOM?
OUT OF ORDER
HAVE A SEAT.

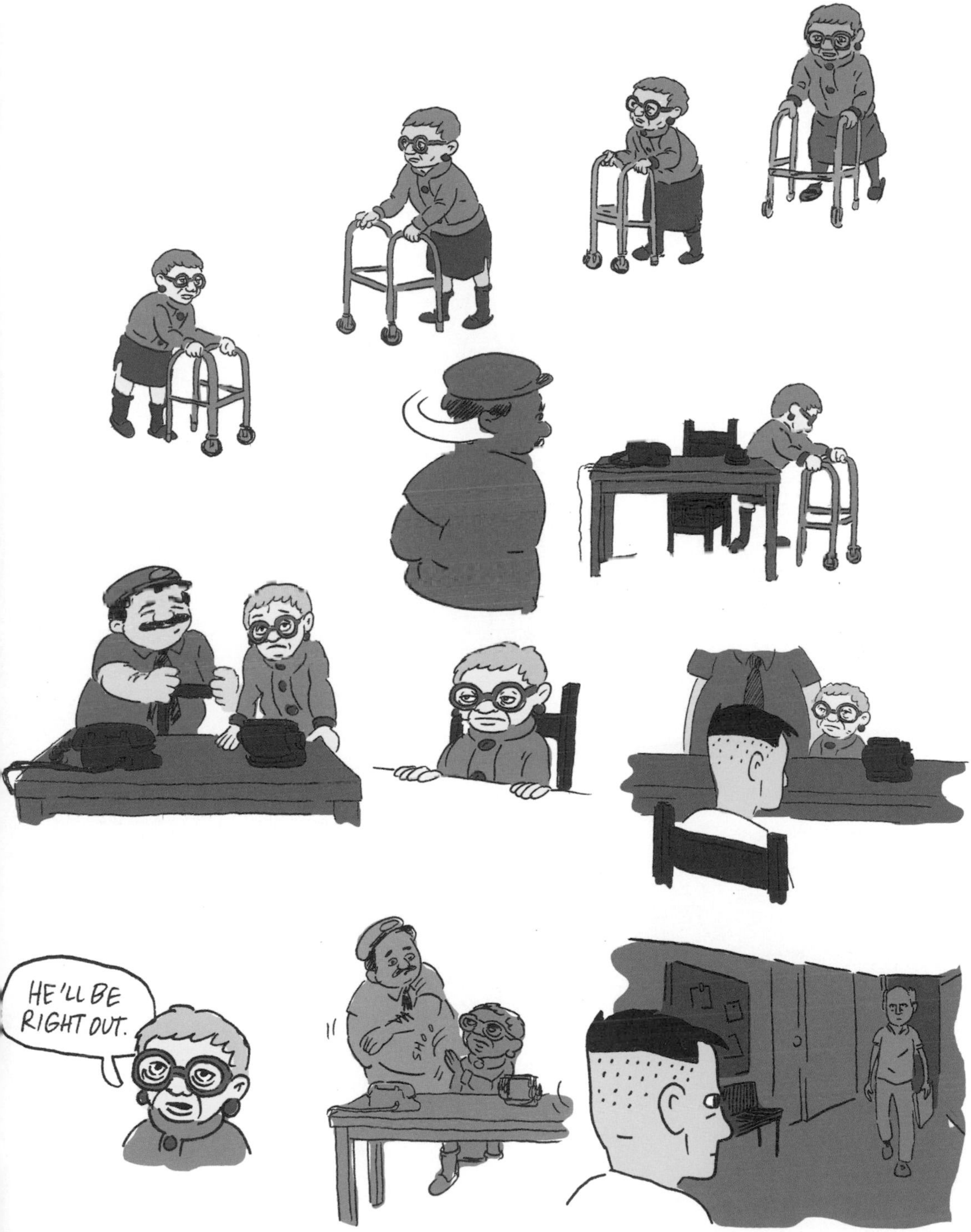
HE'LL BE RIGHT OUT.
SHOO

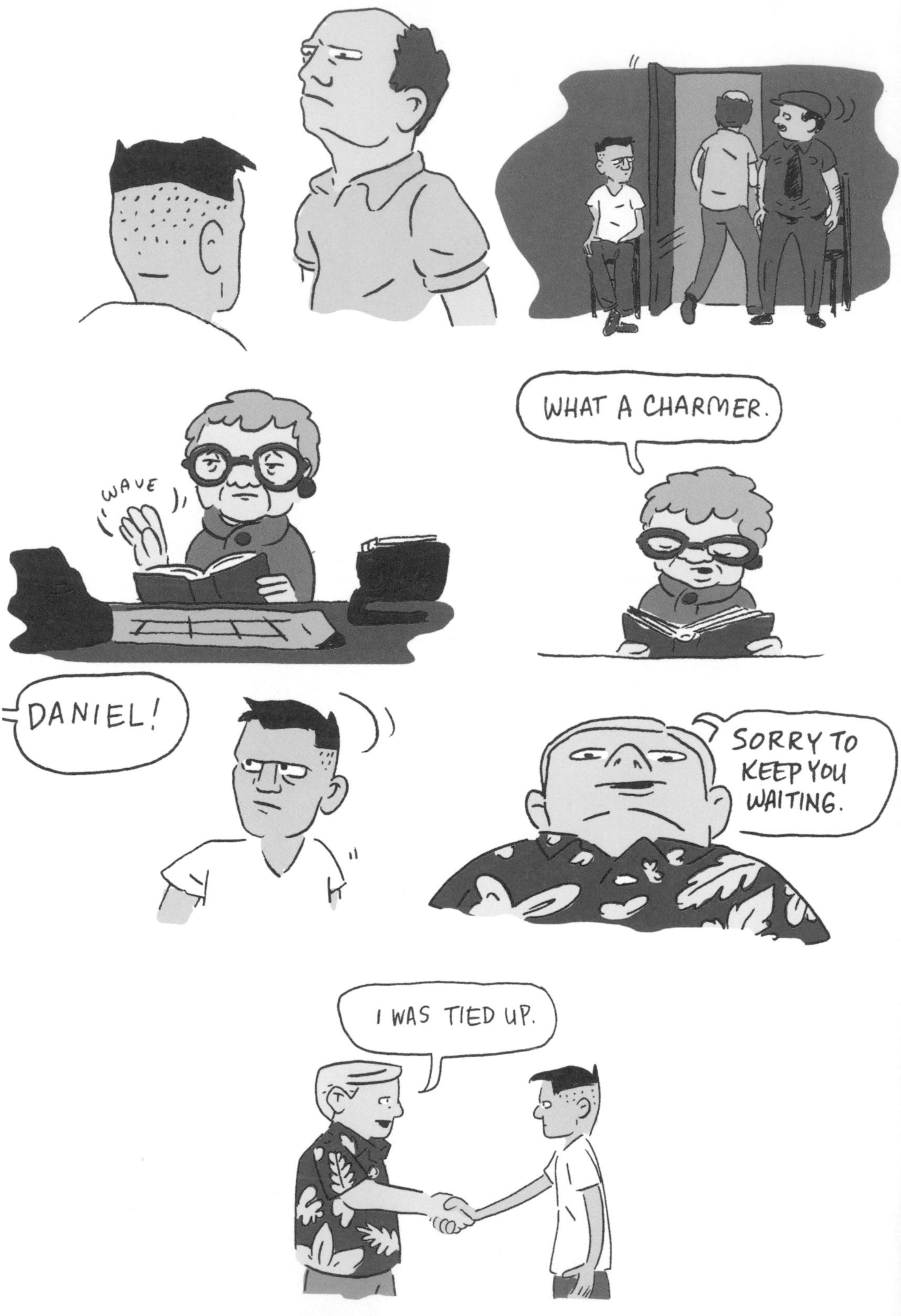
WAVE
WHAT A CHARMER.
DANIEL!
SORRY TO KEEP YOU WAITING.
I WAS TIED UP.

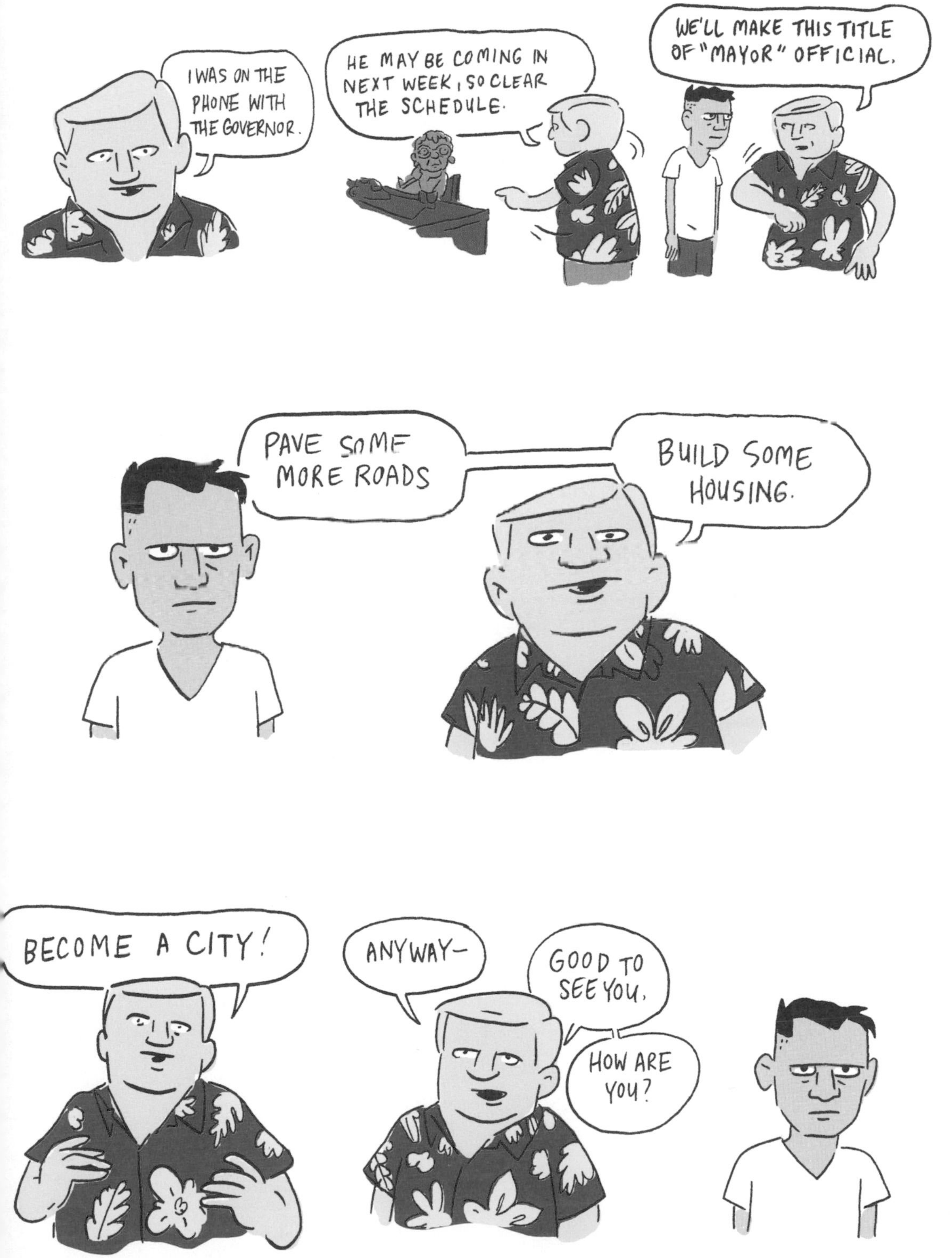
I WAS ON THE PHONE WITH THE GOVERNOR.
HE MAY BE COMING IN NEXT WEEK, SO CLEAR THE SCHEDULE.
WE'LL MAKE THIS TITLE OF "MAYOR" OFFICIAL.
PAVE SOME MORE ROADS
BUILD SOME HOUSING.
BECOME A CITY!
ANYWAY-
GOOD TO SEE YOU.
HOW ARE YOU?

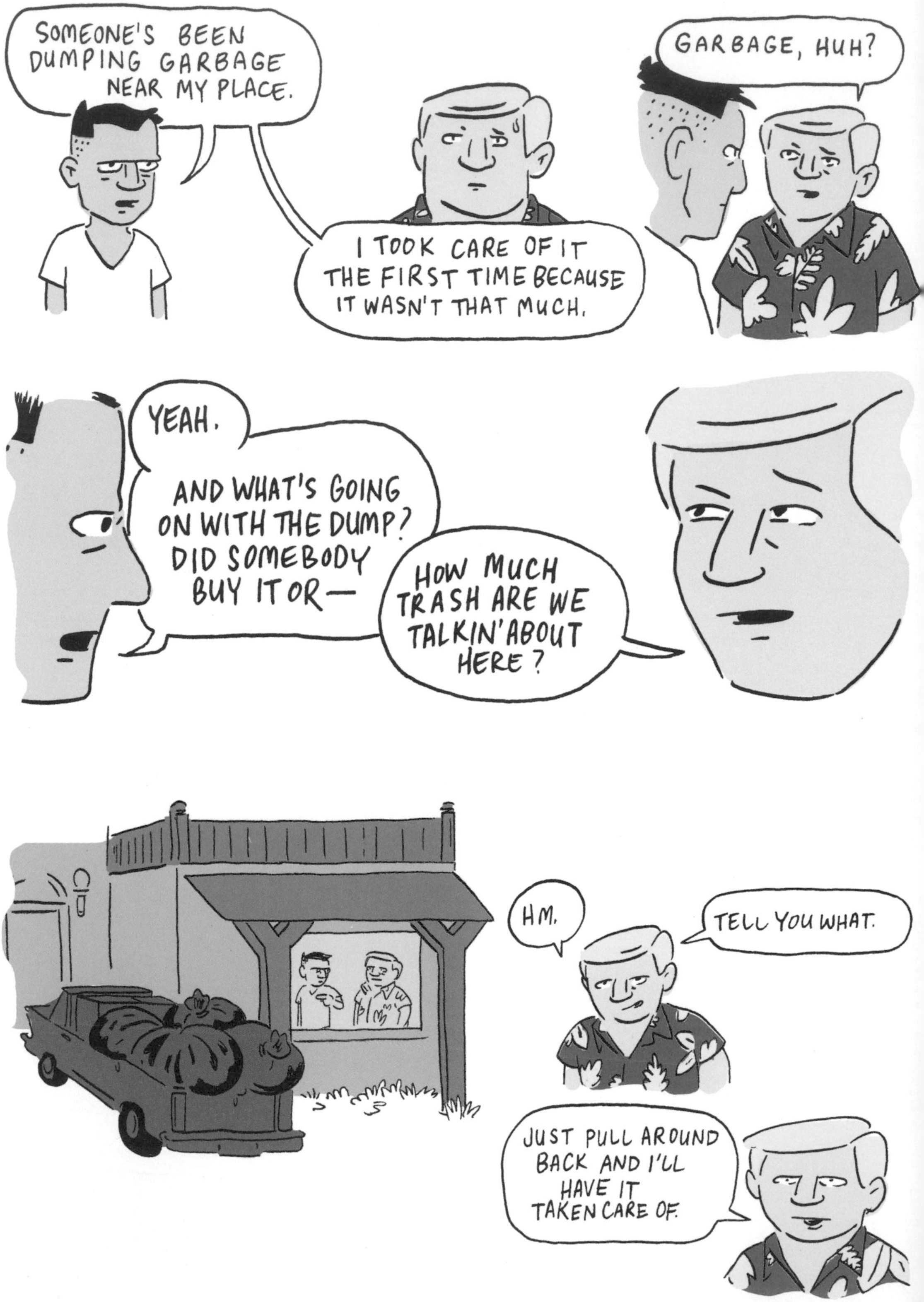
SOMEONE'S BEEN DUMPING GARBAGE NEAR MY PLACE.
I TOOK CARE OF IT THE FIRST TIME BECAUSE IT WASN'T THAT MUCH.
GARBAGE, HUH?
YEAH.
AND WHAT'S GOING ON WITH THE DUMP? DID SOMEBODY BUY IT OR—
HOW MUCH TRASH ARE WE TALKIN' ABOUT HERE?
HM.
TELL YOU WHAT.
JUST PULL AROUND BACK AND I'LL HAVE IT TAKEN CARE OF.

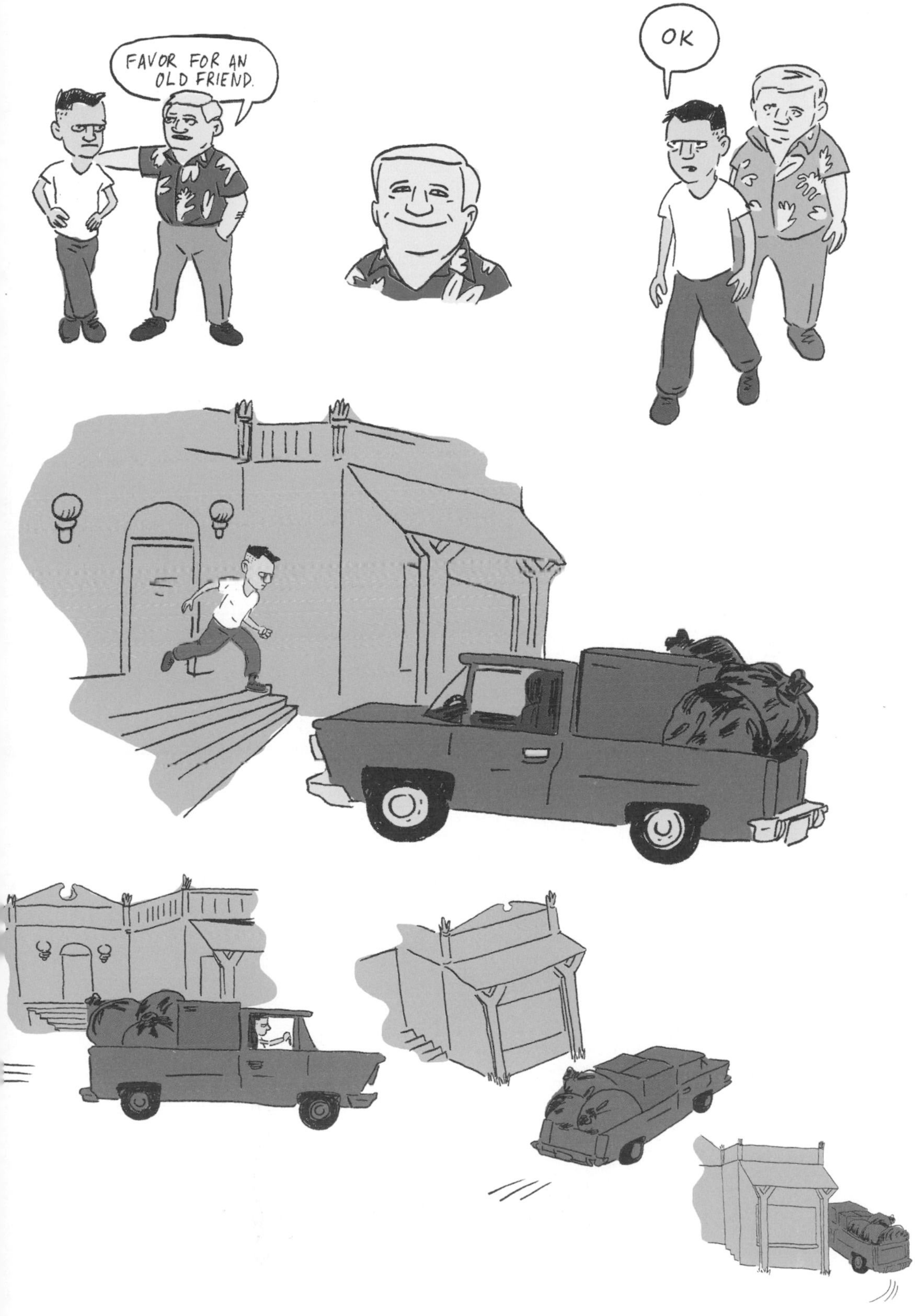
FAVOR FOR AN OLD FRIEND.
OK

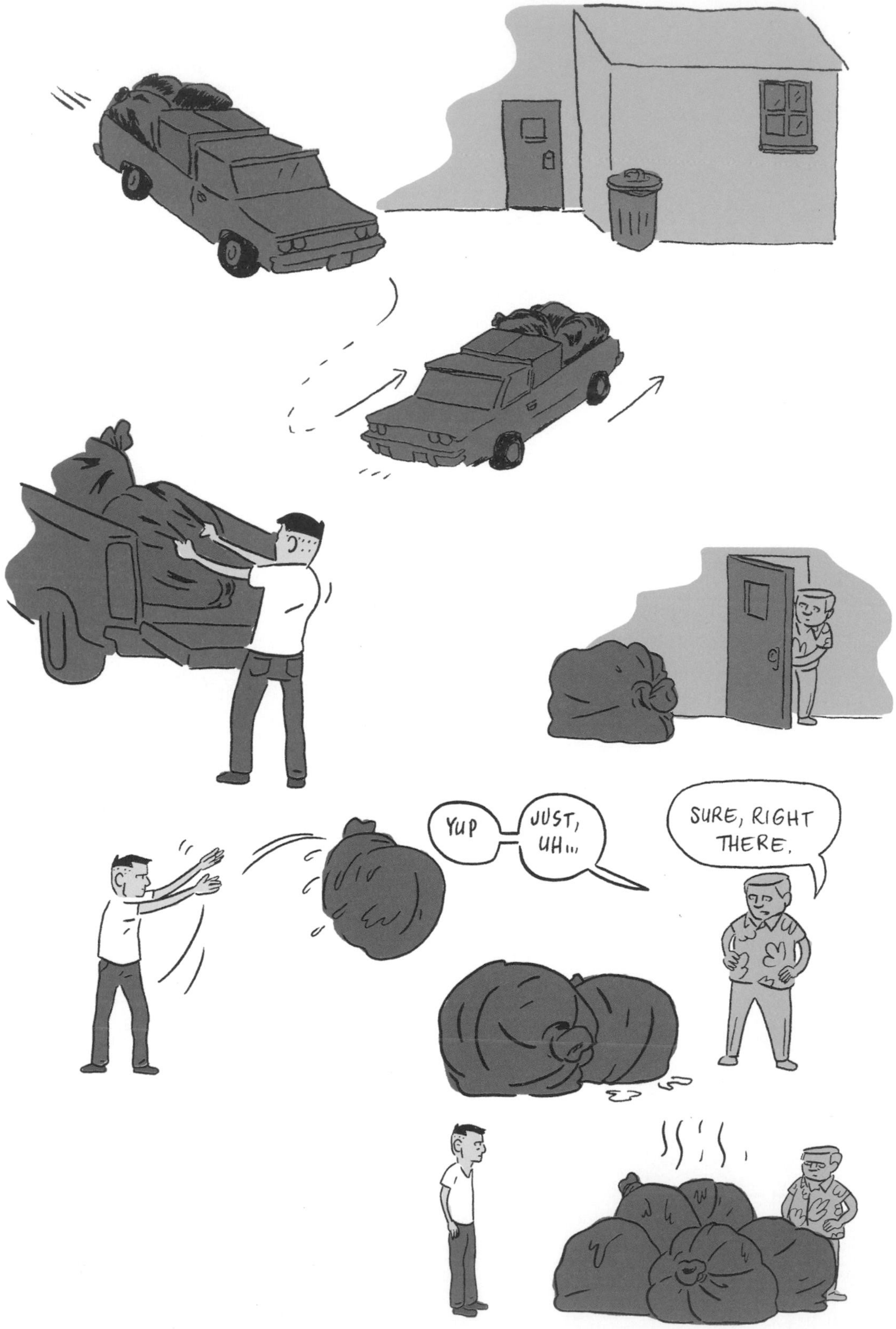
YUP
JUST, UH...
SURE, RIGHT THERE.

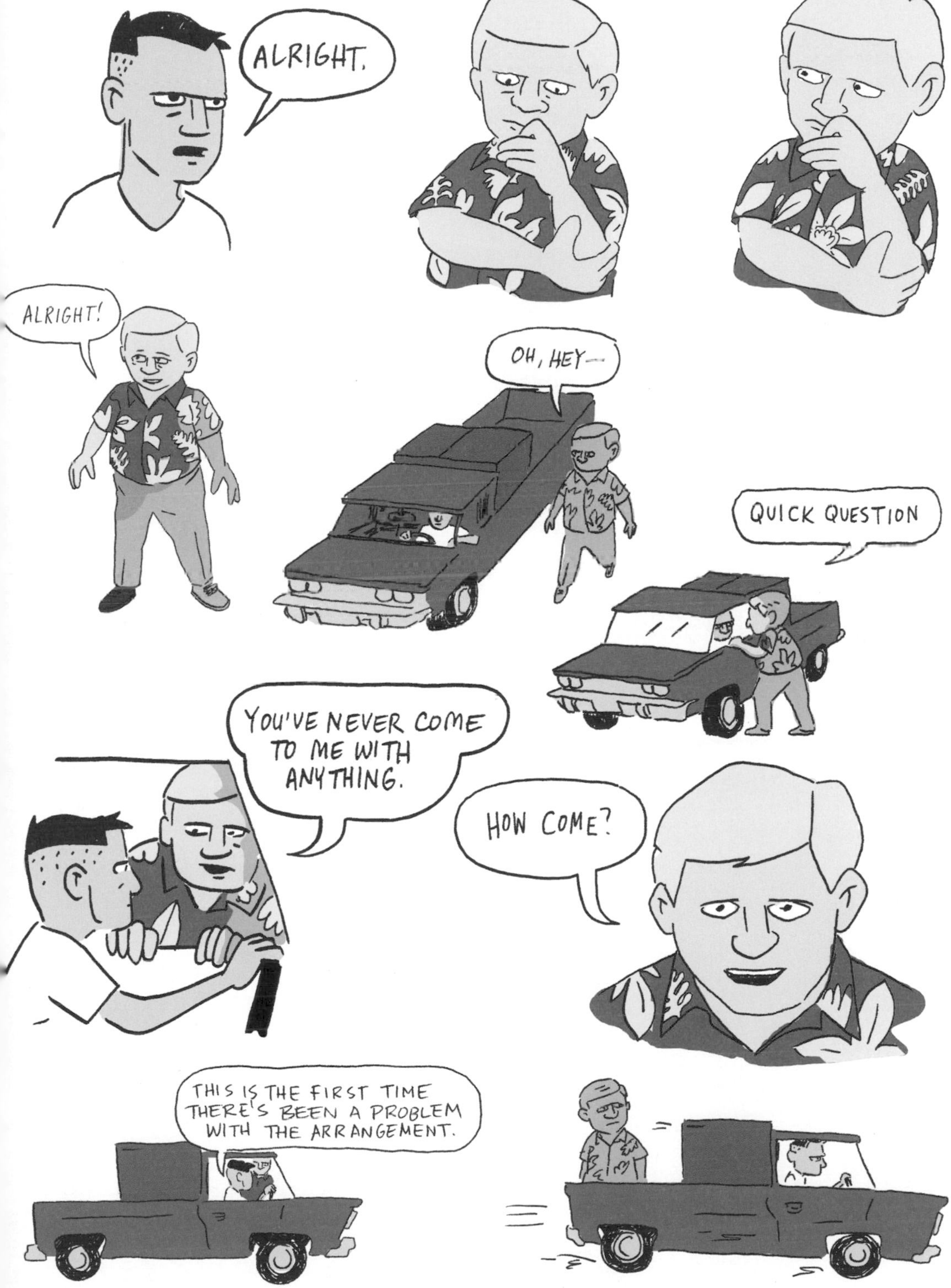
ALRIGHT.
ALRIGHT!
OH, HEY—
QUICK QUESTION
YOU'VE NEVER COME TO ME WITH ANYTHING.
HOW COME?
THIS IS THE FIRST TIME THERE'S BEEN A PROBLEM WITH THE ARRANGEMENT.

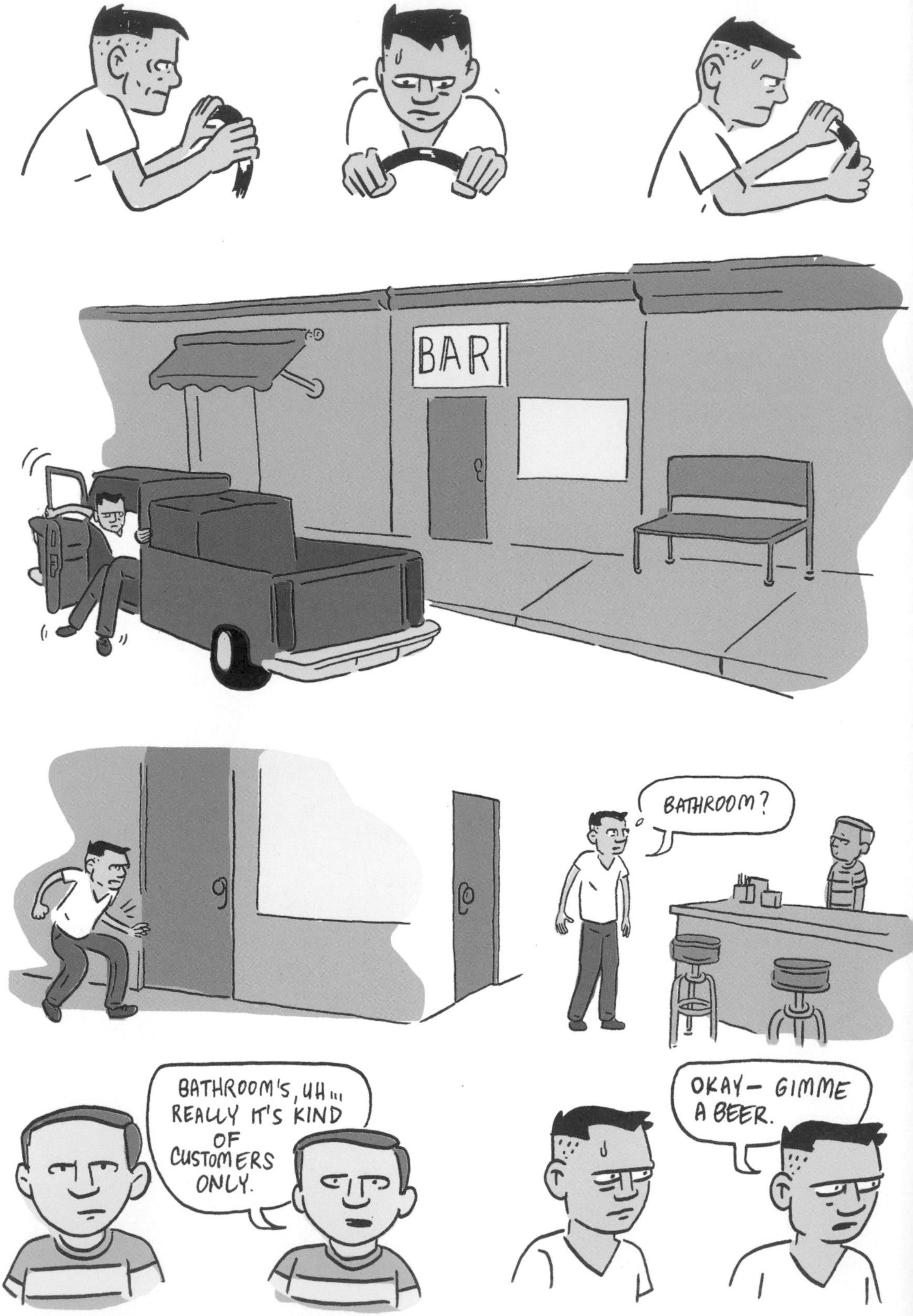
BAR
BATHROOM?
BATHROOM'S, UH... REALLY IT'S KIND OF CUSTOMERS ONLY.
OKAY— GIMME A BEER.

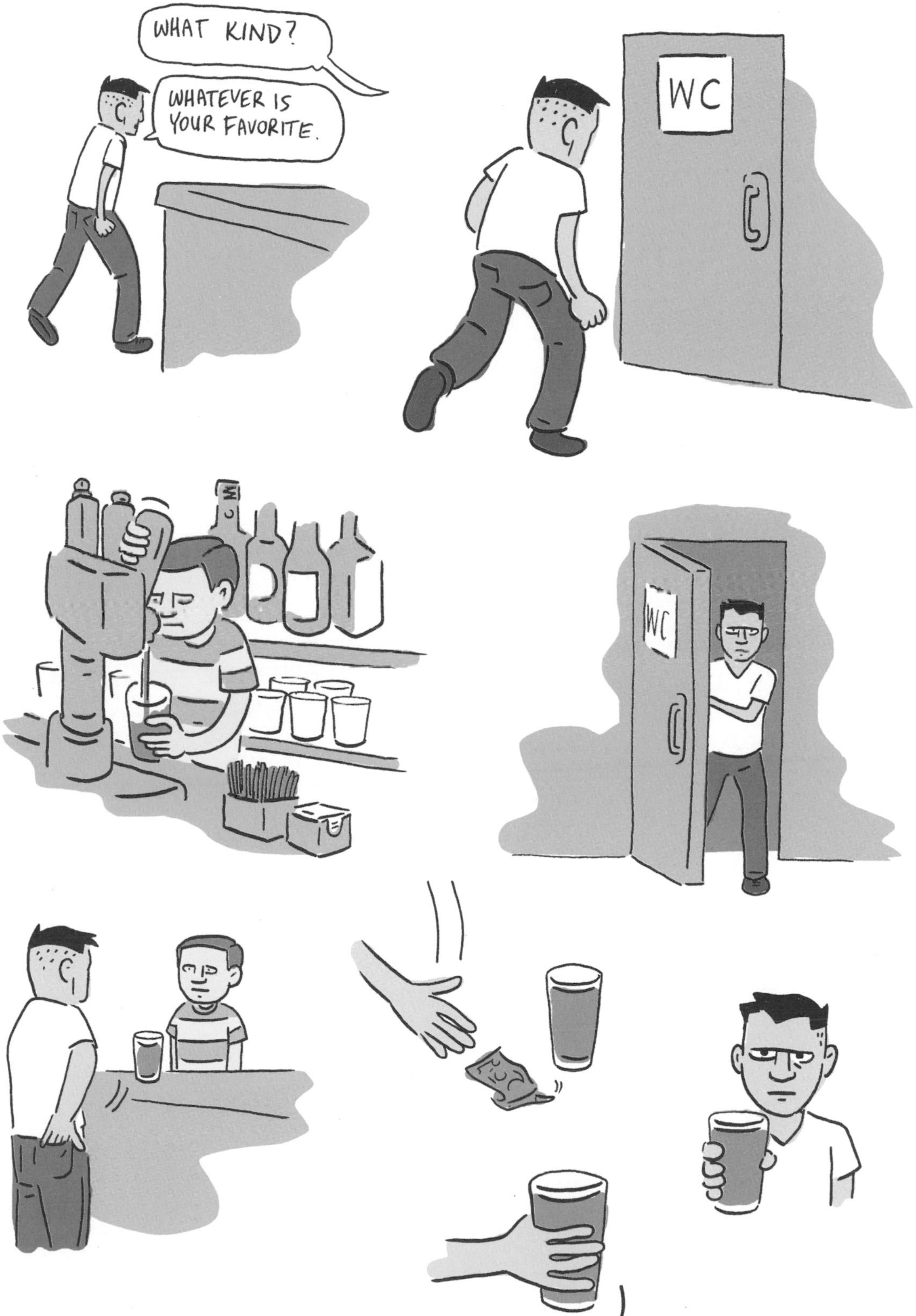
WHAT KIND?
WHATEVER IS YOUR FAVORITE.
WC
WC

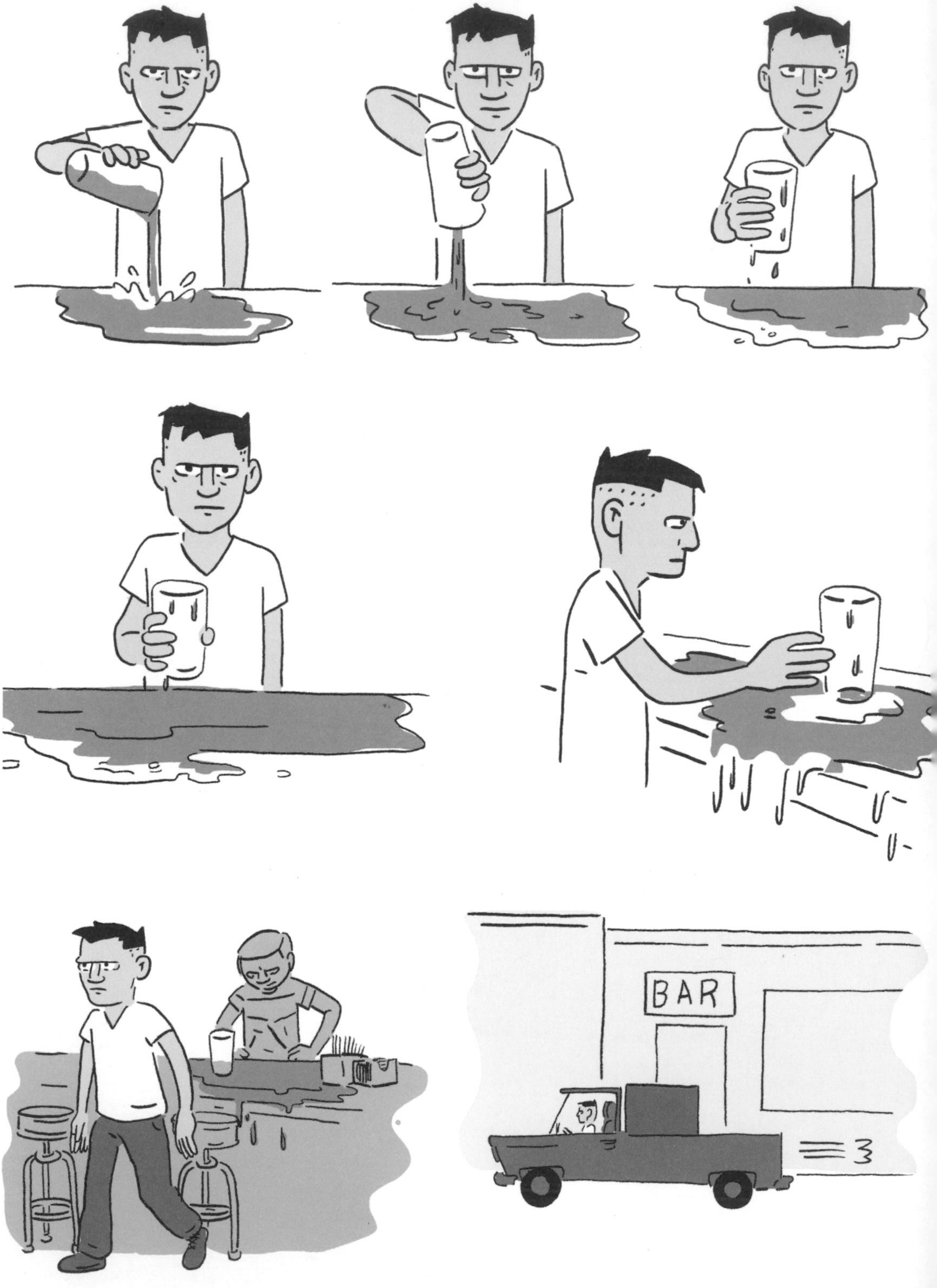
BAR

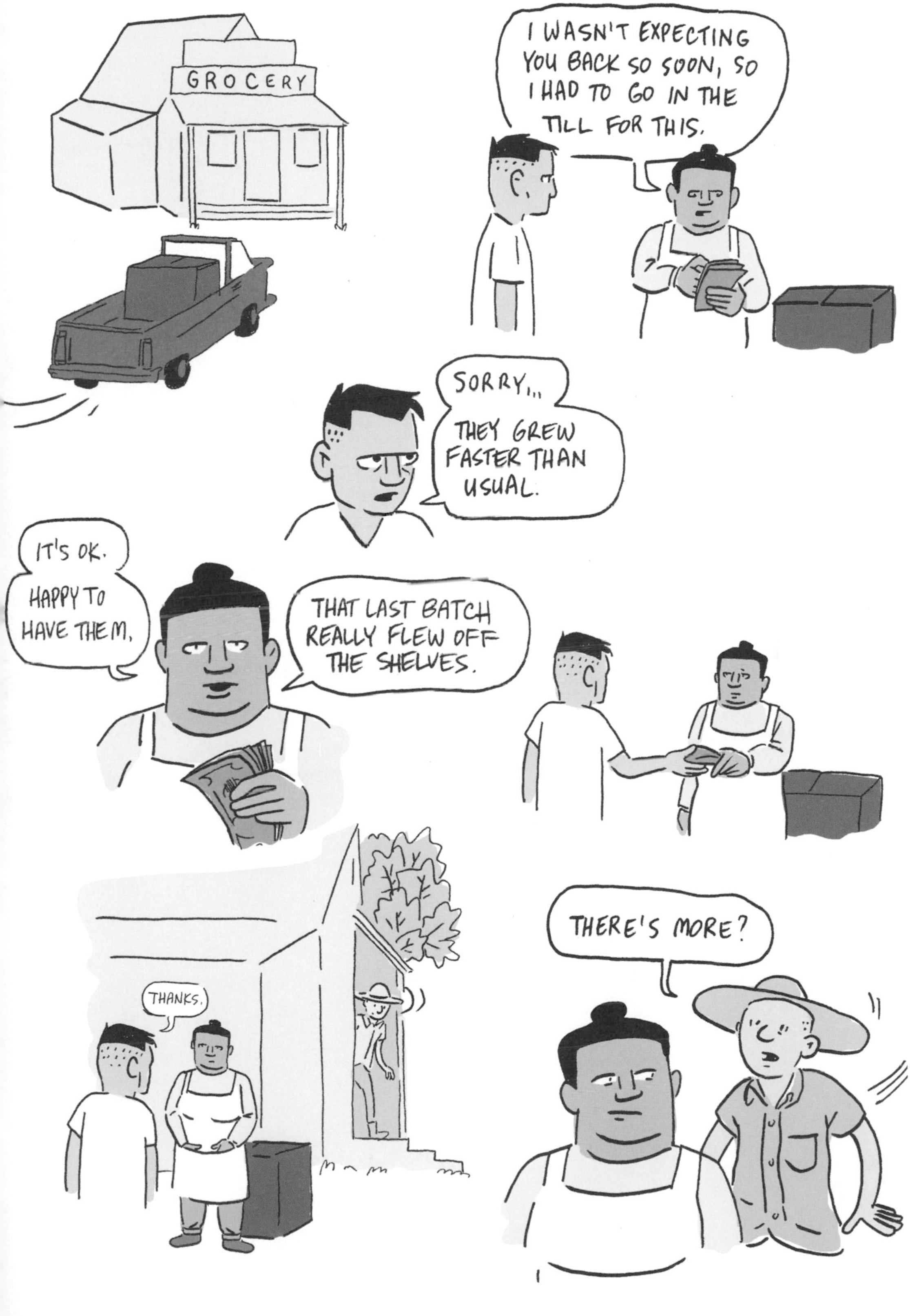
GROCERY
I WASN'T EXPECTING YOU BACK SO SOON, SO I HAD TO GO IN THE TILL FOR THIS.
SORRY...
THEY GREW FASTER THAN USUAL.
IT'S OK.
HAPPY TO HAVE THEM.
THAT LAST BATCH REALLY FLEW OFF THE SHELVES.
THANKS.
THERE'S MORE?

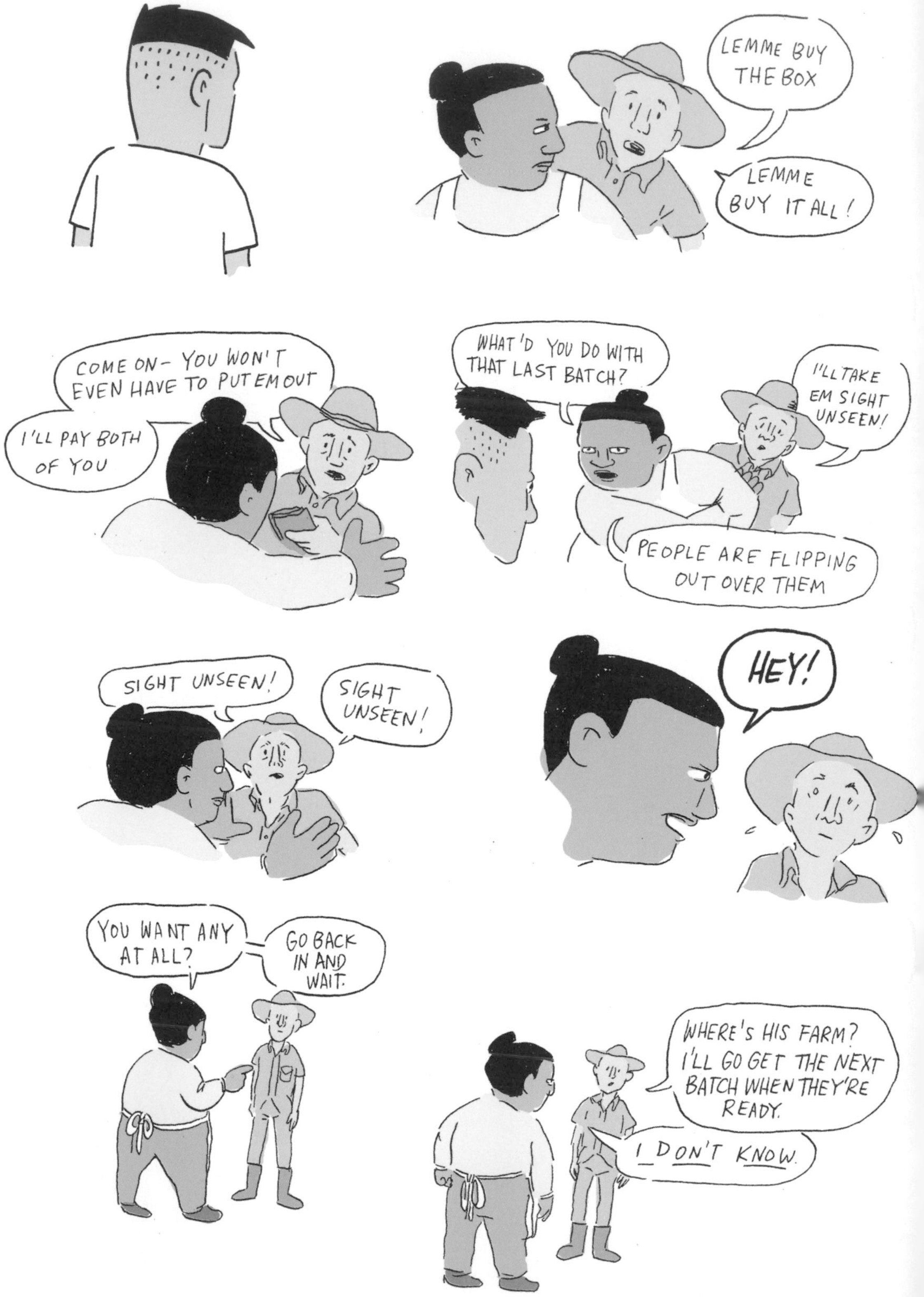
LEMME BUY THE BOX
LEMME BUY IT ALL!
COME ON- YOU WON'T EVEN HAVE TO PUT EM OUT
I'LL PAY BOTH OF YOU
WHAT'D YOU DO WITH THAT LAST BATCH?
I'LL TAKE EM SIGHT UNSEEN!
PEOPLE ARE FLIPPING OUT OVER THEM
SIGHT UNSEEN!
SIGHT UNSEEN!
HEY!
YOU WANT ANY AT ALL?
GO BACK IN AND WAIT.
WHERE'S HIS FARM? I'LL GO GET THE NEXT BATCH WHEN THEY'RE READY.
I DON'T KNOW.

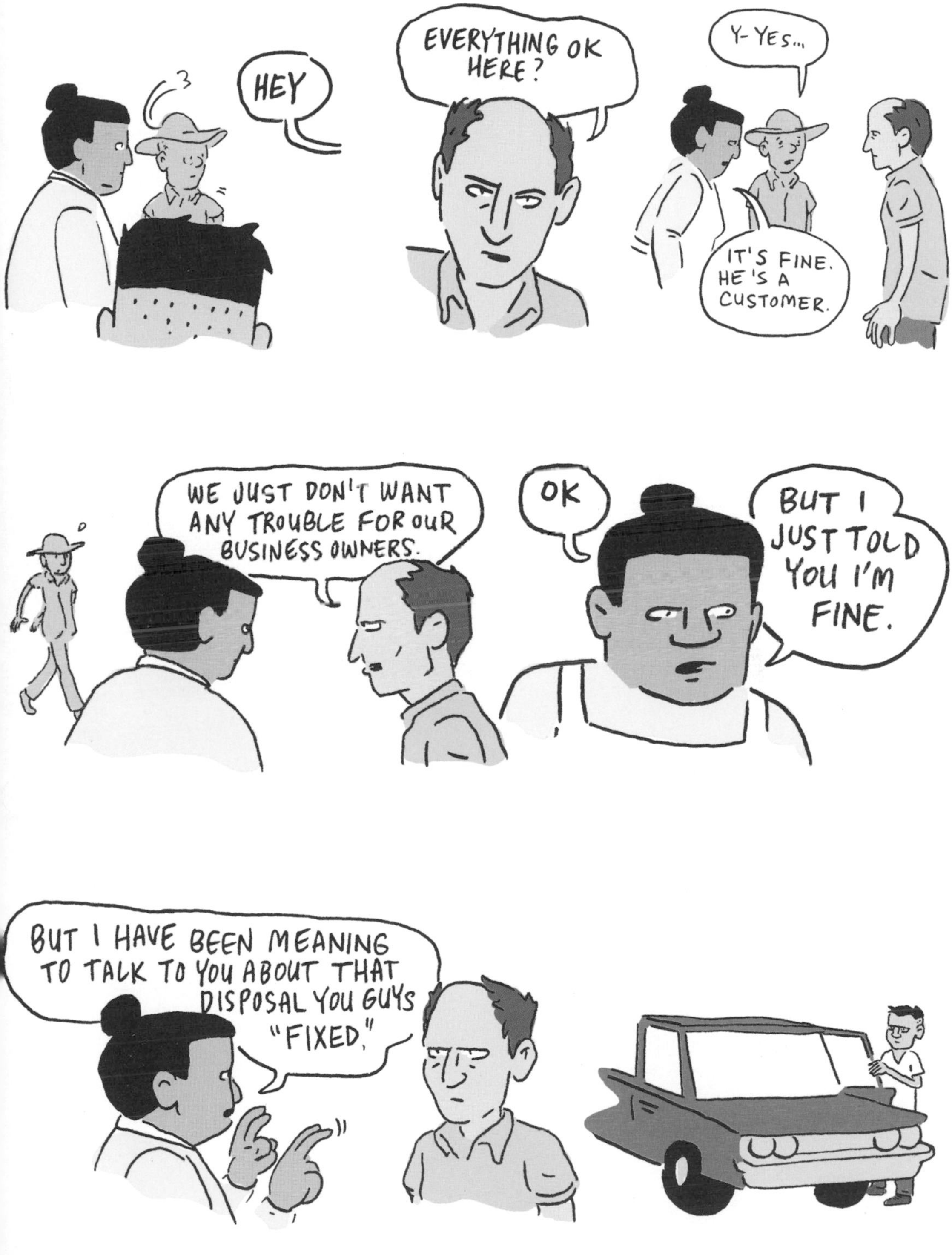
HEY
EVERYTHING OK HERE?
Y- YES...
IT'S FINE. HE'S A CUSTOMER.
WE JUST DON'T WANT ANY TROUBLE FOR OUR BUSINESS OWNERS.
OK
BUT I JUST TOLD YOU I'M FINE.
BUT I HAVE BEEN MEANING TO TALK TO YOU ABOUT THAT DISPOSAL YOU GUYS "FIXED."

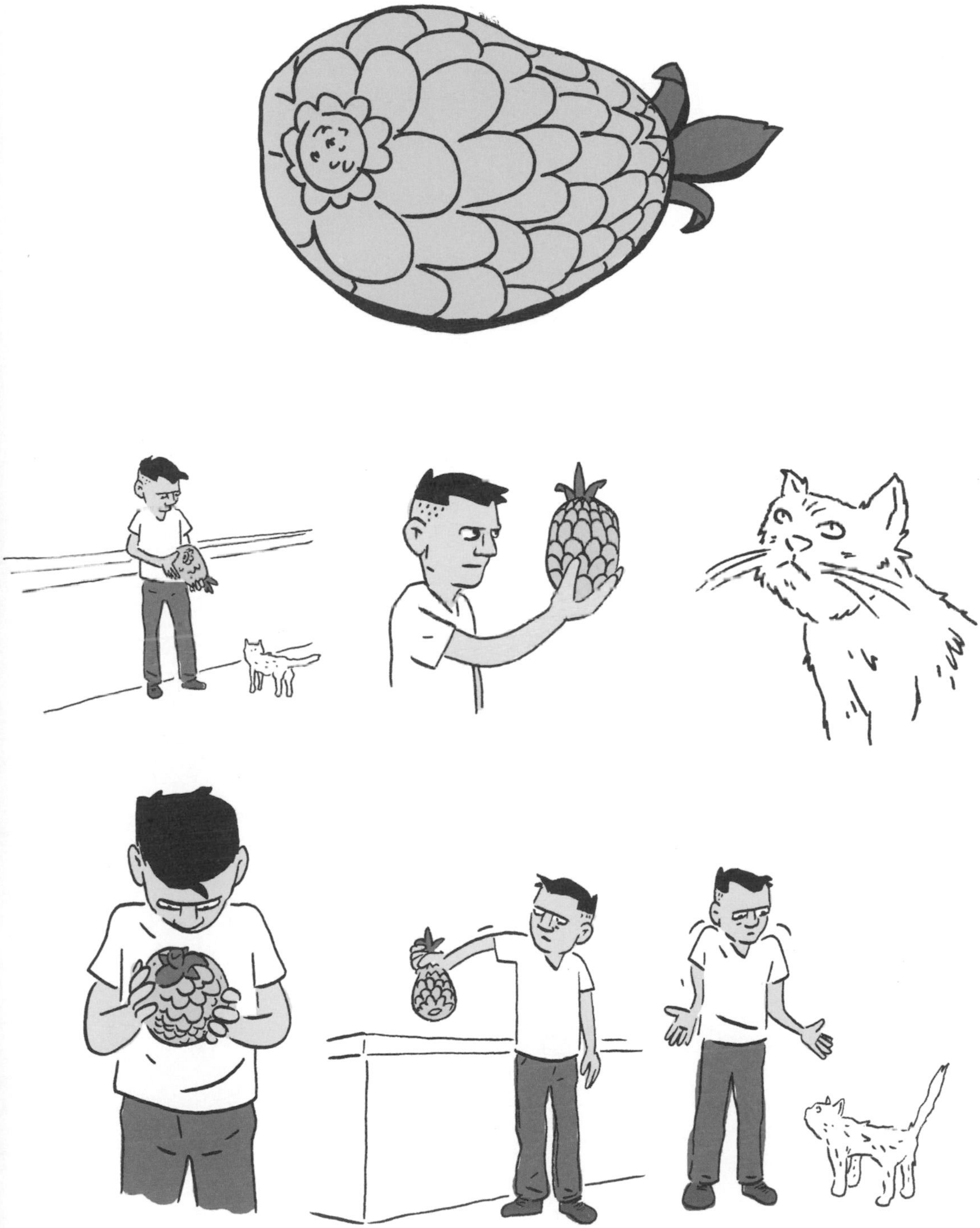

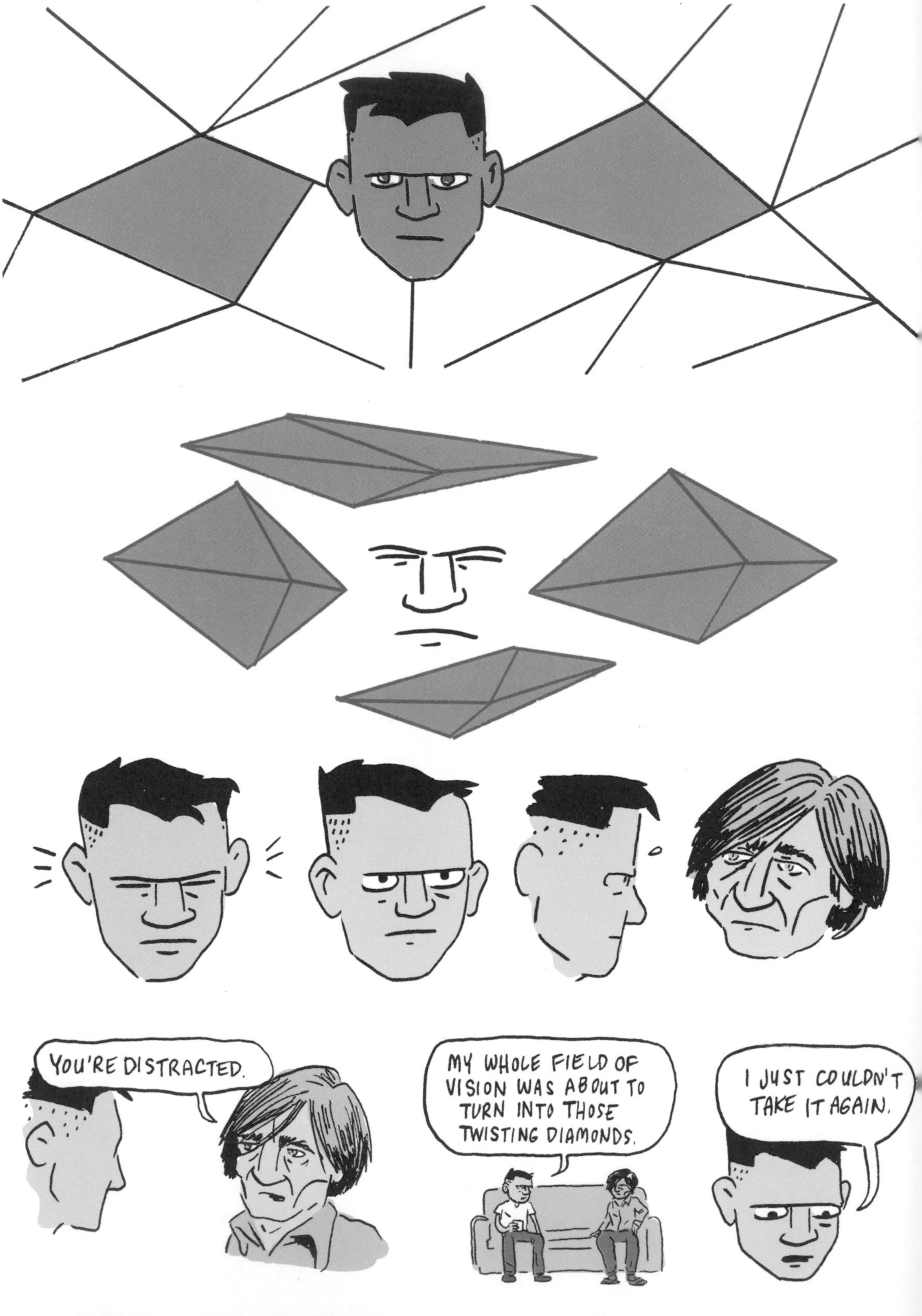
YOU'RE DISTRACTED.
MY WHOLE FIELD OF VISION WAS ABOUT TO TURN INTO THOSE TWISTING DIAMONDS.
I JUST COULDN'T TAKE IT AGAIN.

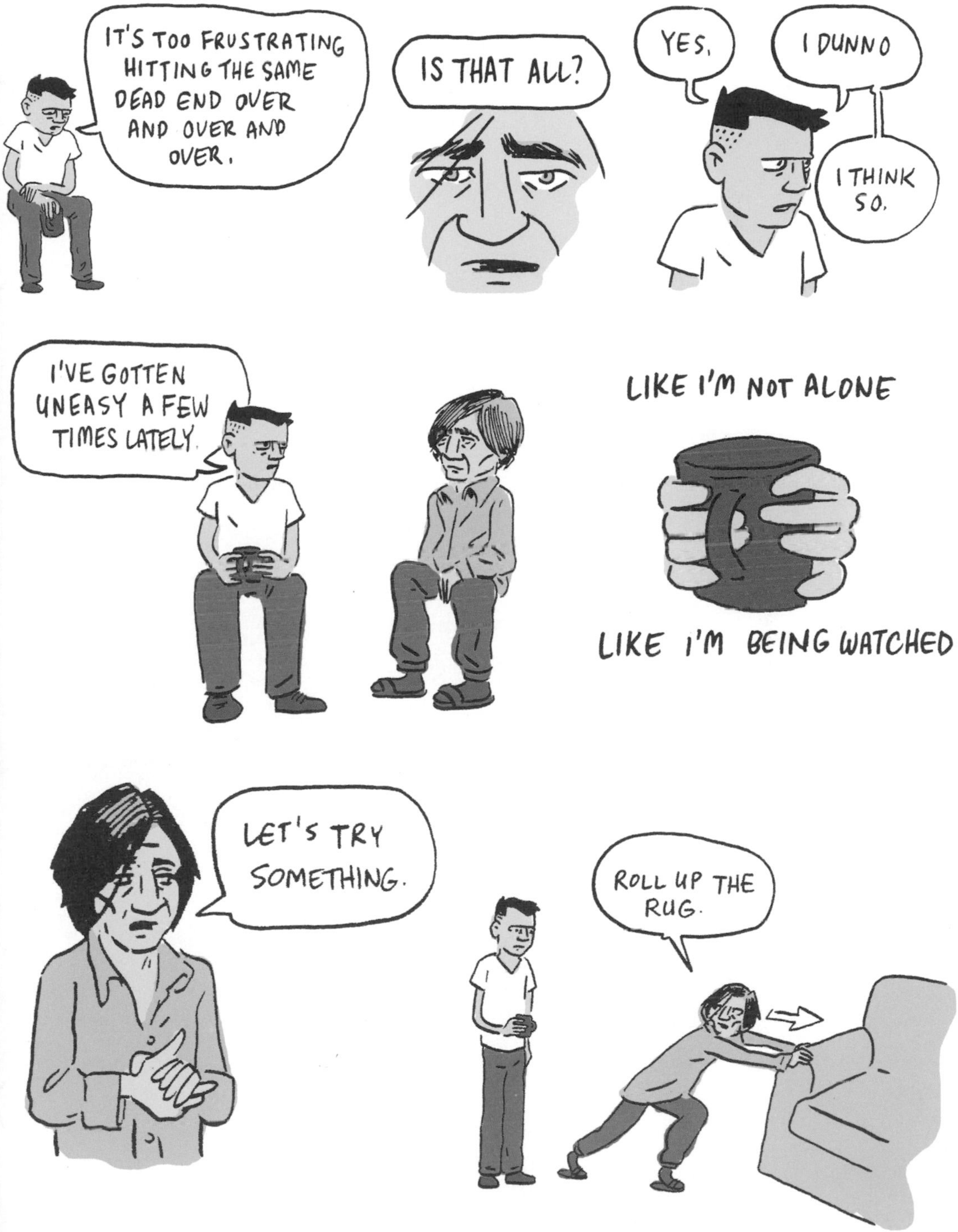
IT'S TOO FRUSTRATING HITTING THE SAME DEAD END OVER AND OVER AND OVER.
IS THAT ALL?
YES.
I DUNNO
I THINK SO.
I'VE GOTTEN UNEASY A FEW TIMES LATELY.
LIKE I'M NOT ALONE
LIKE I'M BEING WATCHED
LET'S TRY SOMETHING.
ROLL UP THE RUG.

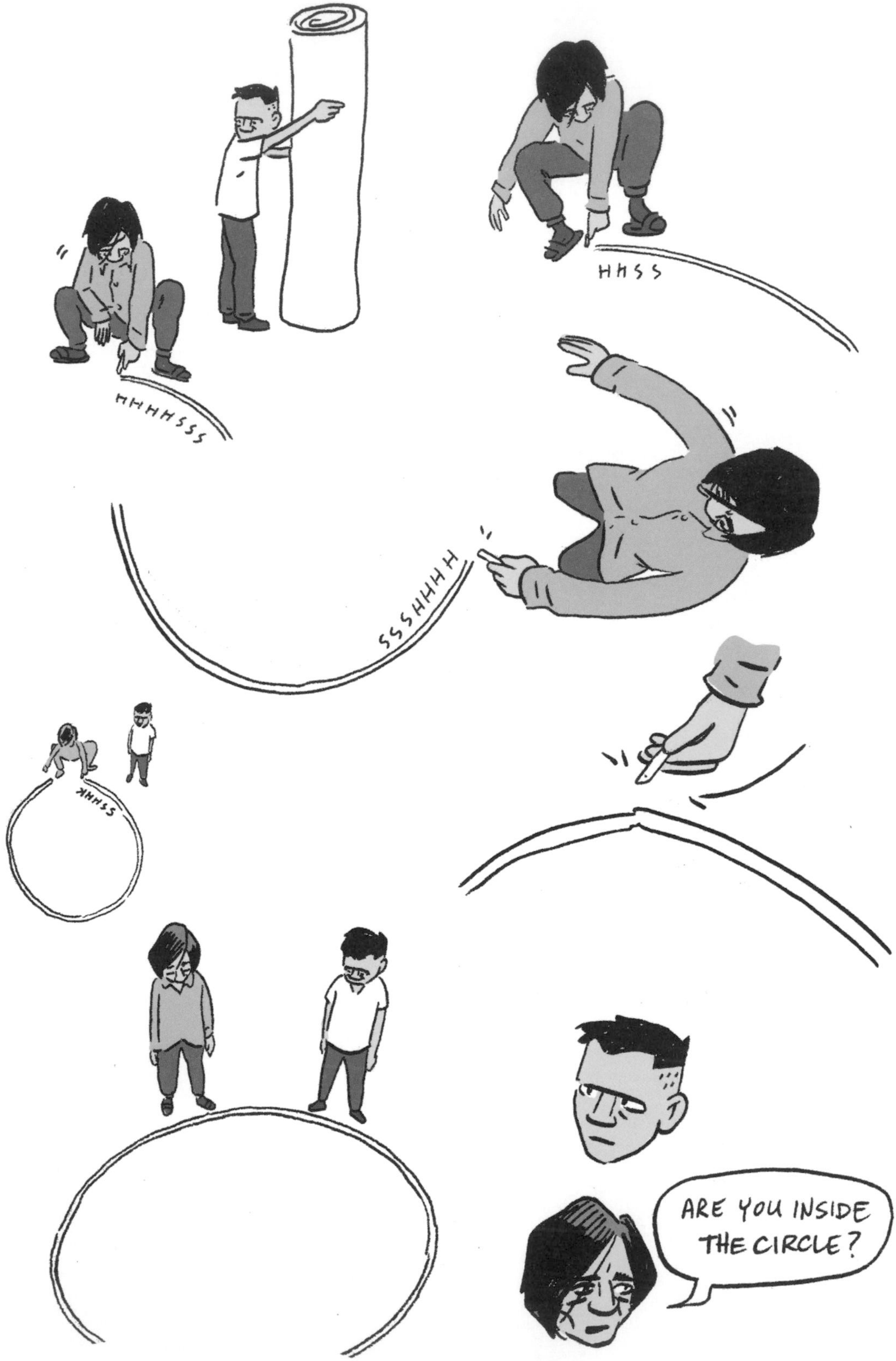
HHHHSSS
HHSS
SSSHHHH
SSHHK
ARE YOU INSIDE THE CIRCLE?

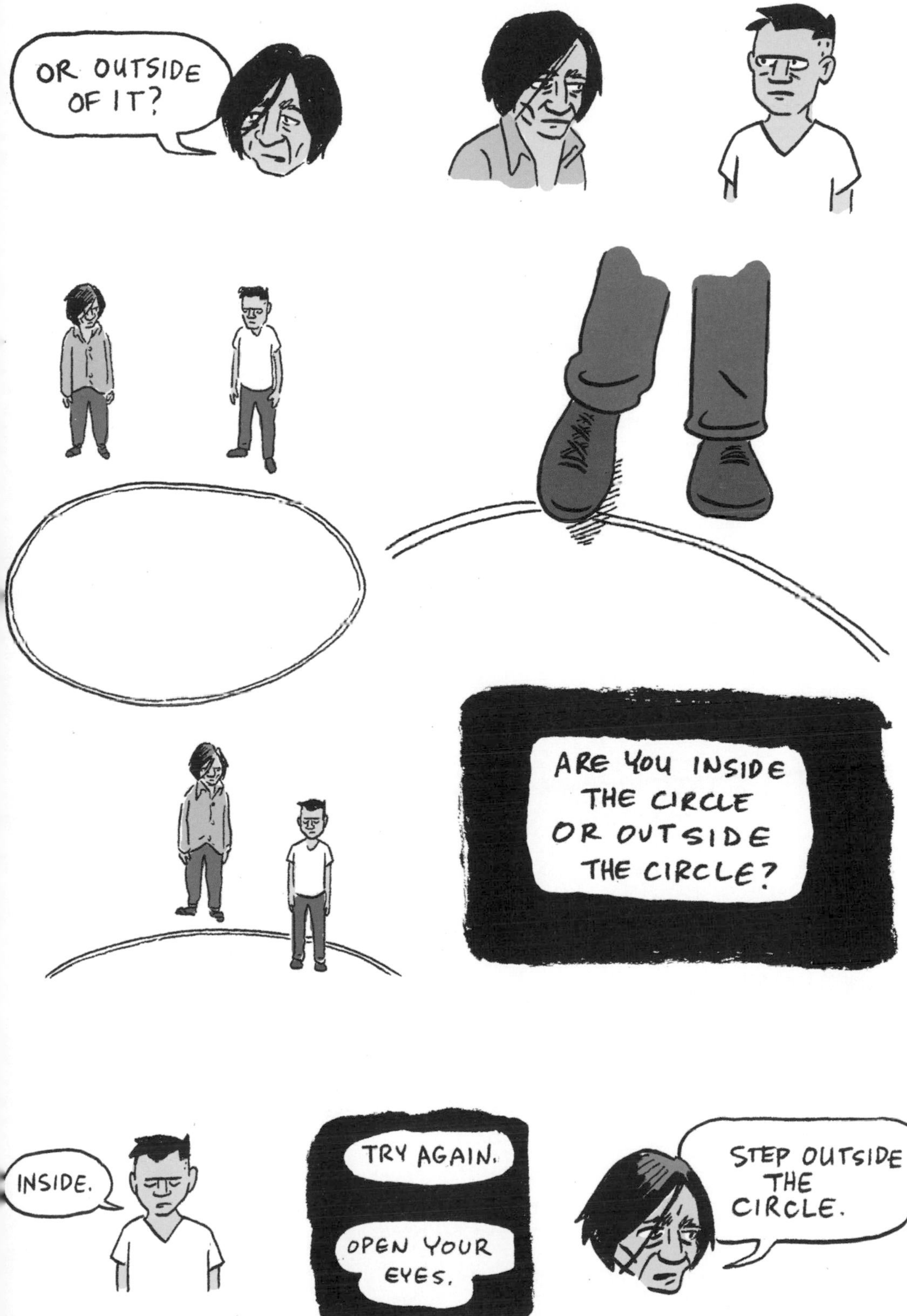
OR OUTSIDE OF IT?
ARE YOU INSIDE THE CIRCLE OR OUTSIDE THE CIRCLE?
INSIDE.
TRY AGAIN.
OPEN YOUR EYES.
STEP OUTSIDE THE CIRCLE.

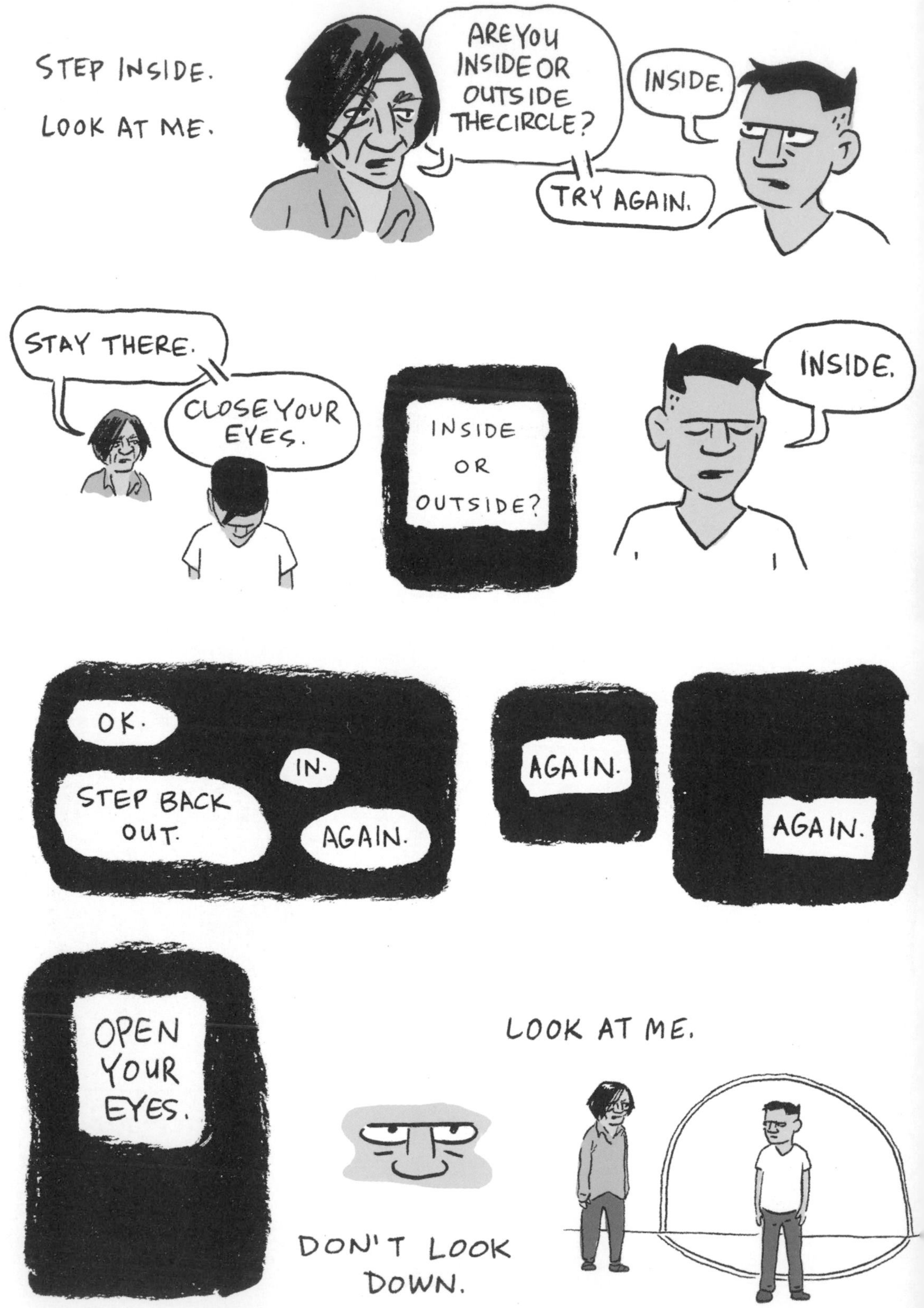
STEP INSIDE.
LOOK AT ME.
ARE YOU INSIDE OR OUTSIDE THE CIRCLE?
INSIDE.
TRY AGAIN.
STAY THERE.
CLOSE YOUR EYES.
INSIDE OR OUTSIDE?
INSIDE.
OK.
IN.
STEP BACK OUT.
AGAIN.
AGAIN.
AGAIN.
OPEN YOUR EYES.
LOOK AT ME.
DON'T LOOK DOWN.

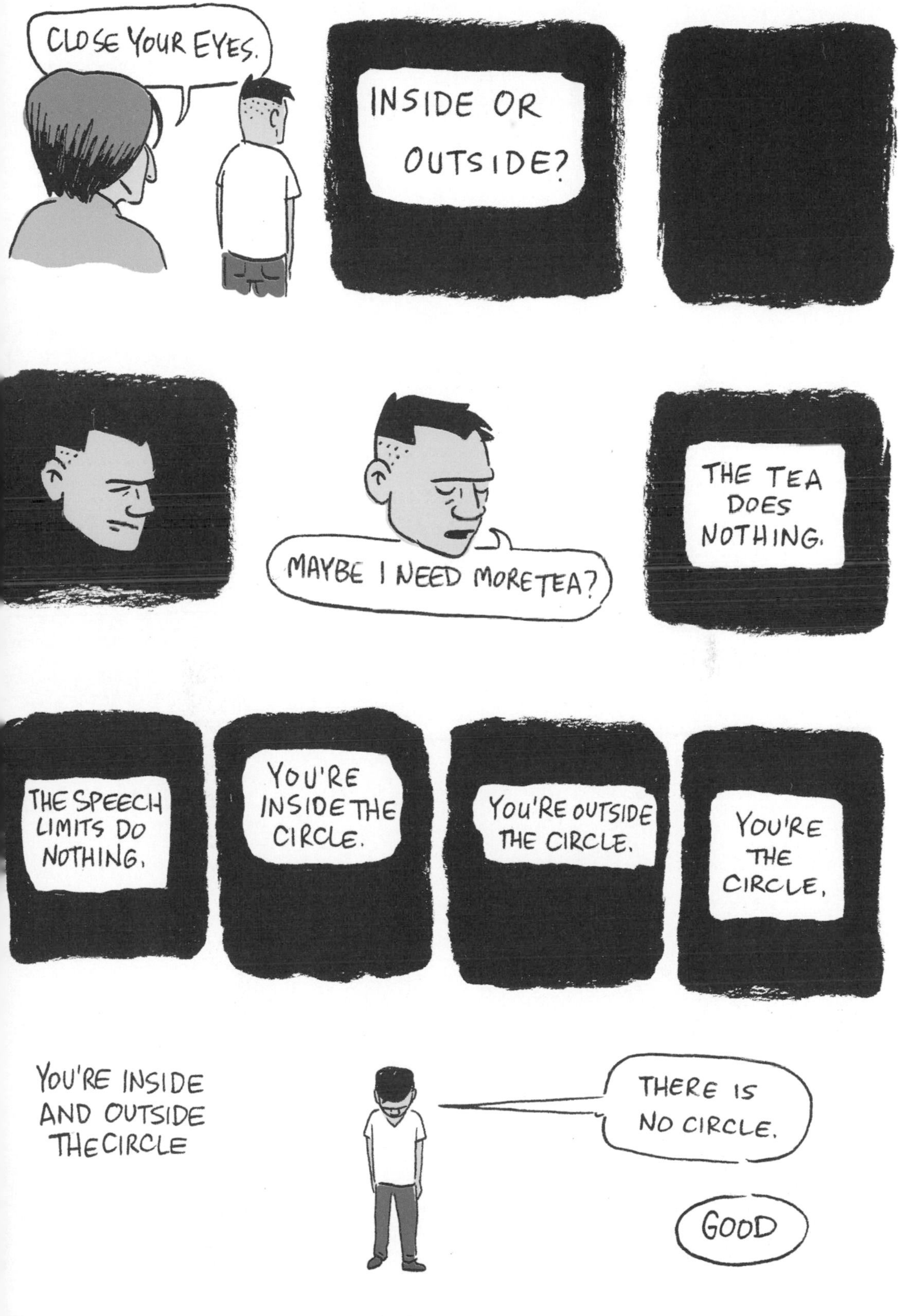
CLOSE YOUR EYES.
INSIDE OR OUTSIDE?
MAYBE I NEED MORE TEA?
THE TEA DOES NOTHING.
THE SPEECH LIMITS DO NOTHING.
YOU'RE INSIDE THE CIRCLE.
YOU'RE OUTSIDE THE CIRCLE.
YOU'RE THE CIRCLE.
YOU'RE INSIDE AND OUTSIDE THE CIRCLE
THERE IS NO CIRCLE.
GOOD

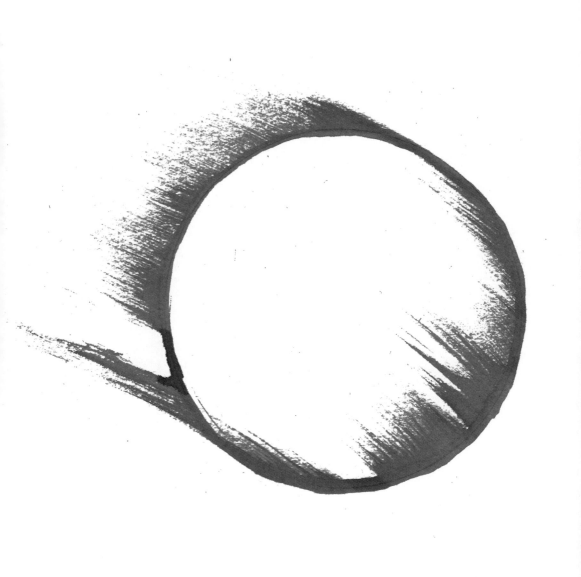

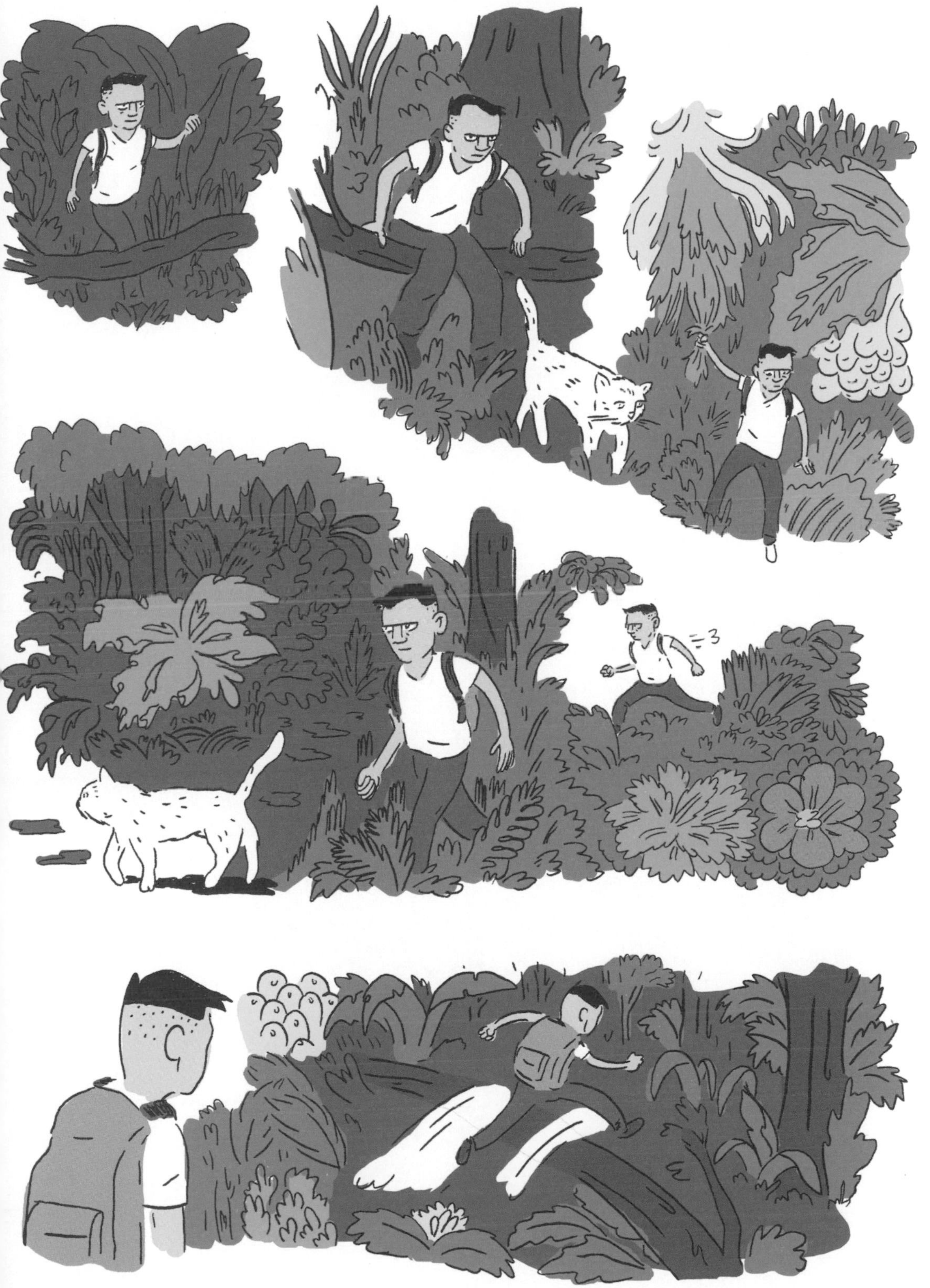

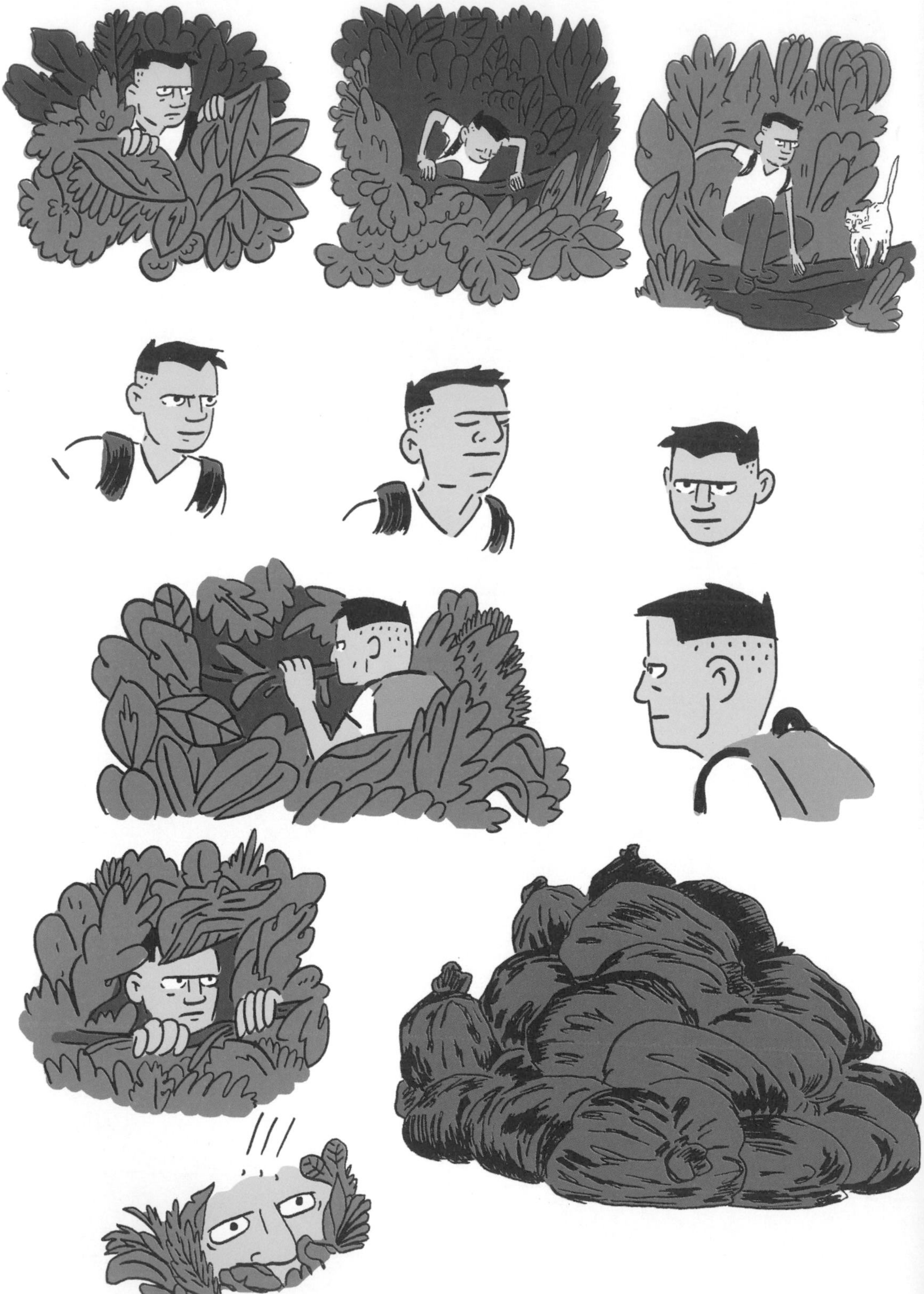

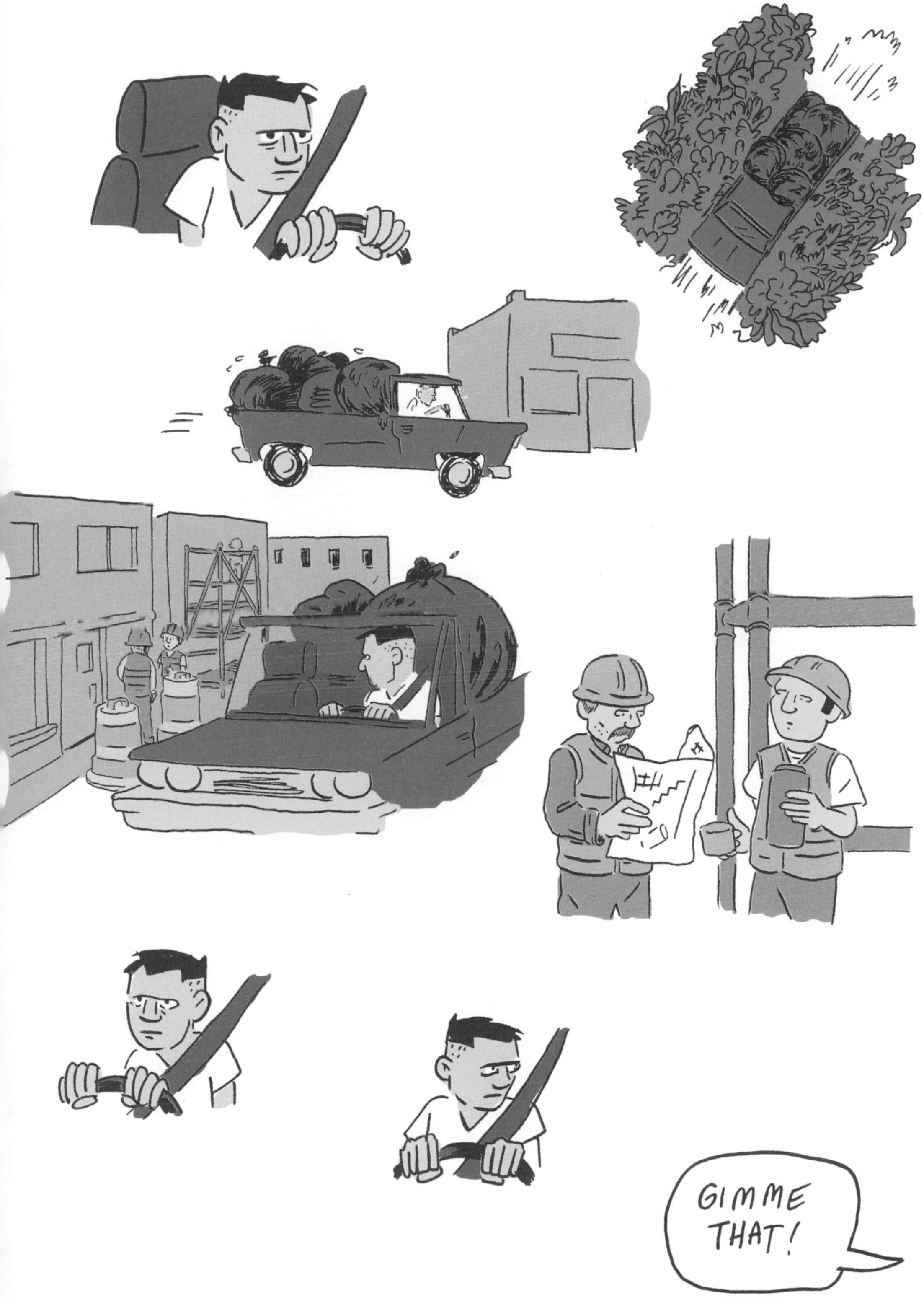
GIMME THAT!

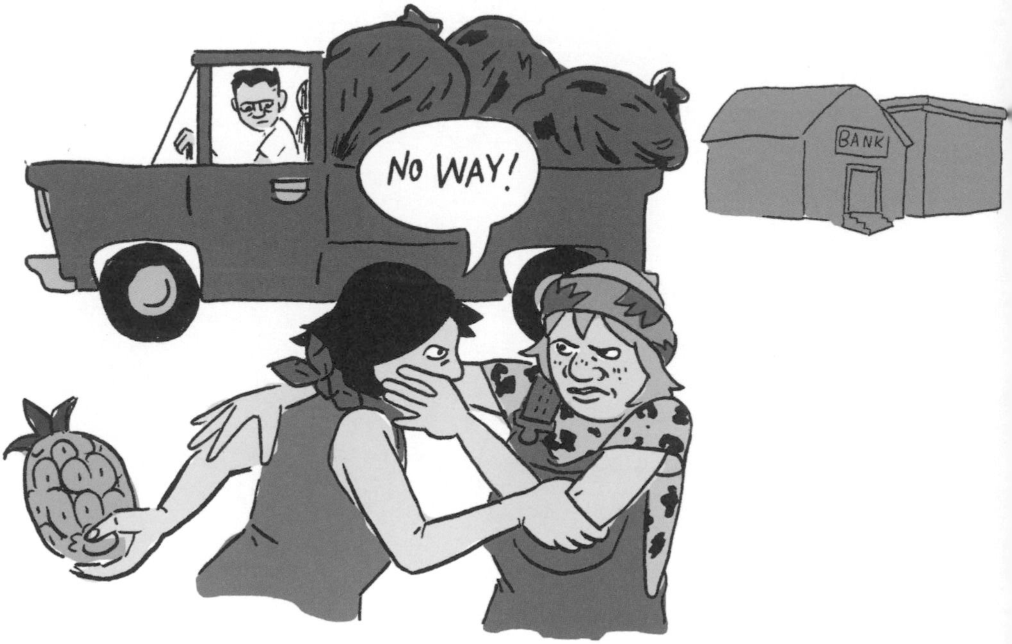
NO WAY!
BANK

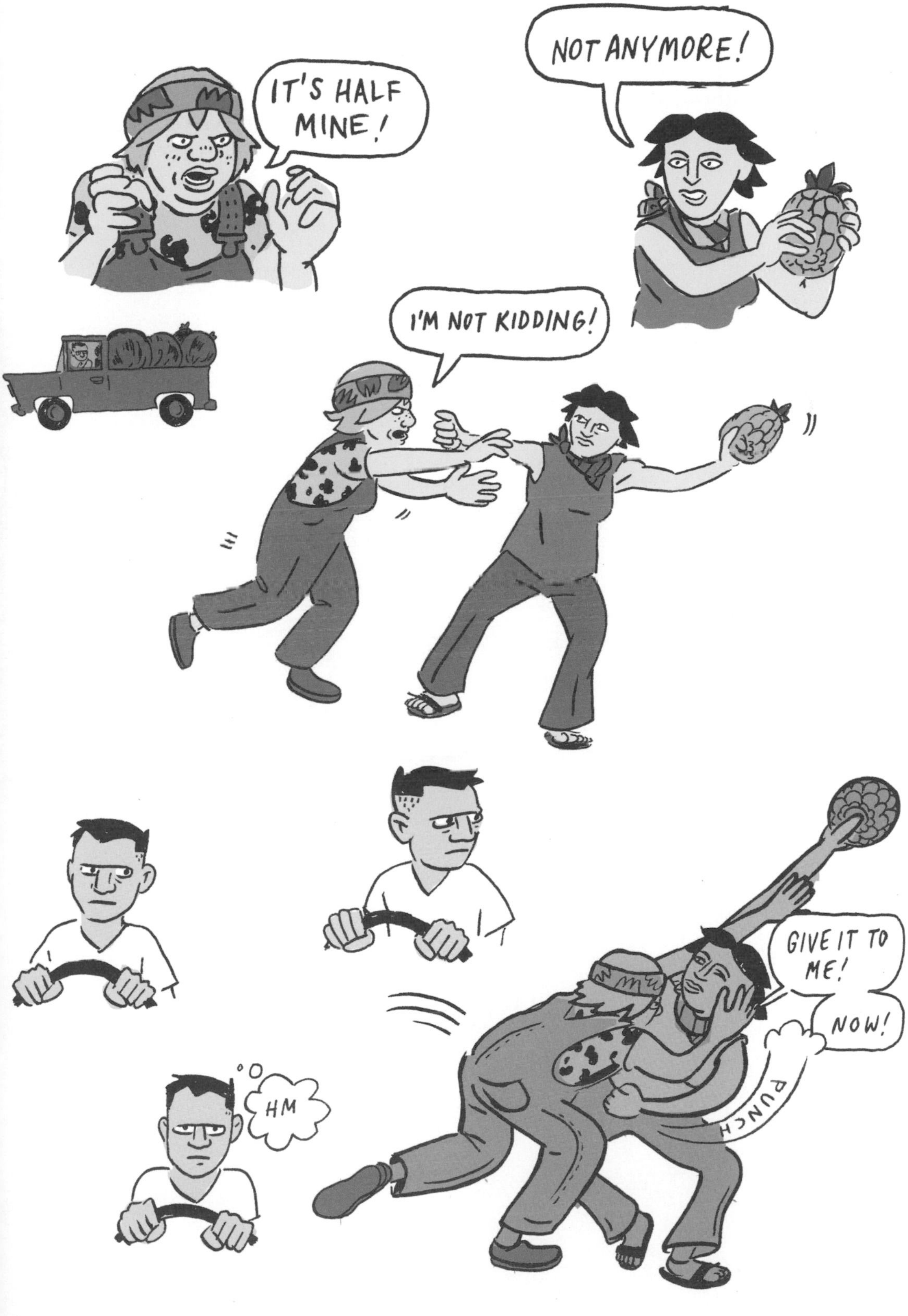
IT'S HALF MINE!
NOT ANYMORE!
I'M NOT KIDDING!
HM
GIVE IT TO ME!
NOW!
PUNCH

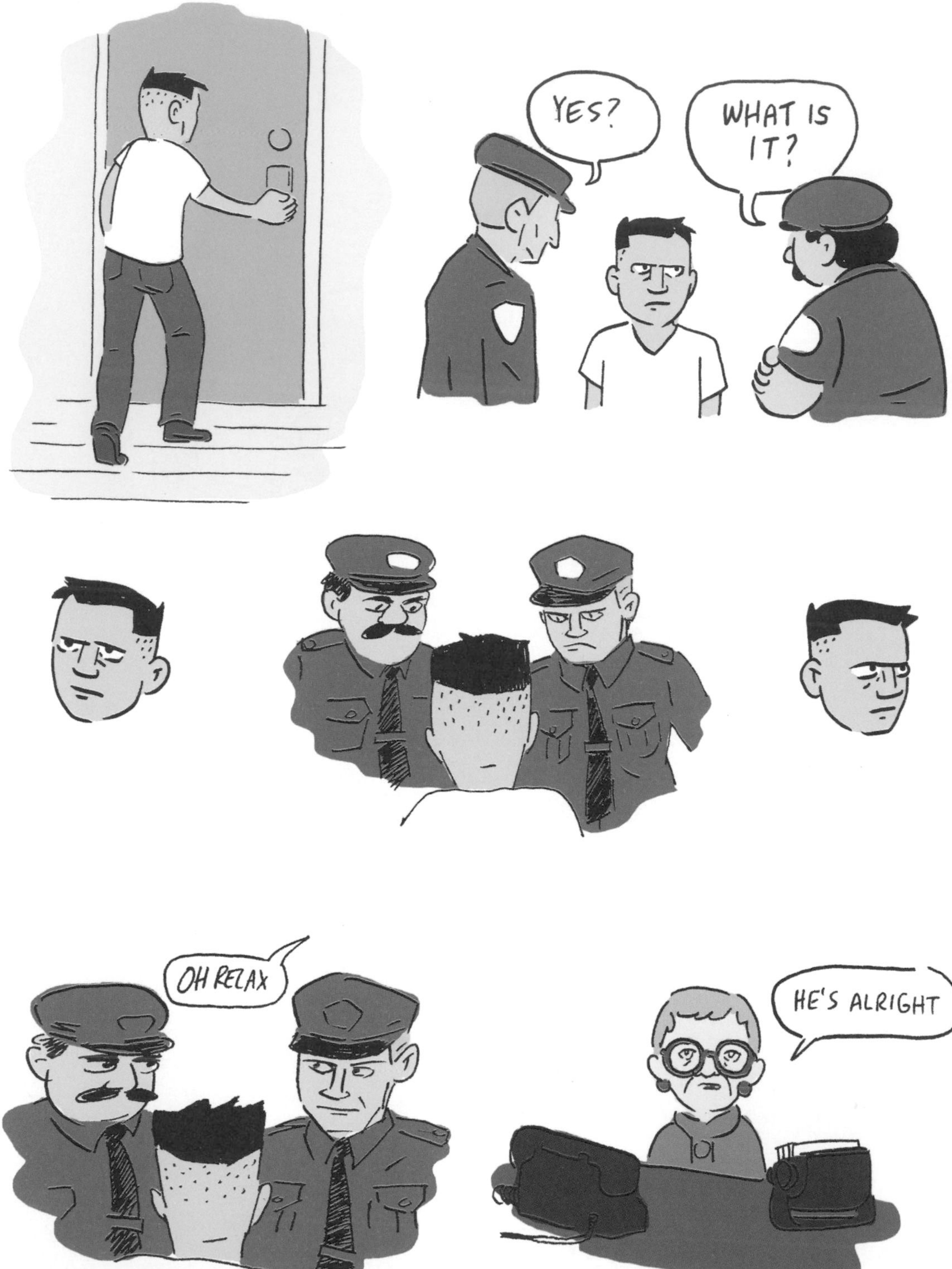
YES?
WHAT IS IT?
OH RELAX
HE'S ALRIGHT

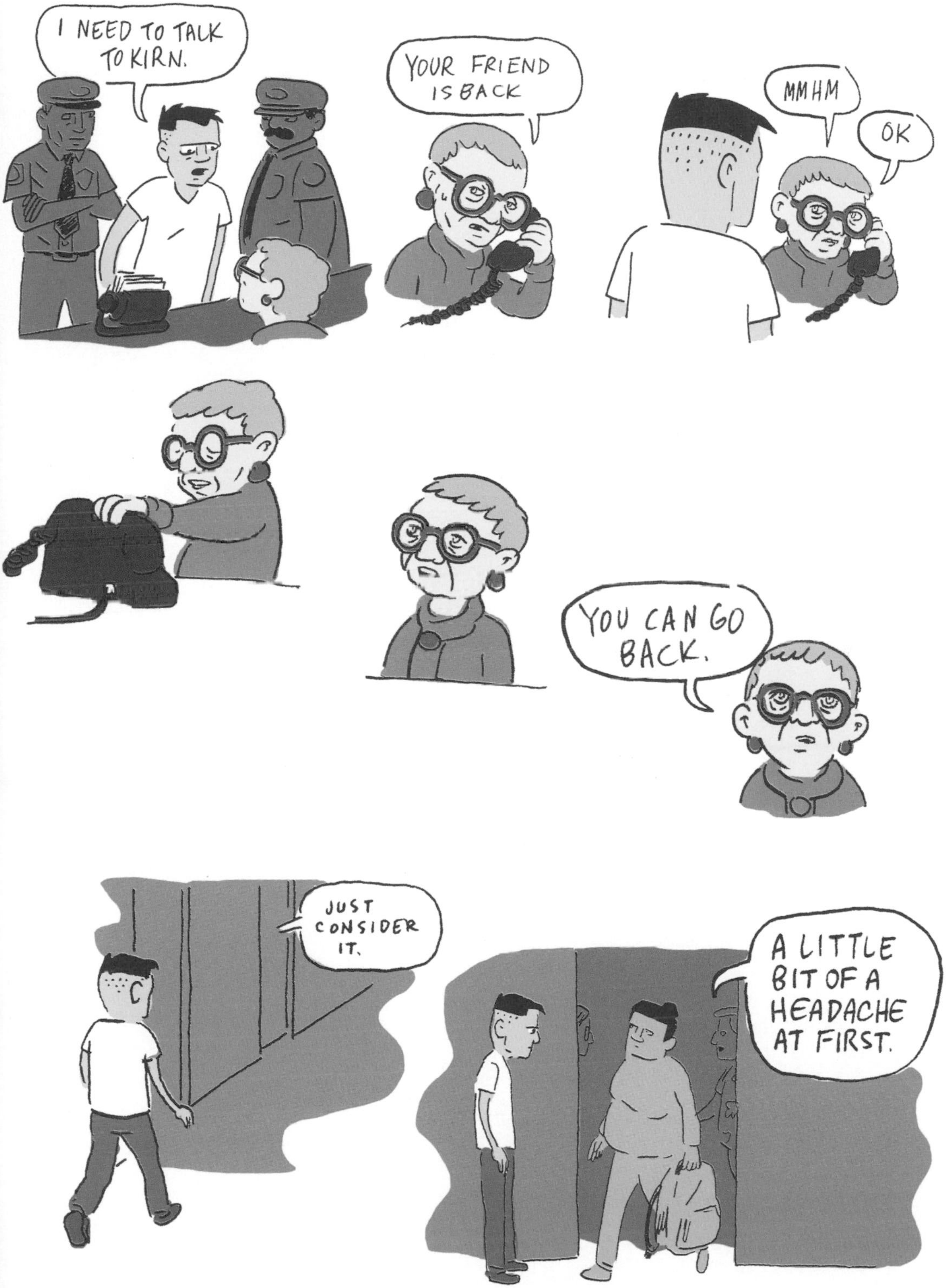
I NEED TO TALK TO KIRN.
YOUR FRIEND IS BACK
MMHM
OK
YOU CAN GO BACK.
JUST CONSIDER IT.
A LITTLE BIT OF A HEADACHE AT FIRST.

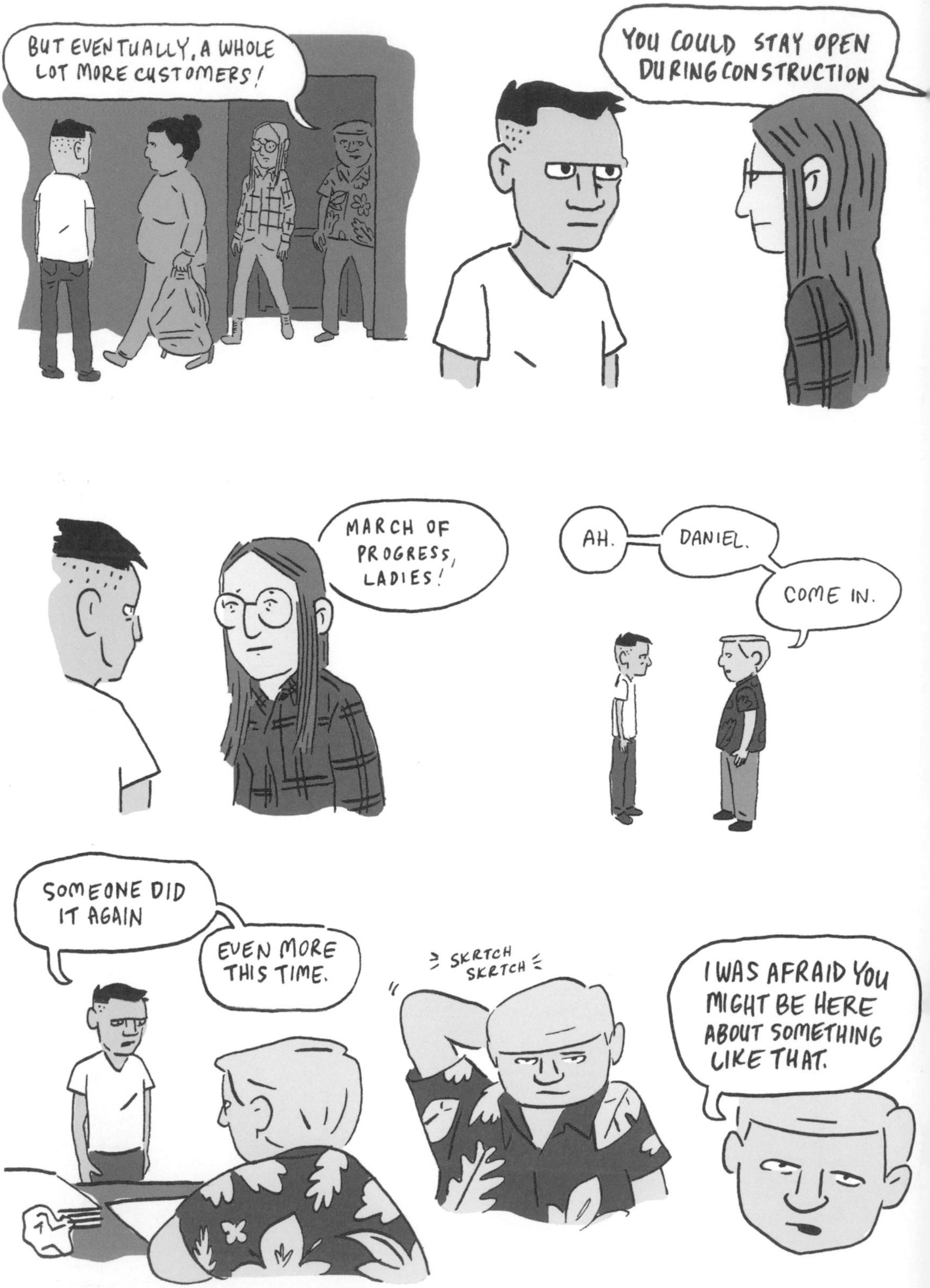
BUT EVENTUALLY, A WHOLE LOT MORE CUSTOMERS!
YOU COULD STAY OPEN DURING CONSTRUCTION
MARCH OF PROGRESS, LADIES!
AH.
DANIEL.
COME IN.
SOMEONE DID IT AGAIN
EVEN MORE THIS TIME.
SKRTCH SKRTCH
I WAS AFRAID YOU MIGHT BE HERE ABOUT SOMETHING LIKE THAT.

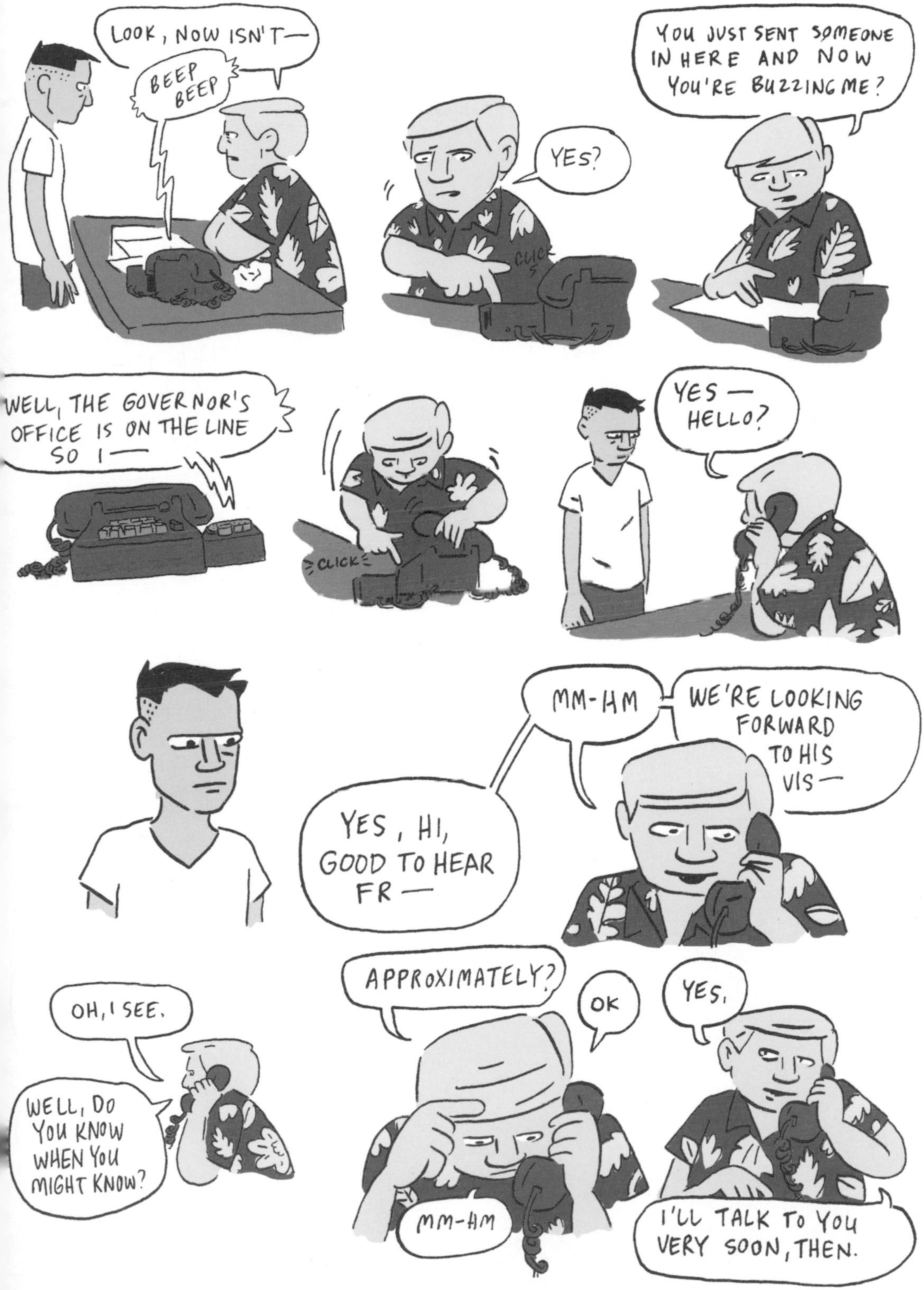
LOOK, NOW ISN'T—
BEEP BEEP
YES?
YOU JUST SENT SOMEONE IN HERE AND NOW YOU'RE BUZZING ME?
WELL, THE GOVERNOR'S OFFICE IS ON THE LINE SO I—
CLICK
YES — HELLO?
YES, HI, GOOD TO HEAR FR—
MM-HM
WE'RE LOOKING FORWARD TO HIS VIS—
OH, I SEE.
WELL, DO YOU KNOW WHEN YOU MIGHT KNOW?
APPROXIMATELY?
MM-HM
OK
YES.
I'LL TALK TO YOU VERY SOON, THEN.

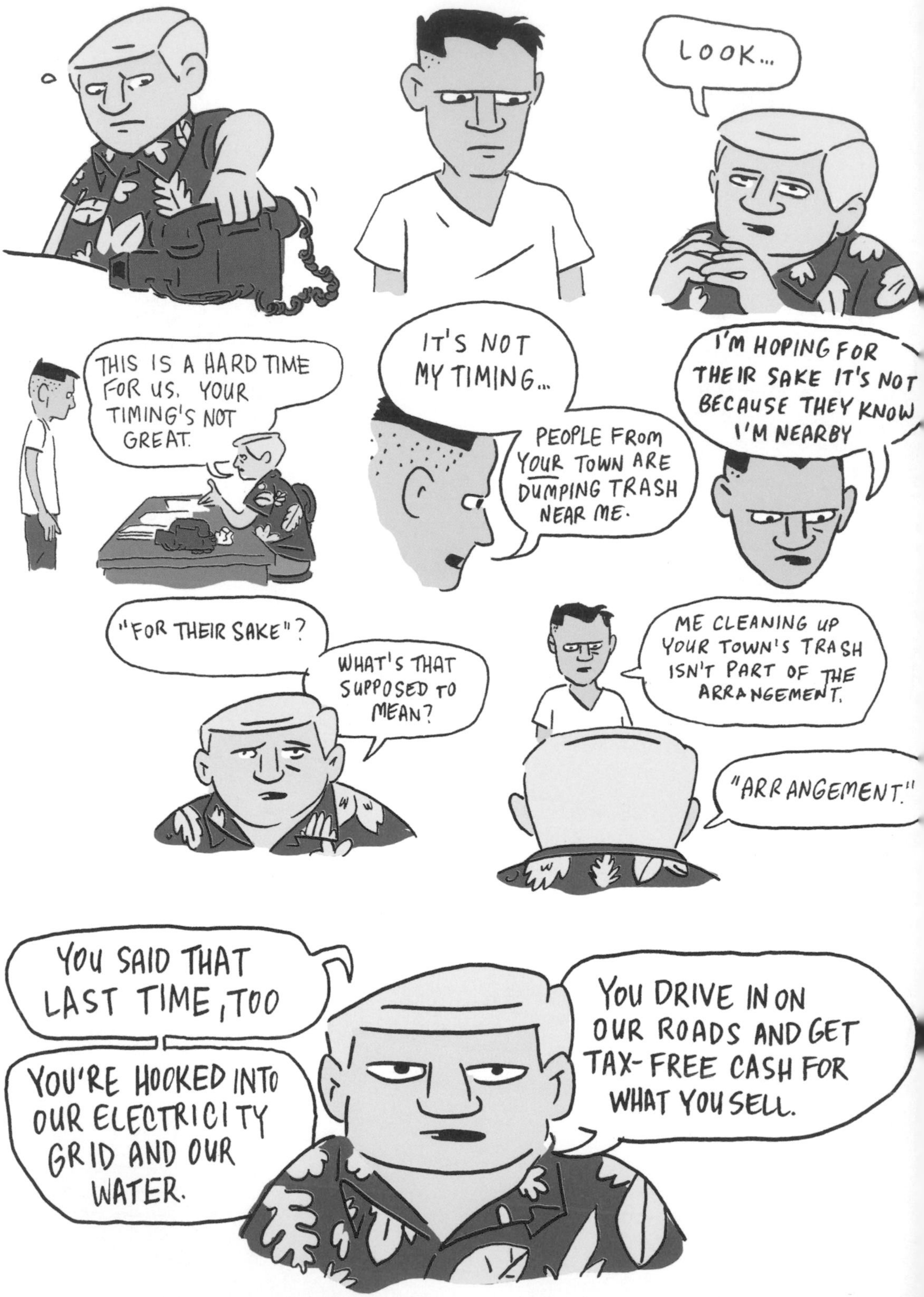
LOOK...
THIS IS A HARD TIME FOR US. YOUR TIMING'S NOT GREAT.
IT'S NOT MY TIMING...
PEOPLE FROM YOUR TOWN ARE DUMPING TRASH NEAR ME.
I'M HOPING FOR THEIR SAKE IT'S NOT BECAUSE THEY KNOW I'M NEARBY
"FOR THEIR SAKE"?
WHAT'S THAT SUPPOSED TO MEAN?
ME CLEANING UP YOUR TOWN'S TRASH ISN'T PART OF THE ARRANGEMENT.
"ARRANGEMENT."
YOU SAID THAT LAST TIME, TOO
YOU'RE HOOKED INTO OUR ELECTRICITY GRID AND OUR WATER.
YOU DRIVE IN ON OUR ROADS AND GET TAX-FREE CASH FOR WHAT YOU SELL.

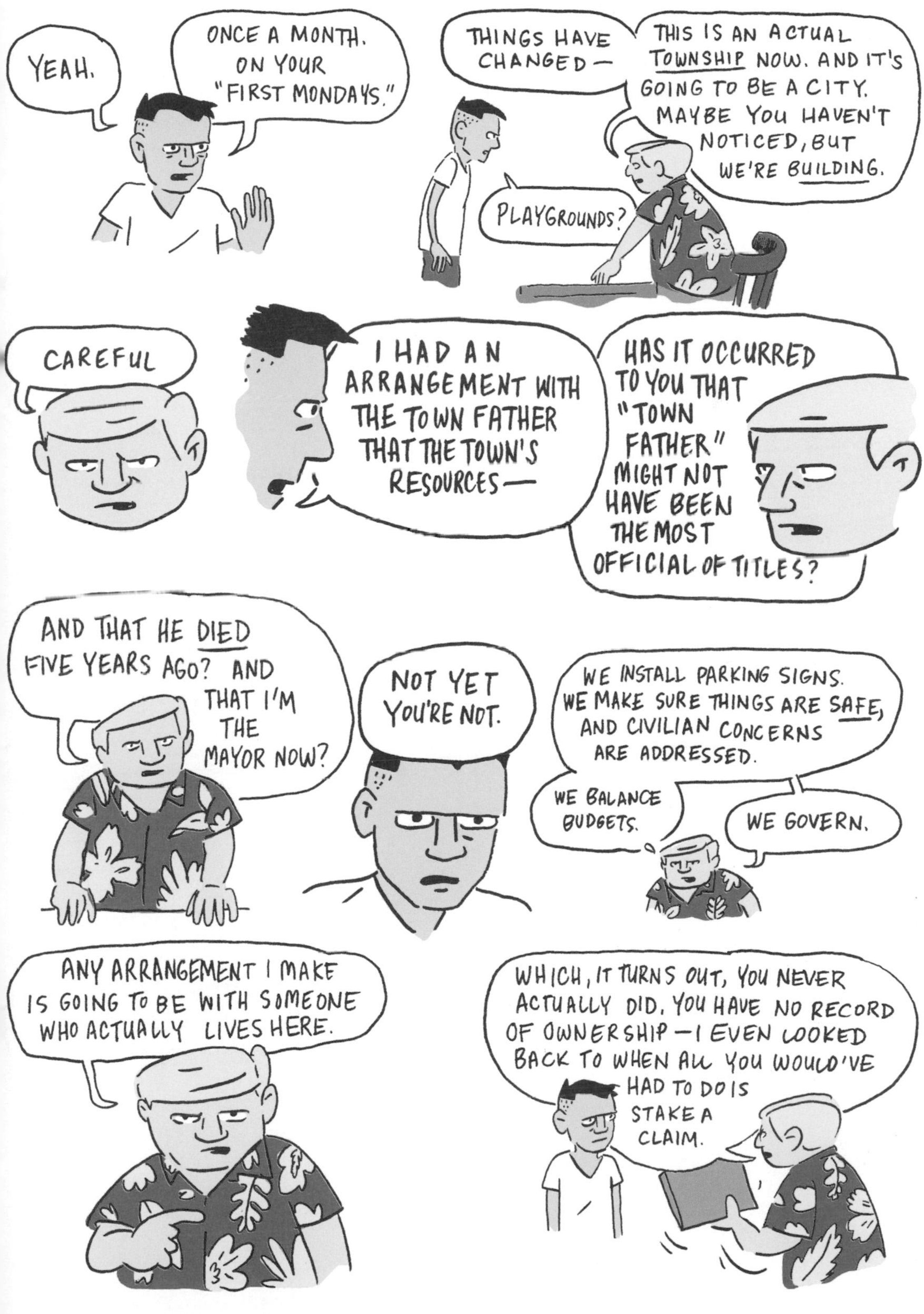

YEAH.
ONCE A MONTH. ON YOUR "FIRST MONDAYS."
THINGS HAVE CHANGED—
THIS IS AN ACTUAL TOWNSHIP NOW. AND IT'S GOING TO BE A CITY. MAYBE YOU HAVEN'T NOTICED, BUT WE'RE BUILDING.
PLAYGROUNDS?
CAREFUL
I HAD AN ARRANGEMENT WITH THE TOWN FATHER THAT THE TOWN'S RESOURCES—
HAS IT OCCURRED TO YOU THAT "TOWN FATHER" MIGHT NOT HAVE BEEN THE MOST OFFICIAL OF TITLES?
AND THAT HE DIED FIVE YEARS AGO? AND THAT I'M THE MAYOR NOW?
NOT YET YOU'RE NOT.
WE INSTALL PARKING SIGNS. WE MAKE SURE THINGS ARE SAFE, AND CIVILIAN CONCERNS ARE ADDRESSED.
WE BALANCE BUDGETS.
WE GOVERN.
ANY ARRANGEMENT I MAKE IS GOING TO BE WITH SOMEONE WHO ACTUALLY LIVES HERE.
WHICH, IT TURNS OUT, YOU NEVER ACTUALLY DID. YOU HAVE NO RECORD OF OWNERSHIP—I EVEN LOOKED BACK TO WHEN ALL YOU WOULD'VE HAD TO DO IS STAKE A CLAIM.

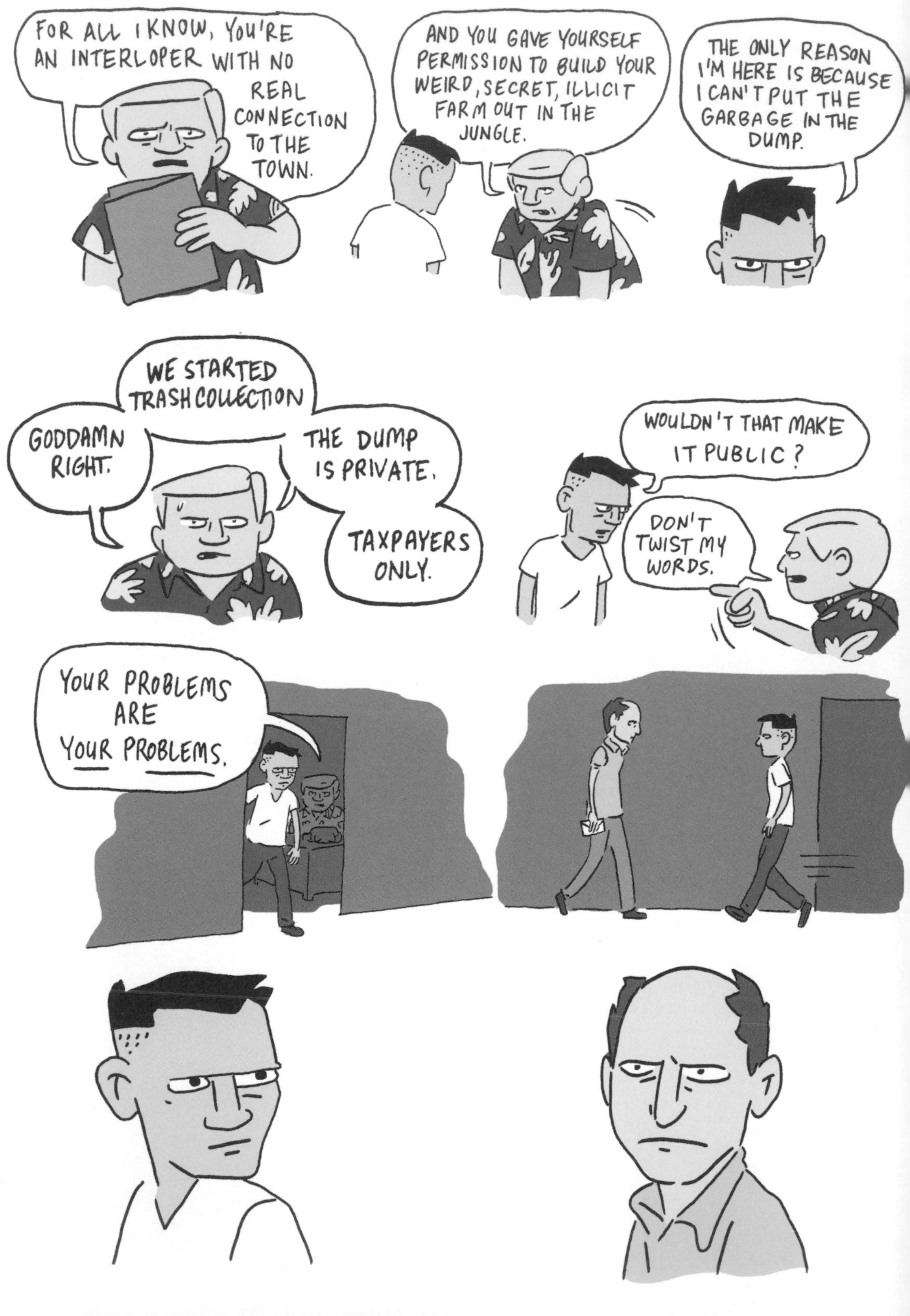
FOR ALL I KNOW, YOU'RE AN INTERLOPER WITH NO REAL CONNECTION TO THE TOWN.
AND YOU GAVE YOURSELF PERMISSION TO BUILD YOUR WEIRD, SECRET, ILLICIT FARM OUT IN THE JUNGLE.
THE ONLY REASON I'M HERE IS BECAUSE I CAN'T PUT THE GARBAGE IN THE DUMP.
WE STARTED TRASH COLLECTION
GODDAMN RIGHT.
THE DUMP IS PRIVATE.
TAXPAYERS ONLY.
WOULDN'T THAT MAKE IT PUBLIC?
DON'T TWIST MY WORDS.
YOUR PROBLEMS ARE YOUR PROBLEMS.

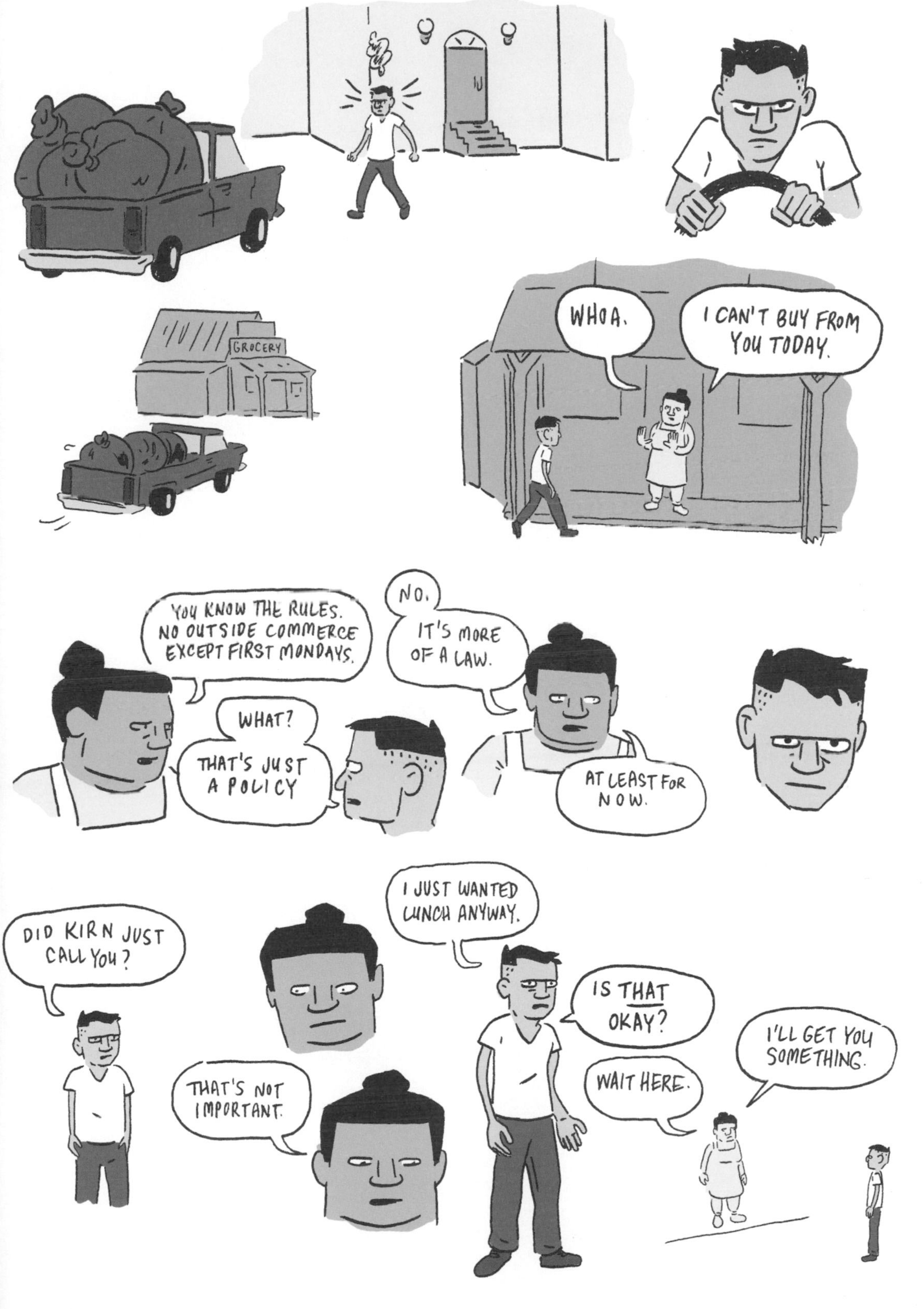
WHOA.
I CAN'T BUY FROM YOU TODAY.
YOU KNOW THE RULES. NO OUTSIDE COMMERCE EXCEPT FIRST MONDAYS.
WHAT?
THAT'S JUST A POLICY
NO.
IT'S MORE OF A LAW.
AT LEAST FOR NOW.
DID KIRN JUST CALL YOU?
THAT'S NOT IMPORTANT.
I JUST WANTED LUNCH ANYWAY.
IS THAT OKAY?
WAIT HERE.
I'LL GET YOU SOMETHING.

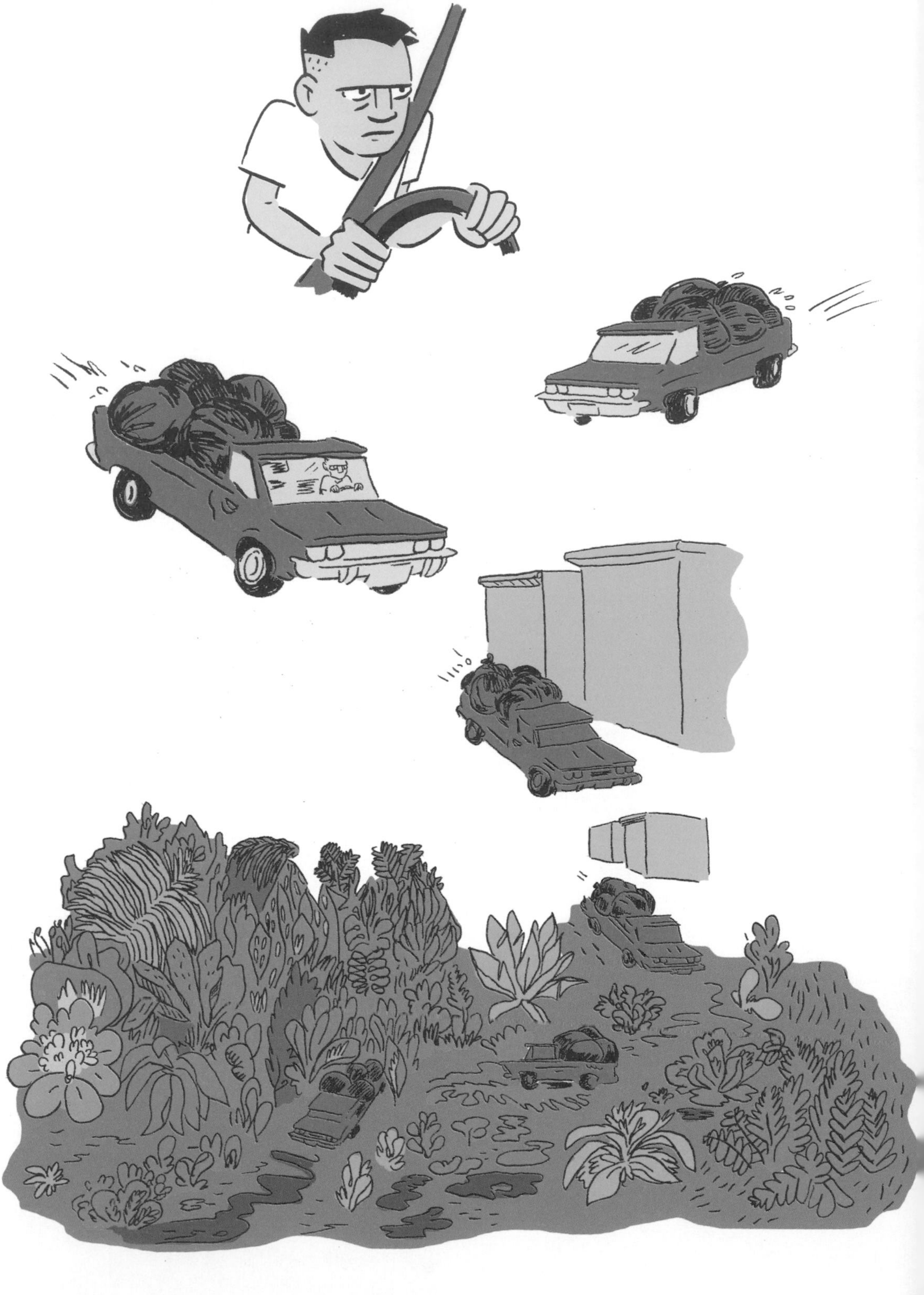

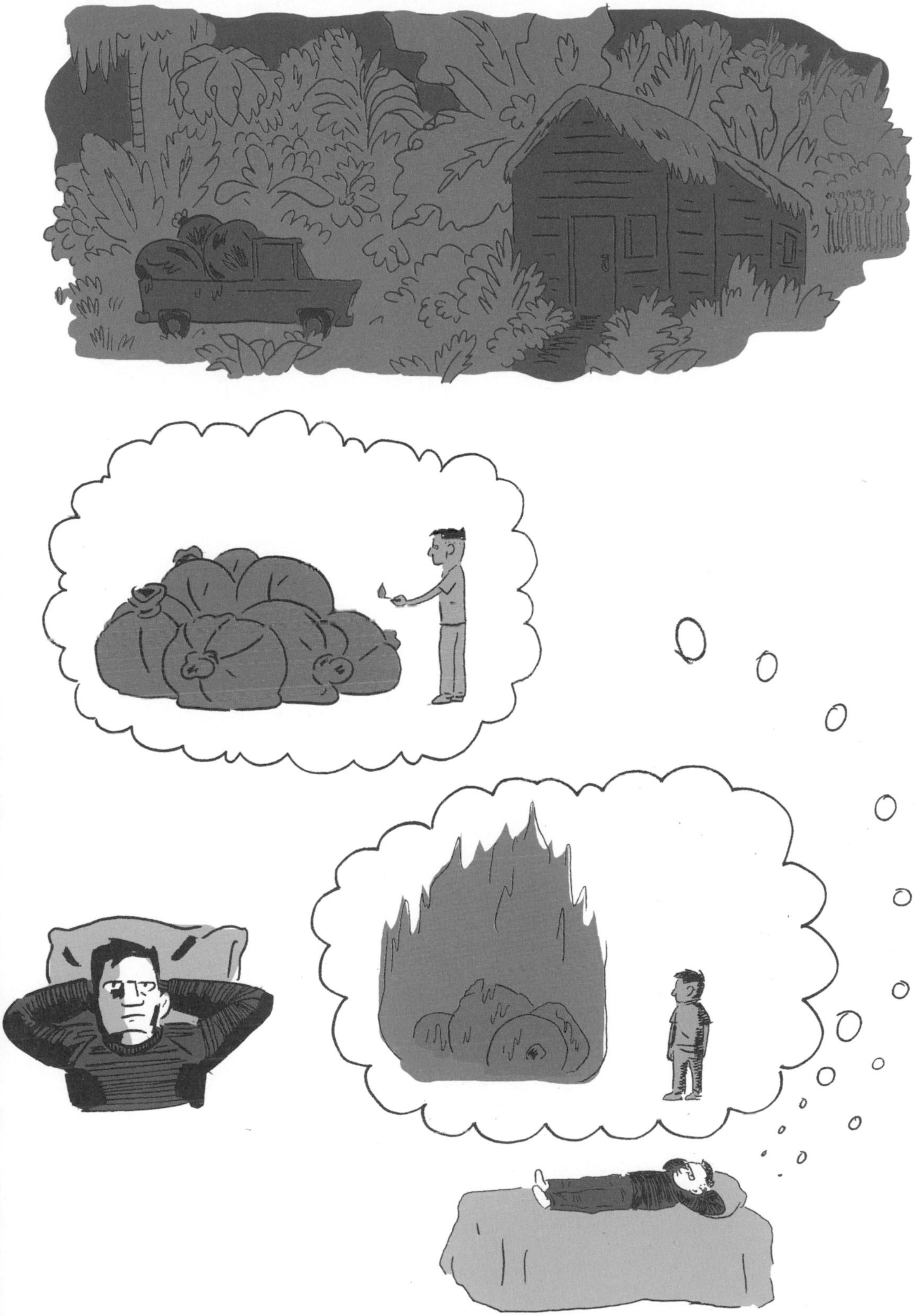

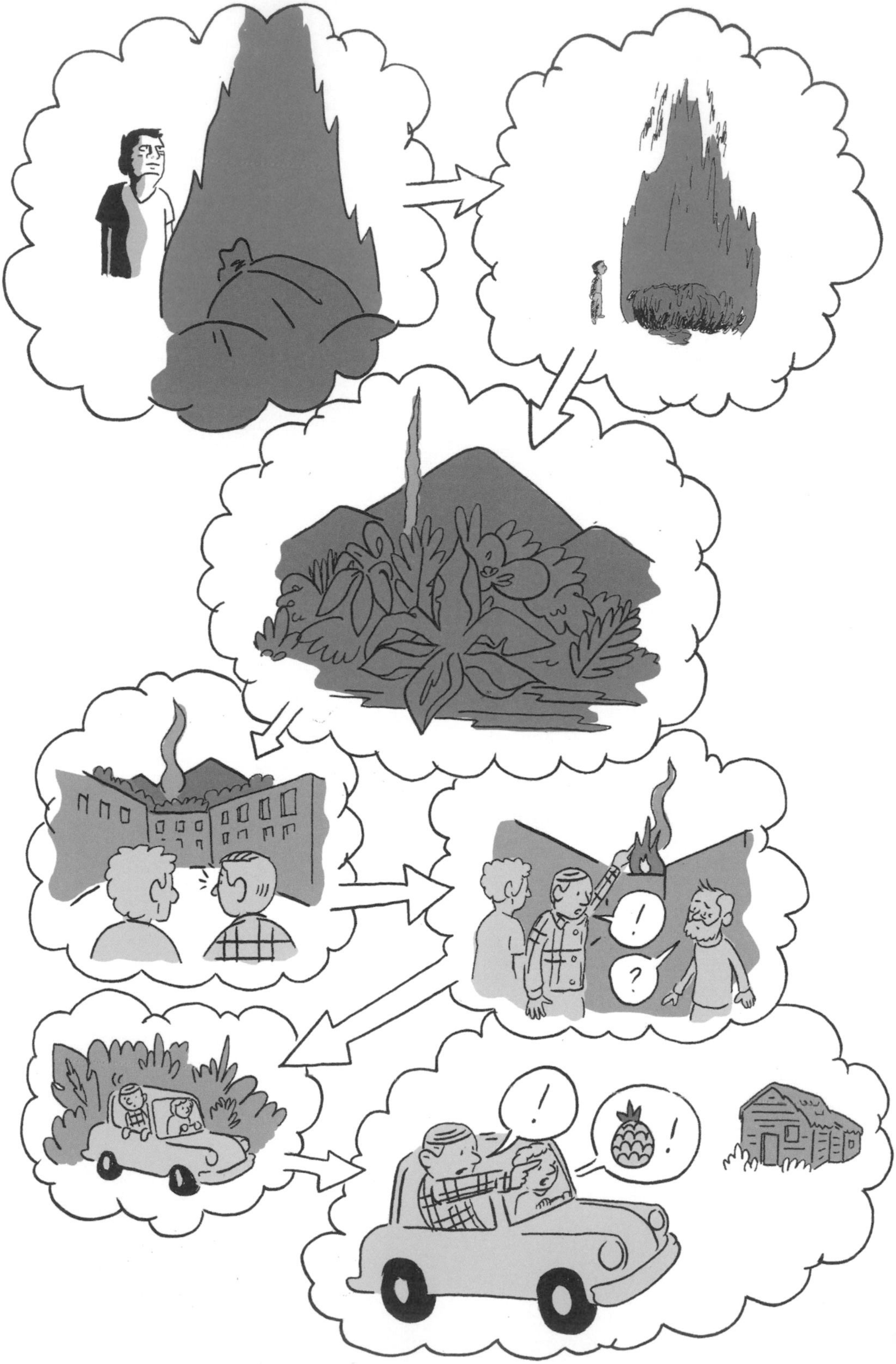
!
?
!
!

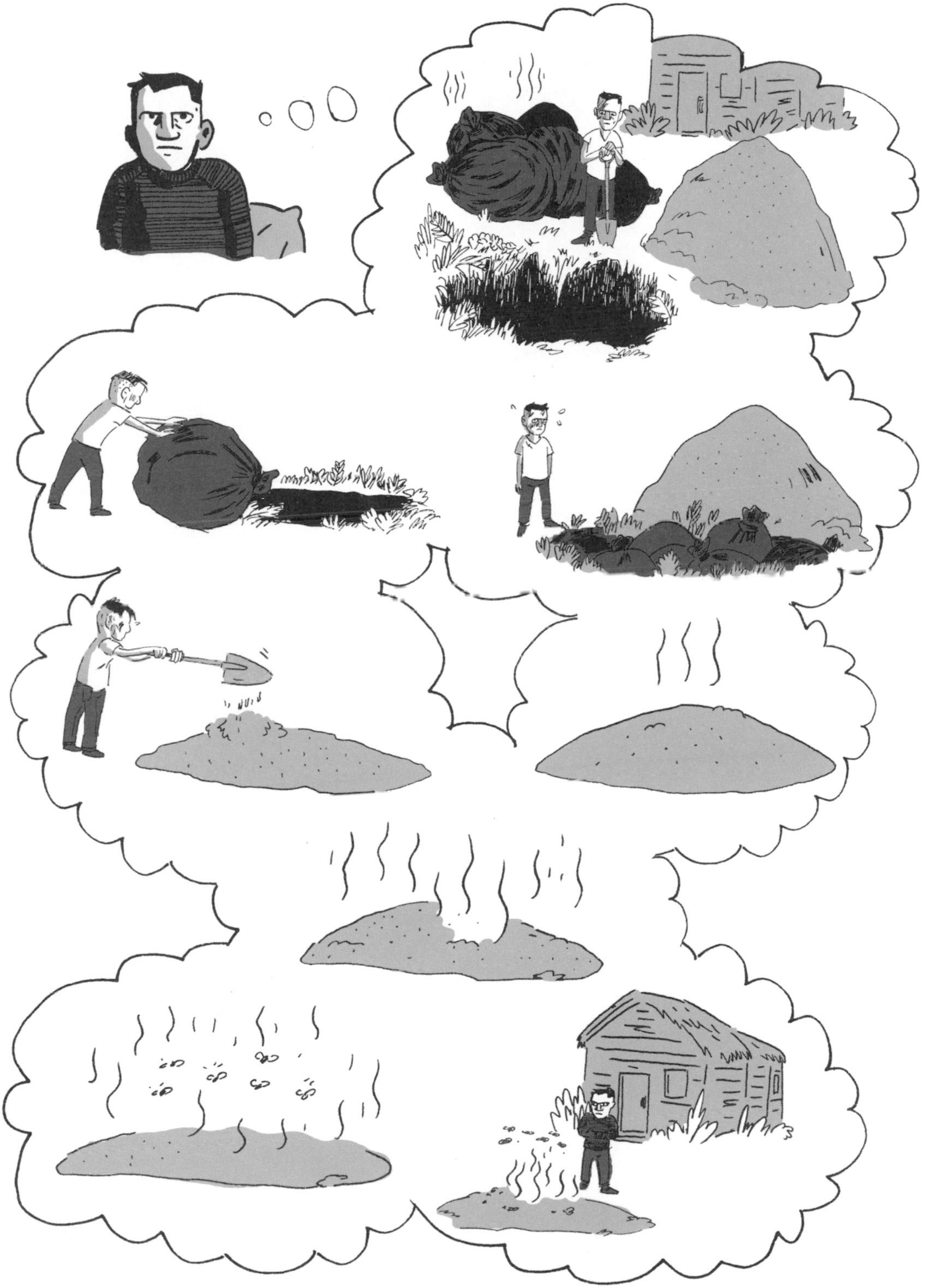

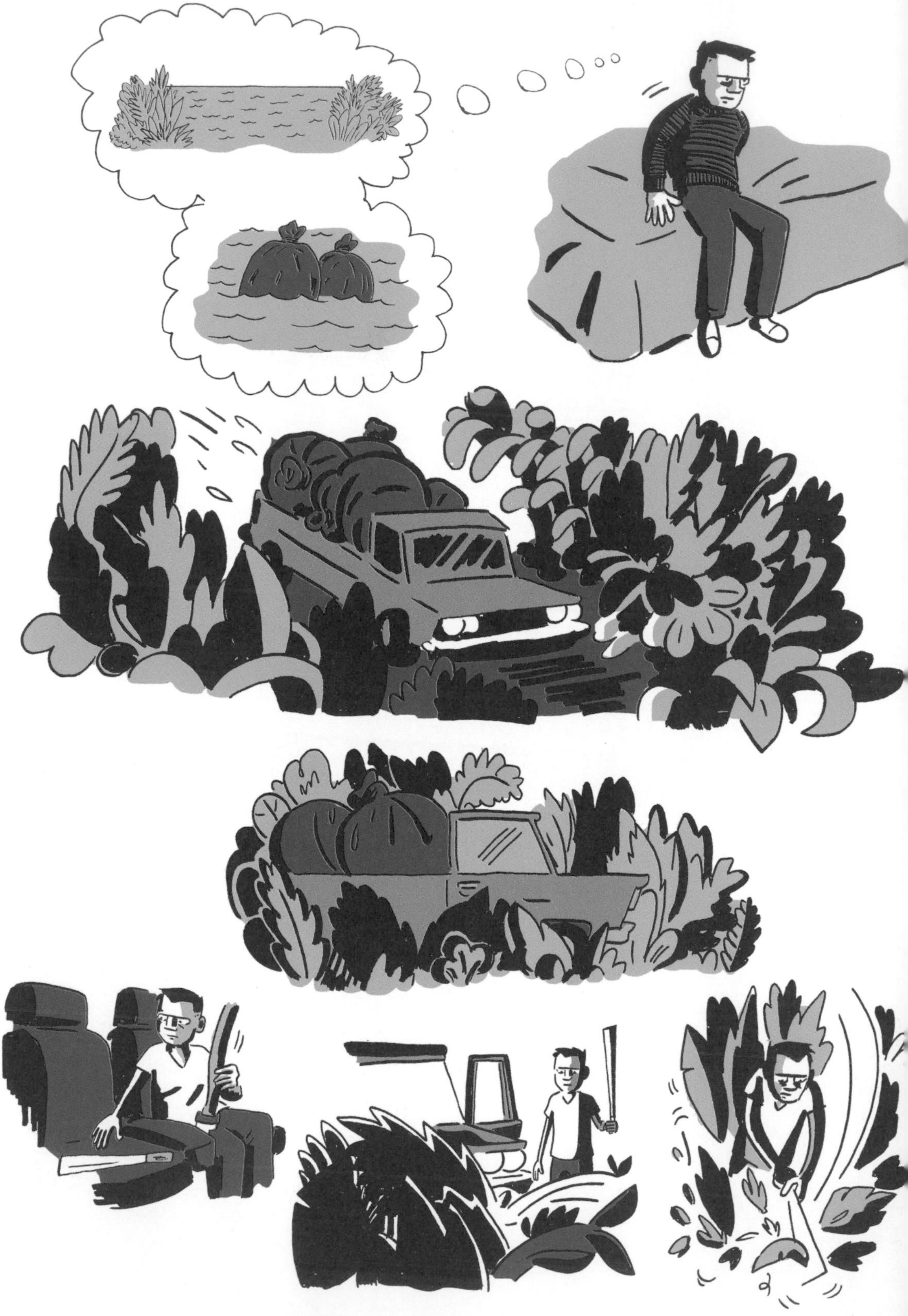

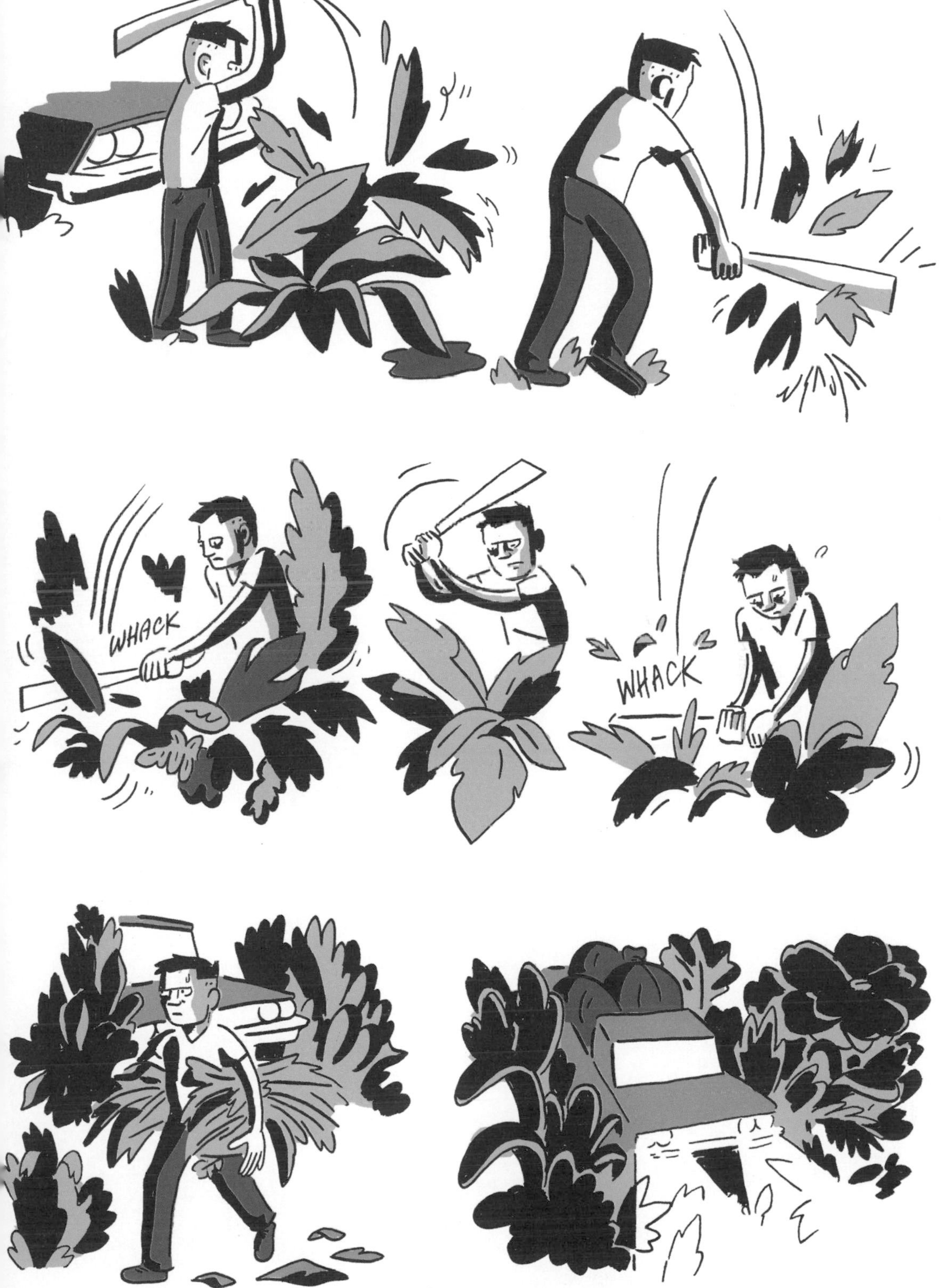
WHACK
WHACK

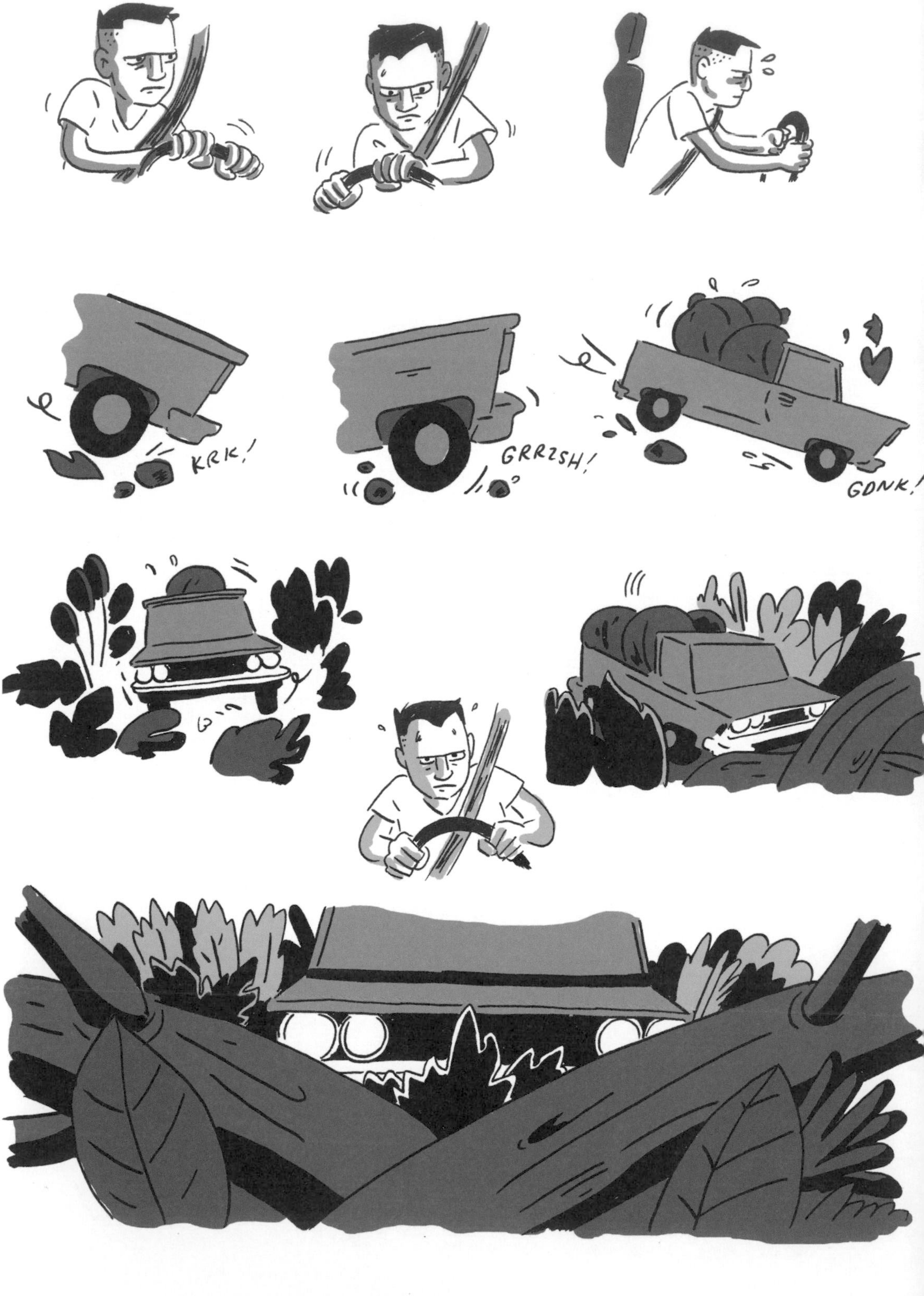
KRK!
GRRZSH!
GONK!

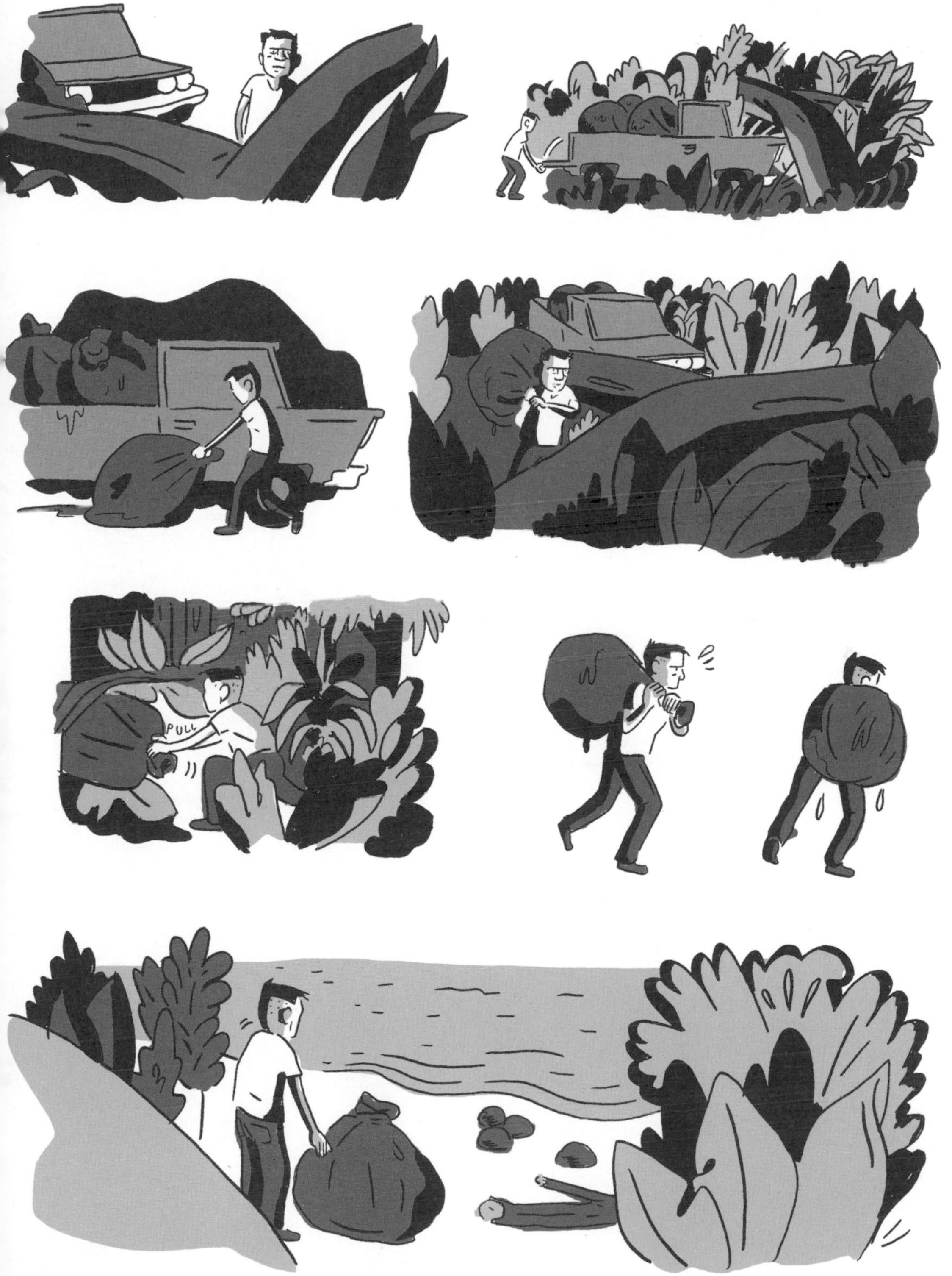
PULL

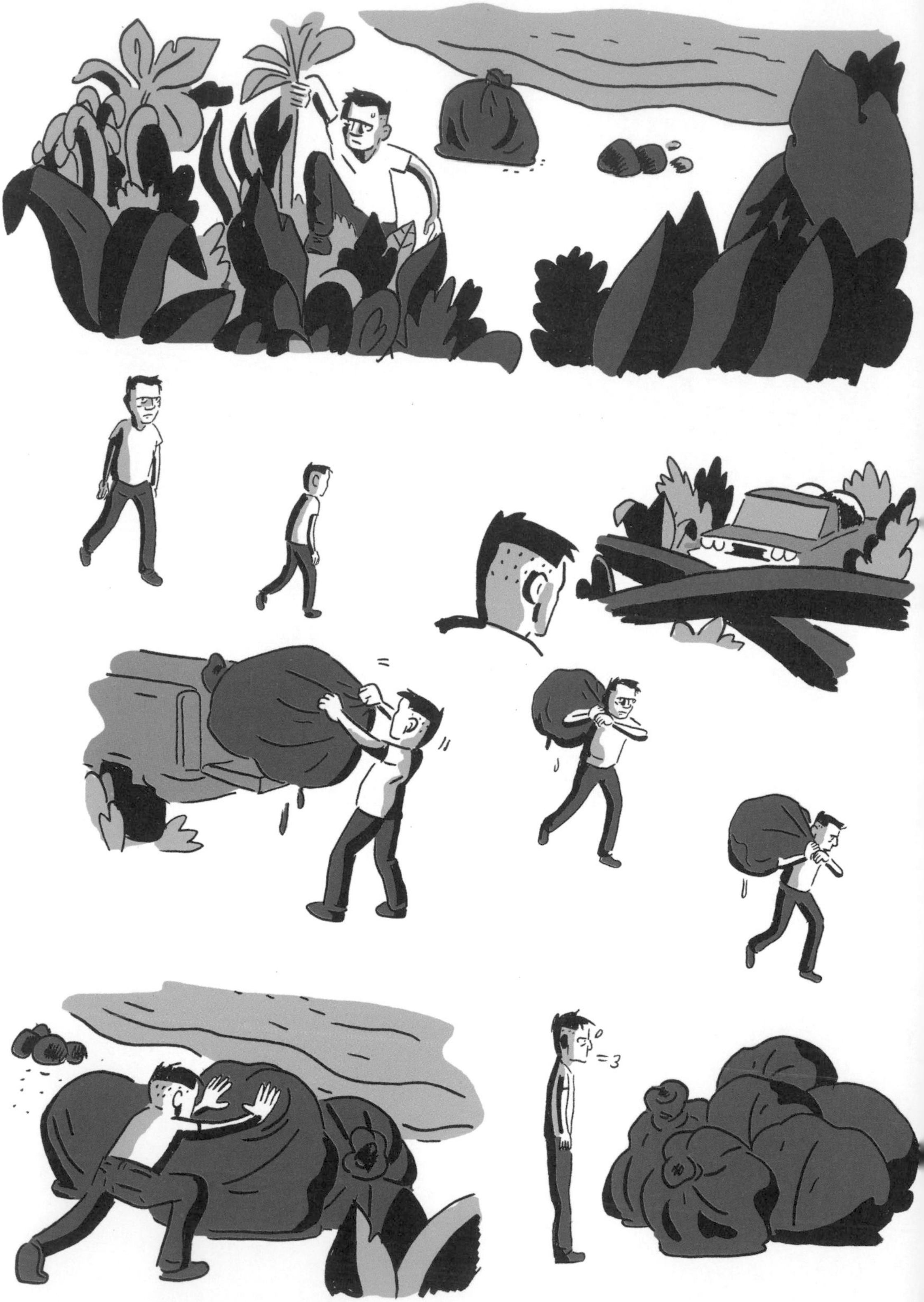

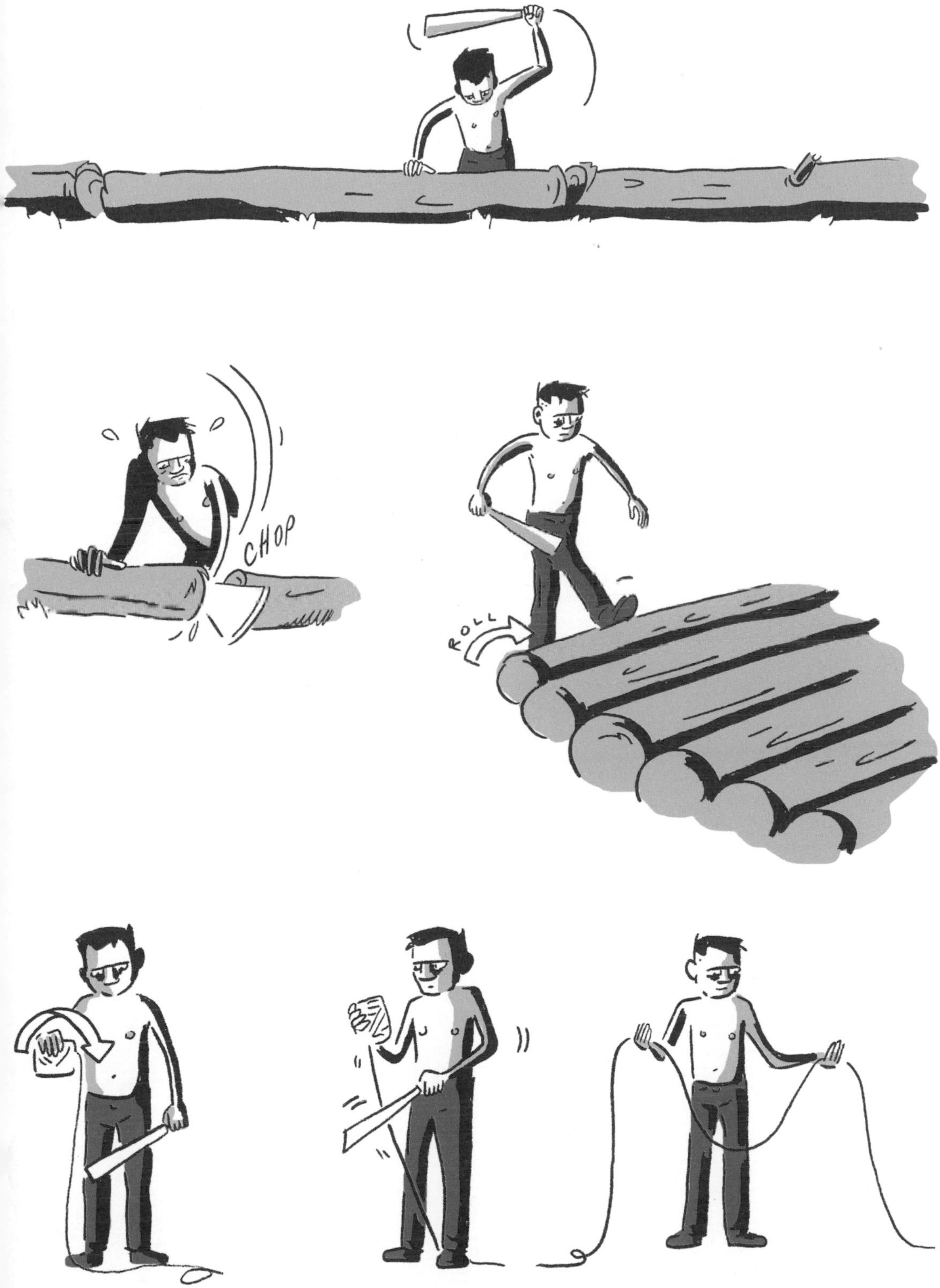
CHOP
ROLL

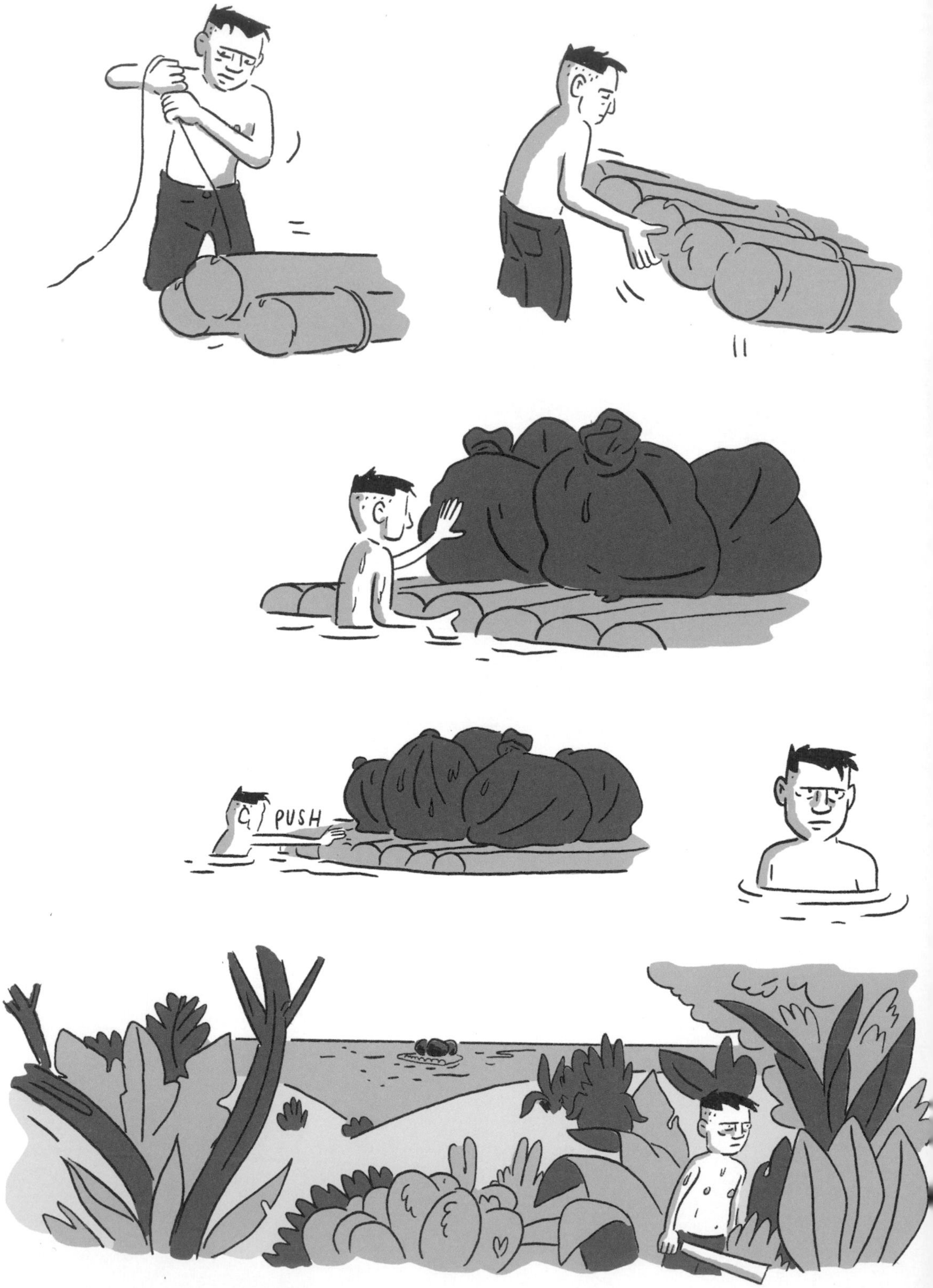
PUSH

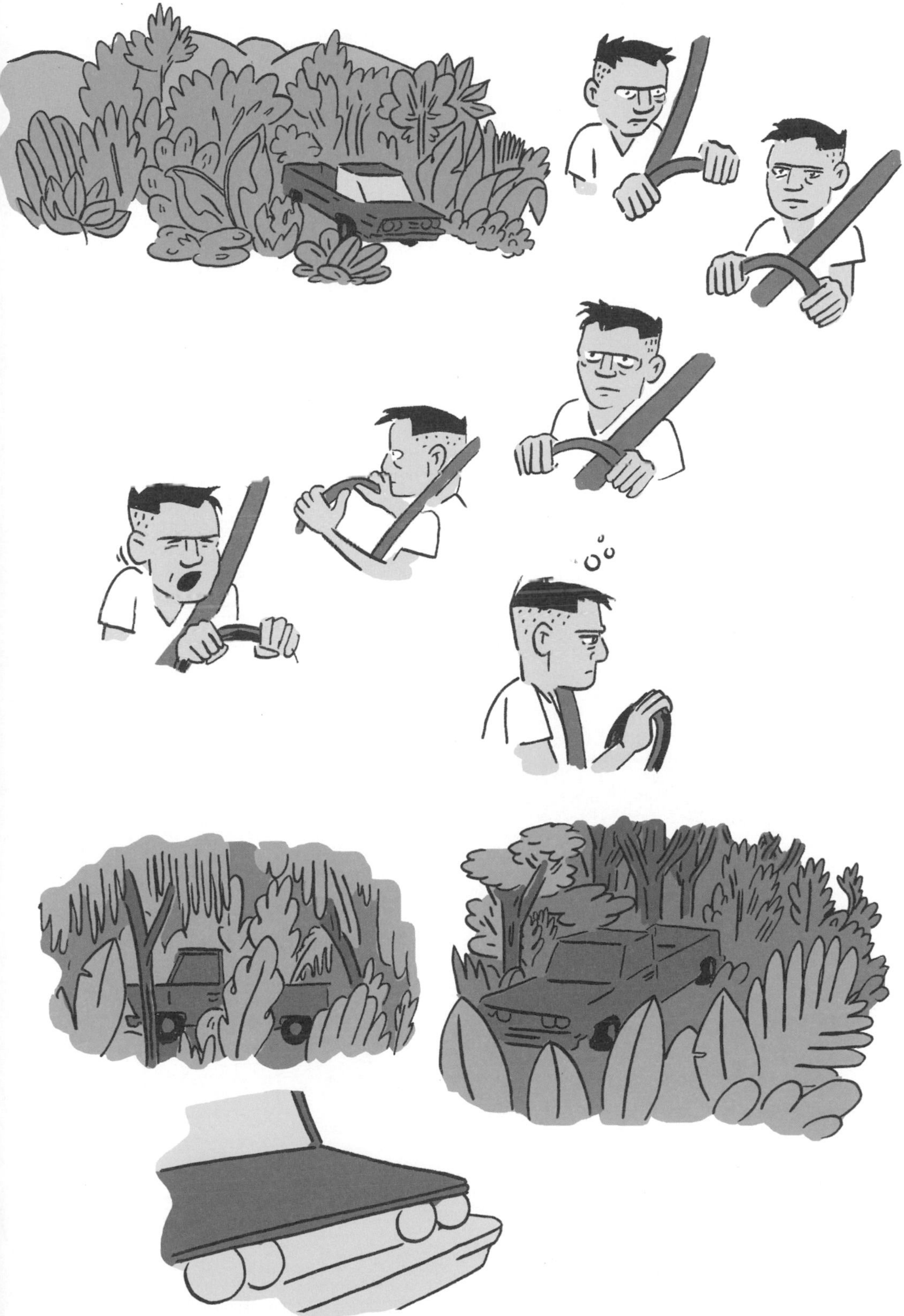

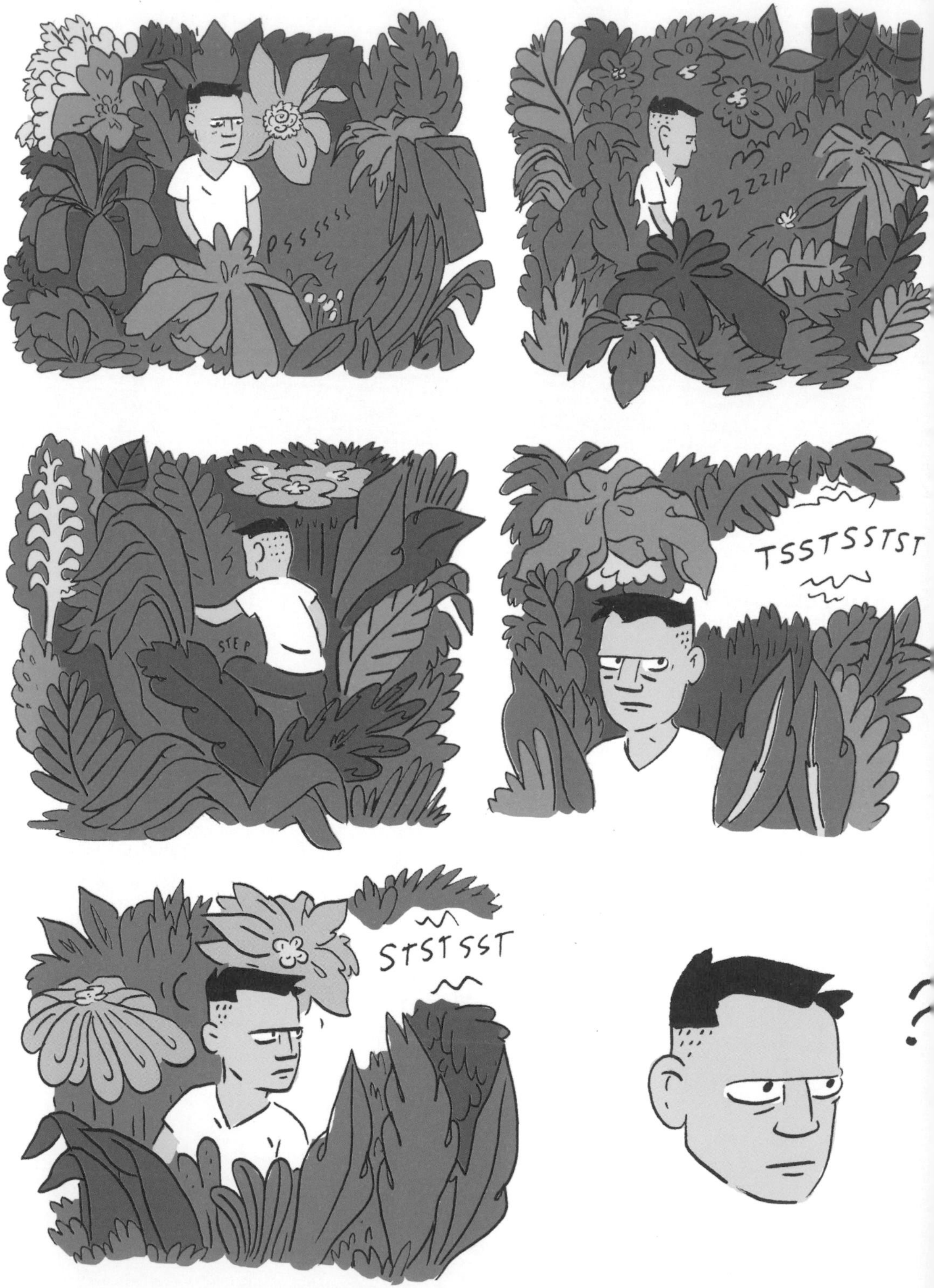
PSSSSSS
ZZZZZIP
STEP
TSSTSSTST
STSTSST
?

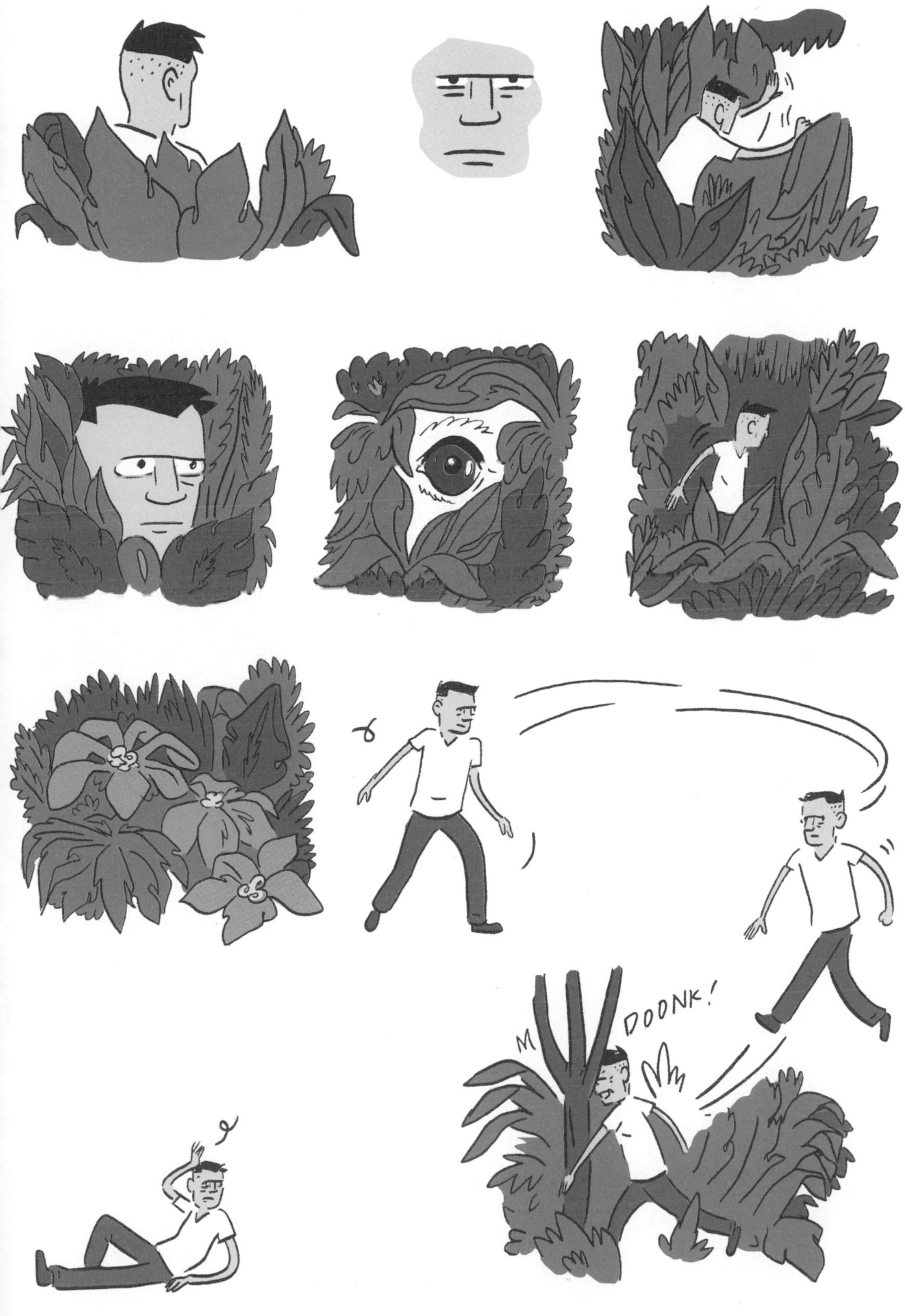
DOONK!

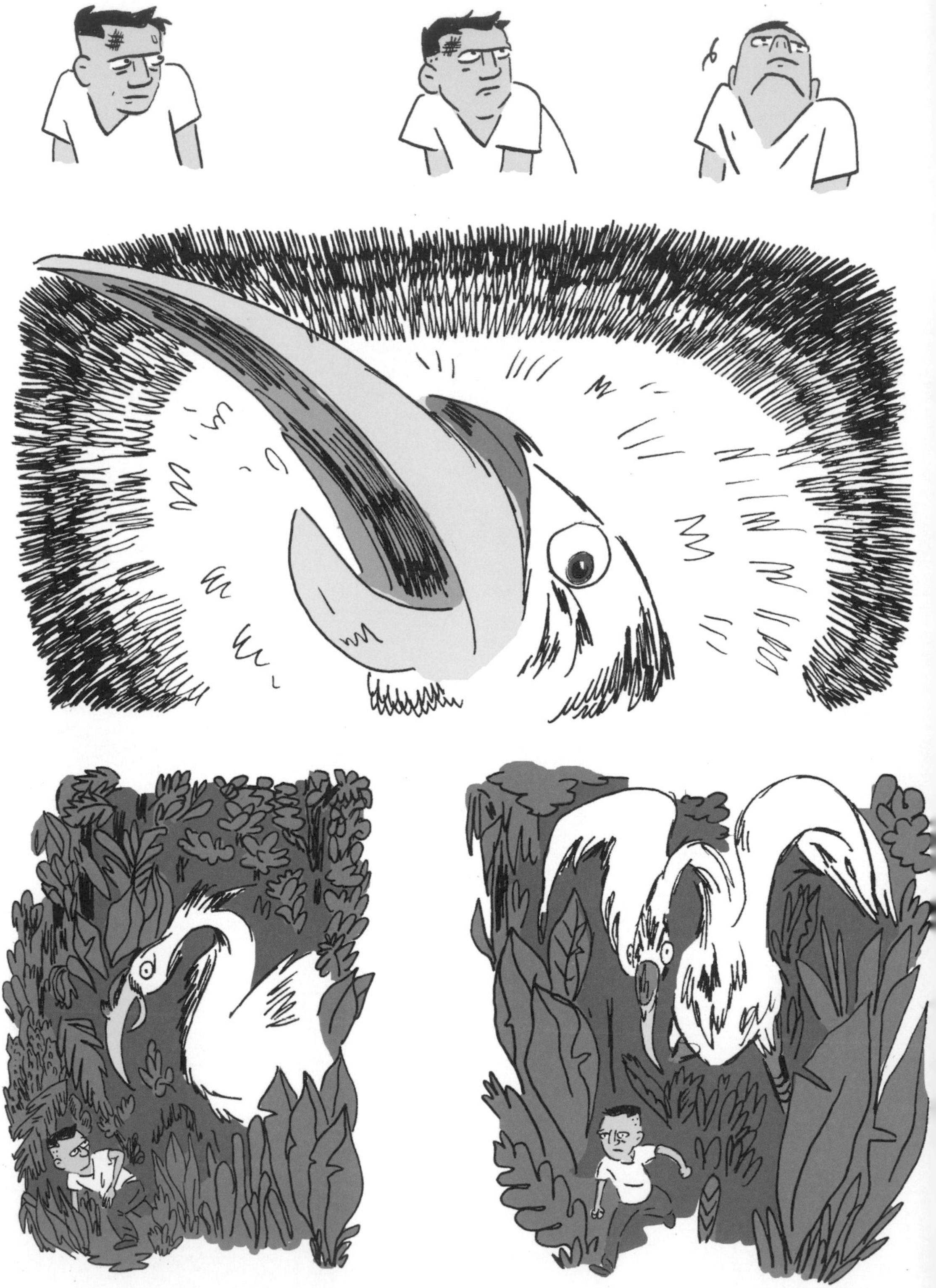

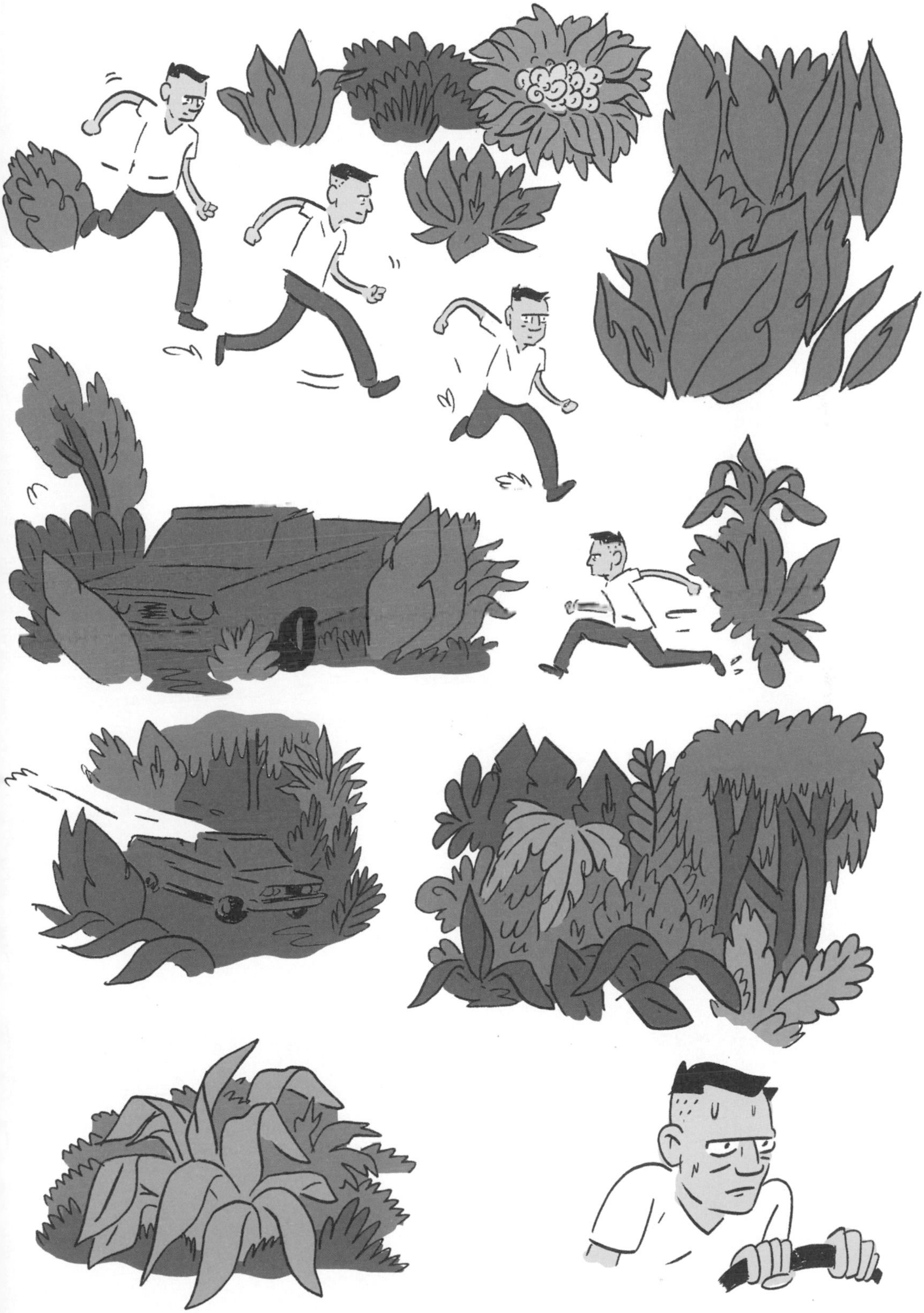

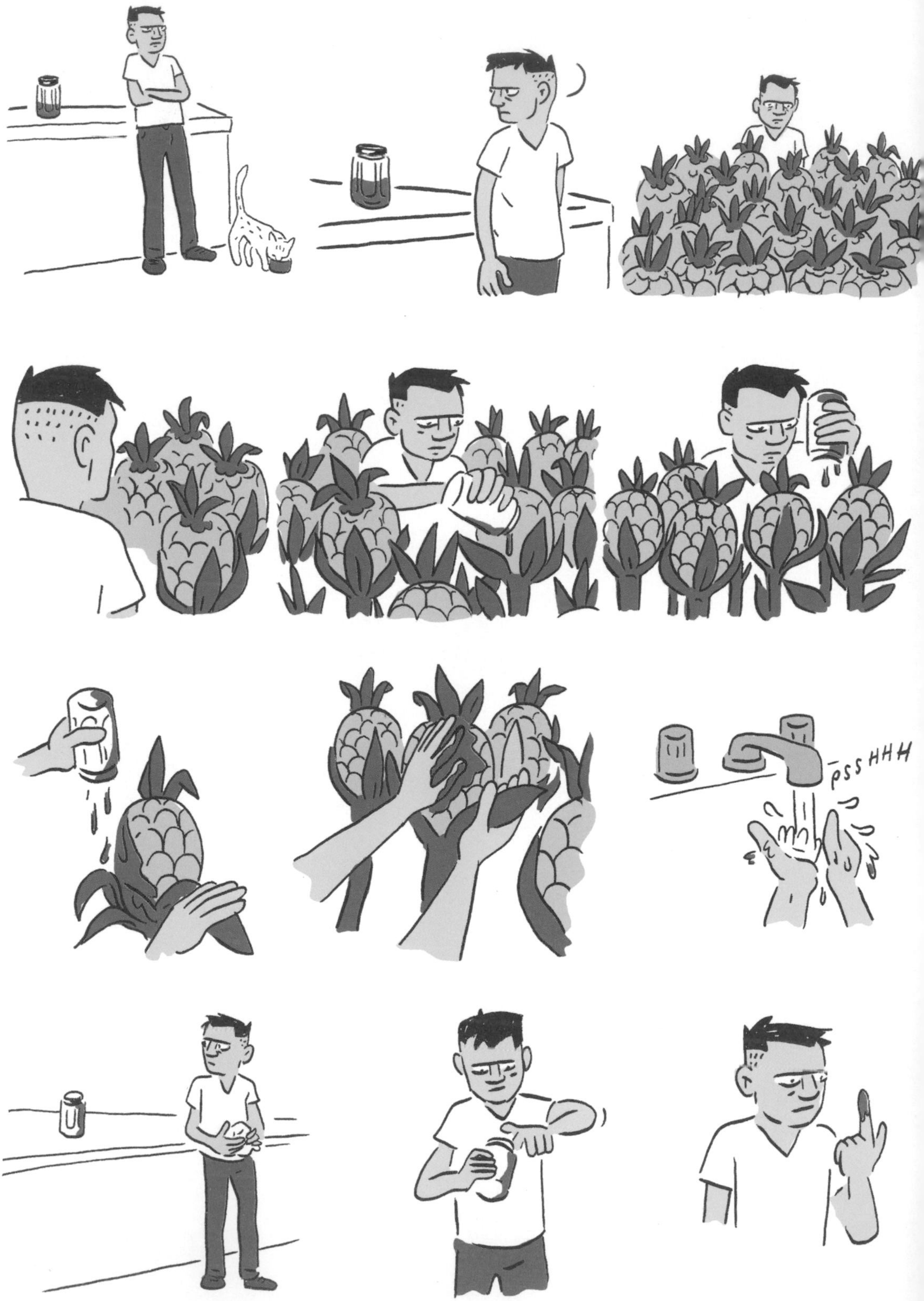
PSSHHH

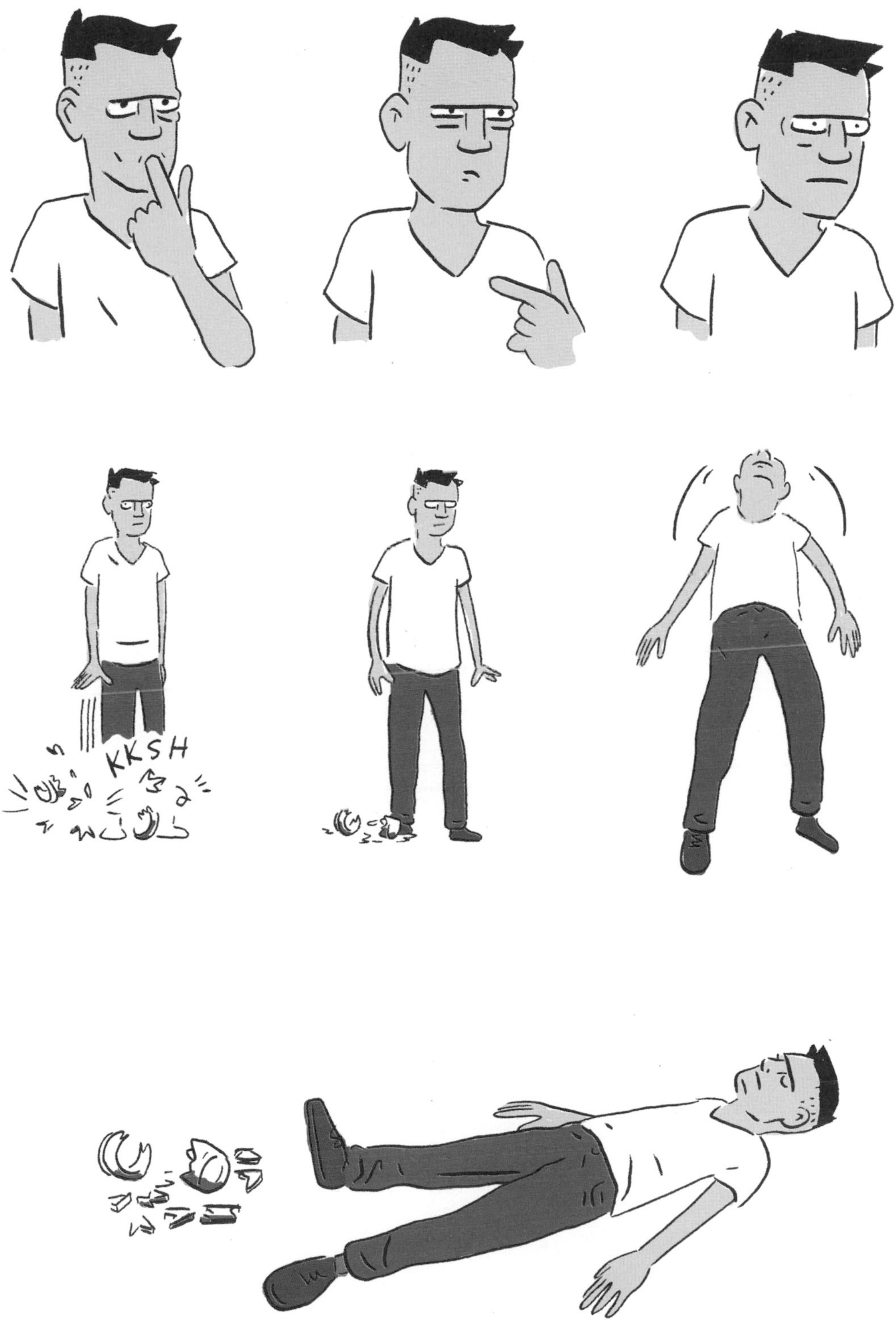
KKSH

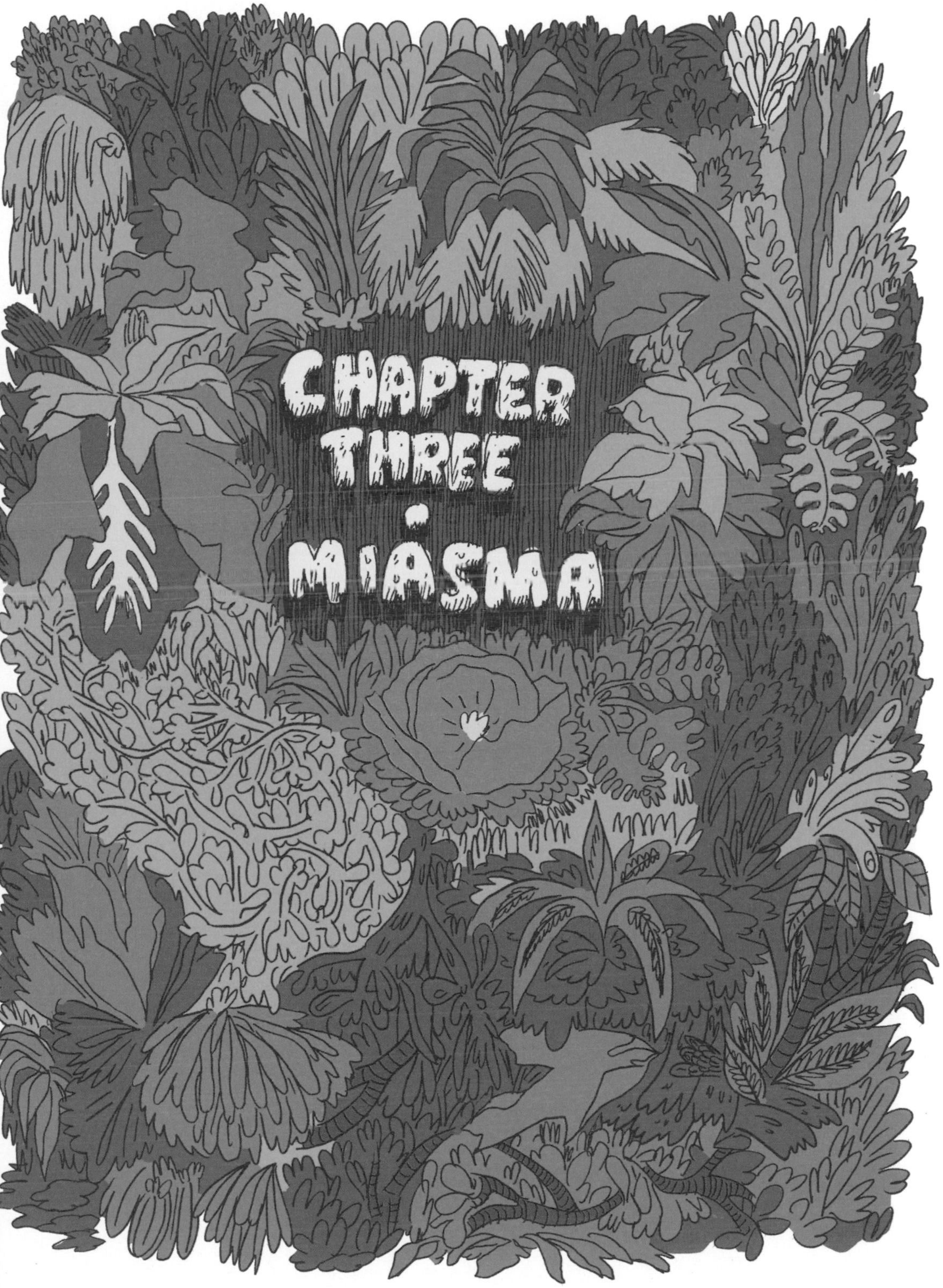
CHAPTER THREE
•
MIASMA

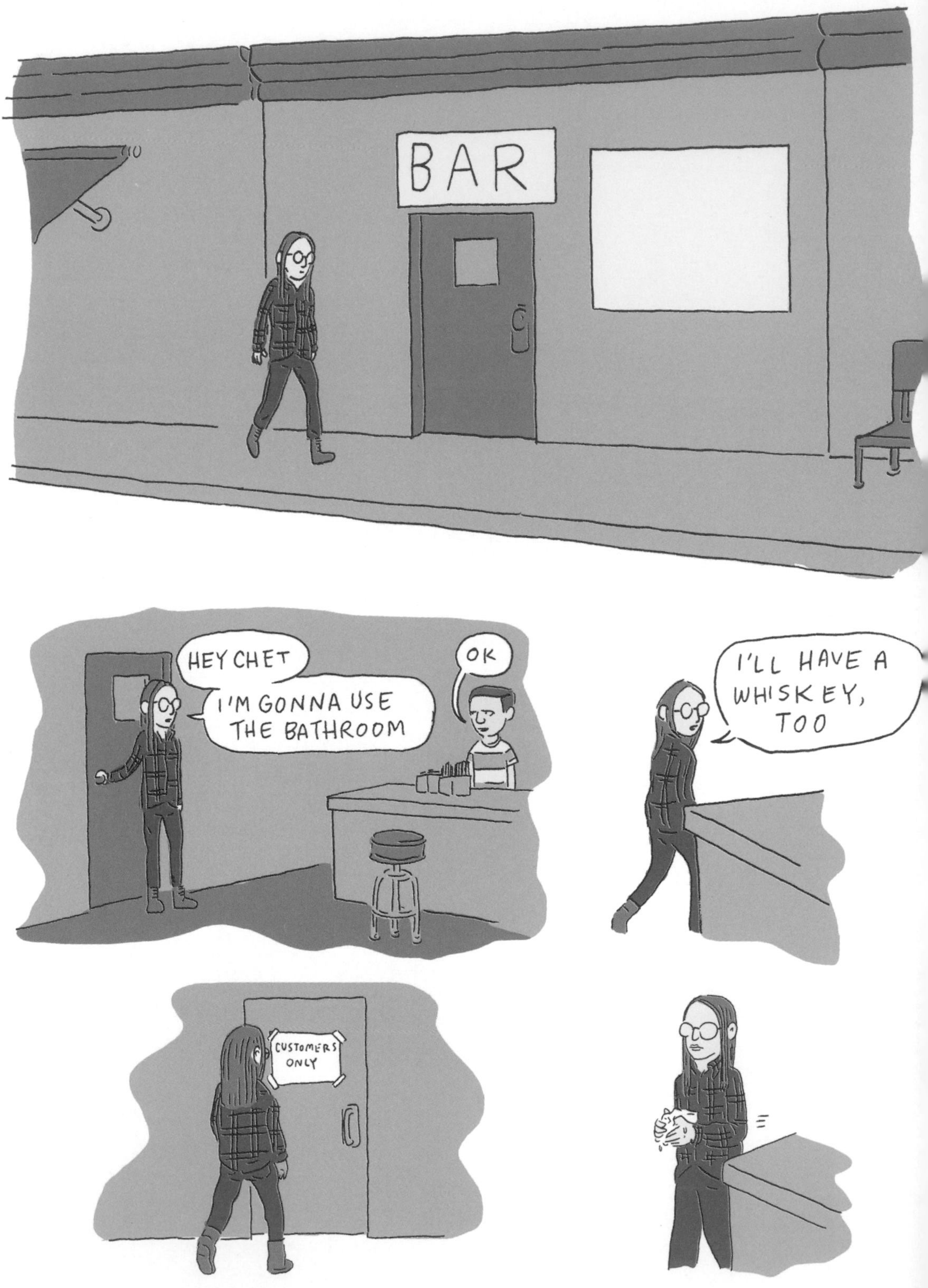
BAR
HEY CHET
I'M GONNA USE THE BATHROOM
OK
I'LL HAVE A WHISKEY, TOO
CUSTOMERS ONLY

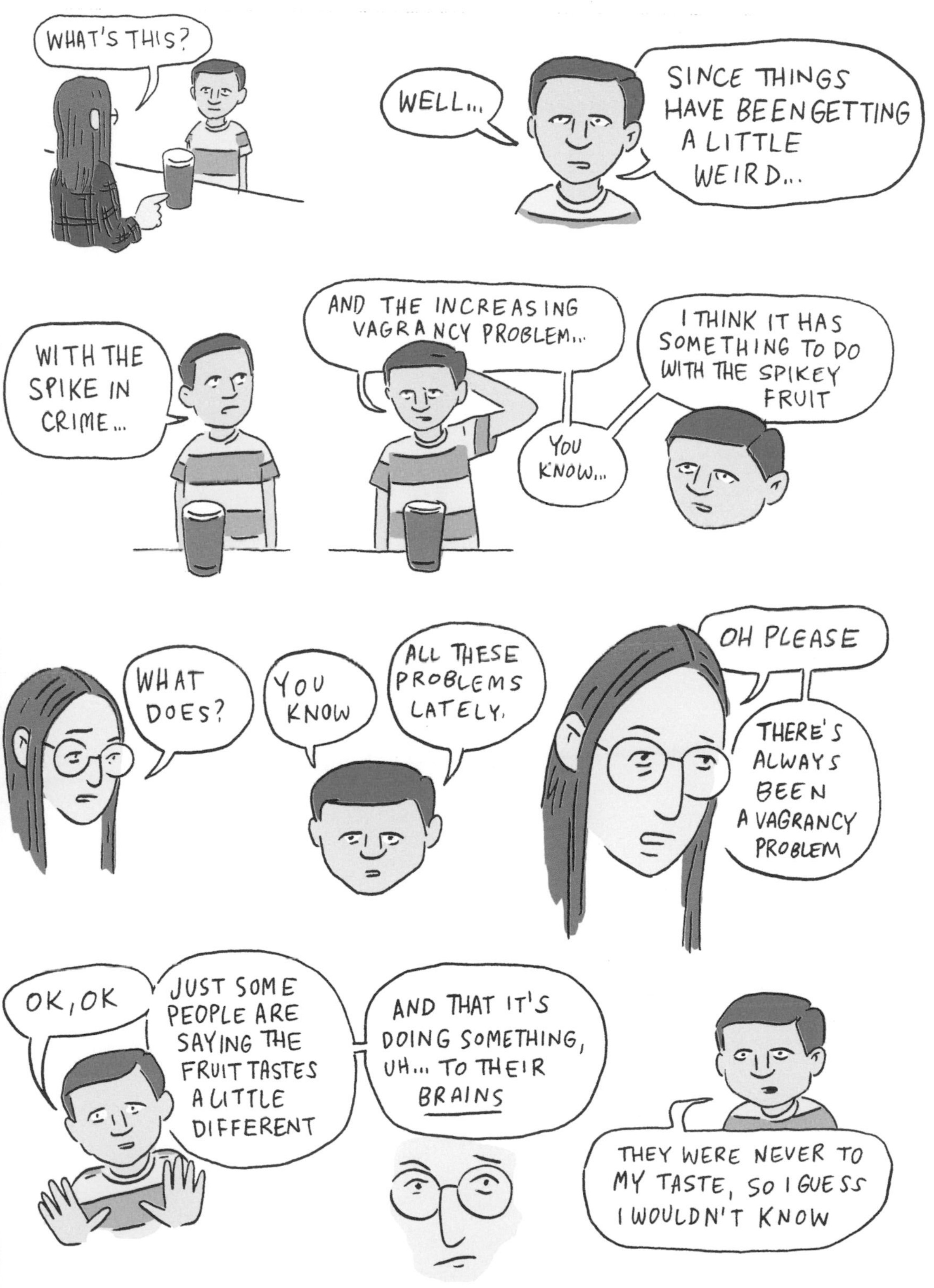
WHAT'S THIS?
WELL...
SINCE THINGS HAVE BEEN GETTING A LITTLE WEIRD...
WITH THE SPIKE IN CRIME...
AND THE INCREASING VAGRANCY PROBLEM...
YOU KNOW...
I THINK IT HAS SOMETHING TO DO WITH THE SPIKEY FRUIT
WHAT DOES?
YOU KNOW
ALL THESE PROBLEMS LATELY.
OH PLEASE
THERE'S ALWAYS BEEN A VAGRANCY PROBLEM
OK, OK
JUST SOME PEOPLE ARE SAYING THE FRUIT TASTES A LITTLE DIFFERENT
AND THAT IT'S DOING SOMETHING, UH... TO THEIR BRAINS
THEY WERE NEVER TO MY TASTE, SO I GUESS I WOULDN'T KNOW

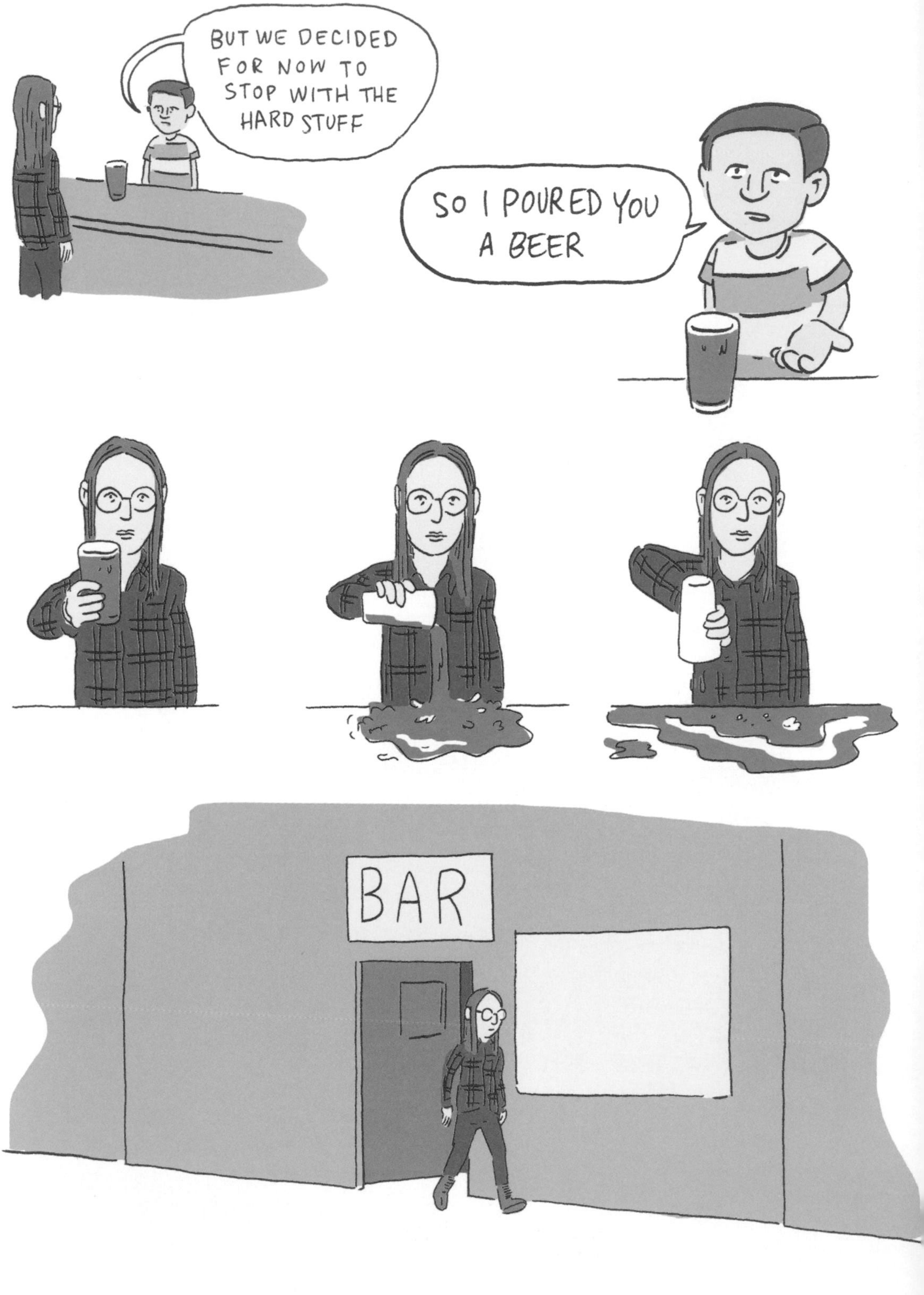
BUT WE DECIDED FOR NOW TO STOP WITH THE HARD STUFF
SO I POURED YOU A BEER
BAR

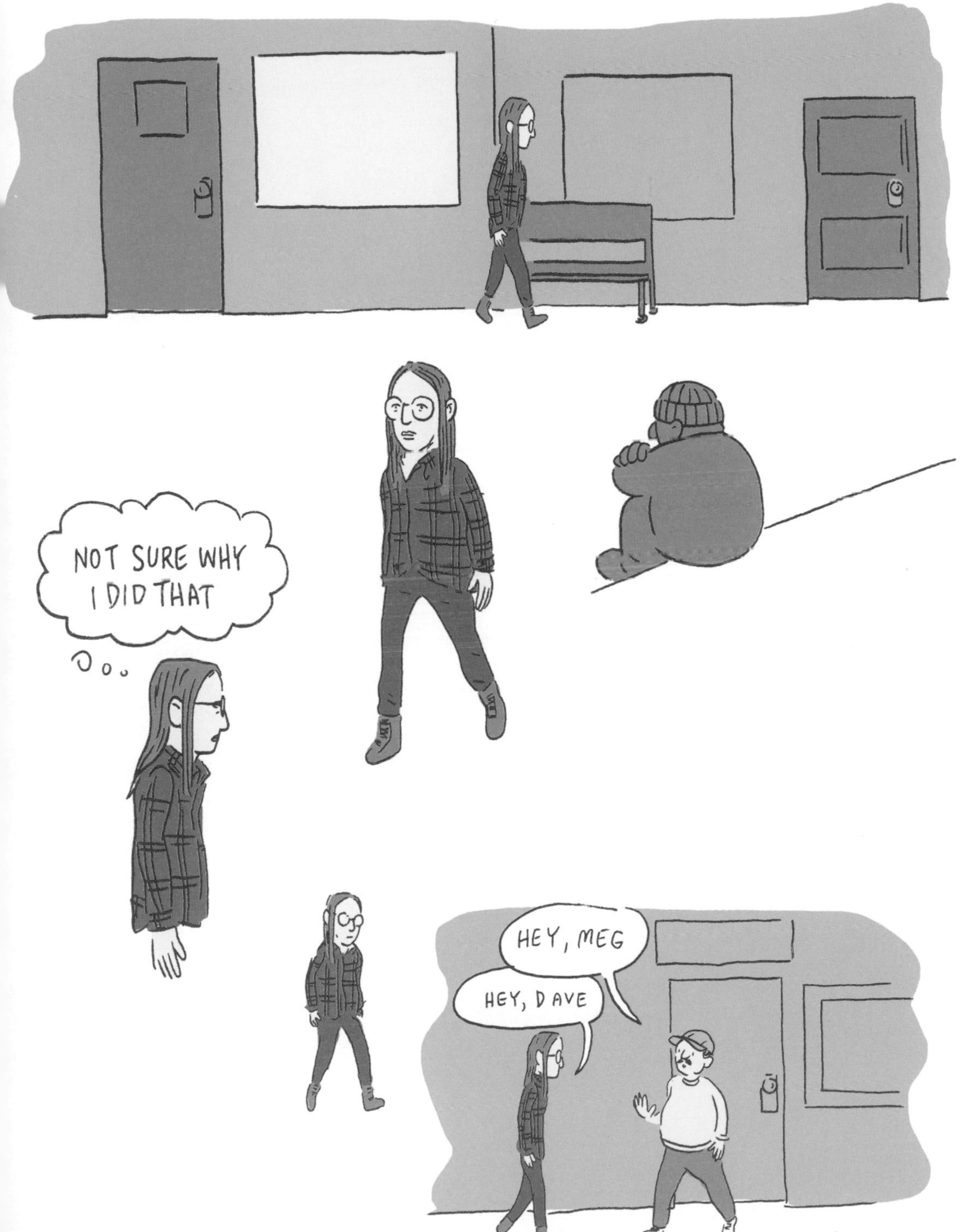
NOT SURE WHY I DID THAT
HEY, MEG
HEY, DAVE

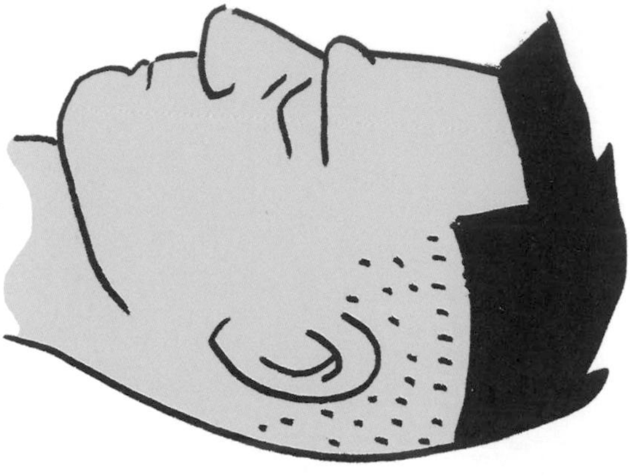

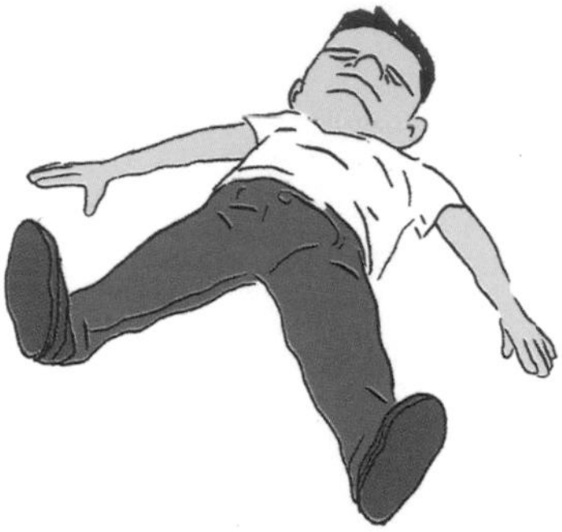

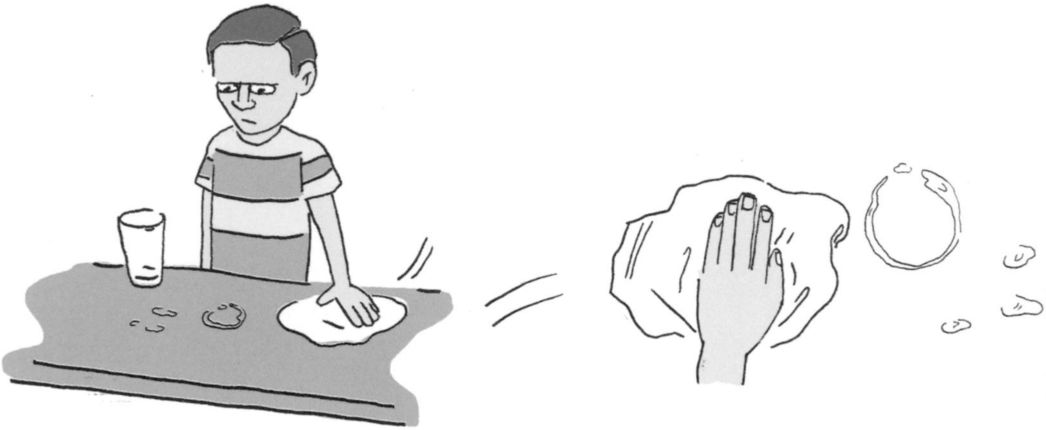

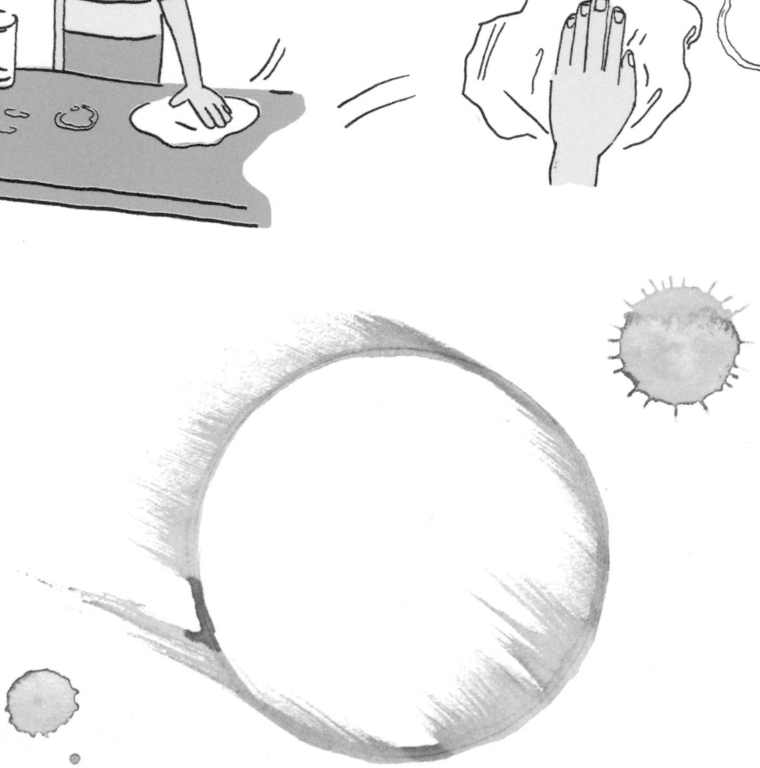

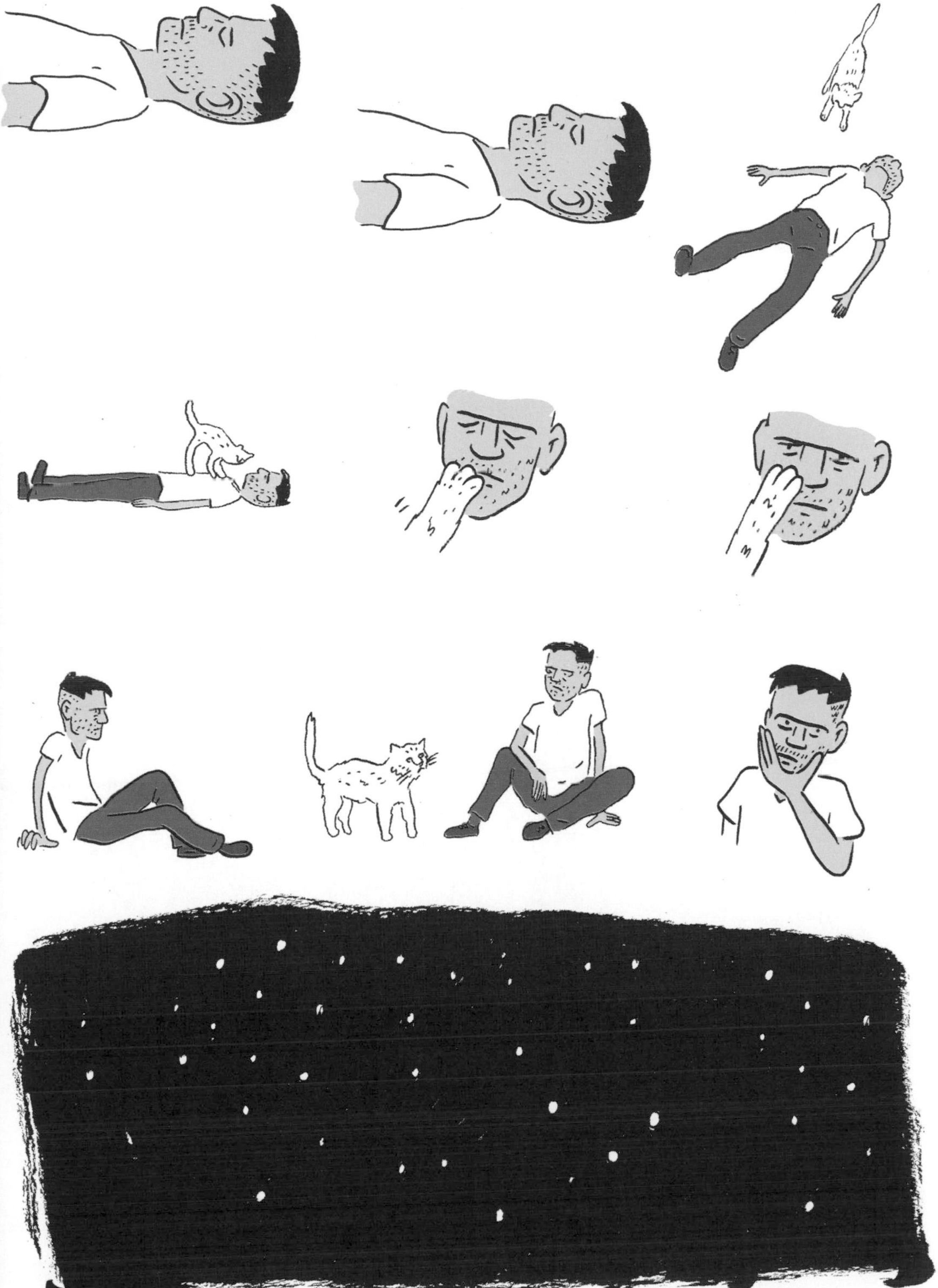

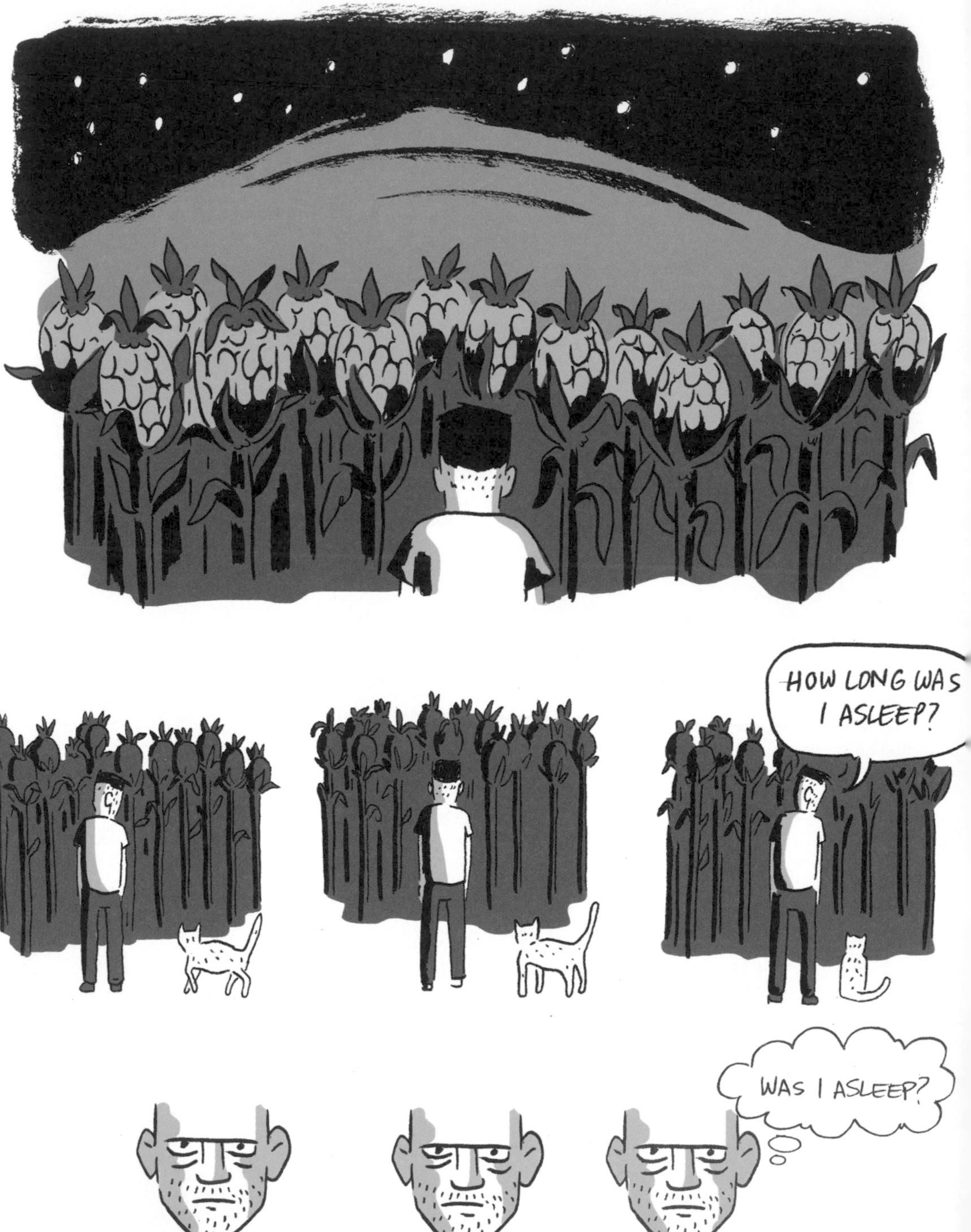
HOW LONG WAS I ASLEEP?
WAS I ASLEEP?

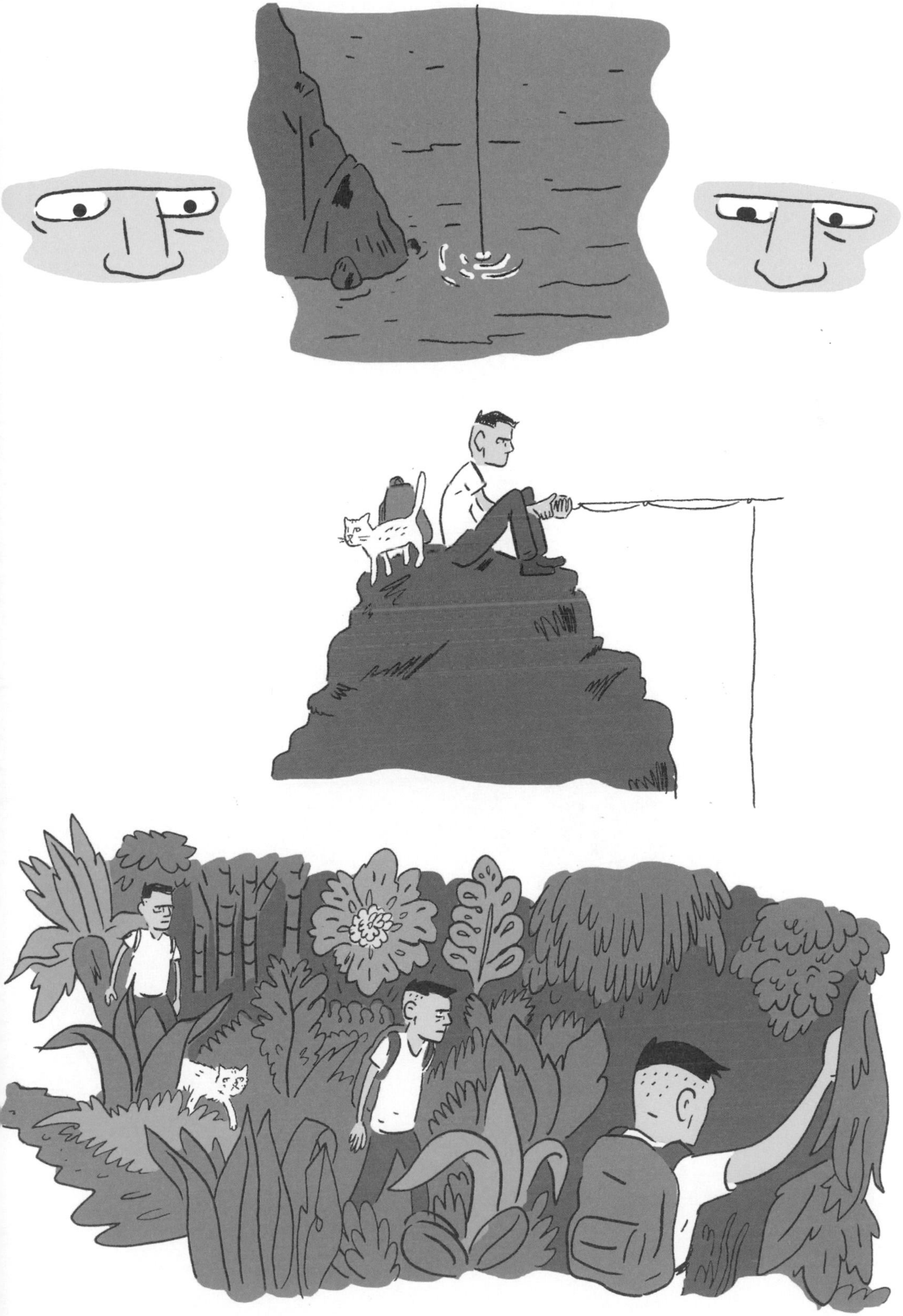

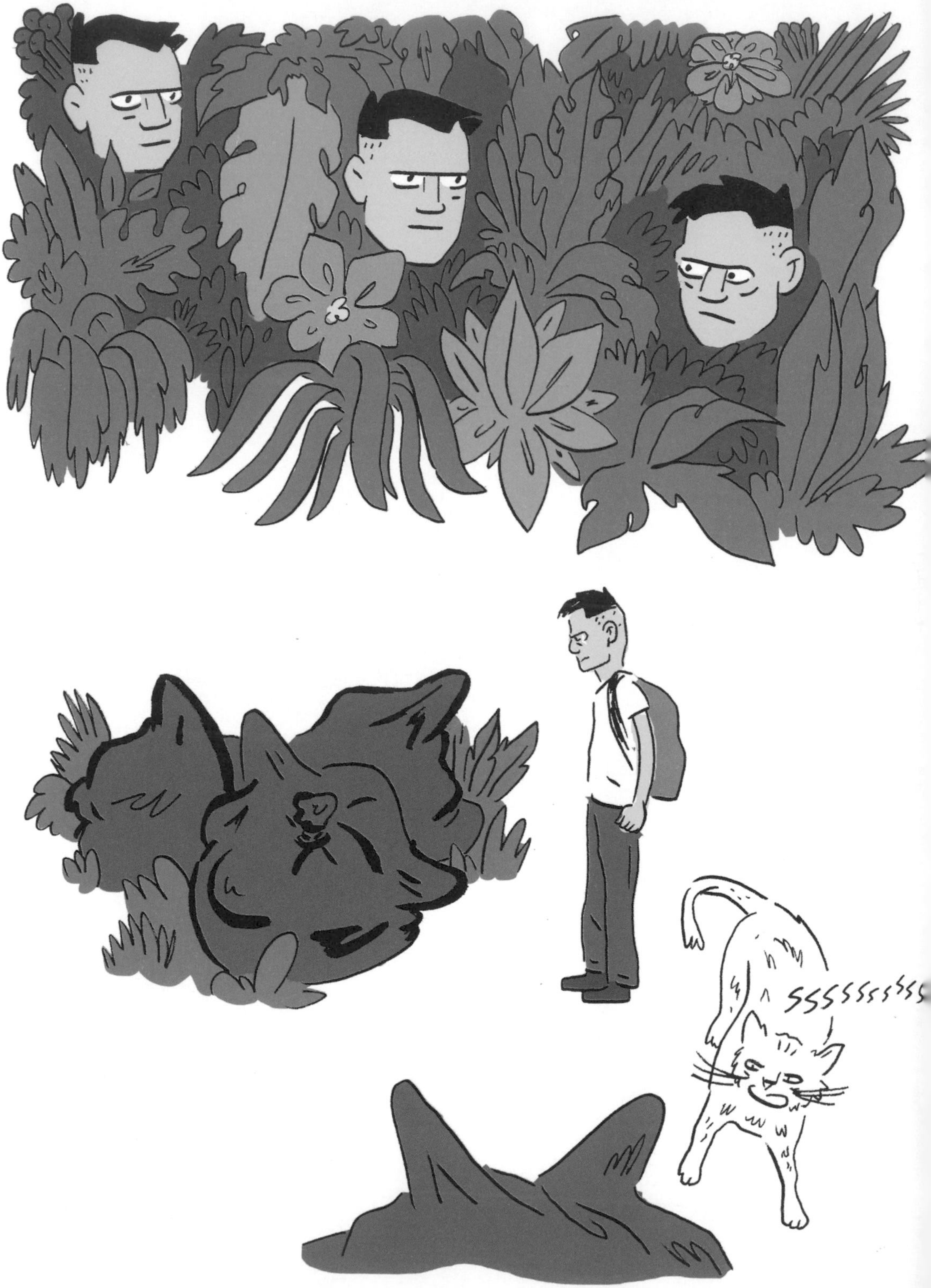
SSSSSSSSSS

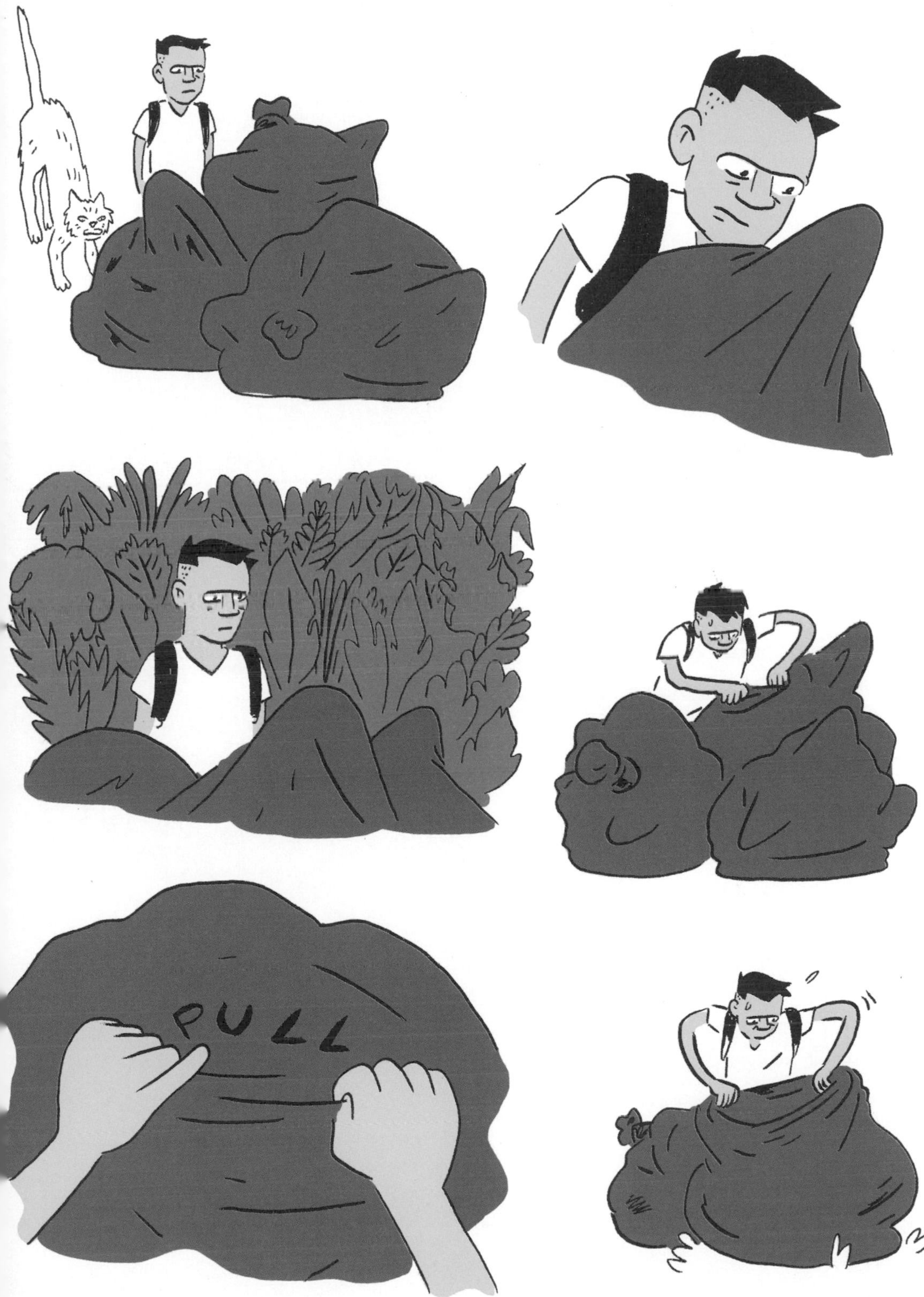
PULL

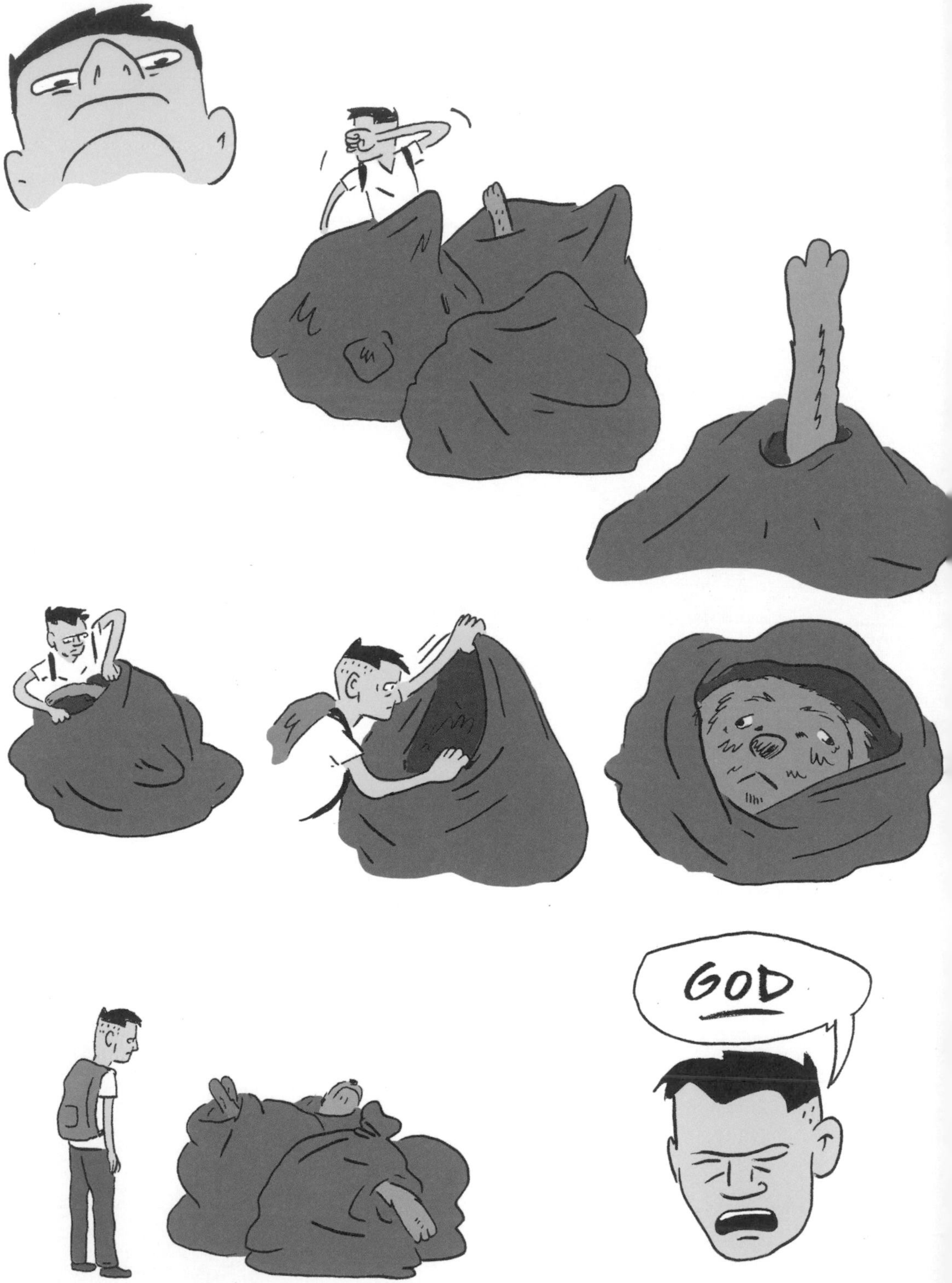
GOD

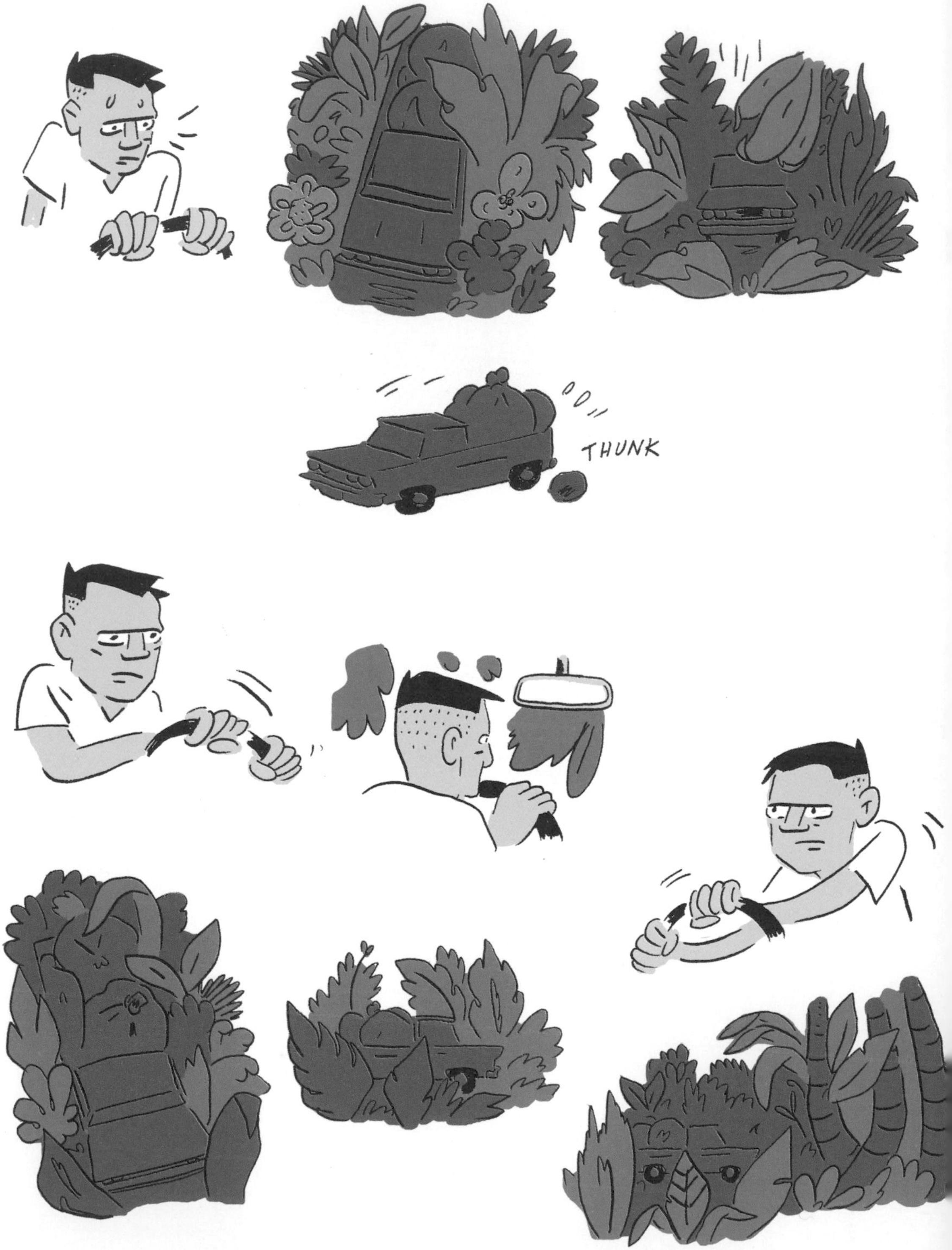
THUNK

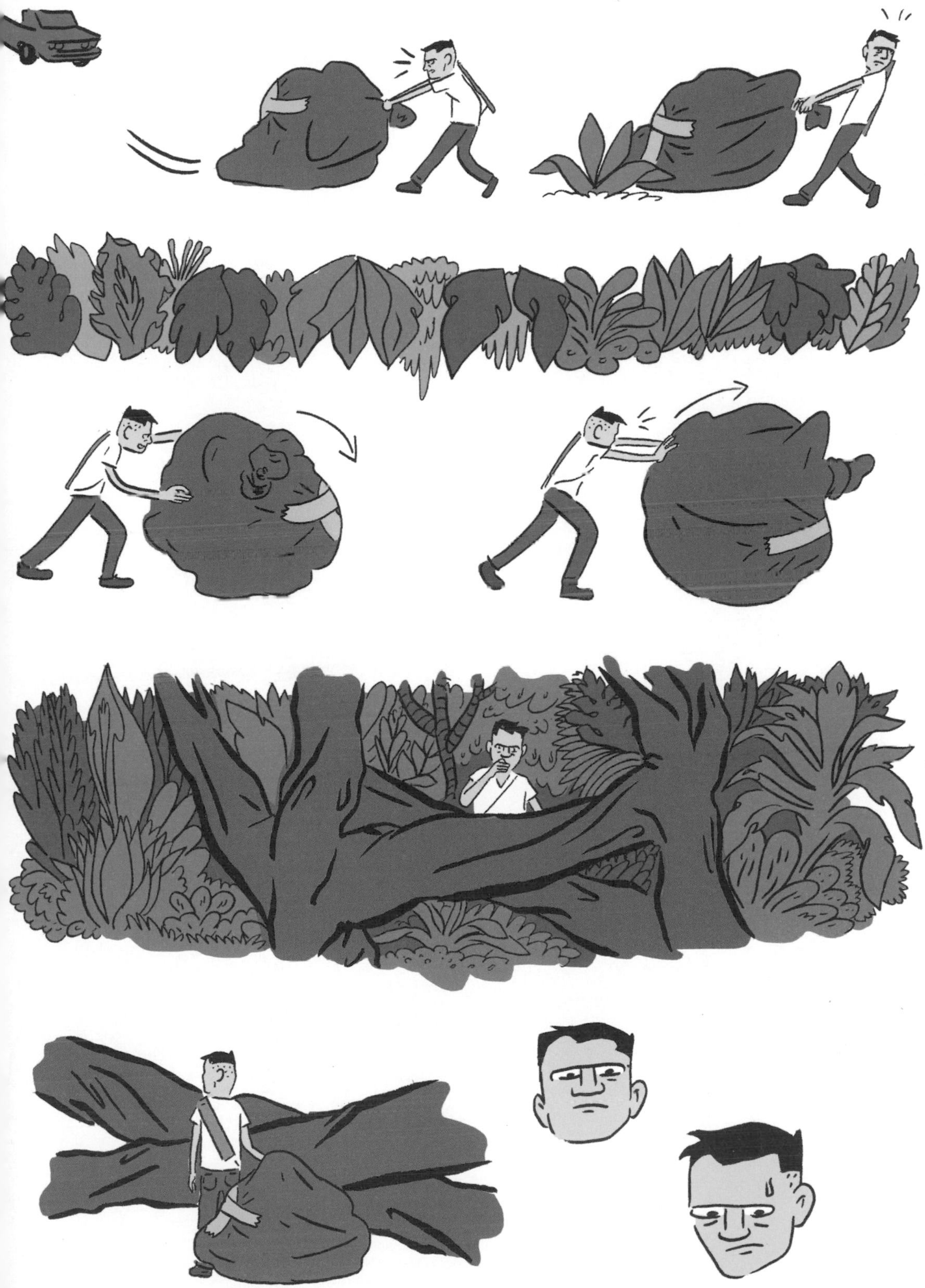

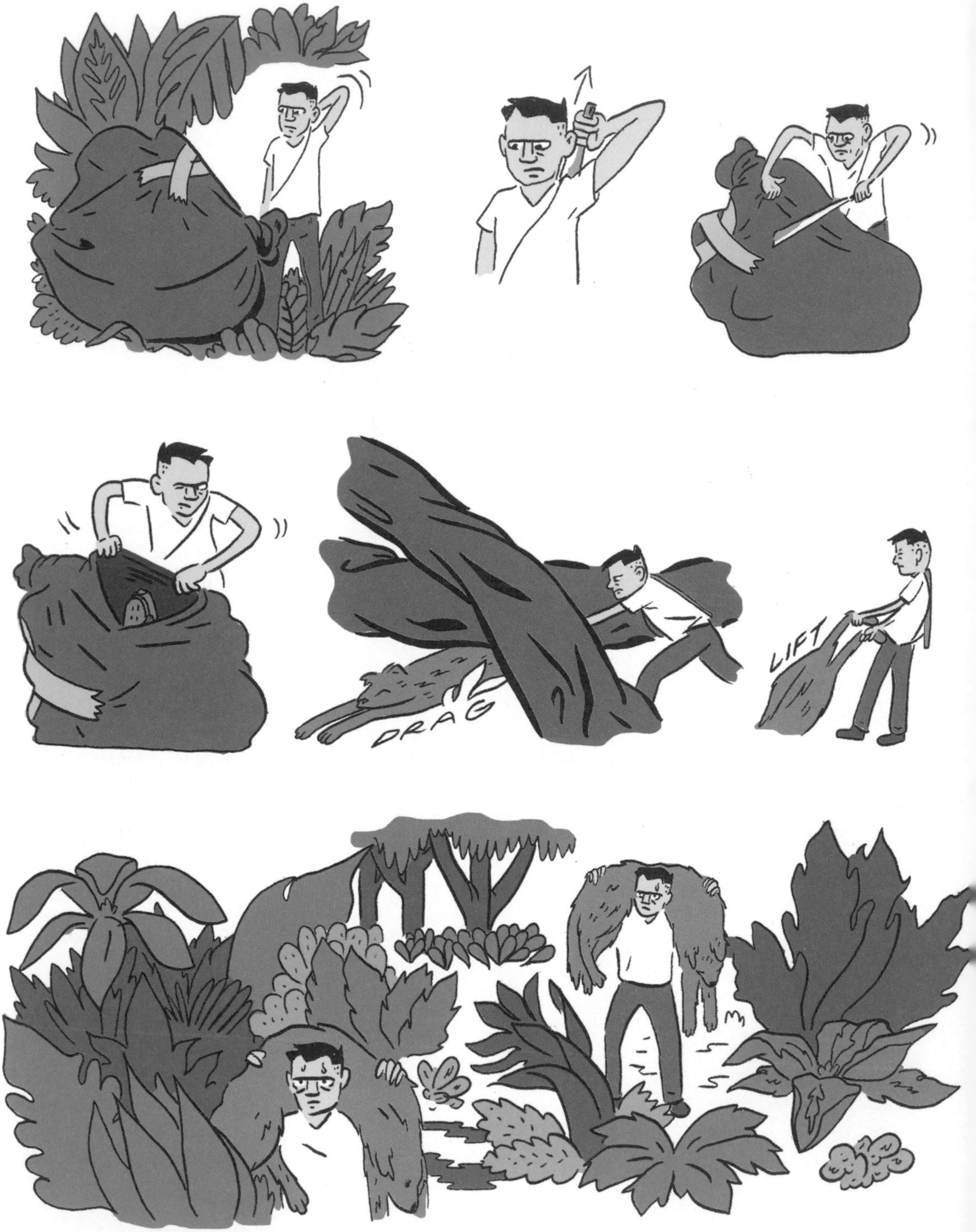
DRAG
LIFT

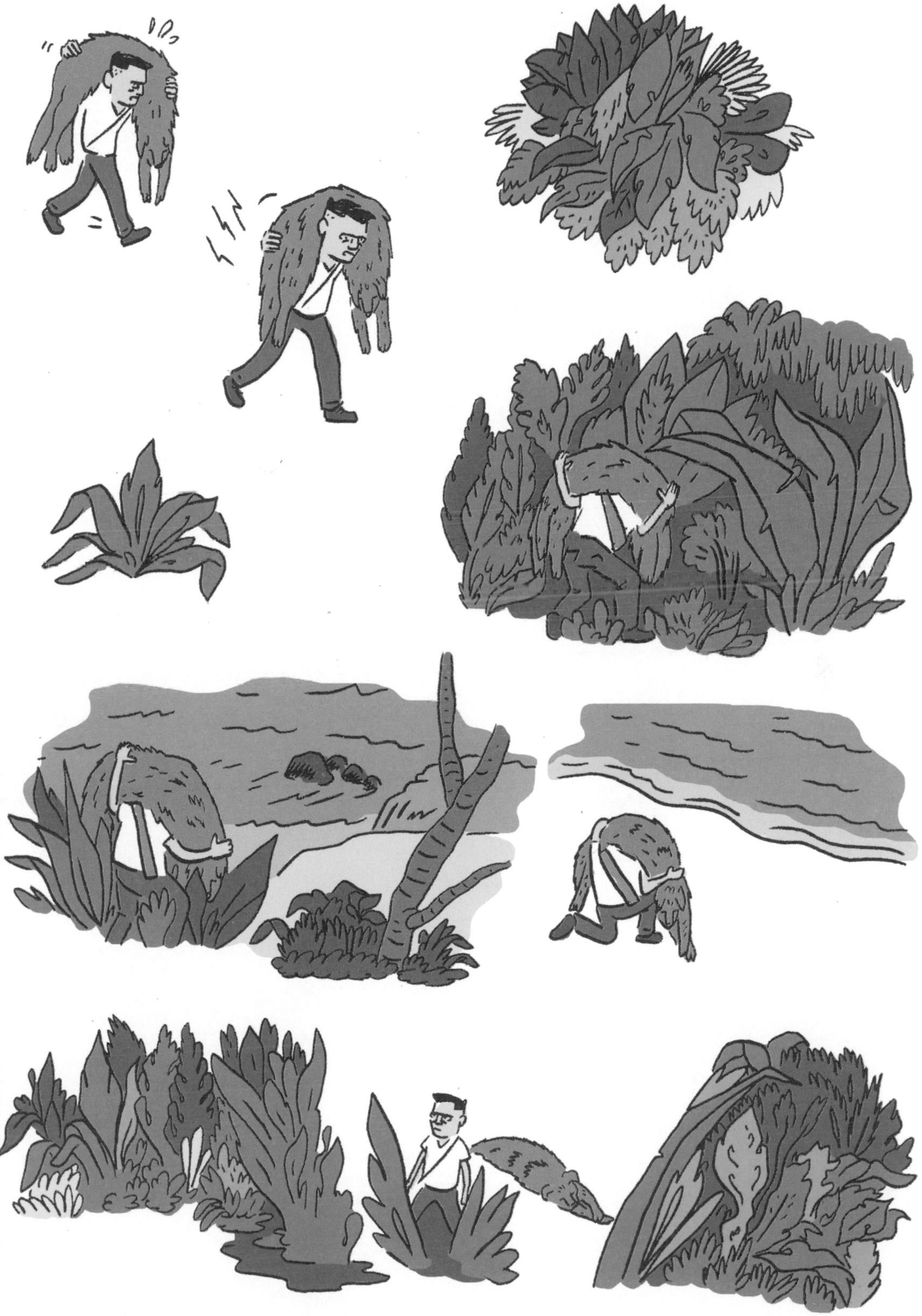

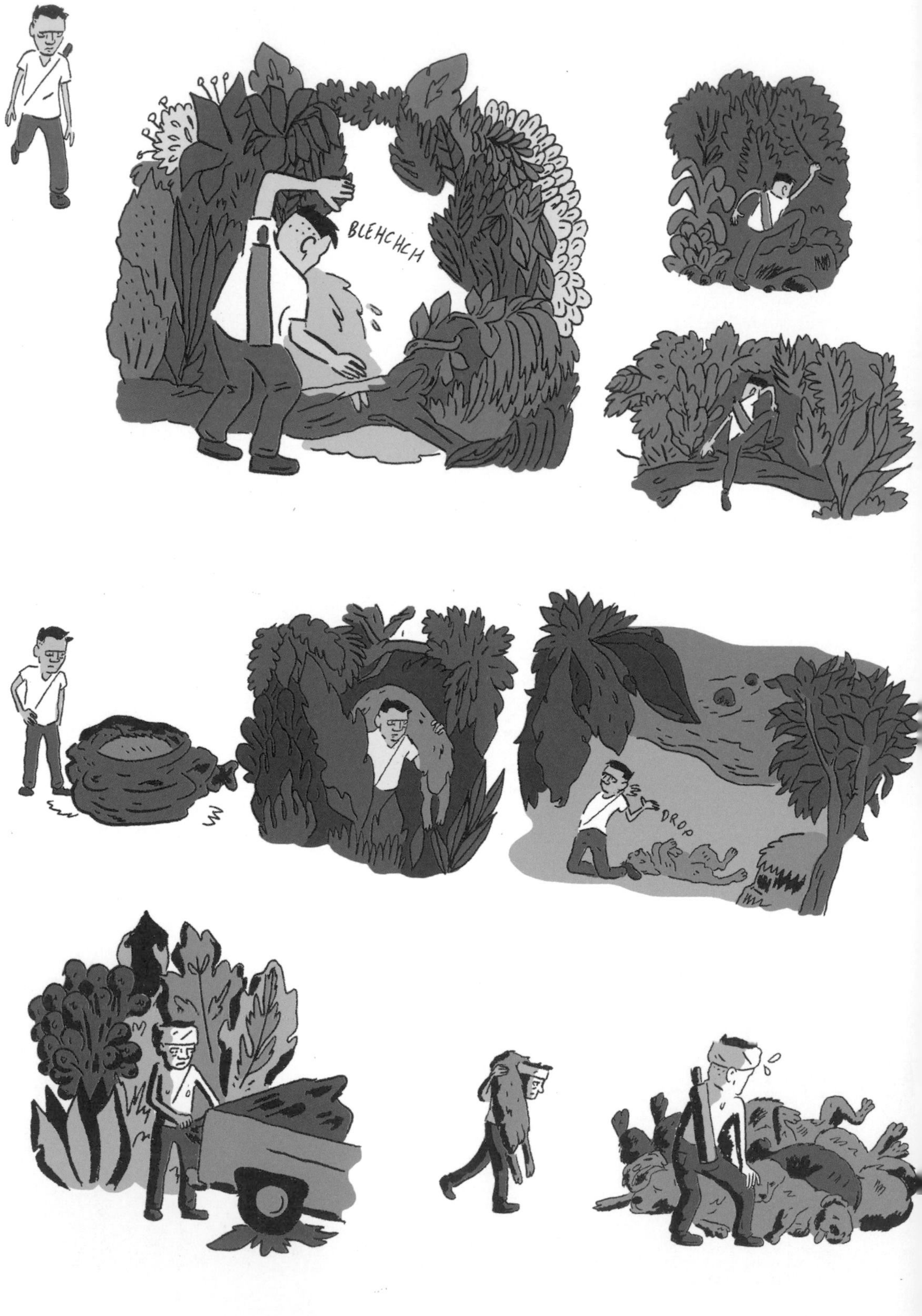
BLEHCHCH
DROP

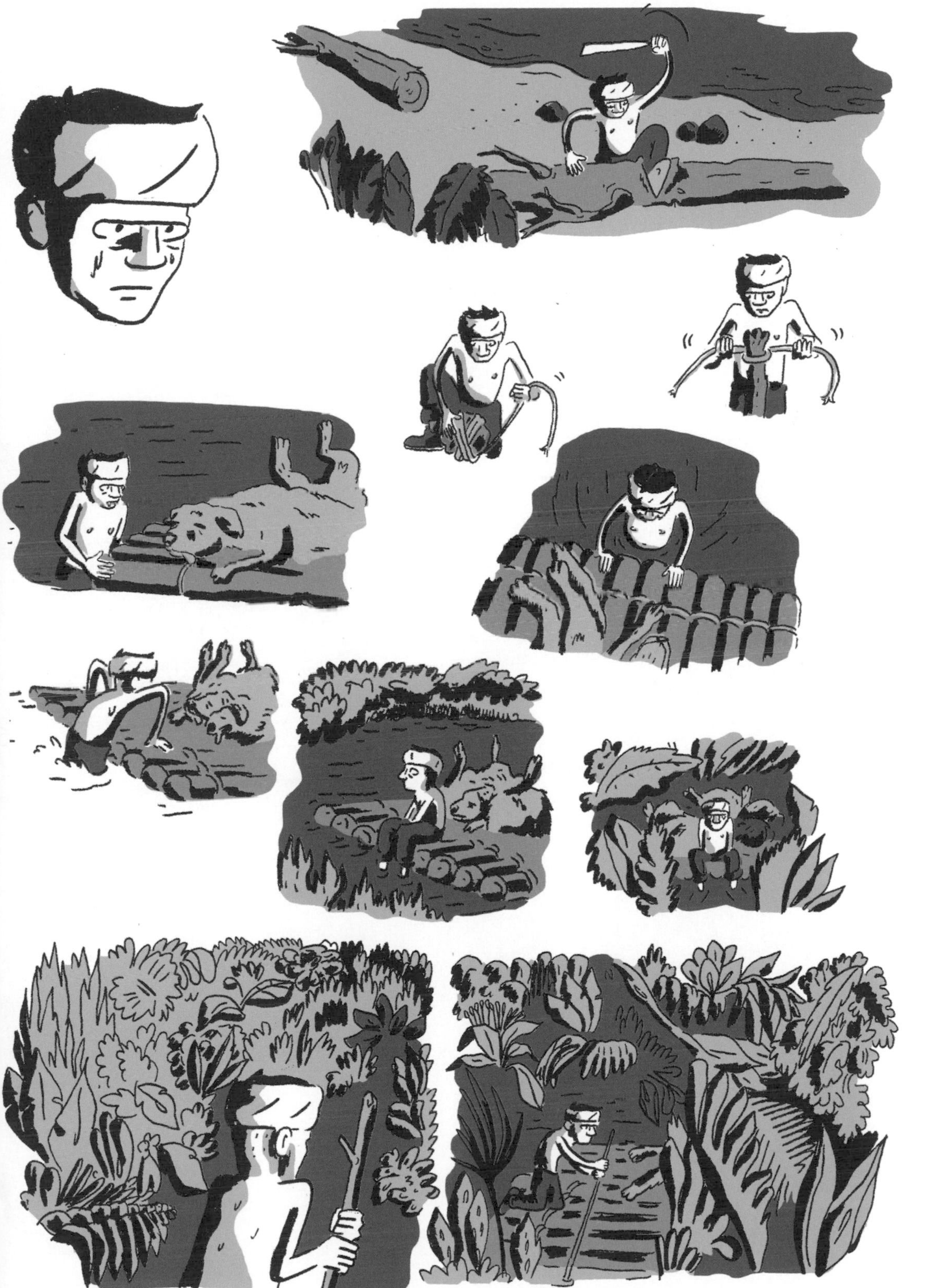

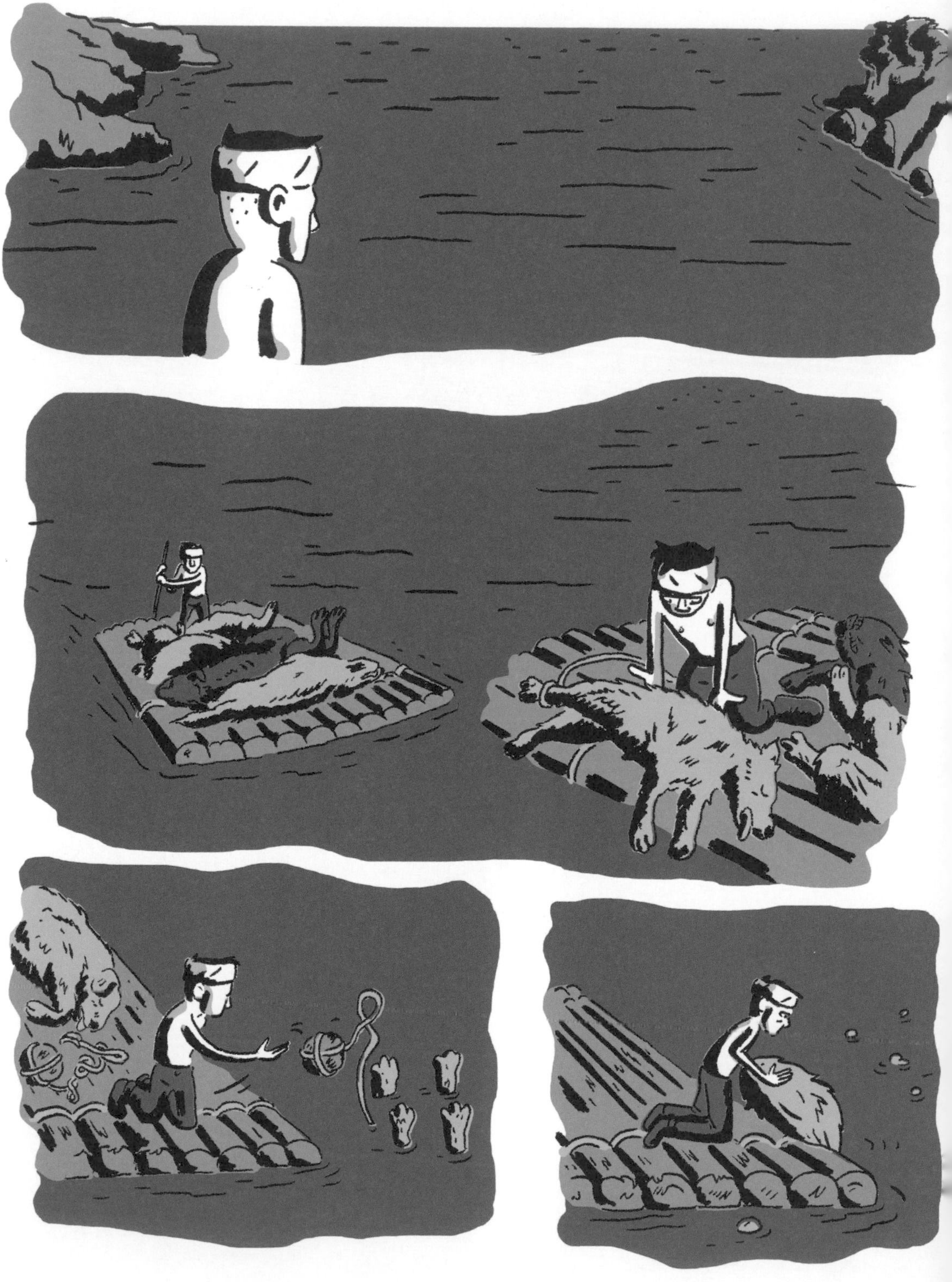

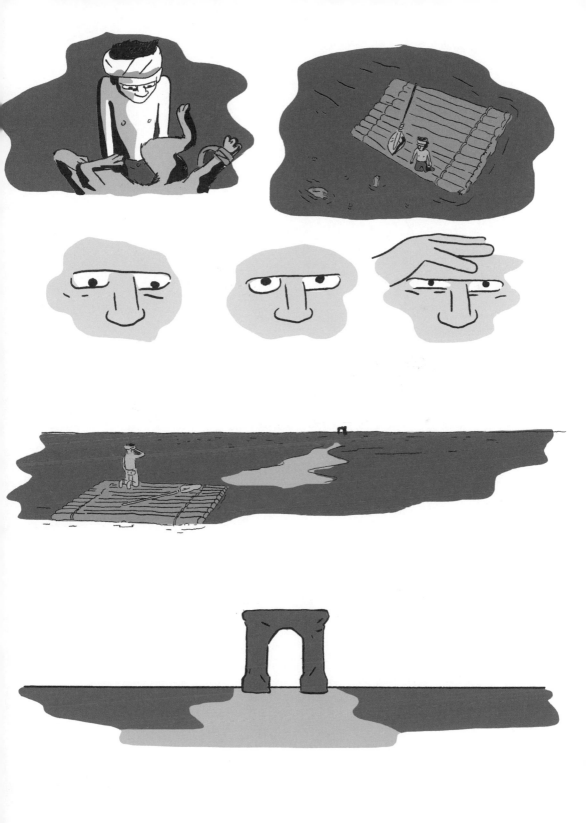

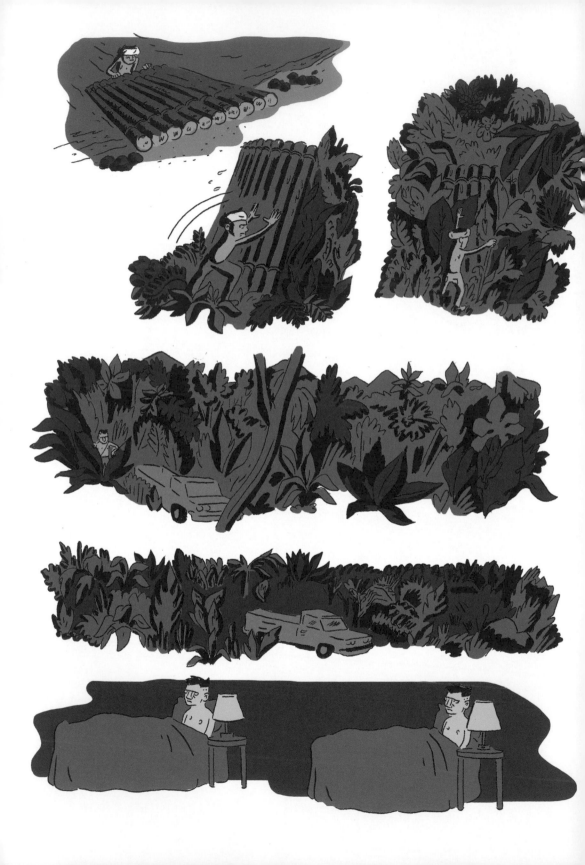

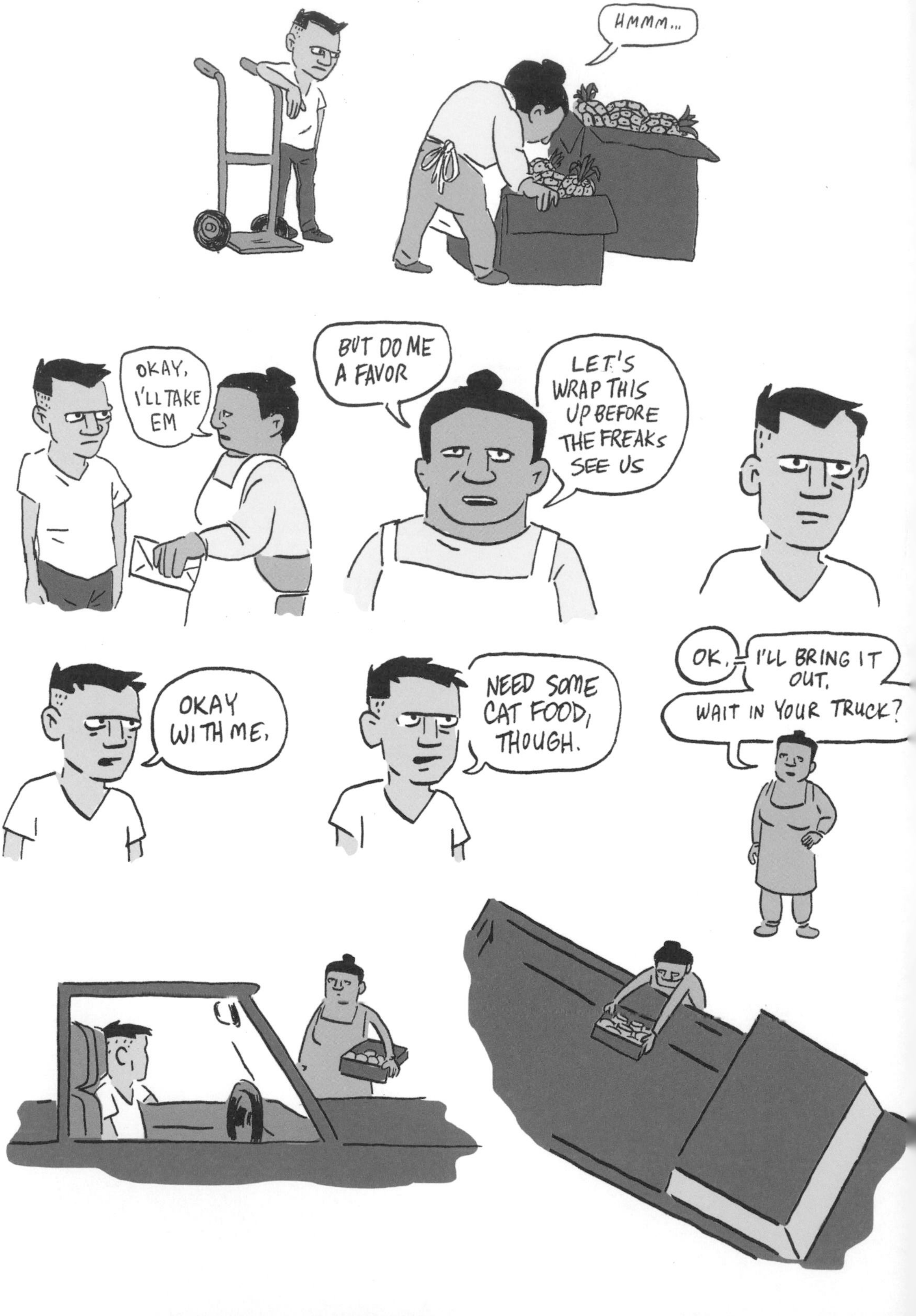
HMMM...
OKAY, I'LL TAKE EM
BUT DO ME A FAVOR
LET'S WRAP THIS UP BEFORE THE FREAKS SEE US
OKAY WITH ME,
NEED SOME CAT FOOD, THOUGH.
OK,
I'LL BRING IT OUT.
WAIT IN YOUR TRUCK?

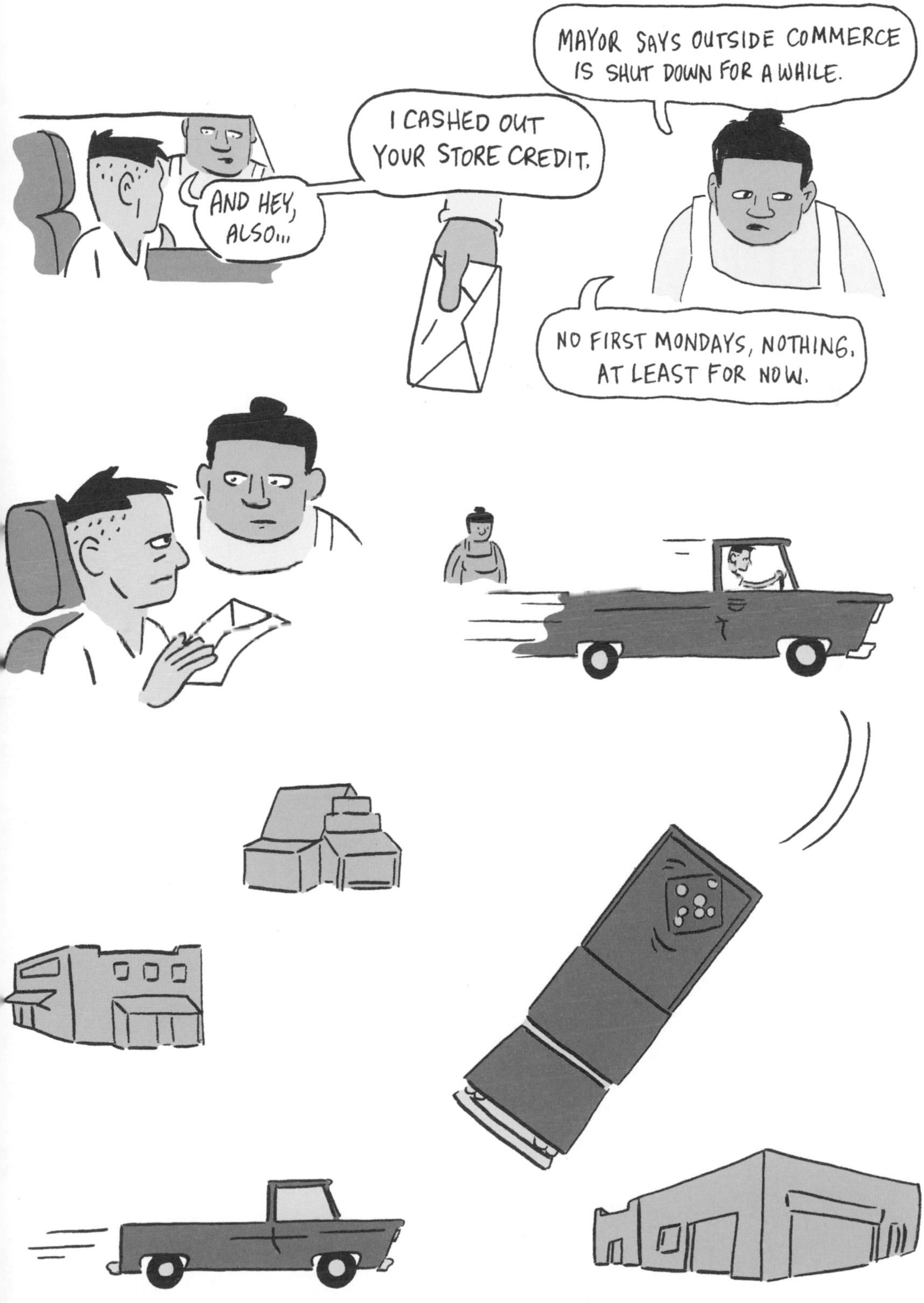
I CASHED OUT YOUR STORE CREDIT.
AND HEY, ALSO...
MAYOR SAYS OUTSIDE COMMERCE IS SHUT DOWN FOR A WHILE.
NO FIRST MONDAYS, NOTHING. AT LEAST FOR NOW.

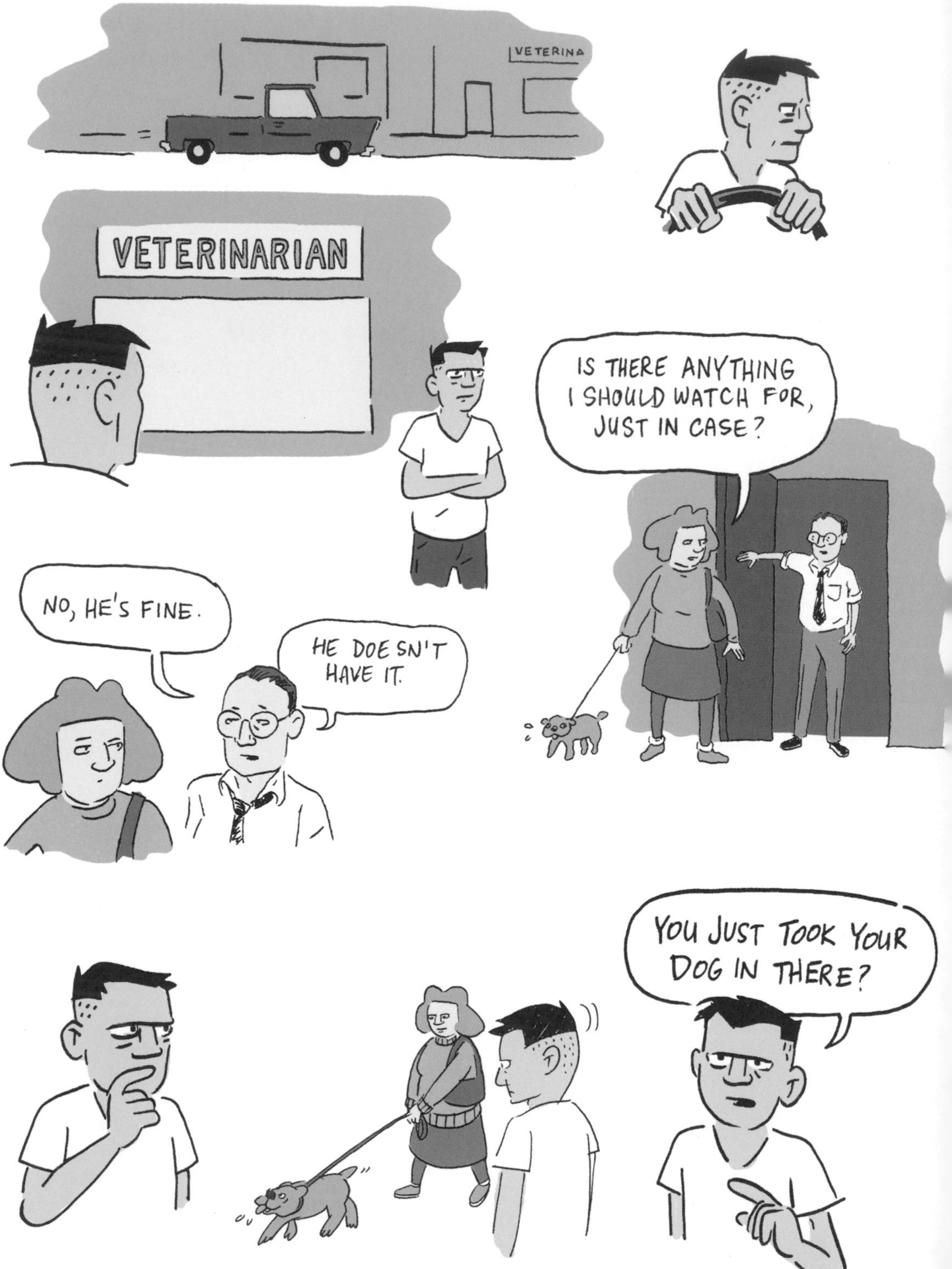
VETERINA
VETERINARIAN
IS THERE ANYTHING I SHOULD WATCH FOR, JUST IN CASE?
NO, HE'S FINE.
HE DOESN'T HAVE IT.
YOU JUST TOOK YOUR DOG IN THERE?

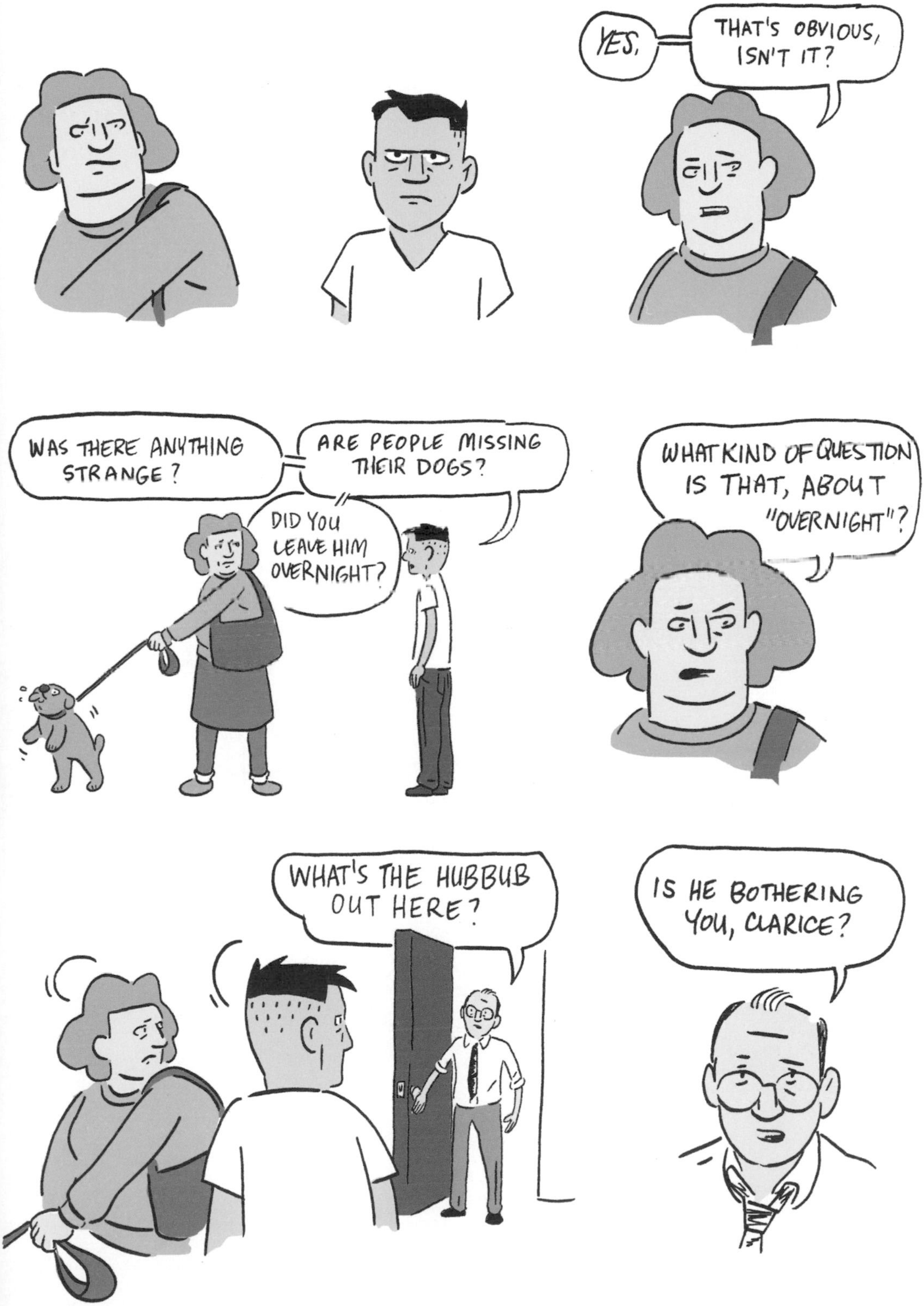
YES,
THAT'S OBVIOUS, ISN'T IT?
WAS THERE ANYTHING STRANGE?
ARE PEOPLE MISSING THEIR DOGS?
DID YOU LEAVE HIM OVERNIGHT?
WHAT KIND OF QUESTION IS THAT, ABOUT "OVERNIGHT"?
WHAT'S THE HUBBUB OUT HERE?
IS HE BOTHERING YOU, CLARICE?

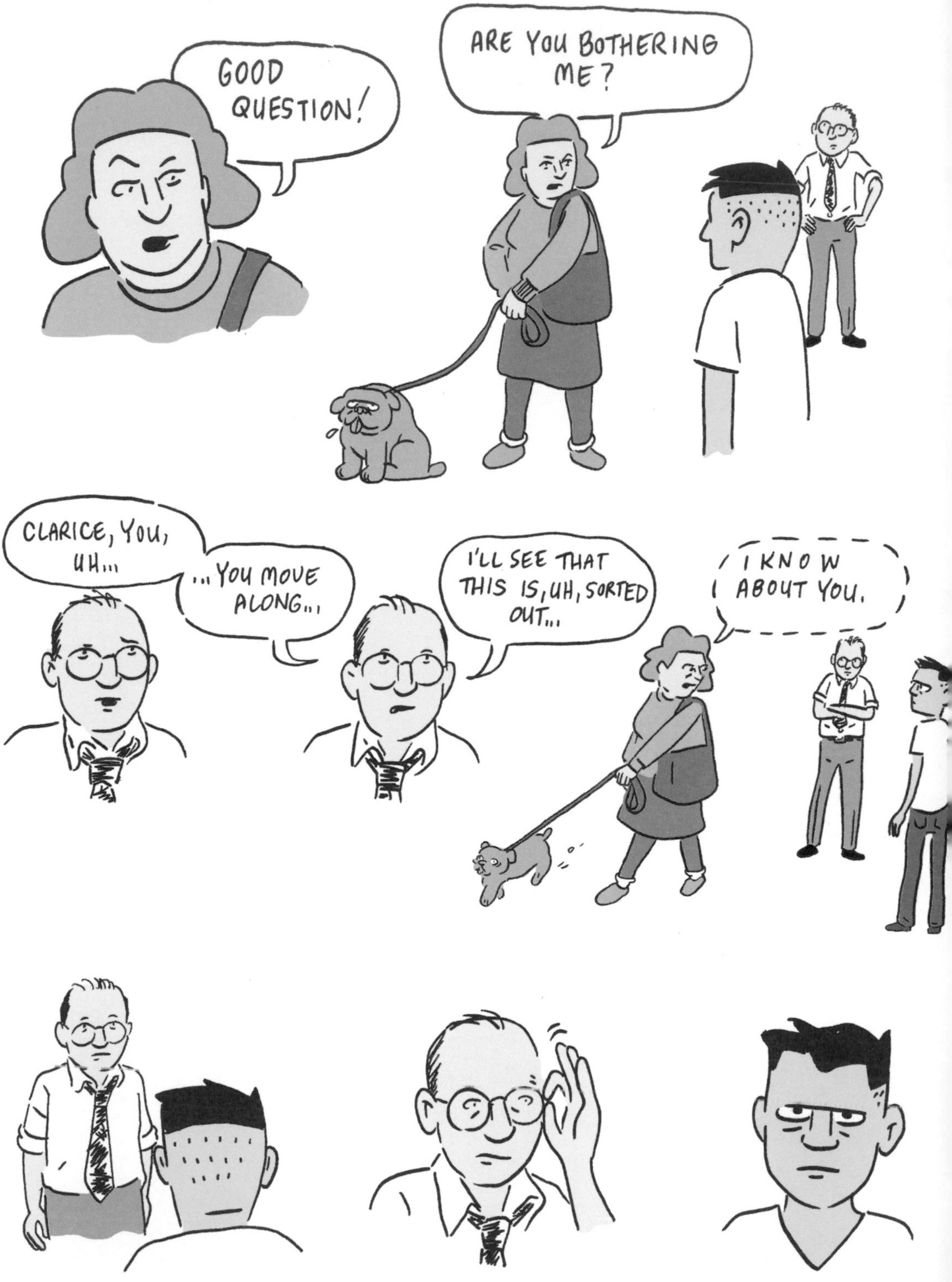
GOOD QUESTION!
ARE YOU BOTHERING ME?
CLARICE, YOU, UH...
...YOU MOVE ALONG...
I'LL SEE THAT THIS IS, UH, SORTED OUT...
I KNOW ABOUT YOU.

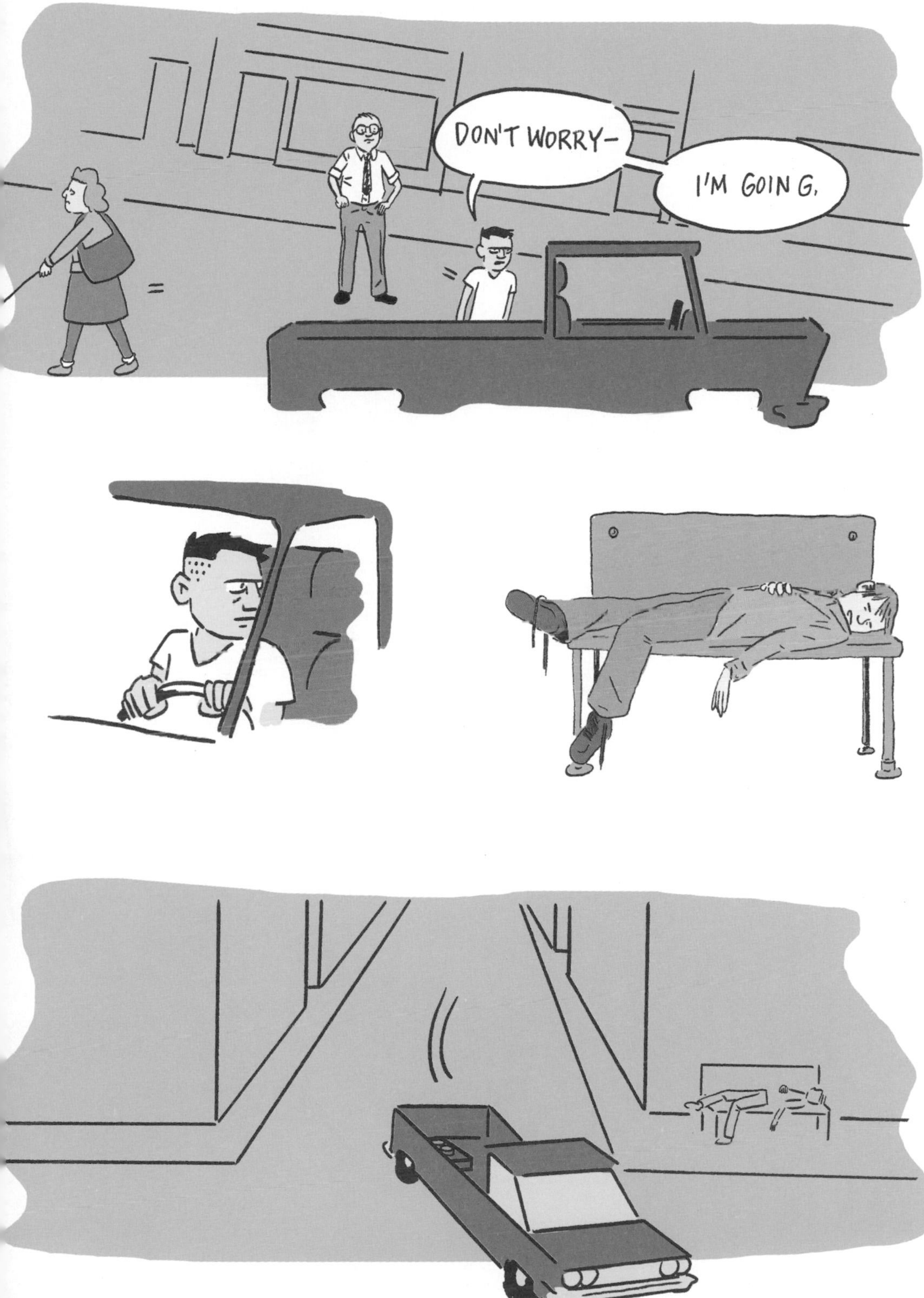
DON'T WORRY-
I'M GOING.

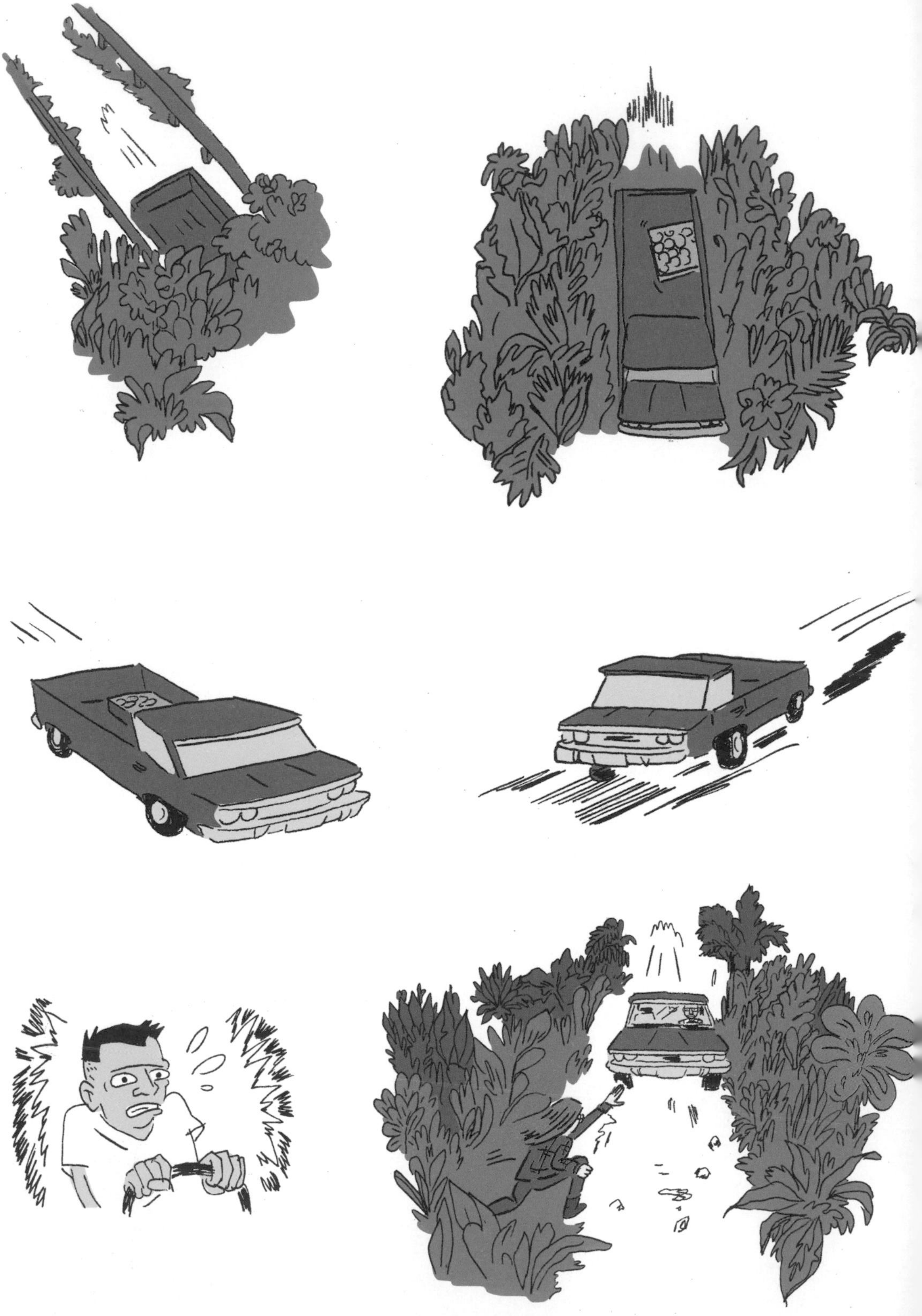

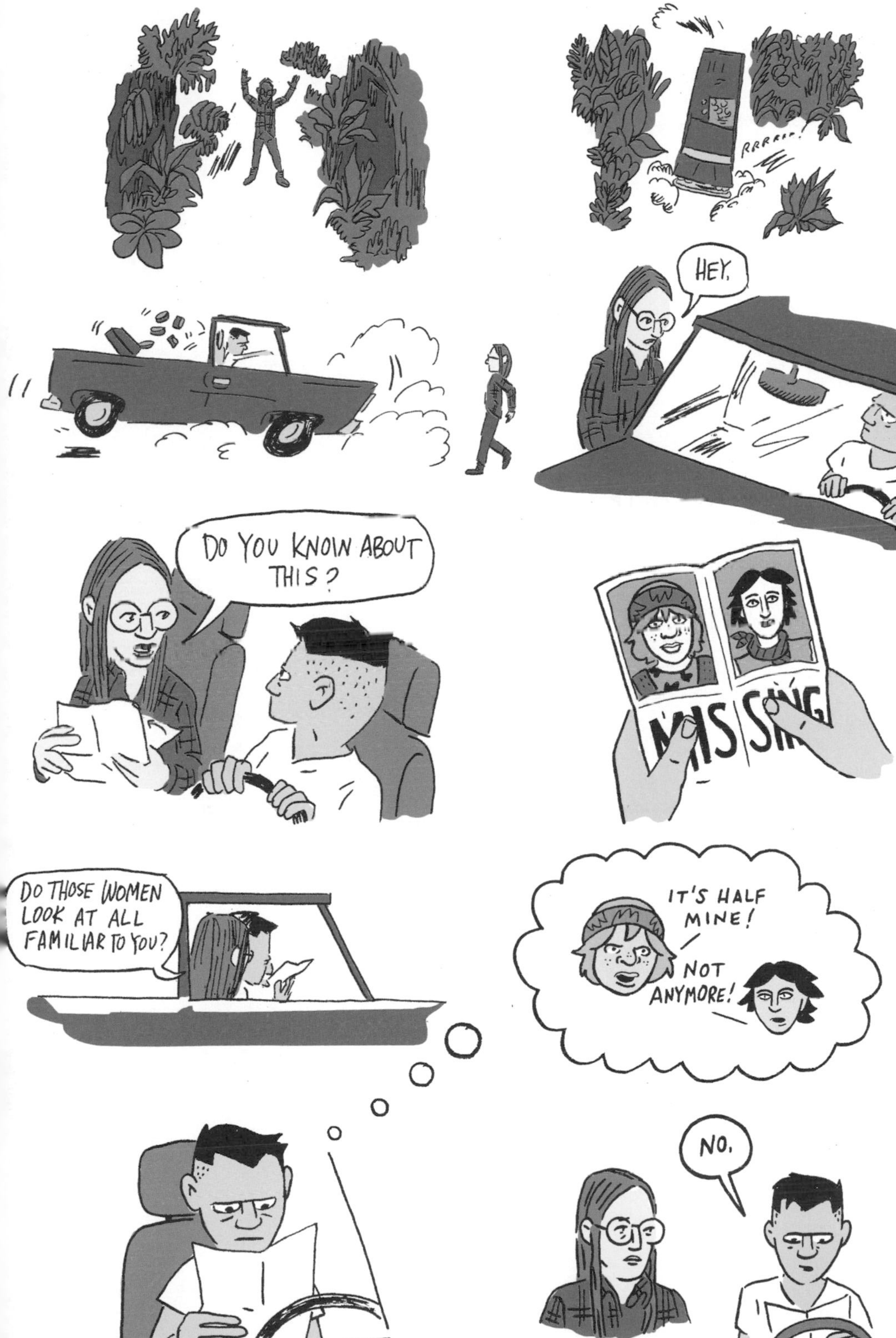
RRRRRR!
HEY.
DO YOU KNOW ABOUT THIS?
MISSING
DO THOSE WOMEN LOOK AT ALL FAMILIAR TO YOU?
IT'S HALF MINE!
NOT ANYMORE!
NO.

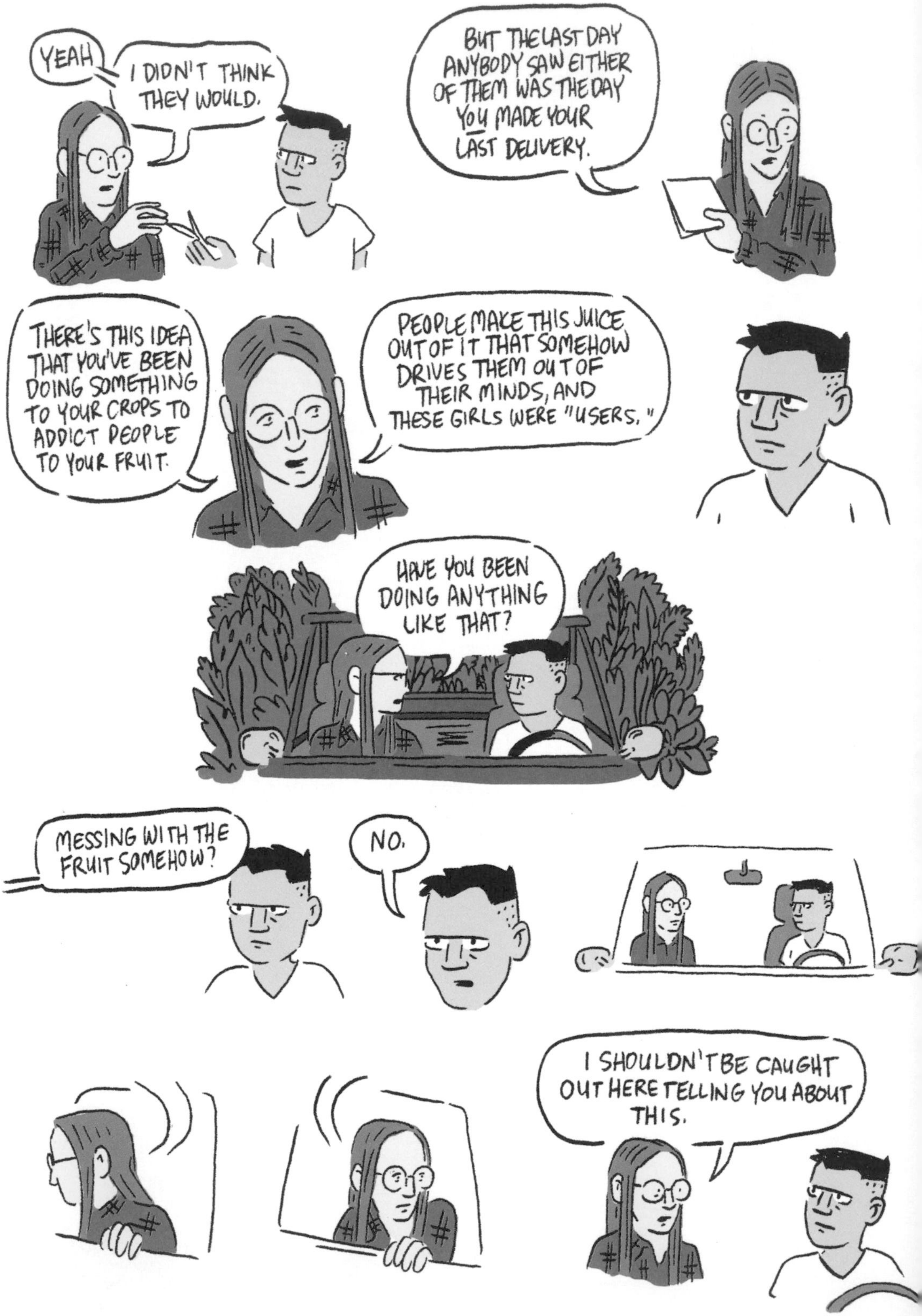
YEAH
I DIDN'T THINK THEY WOULD.
BUT THE LAST DAY ANYBODY SAW EITHER OF THEM WAS THE DAY YOU MADE YOUR LAST DELIVERY.
THERE'S THIS IDEA THAT YOU'VE BEEN DOING SOMETHING TO YOUR CROPS TO ADDICT PEOPLE TO YOUR FRUIT.
PEOPLE MAKE THIS JUICE OUT OF IT THAT SOMEHOW DRIVES THEM OUT OF THEIR MINDS, AND THESE GIRLS WERE "USERS."
HAVE YOU BEEN DOING ANYTHING LIKE THAT?
MESSING WITH THE FRUIT SOMEHOW?
NO.
I SHOULDN'T BE CAUGHT OUT HERE TELLING YOU ABOUT THIS.

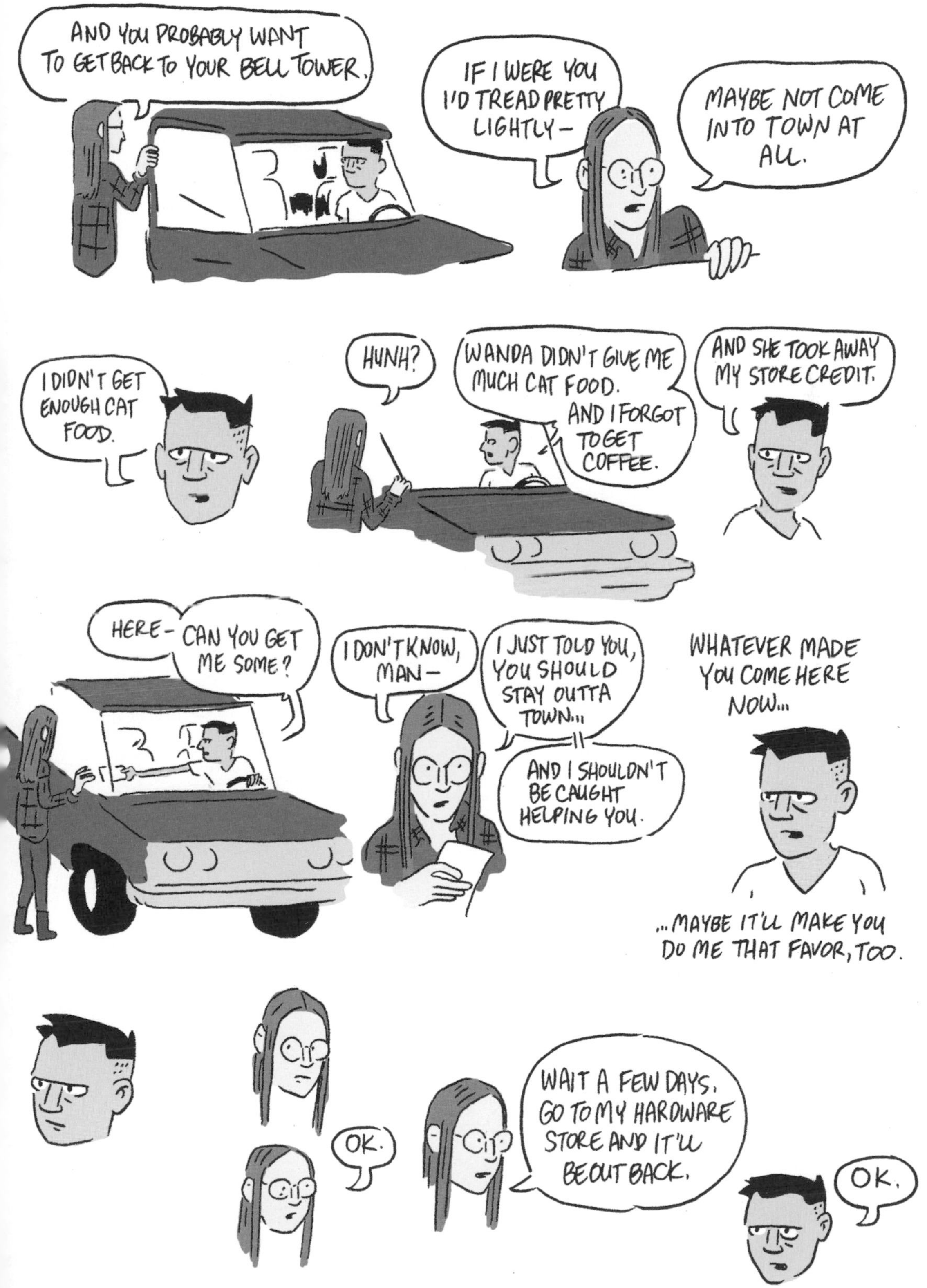

AND YOU PROBABLY WANT TO GET BACK TO YOUR BELL TOWER.
IF I WERE YOU I'D TREAD PRETTY LIGHTLY—
MAYBE NOT COME INTO TOWN AT ALL.
I DIDN'T GET ENOUGH CAT FOOD.
HUNH?
WANDA DIDN'T GIVE ME MUCH CAT FOOD.
AND I FORGOT TO GET COFFEE.
AND SHE TOOK AWAY MY STORE CREDIT.
HERE—
CAN YOU GET ME SOME?
I DON'T KNOW, MAN—
I JUST TOLD YOU, YOU SHOULD STAY OUTTA TOWN...
AND I SHOULDN'T BE CAUGHT HELPING YOU.
WHATEVER MADE YOU COME HERE NOW...
...MAYBE IT'LL MAKE YOU DO ME THAT FAVOR, TOO.
OK.
WAIT A FEW DAYS. GO TO MY HARDWARE STORE AND IT'LL BE OUT BACK.
OK.

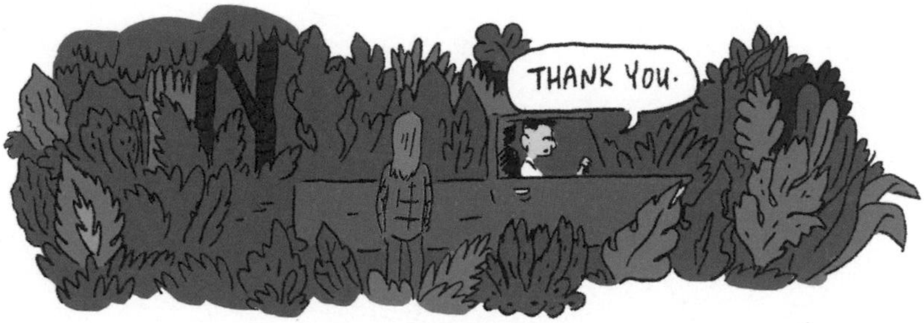
THANK YOU.

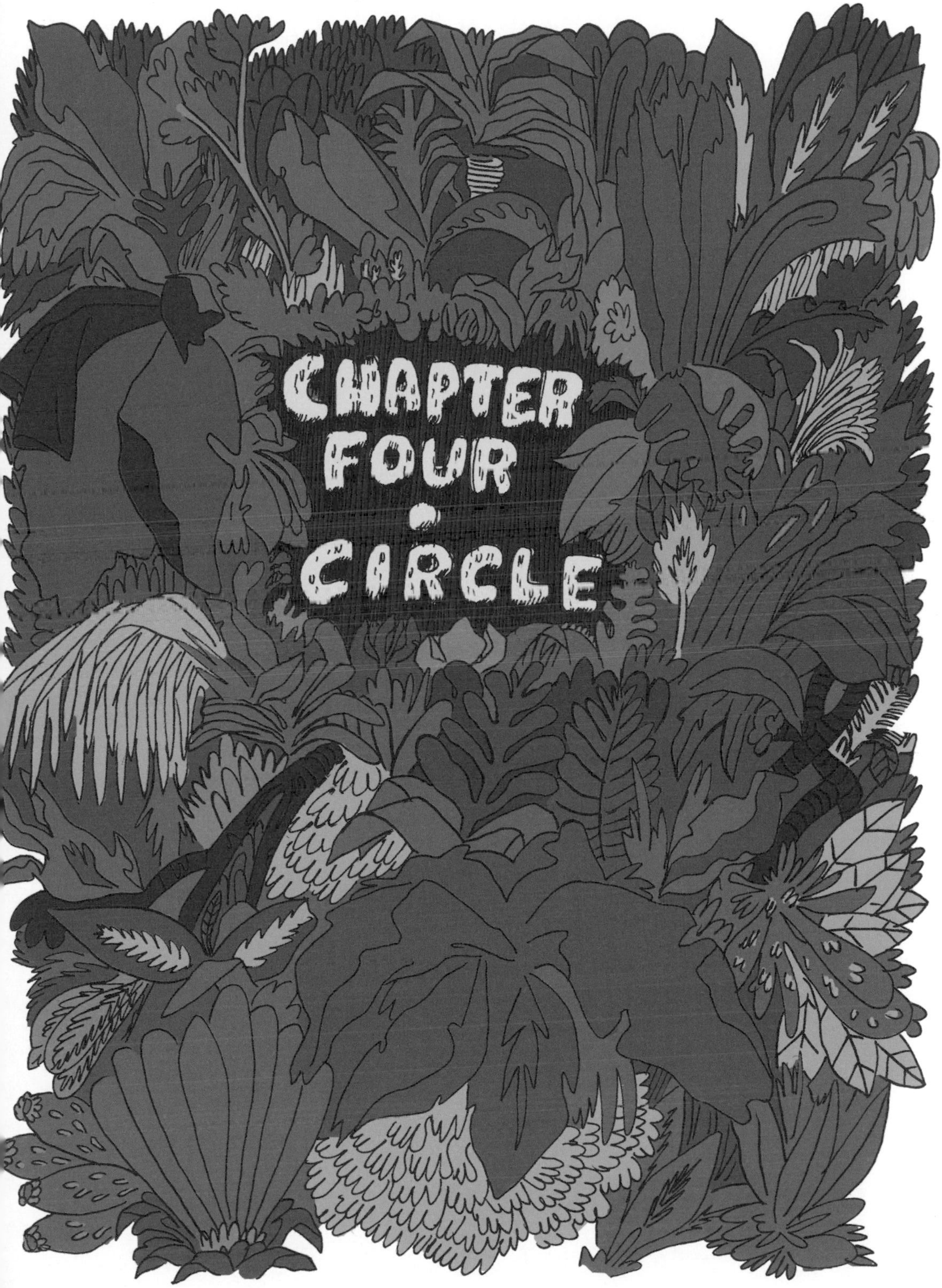
CHAPTER FOUR
CIRCLE

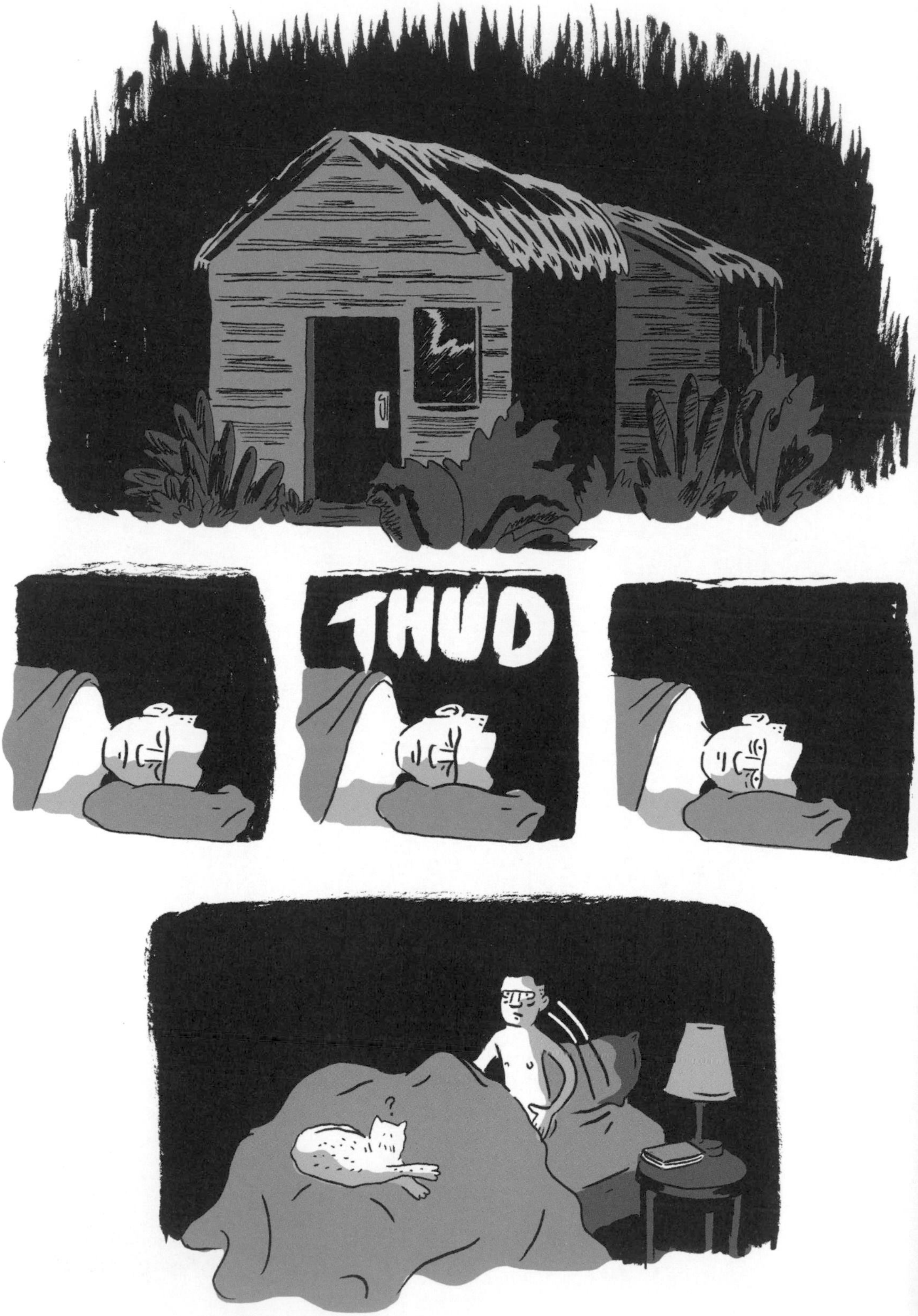
THUD
?

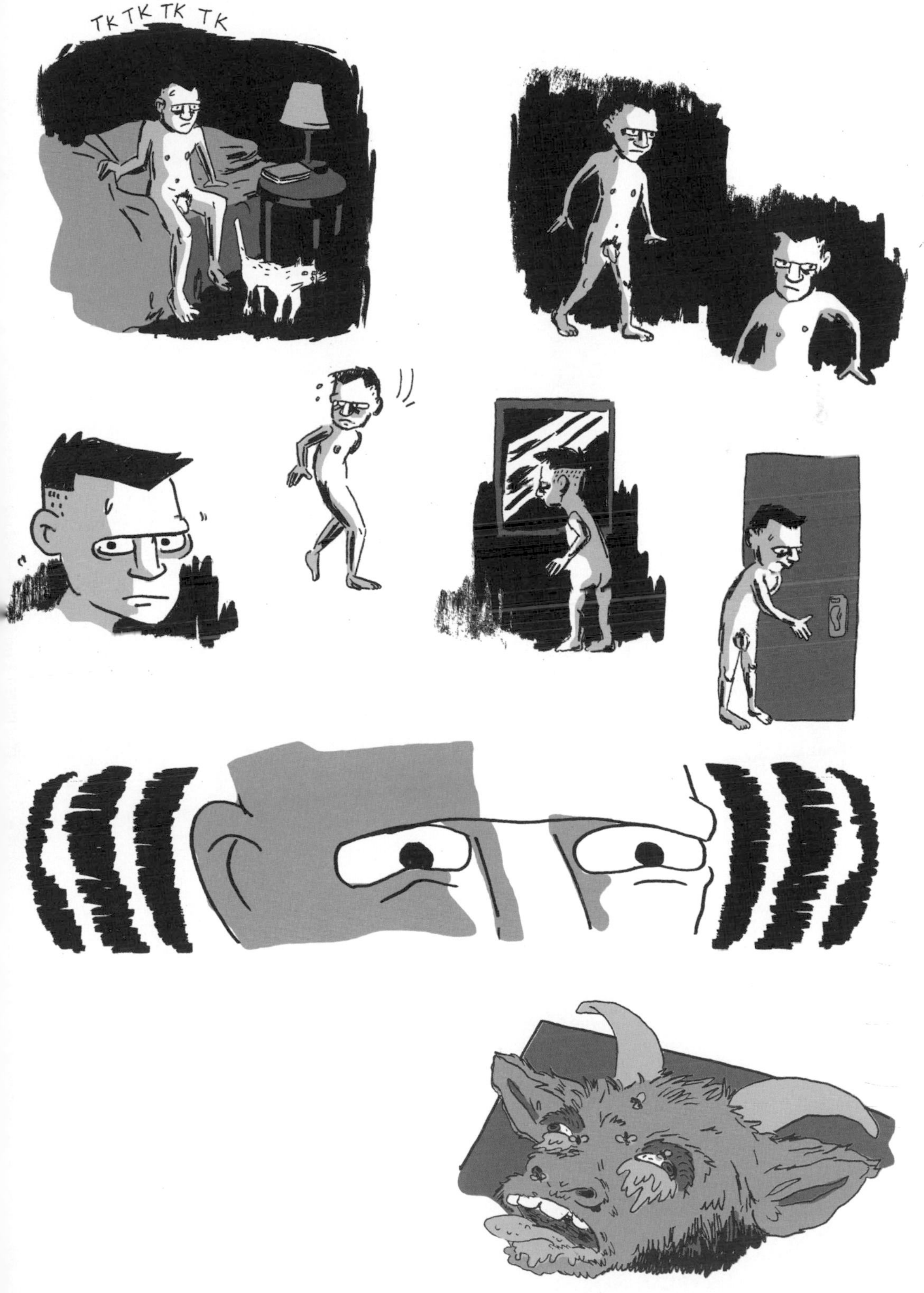
TK TK TK TK

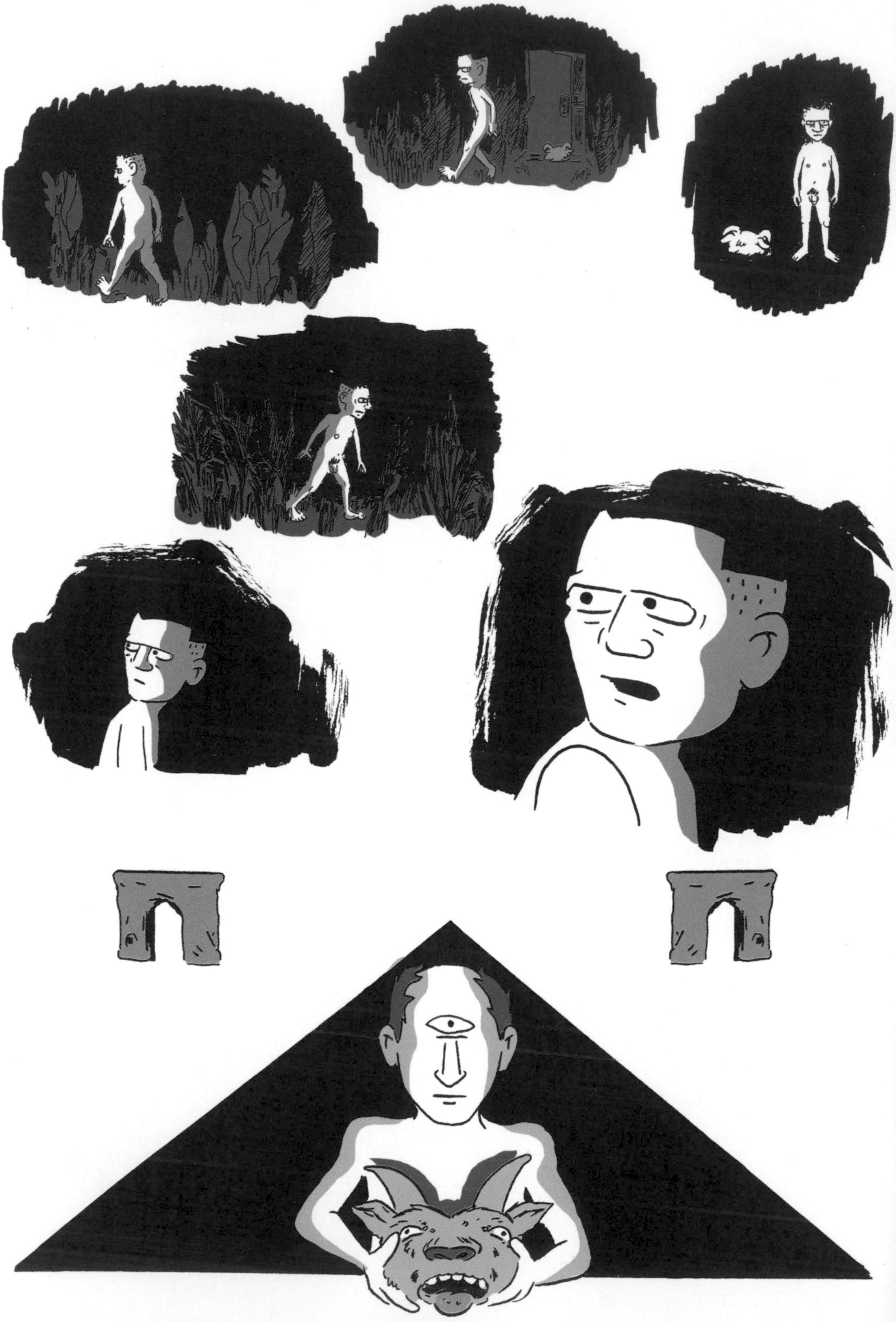

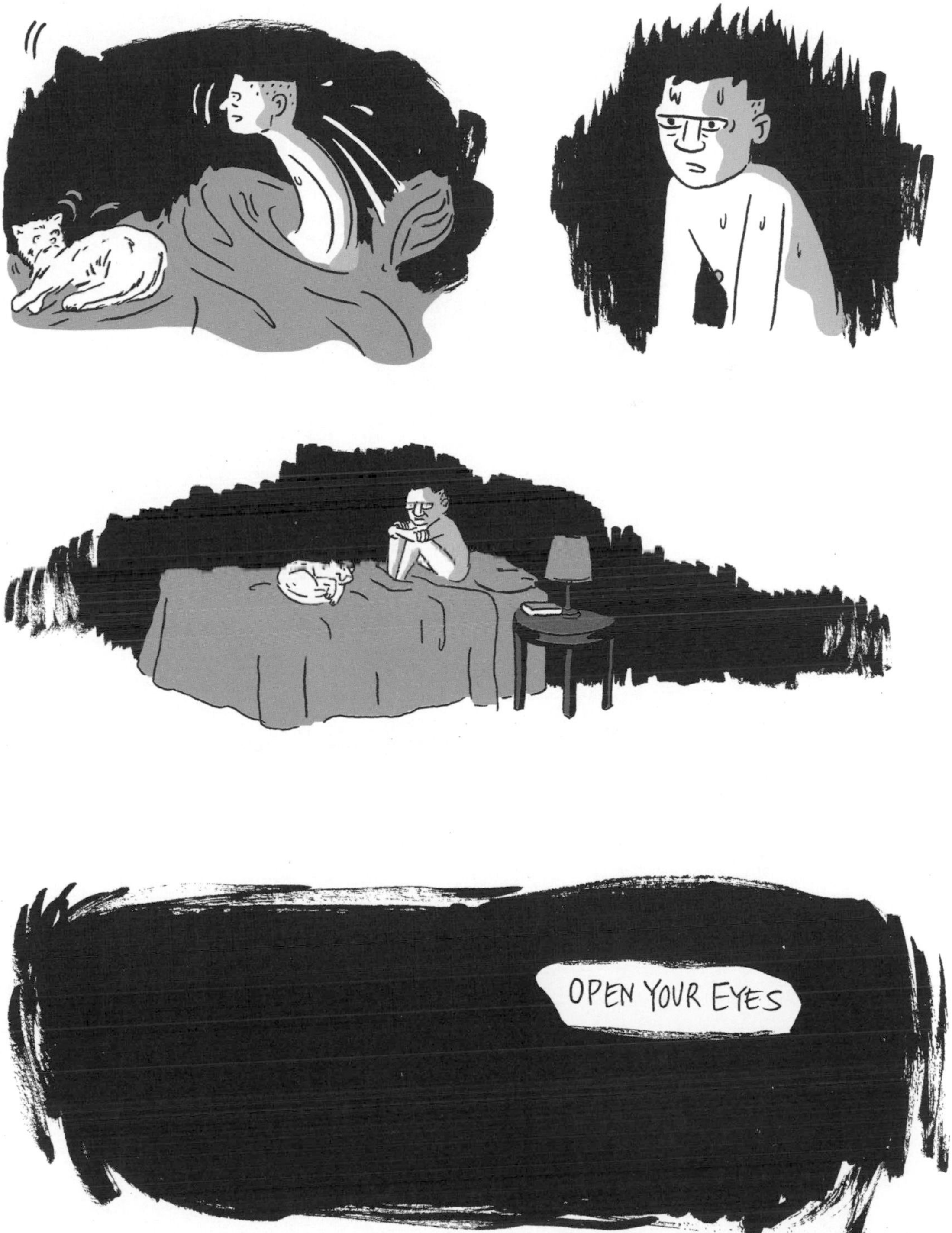
OPEN YOUR EYES

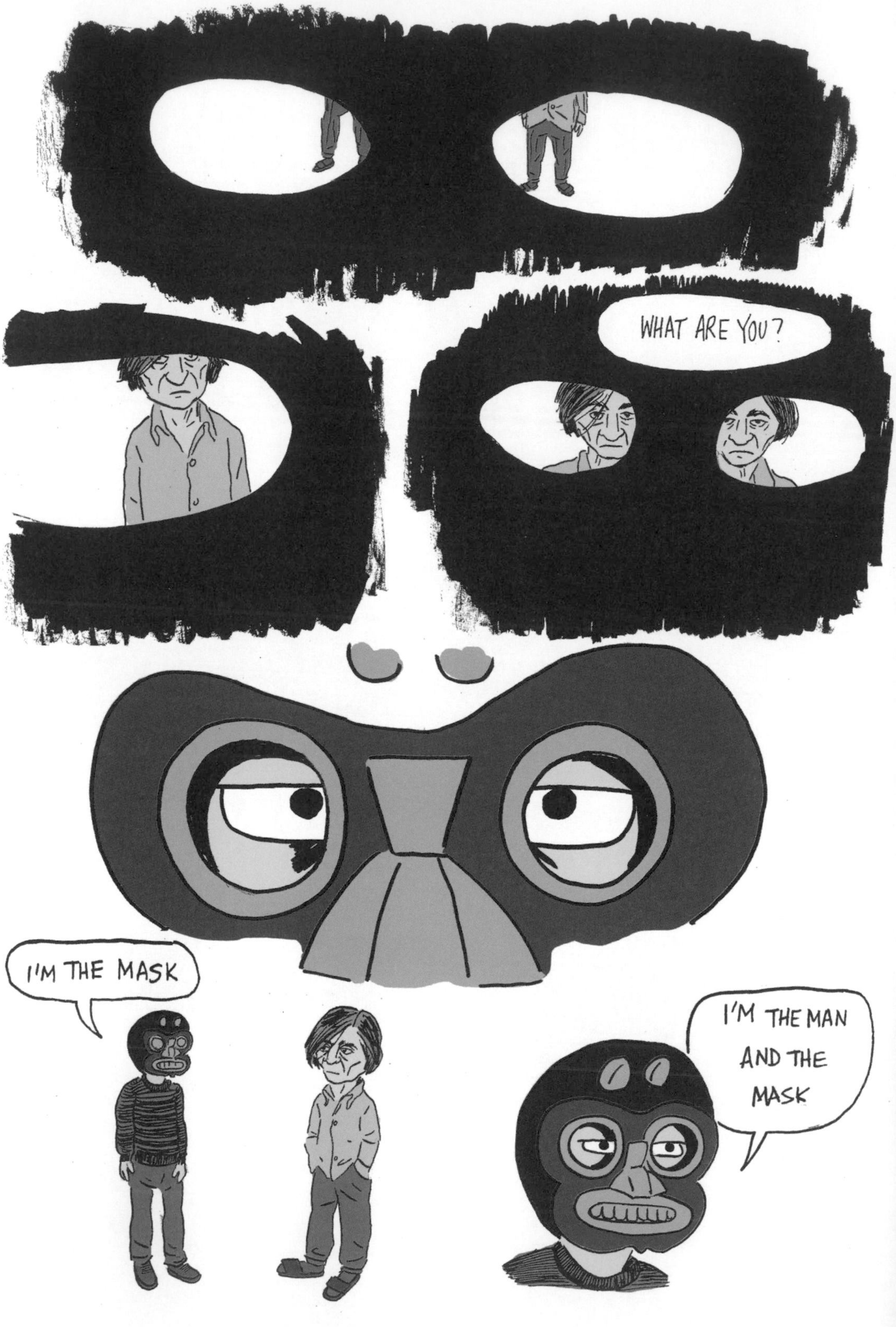
WHAT ARE YOU?
I'M THE MASK
I'M THE MAN AND THE MASK

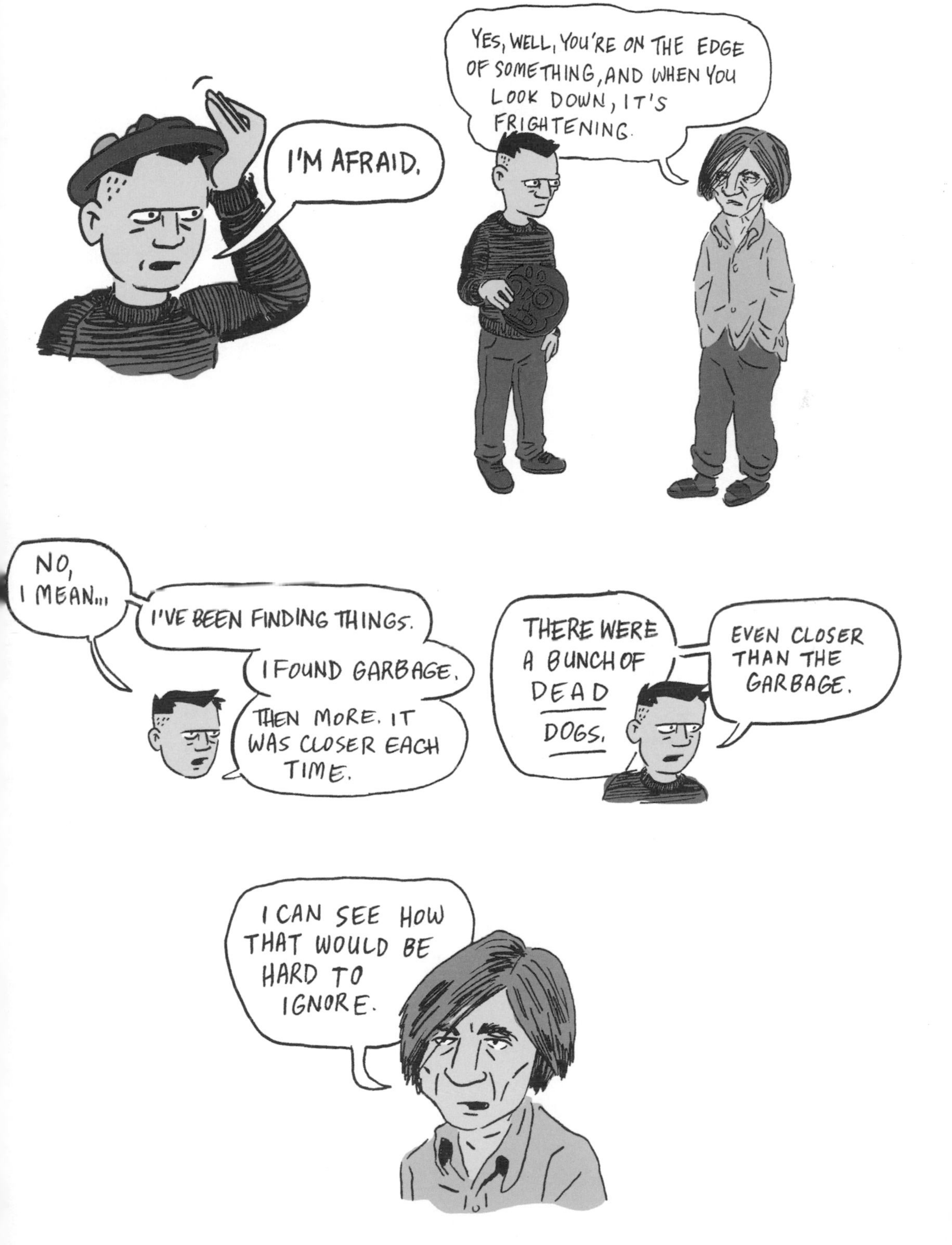
I'M AFRAID.
YES, WELL, YOU'RE ON THE EDGE OF SOMETHING, AND WHEN YOU LOOK DOWN, IT'S FRIGHTENING.
NO, I MEAN...
I'VE BEEN FINDING THINGS.
I FOUND GARBAGE.
THEN MORE. IT WAS CLOSER EACH TIME.
THERE WERE A BUNCH OF DEAD DOGS.
EVEN CLOSER THAN THE GARBAGE.
I CAN SEE HOW THAT WOULD BE HARD TO IGNORE.

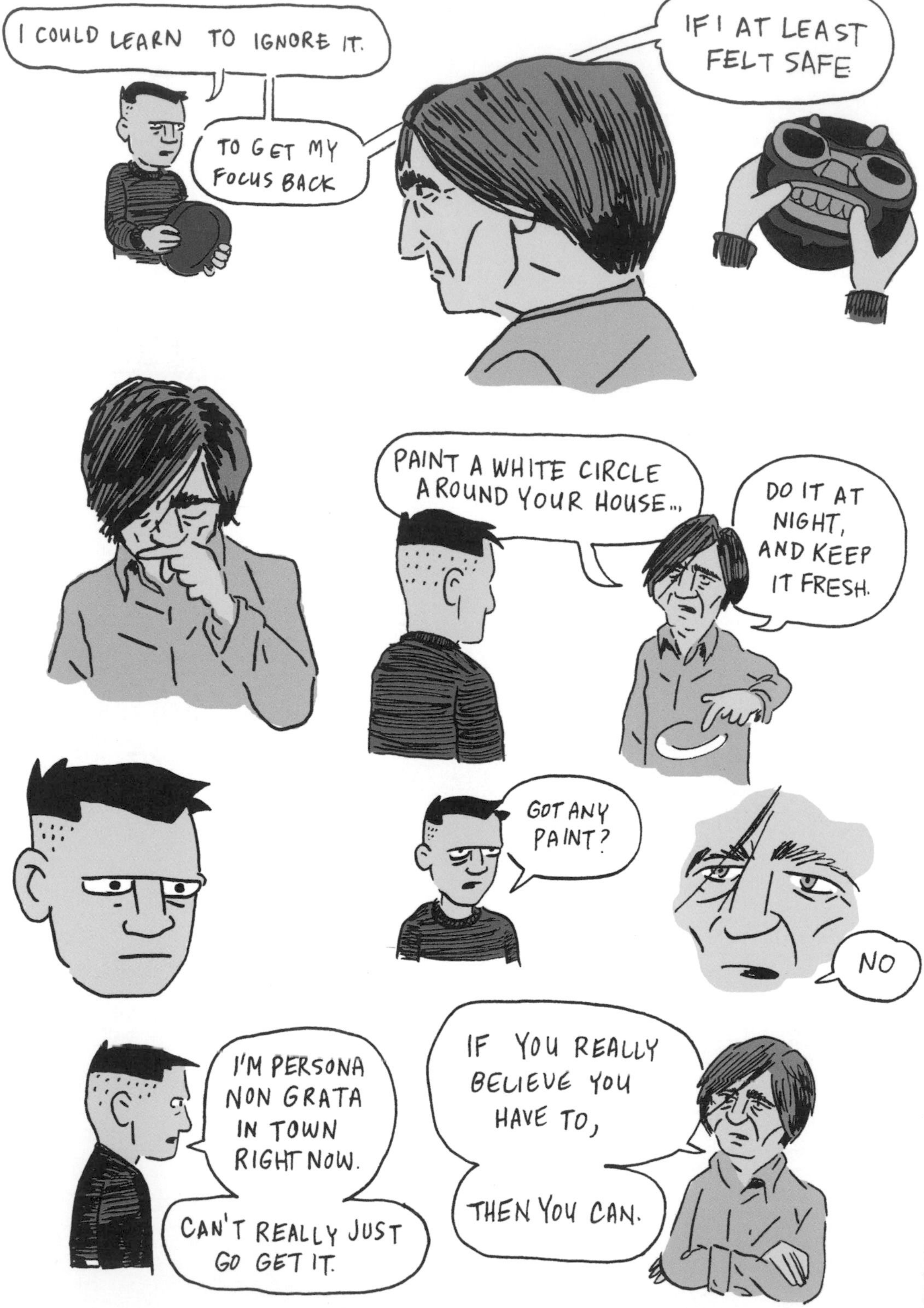
I COULD LEARN TO IGNORE IT.
TO GET MY FOCUS BACK
IF I AT LEAST FELT SAFE
PAINT A WHITE CIRCLE AROUND YOUR HOUSE...
DO IT AT NIGHT, AND KEEP IT FRESH.
GOT ANY PAINT?
NO
I'M PERSONA NON GRATA IN TOWN RIGHT NOW.
CAN'T REALLY JUST GO GET IT.
IF YOU REALLY BELIEVE YOU HAVE TO,
THEN YOU CAN.

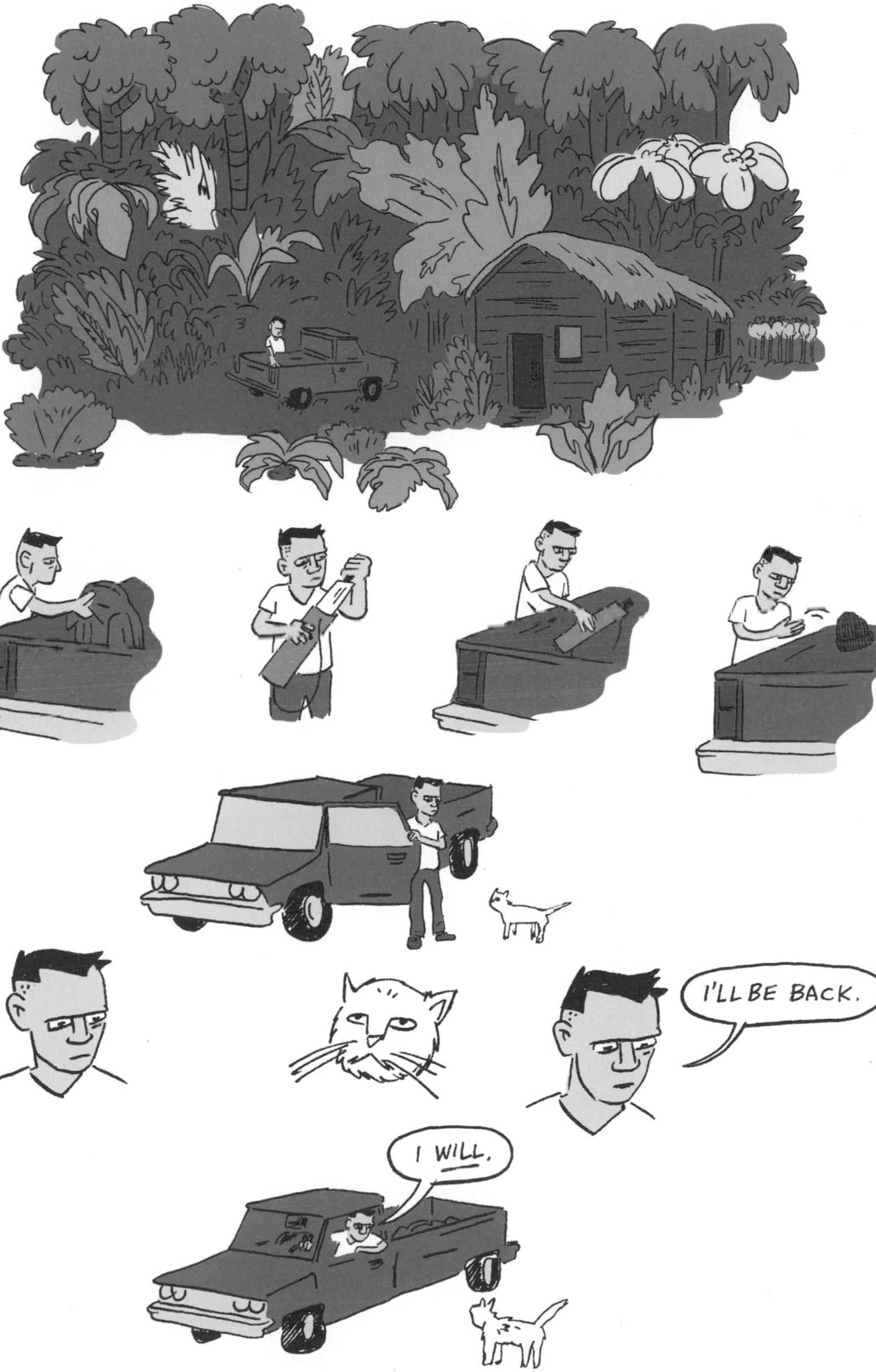
I'LL BE BACK.
I WILL.

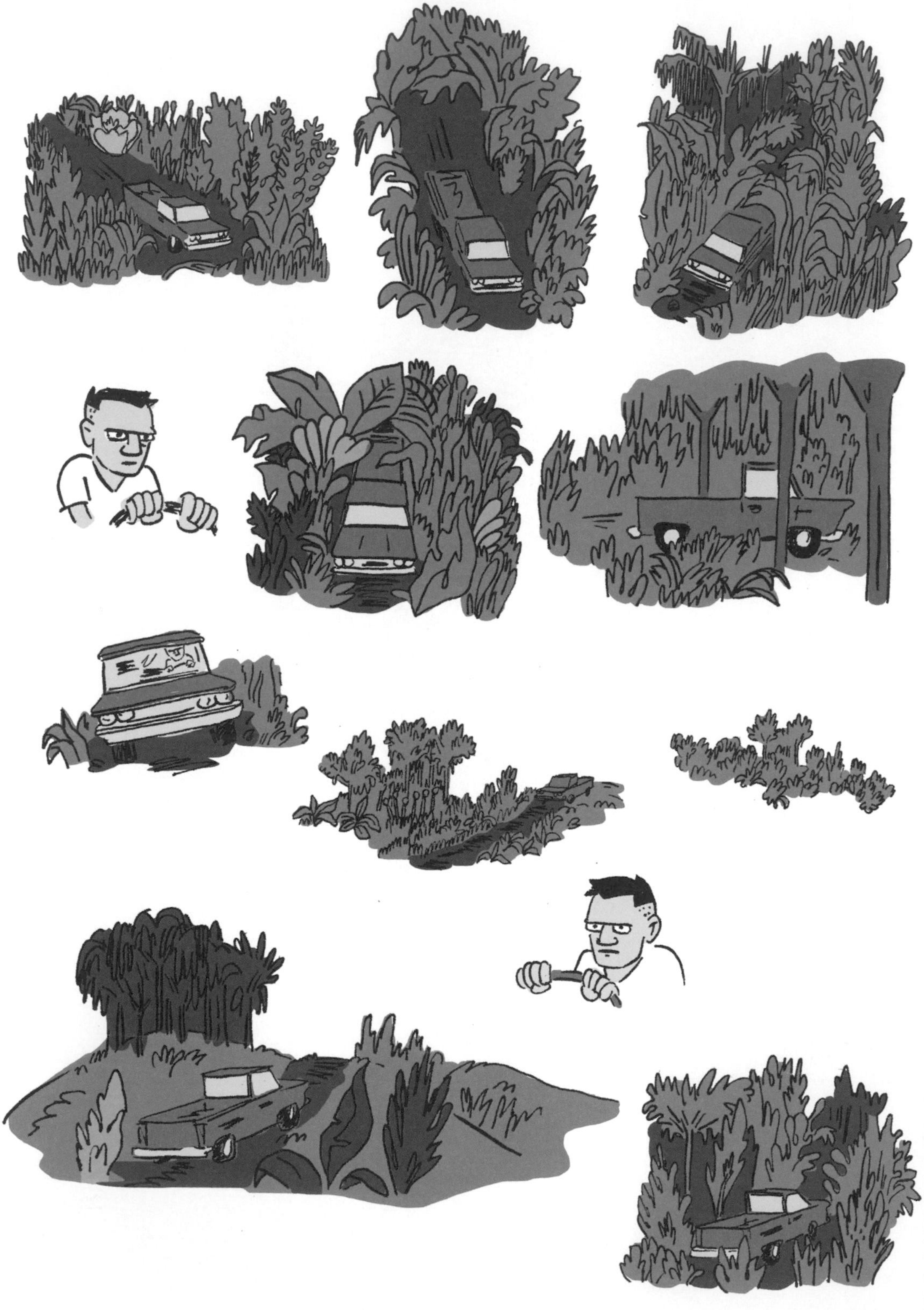

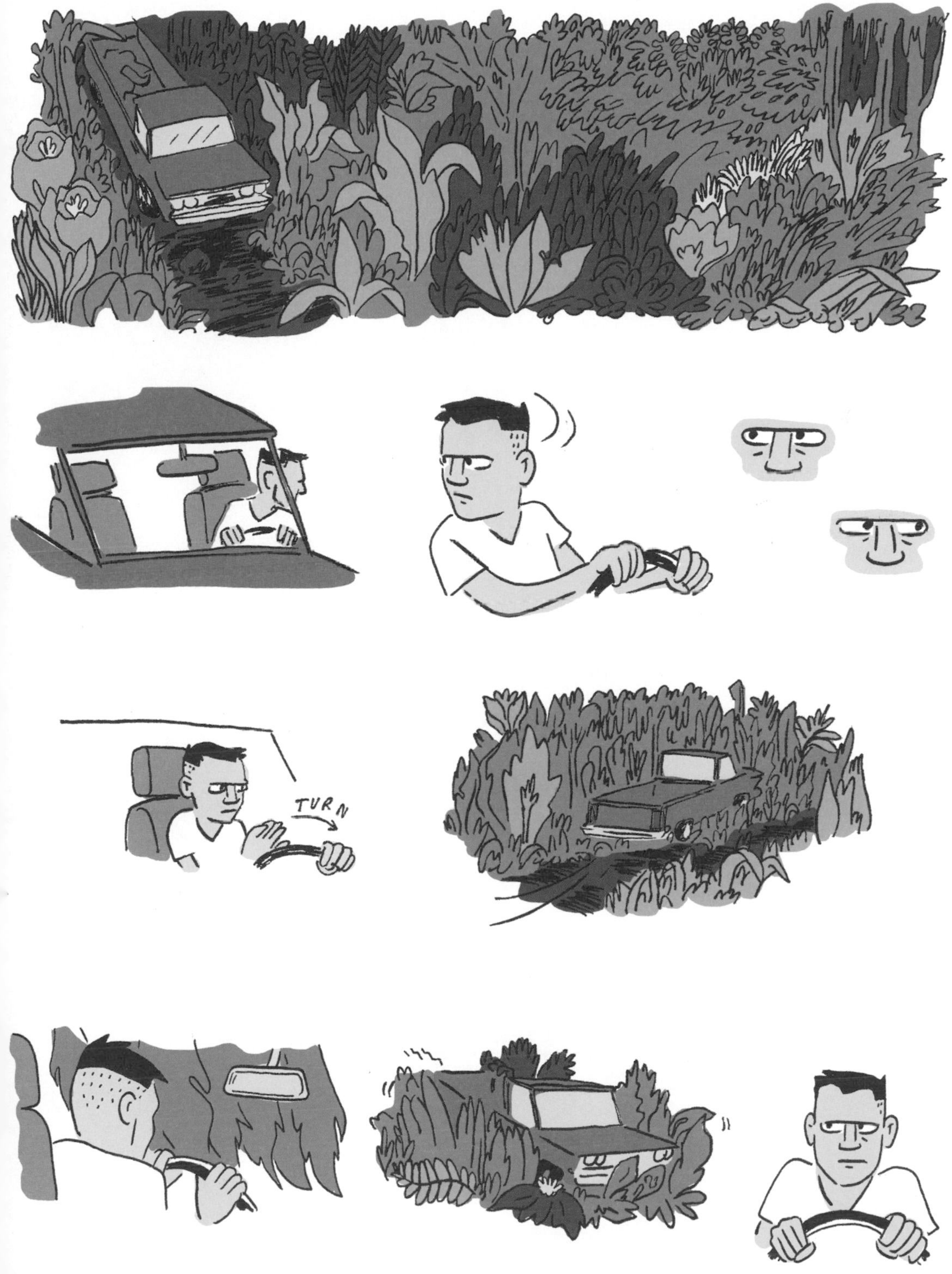
TURN

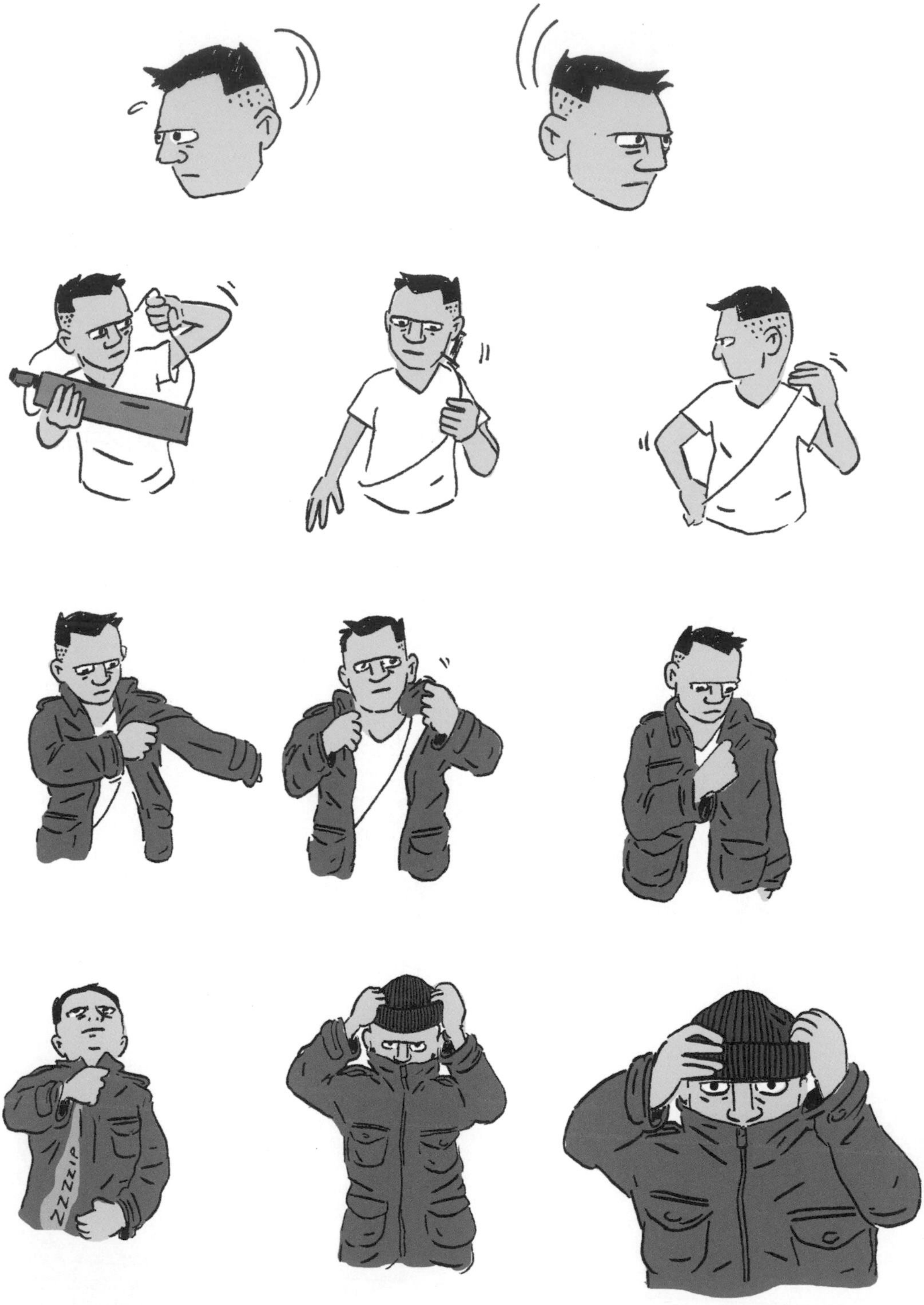
ZZZZZIP

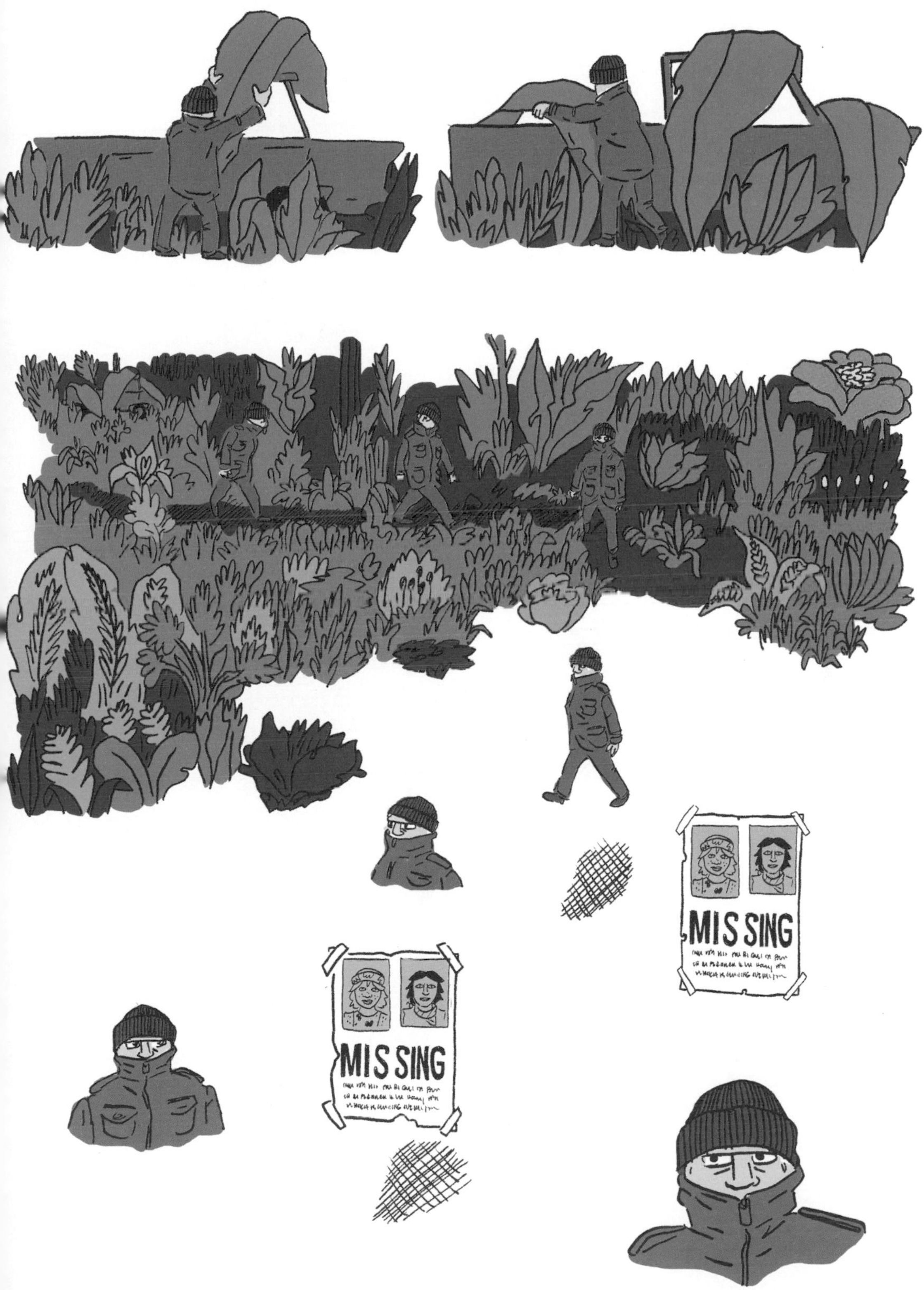
MIS SING
MIS SING

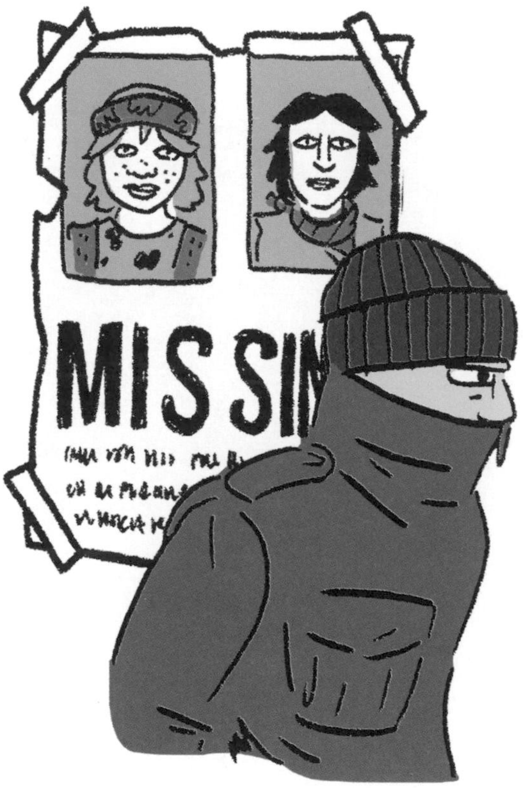
MIS SIN

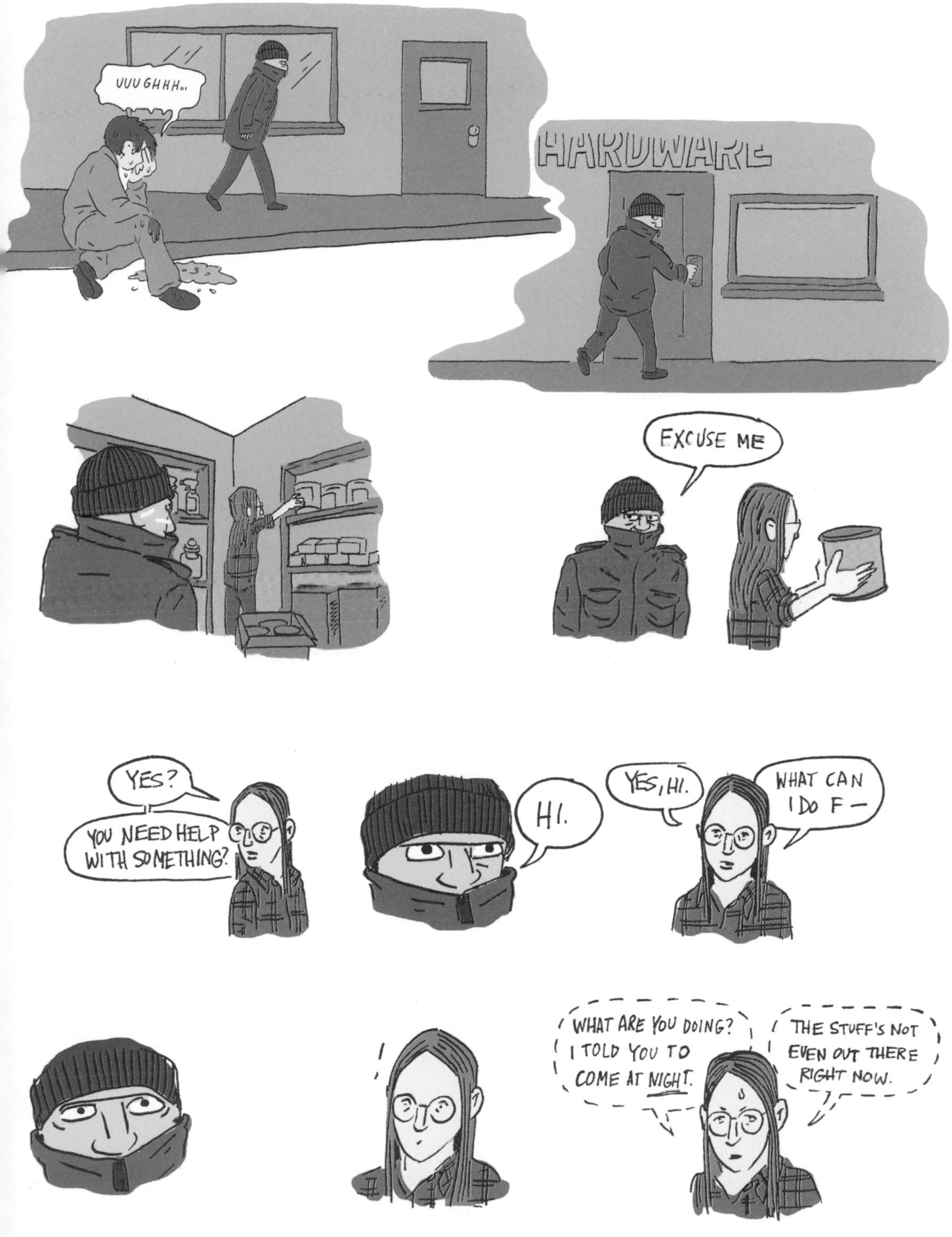
UUUGHHH...
HARDWARE
EXCUSE ME
YES?
YOU NEED HELP WITH SOMETHING?
HI.
YES, HI.
WHAT CAN I DO F—
!
WHAT ARE YOU DOING? I TOLD YOU TO COME AT NIGHT.
THE STUFF'S NOT EVEN OUT THERE RIGHT NOW.

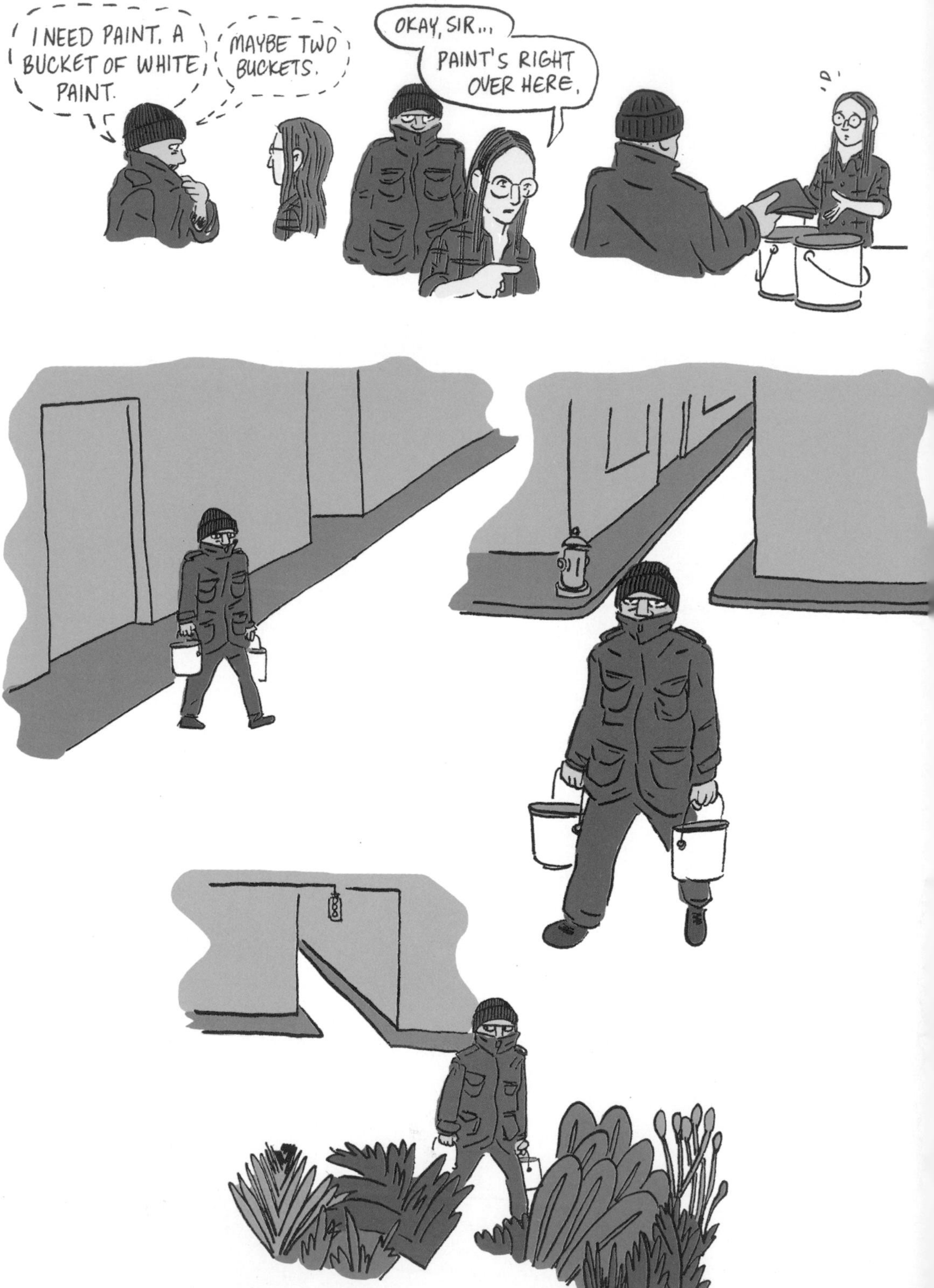
I NEED PAINT. A BUCKET OF WHITE PAINT.
MAYBE TWO BUCKETS.
OKAY, SIR...
PAINT'S RIGHT OVER HERE.

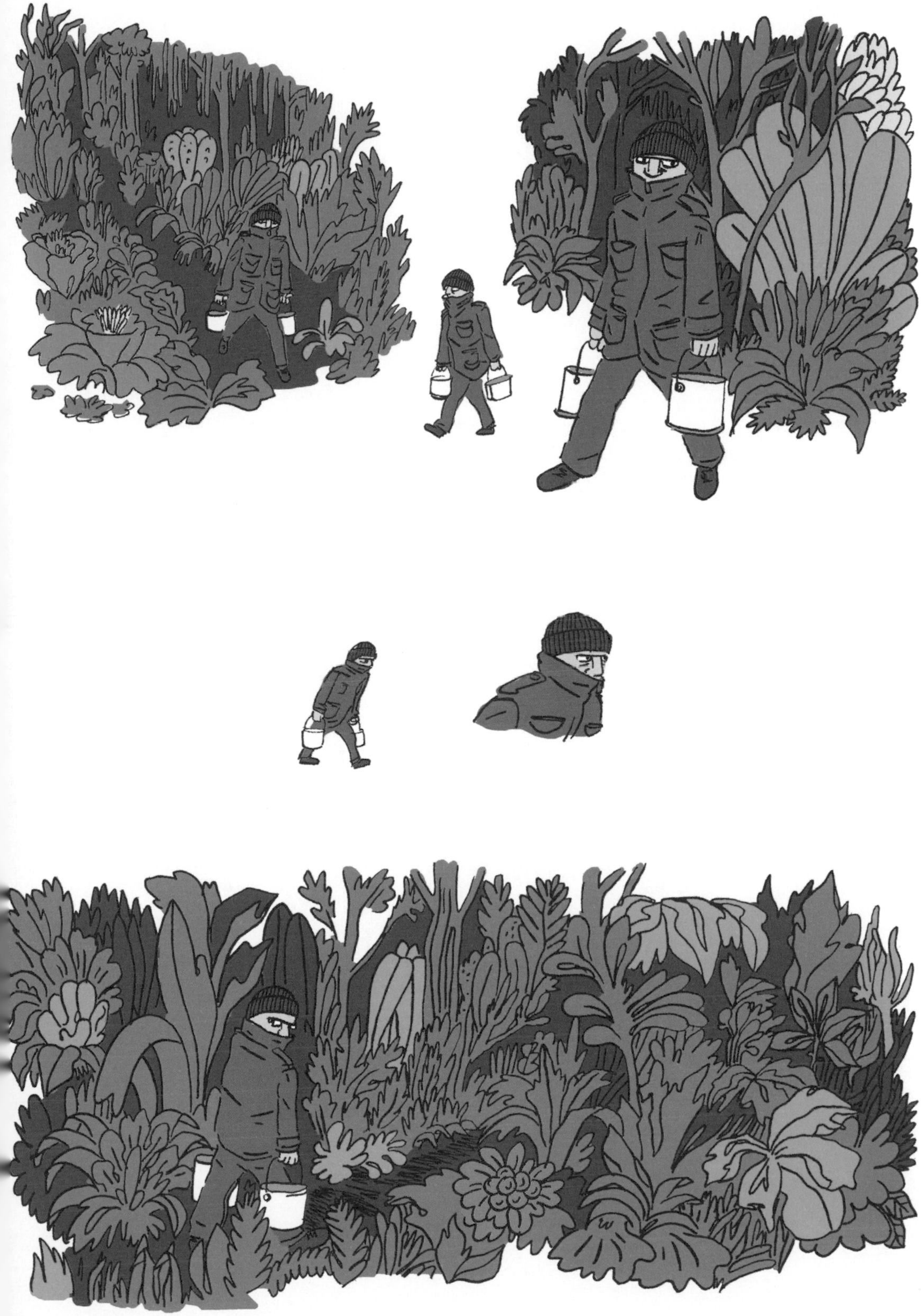

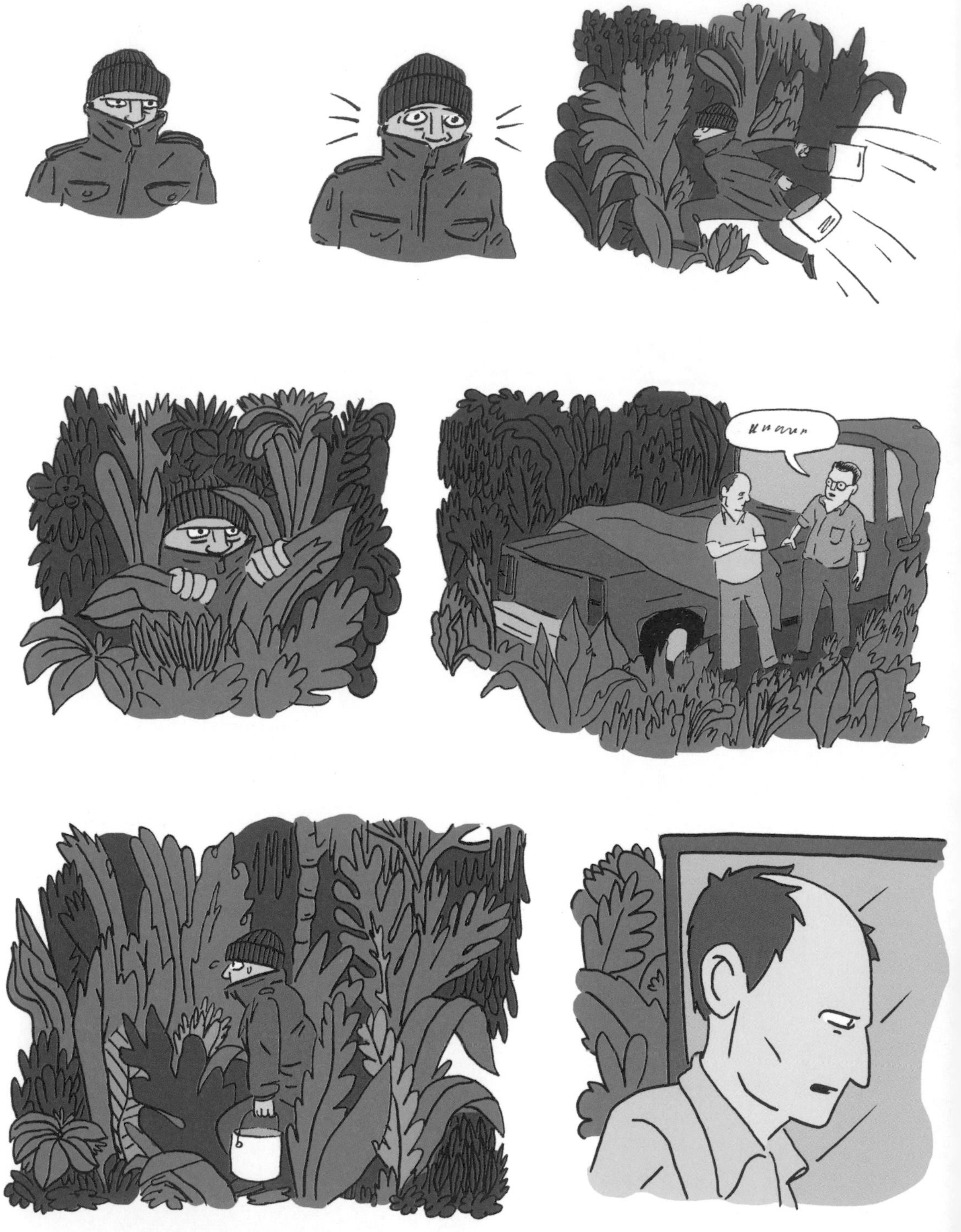

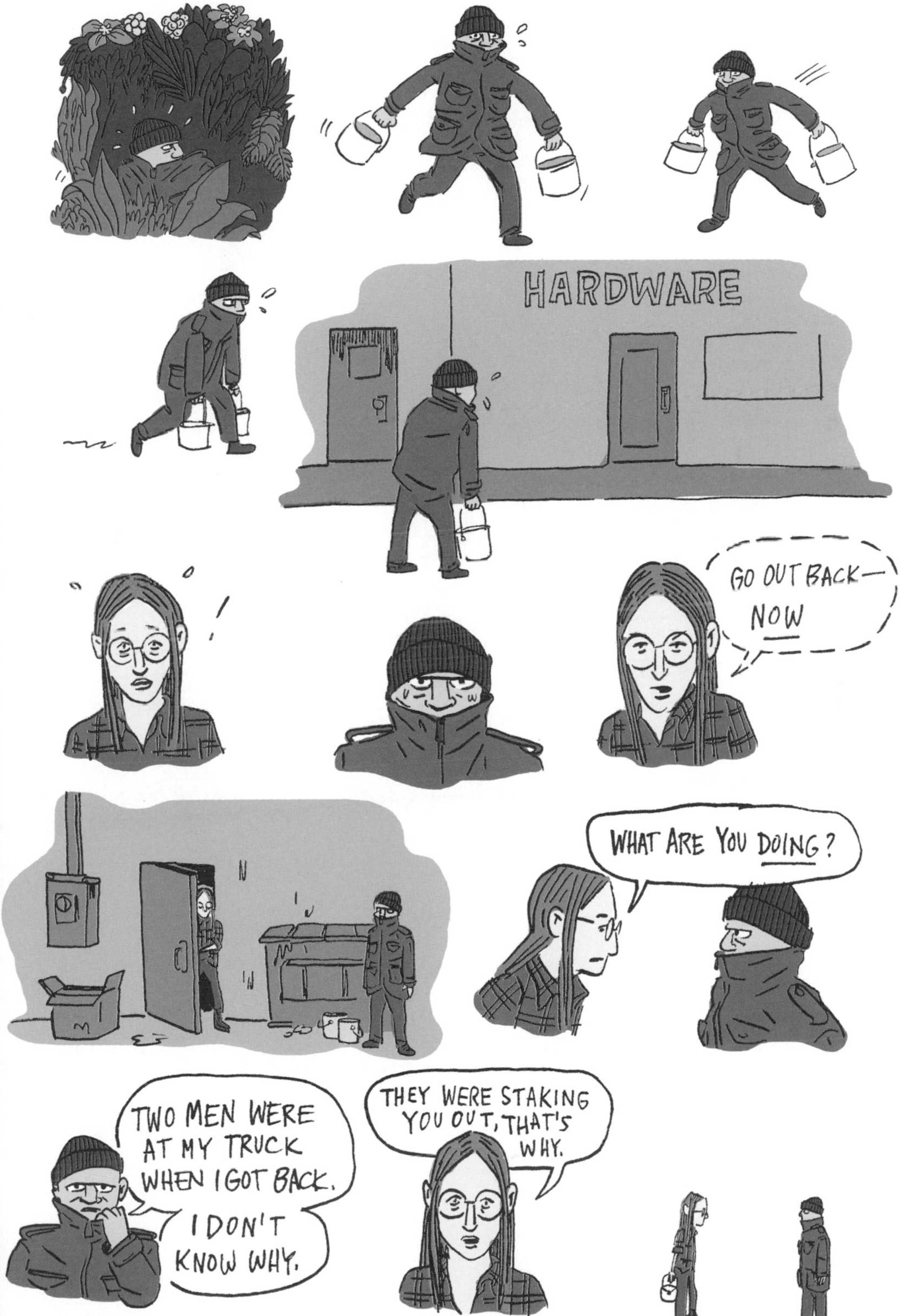
HARDWARE
GO OUT BACK— NOW
WHAT ARE YOU DOING?
TWO MEN WERE AT MY TRUCK WHEN I GOT BACK.
I DON'T KNOW WHY.
THEY WERE STAKING YOU OUT, THAT'S WHY.

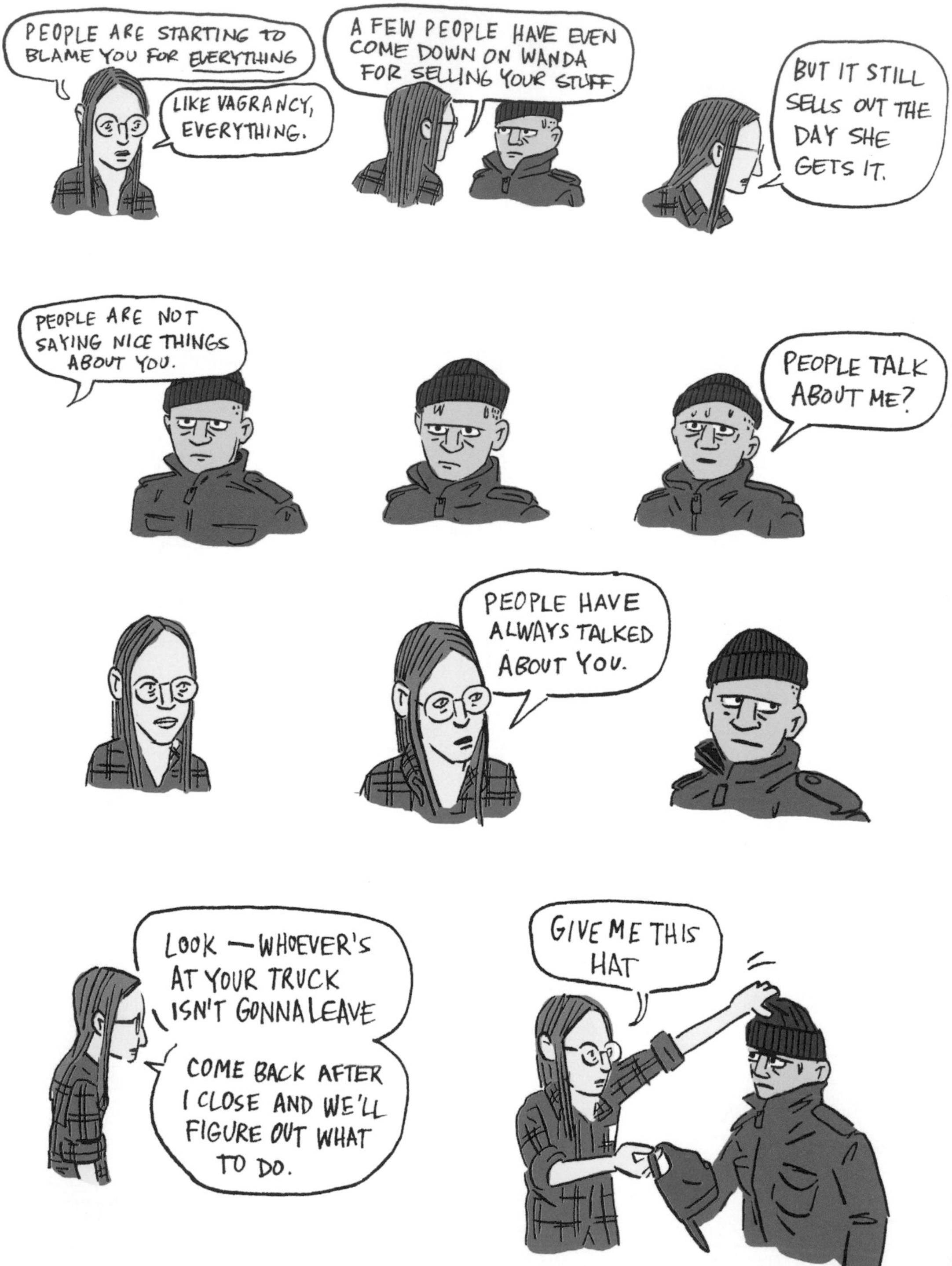
PEOPLE ARE STARTING TO BLAME YOU FOR EVERYTHING
LIKE VAGRANCY, EVERYTHING.
A FEW PEOPLE HAVE EVEN COME DOWN ON WANDA FOR SELLING YOUR STUFF.
BUT IT STILL SELLS OUT THE DAY SHE GETS IT.
PEOPLE ARE NOT SAYING NICE THINGS ABOUT YOU.
PEOPLE TALK ABOUT ME?
PEOPLE HAVE ALWAYS TALKED ABOUT YOU.
LOOK — WHOEVER'S AT YOUR TRUCK ISN'T GONNA LEAVE
COME BACK AFTER I CLOSE AND WE'LL FIGURE OUT WHAT TO DO.
GIVE ME THIS HAT

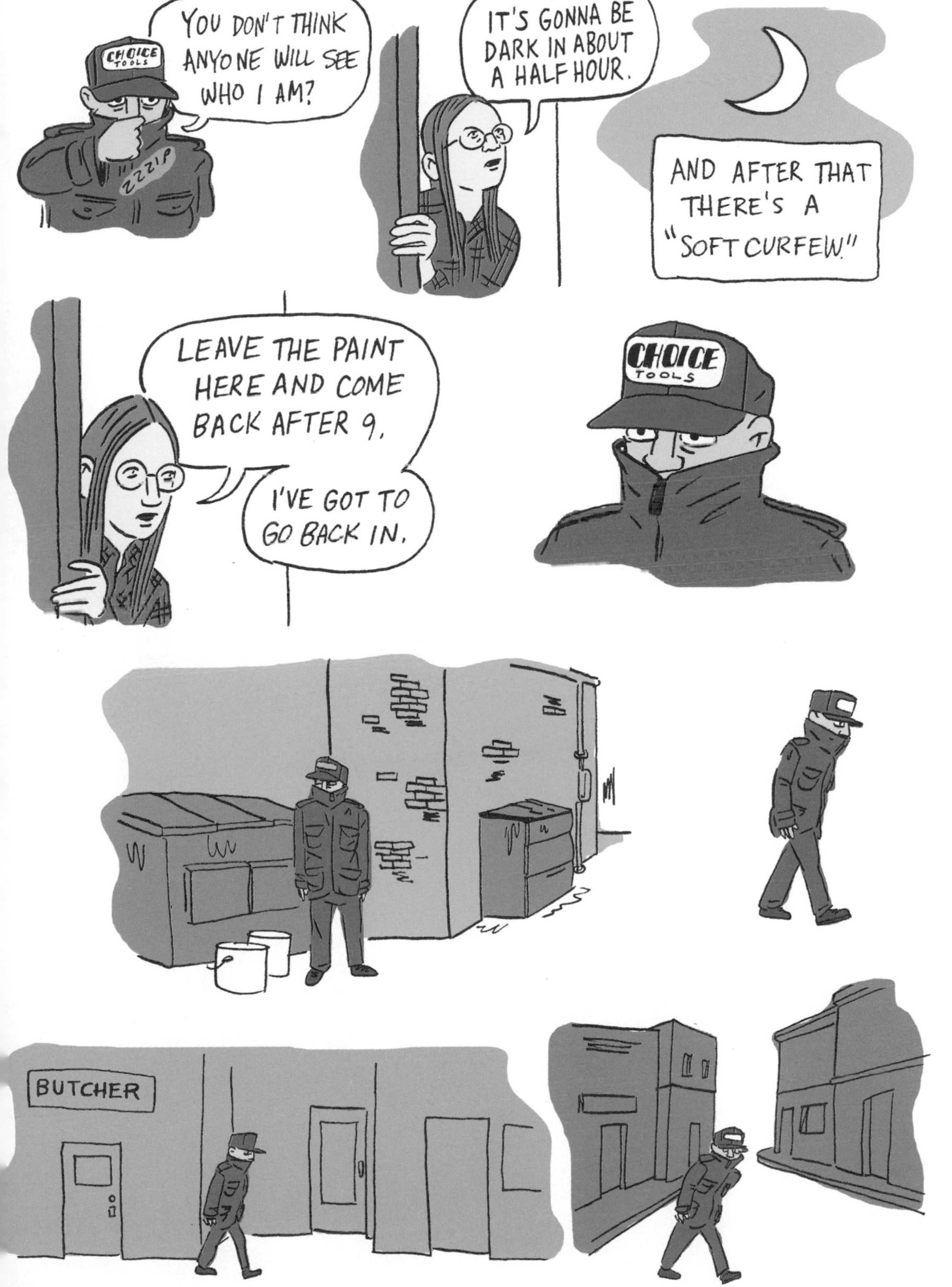
CHOICE TOOLS
YOU DON'T THINK ANYONE WILL SEE WHO I AM?
ZZZIP
IT'S GONNA BE DARK IN ABOUT A HALF HOUR.
AND AFTER THAT THERE'S A "SOFT CURFEW."
LEAVE THE PAINT HERE AND COME BACK AFTER 9.
I'VE GOT TO GO BACK IN.
CHOICE TOOLS
BUTCHER

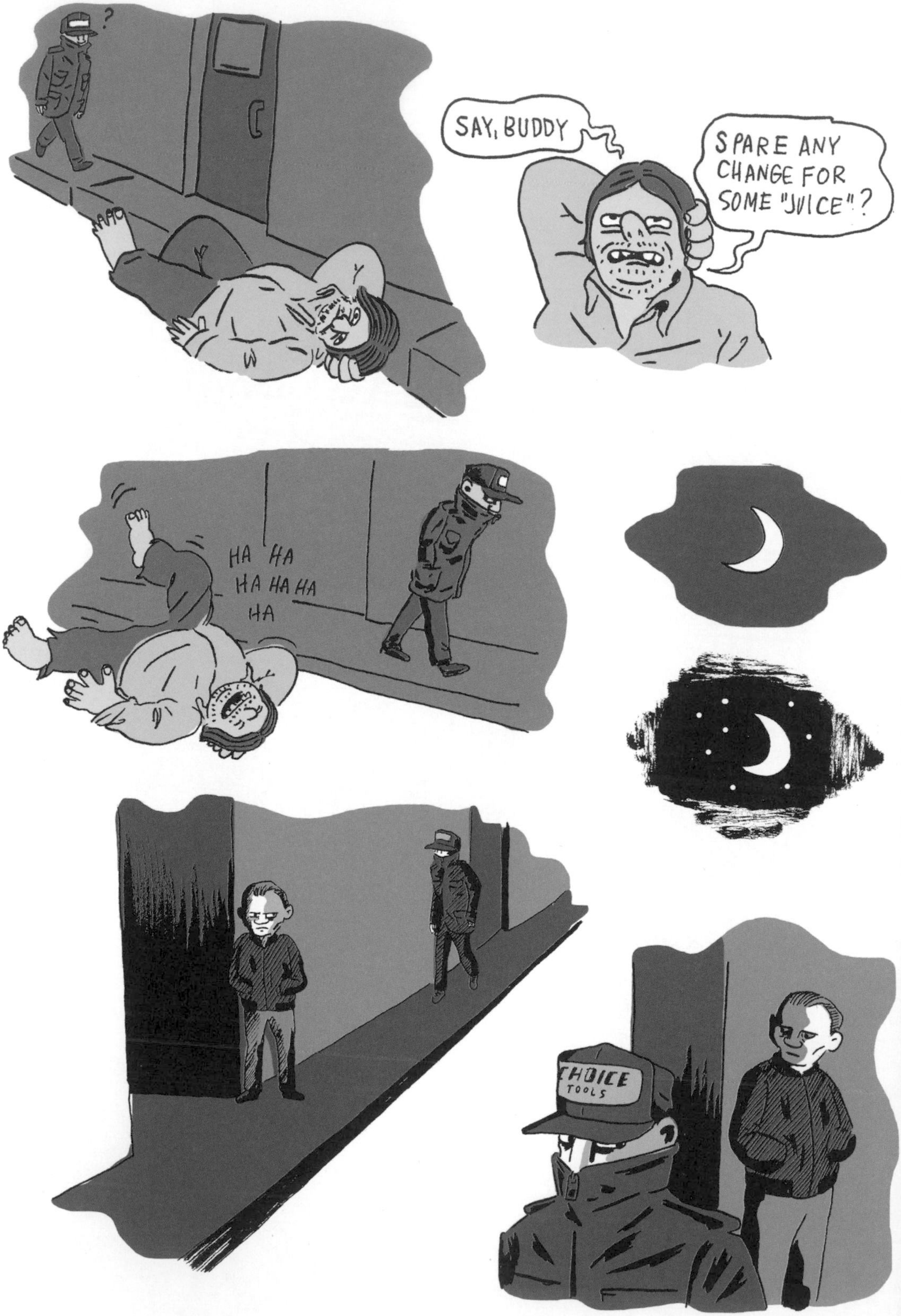
?
SAY, BUDDY
SPARE ANY CHANGE FOR SOME "JUICE"?
HA HA HA HA HA HA
CHOICE TOOLS

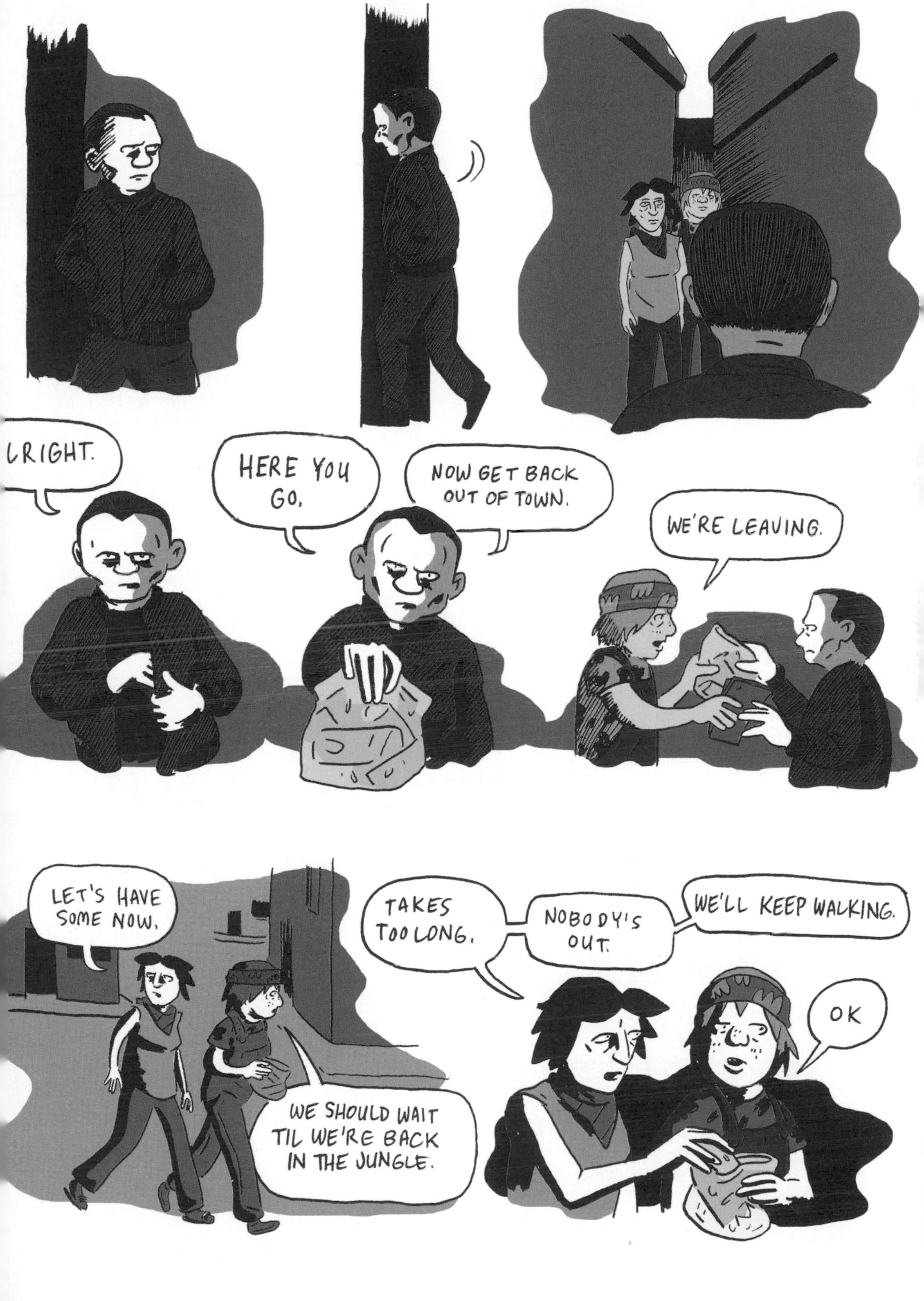
LRIGHT.
HERE YOU GO.
NOW GET BACK OUT OF TOWN.
WE'RE LEAVING.
LET'S HAVE SOME NOW.
WE SHOULD WAIT TIL WE'RE BACK IN THE JUNGLE.
TAKES TOO LONG.
NOBODY'S OUT.
WE'LL KEEP WALKING.
OK

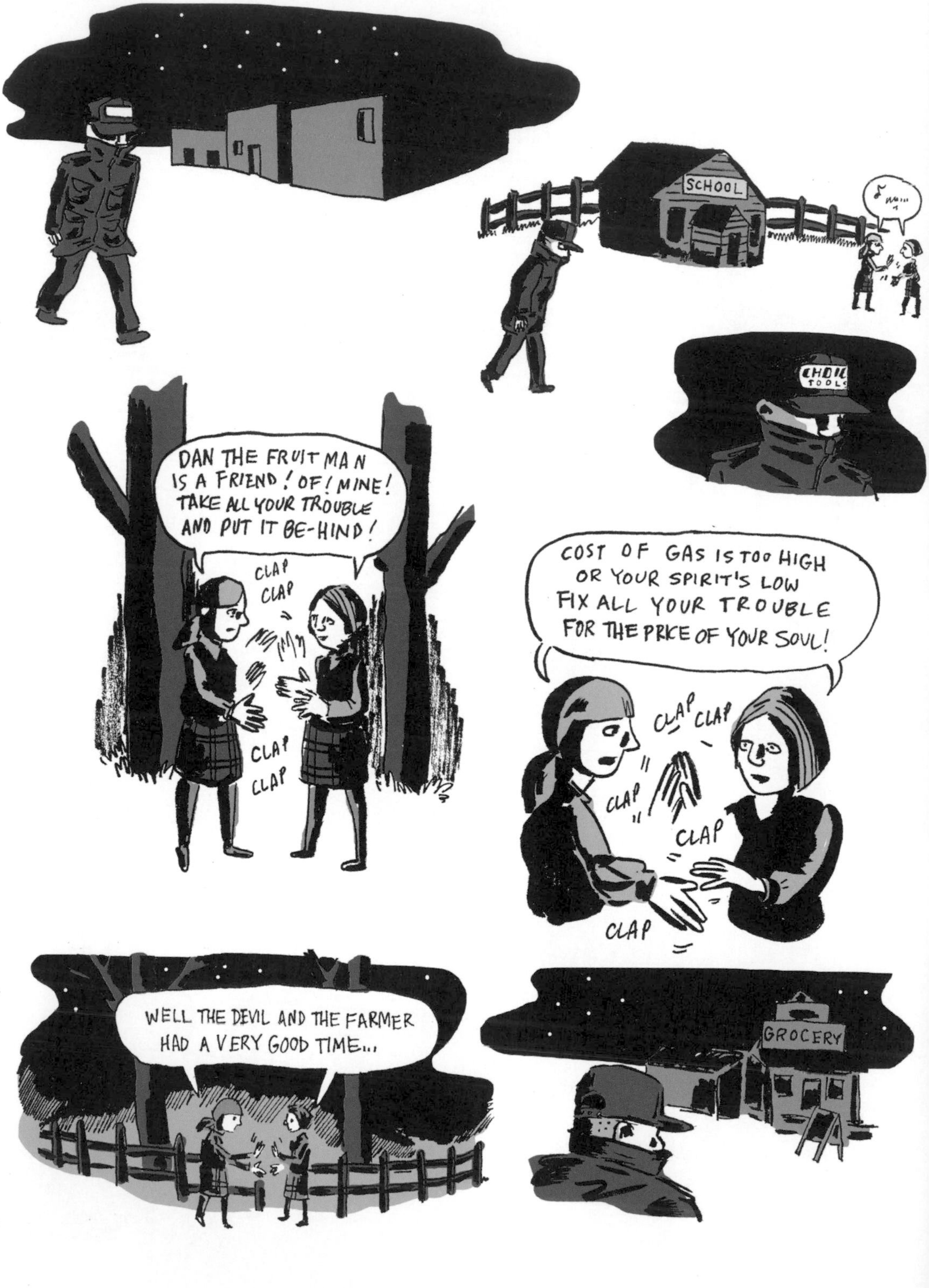
SCHOOL
CHOICE TOOLS
DAN THE FRUIT MAN IS A FRIEND! OF! MINE! TAKE ALL YOUR TROUBLE AND PUT IT BE-HIND!
CLAP CLAP
CLAP CLAP
COST OF GAS IS TOO HIGH OR YOUR SPIRIT'S LOW FIX ALL YOUR TROUBLE FOR THE PRICE OF YOUR SOUL!
CLAP CLAP
CLAP
CLAP
CLAP
WELL THE DEVIL AND THE FARMER HAD A VERY GOOD TIME...
GROCERY

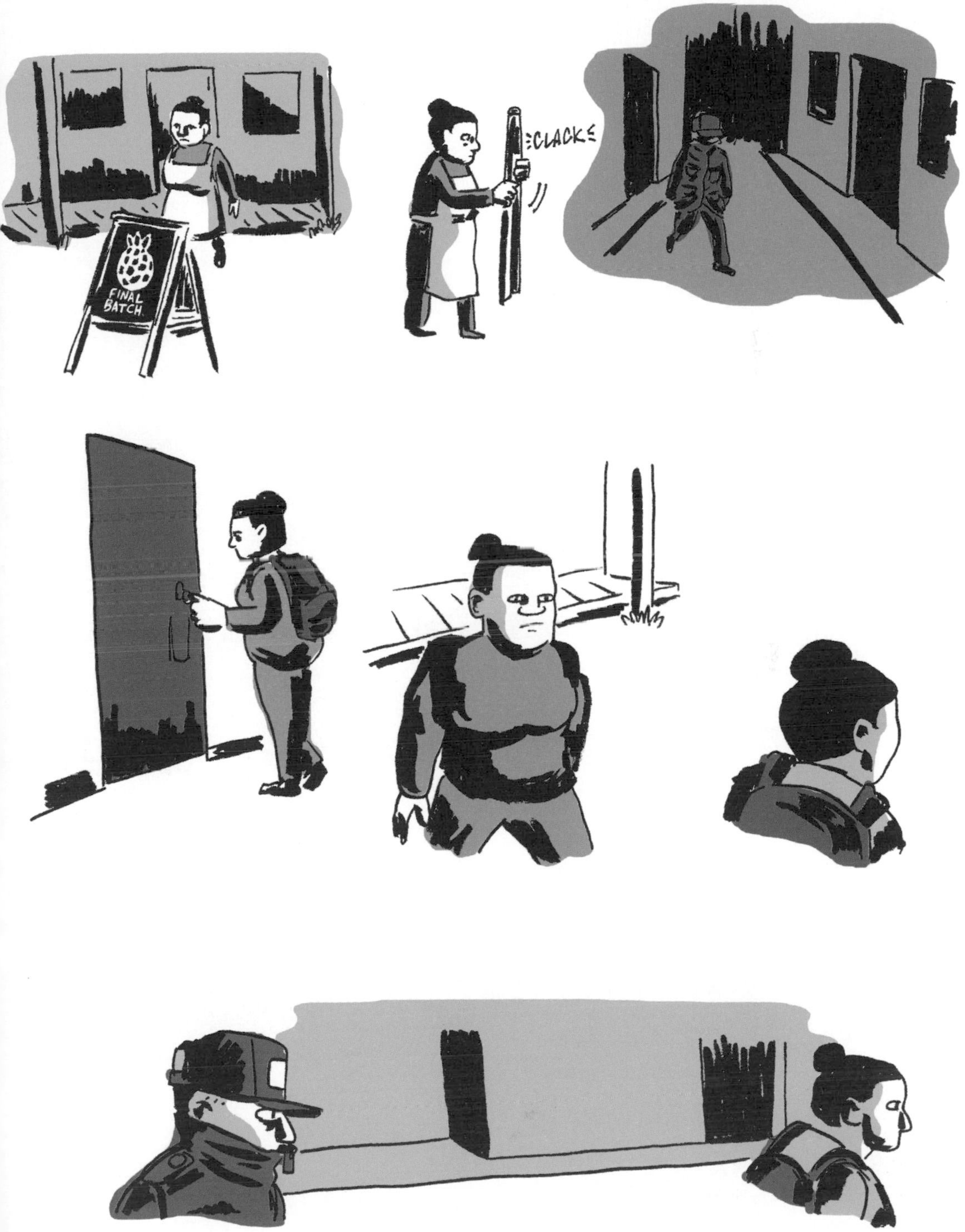
FINAL BATCH
CLACK

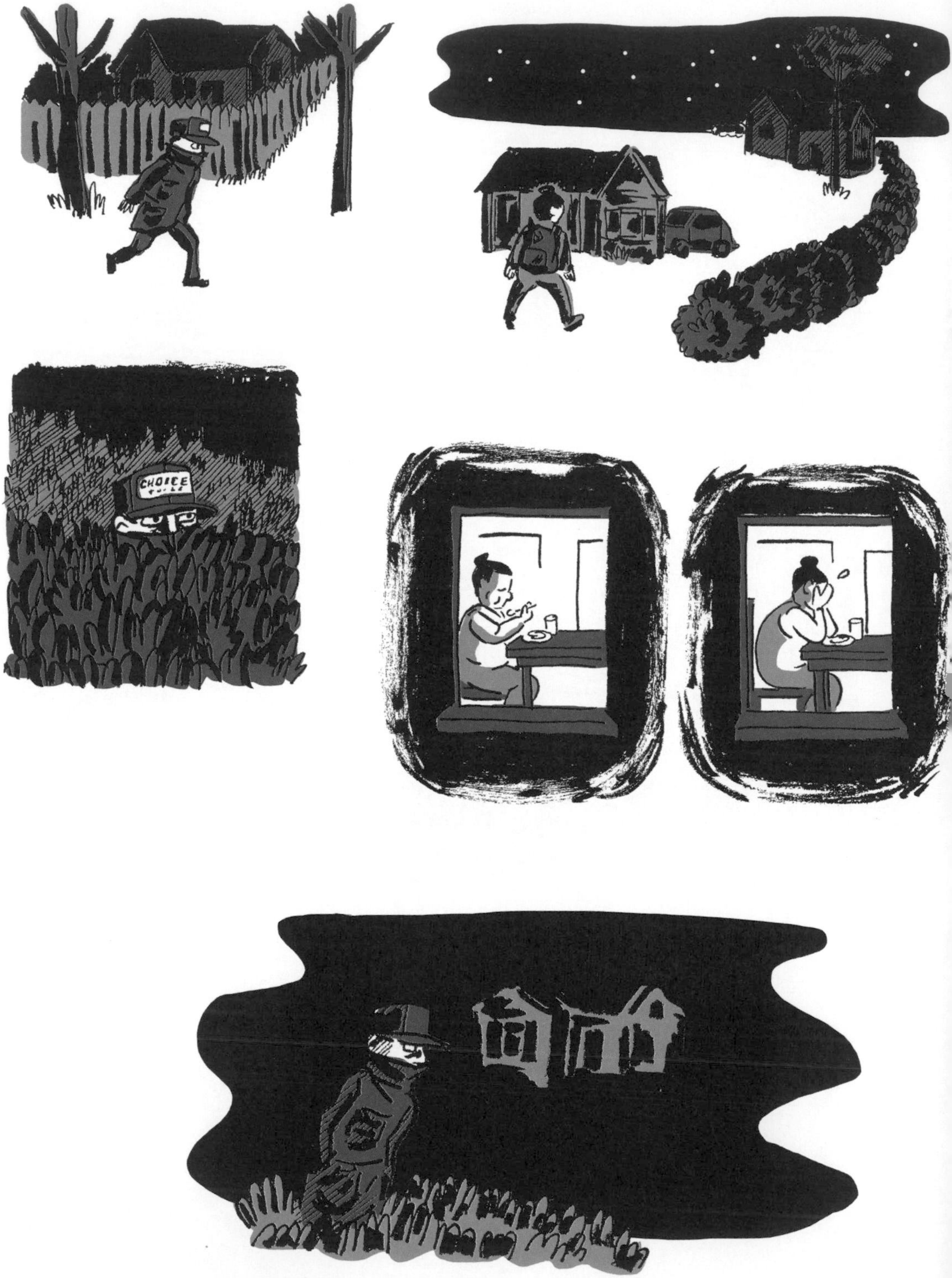
CHOICE

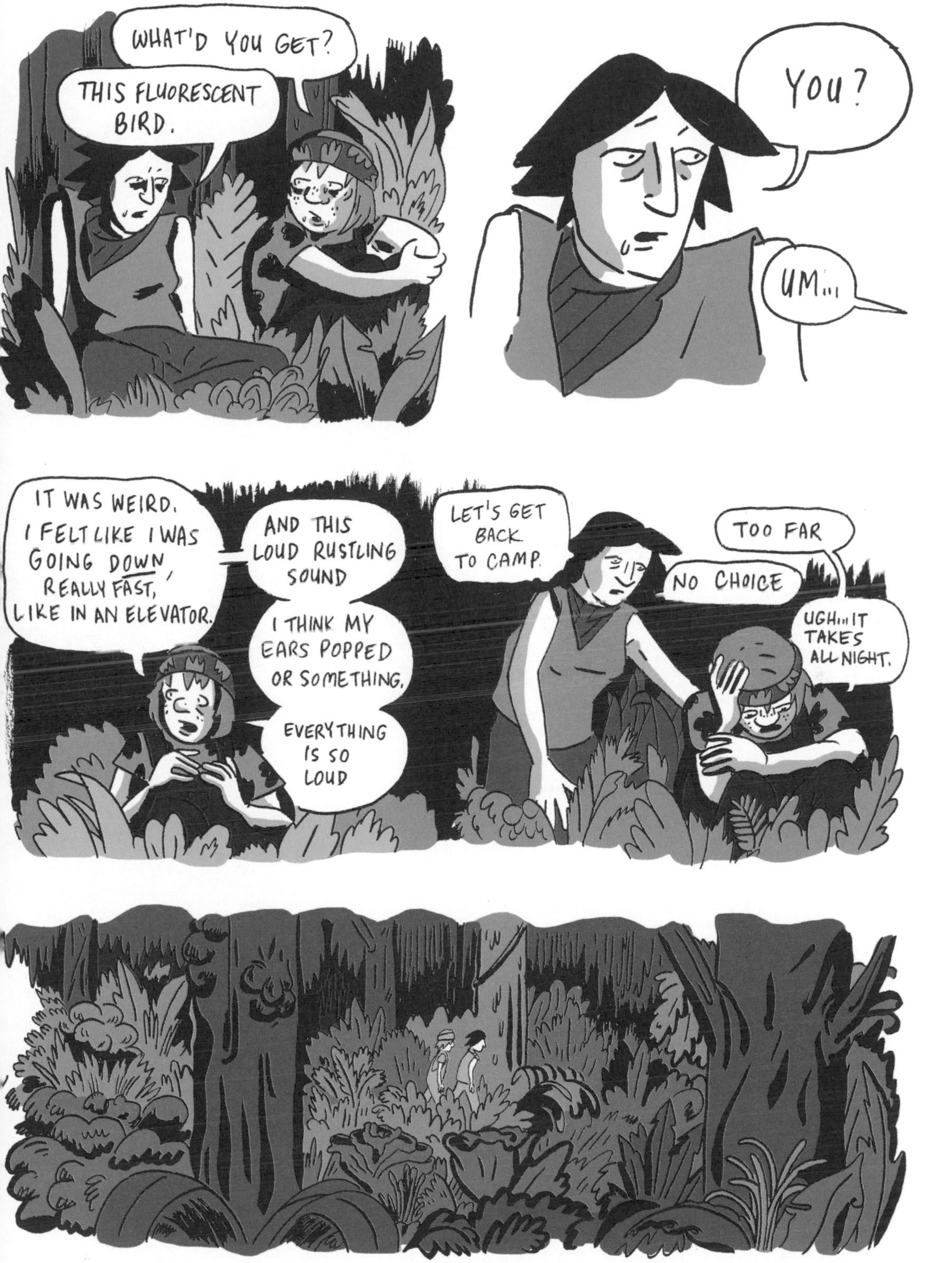
WHAT'D YOU GET?
THIS FLUORESCENT BIRD.
YOU?
UM...
IT WAS WEIRD. I FELT LIKE I WAS GOING DOWN, REALLY FAST, LIKE IN AN ELEVATOR.
AND THIS LOUD RUSTLING SOUND
I THINK MY EARS POPPED OR SOMETHING.
EVERYTHING IS SO LOUD
LET'S GET BACK TO CAMP.
TOO FAR
NO CHOICE
UGH... IT TAKES ALL NIGHT.

HEY.

I'LL GO GET IN MY CAR AROUND FRONT.

GIVE IT A MINUTE THEN COME GET IN THE BACK AND LAY DOWN.

IN?

YEAH

TAKE THE WEST ROAD OUT.

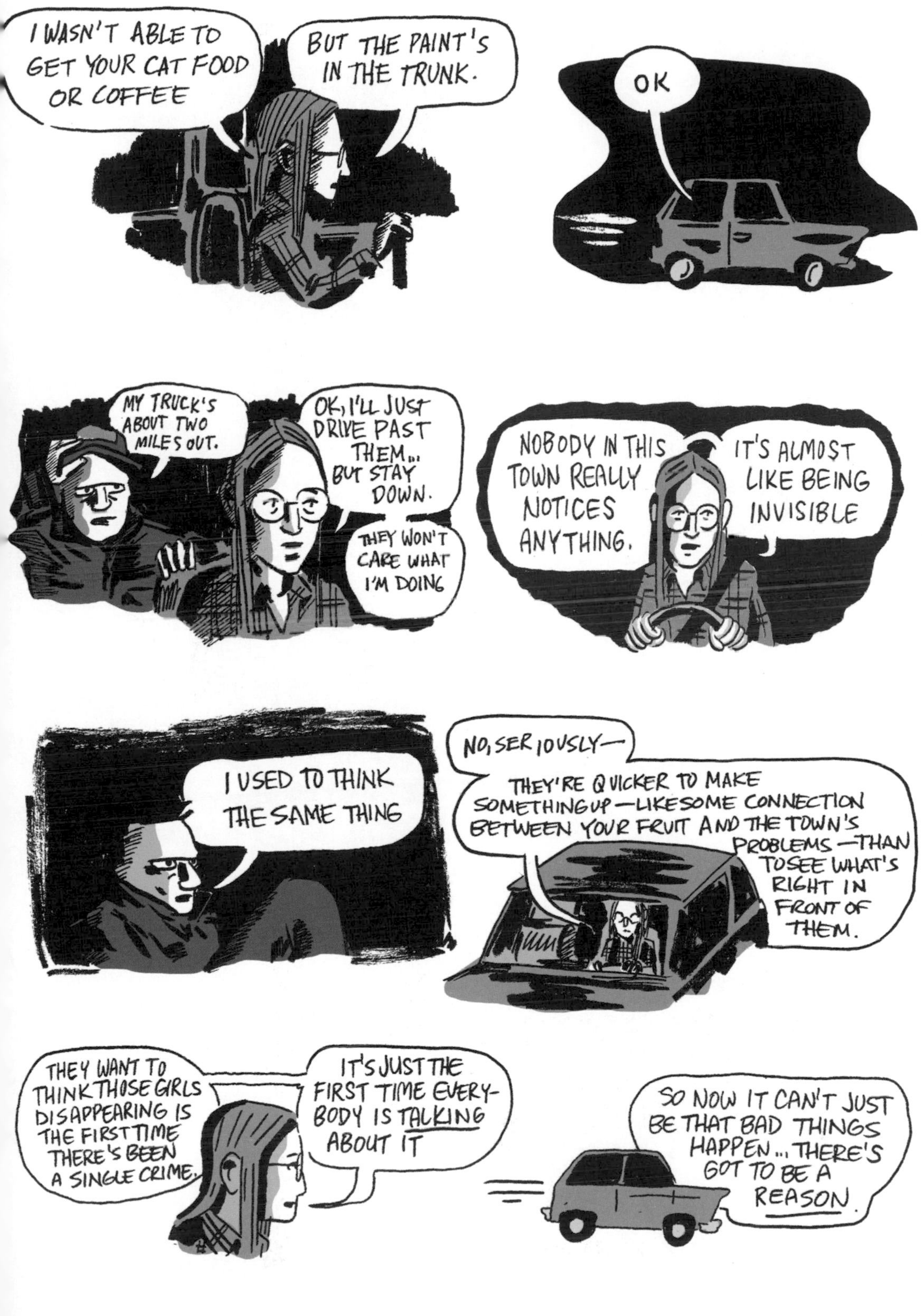

I WASN'T ABLE TO GET YOUR CAT FOOD OR COFFEE
BUT THE PAINT'S IN THE TRUNK.
OK
MY TRUCK'S ABOUT TWO MILES OUT.
OK, I'LL JUST DRIVE PAST THEM... BUT STAY DOWN.
THEY WON'T CARE WHAT I'M DOING
NOBODY IN THIS TOWN REALLY NOTICES ANYTHING.
IT'S ALMOST LIKE BEING INVISIBLE
I USED TO THINK THE SAME THING
NO, SERIOUSLY—
THEY'RE QUICKER TO MAKE SOMETHING UP—LIKE SOME CONNECTION BETWEEN YOUR FRUIT AND THE TOWN'S PROBLEMS—THAN TO SEE WHAT'S RIGHT IN FRONT OF THEM.
THEY WANT TO THINK THOSE GIRLS DISAPPEARING IS THE FIRST TIME THERE'S BEEN A SINGLE CRIME.
IT'S JUST THE FIRST TIME EVERYBODY IS TALKING ABOUT IT
SO NOW IT CAN'T JUST BE THAT BAD THINGS HAPPEN... THERE'S GOT TO BE A REASON.

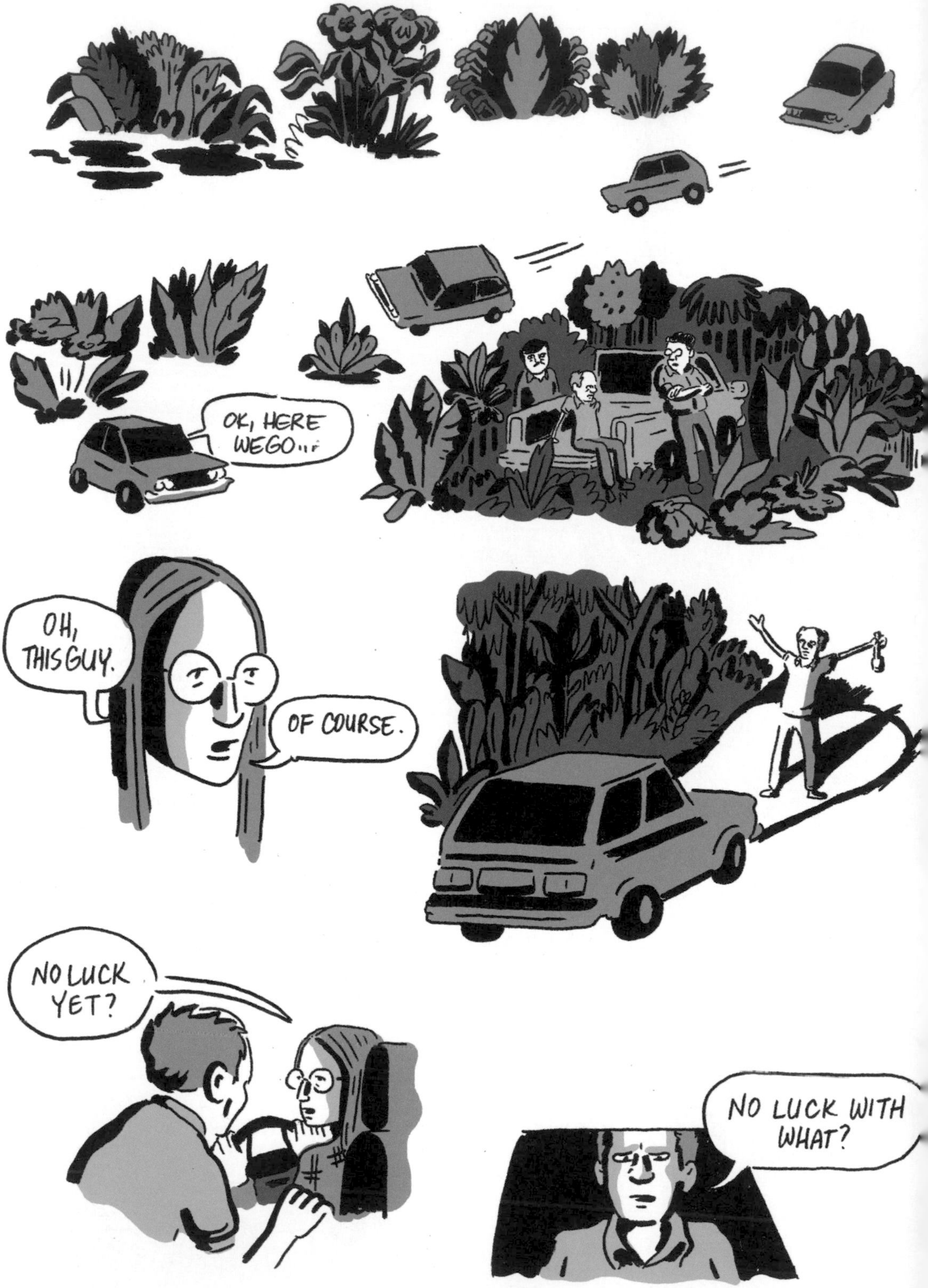
OK, HERE WE GO...
OH, THIS GUY.
OF COURSE.
NO LUCK YET?
NO LUCK WITH WHAT?

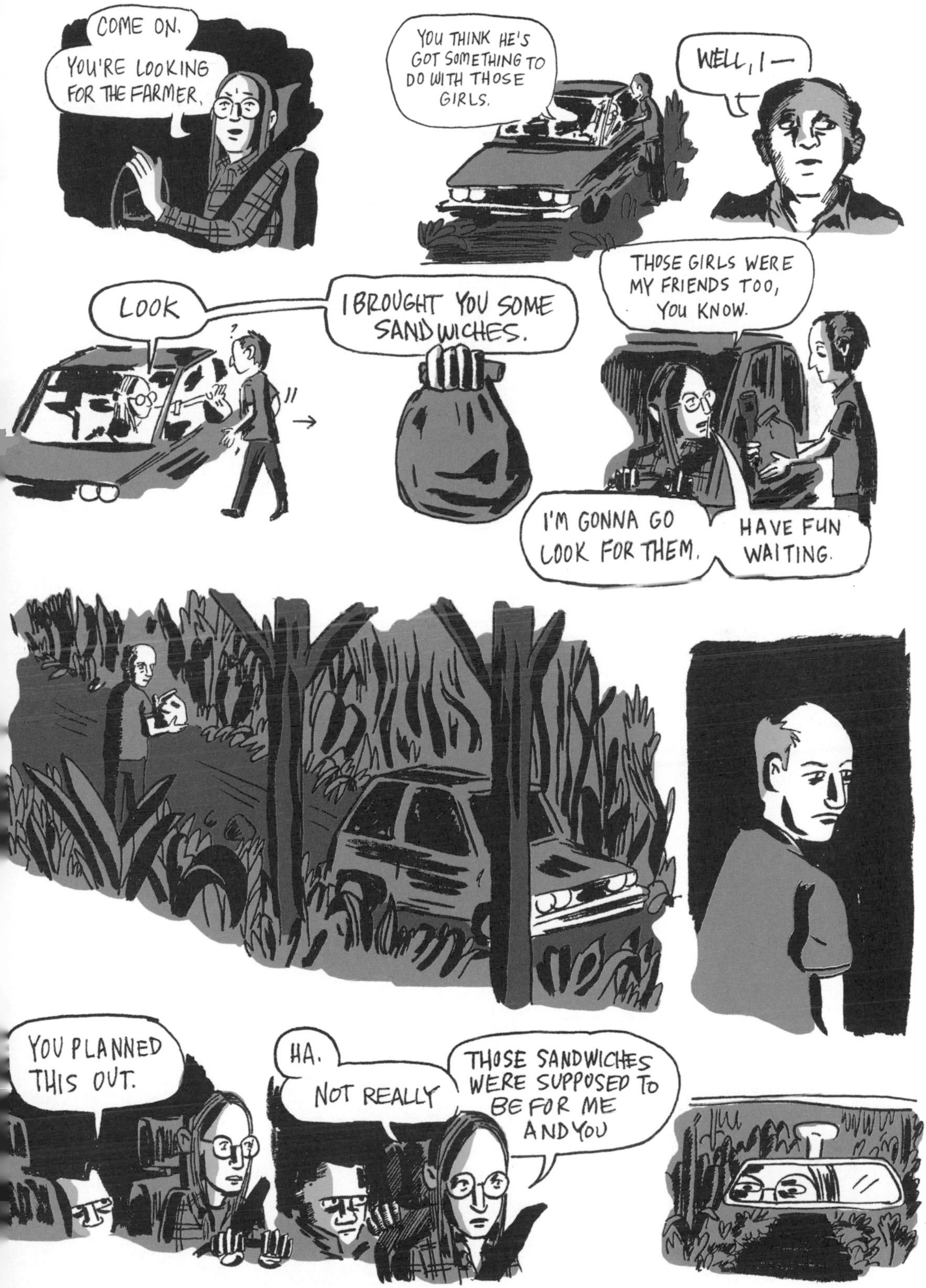
COME ON.
YOU'RE LOOKING FOR THE FARMER.
YOU THINK HE'S GOT SOMETHING TO DO WITH THOSE GIRLS.
WELL, I—
LOOK
I BROUGHT YOU SOME SANDWICHES.
THOSE GIRLS WERE MY FRIENDS TOO, YOU KNOW.
I'M GONNA GO LOOK FOR THEM.
HAVE FUN WAITING.
YOU PLANNED THIS OUT.
HA.
NOT REALLY
THOSE SANDWICHES WERE SUPPOSED TO BE FOR ME AND YOU

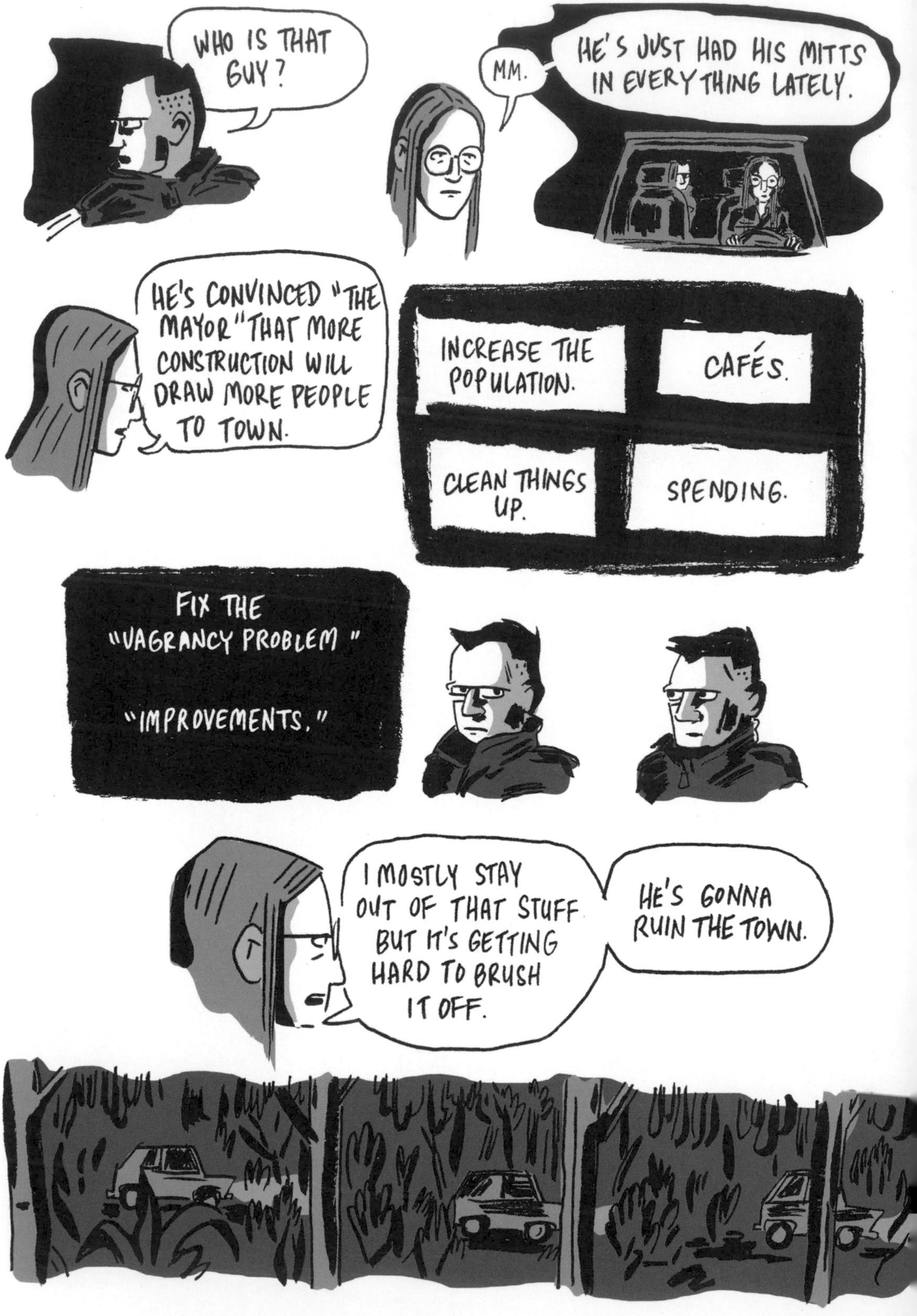
WHO IS THAT GUY?
MM.
HE'S JUST HAD HIS MITTS IN EVERYTHING LATELY.
HE'S CONVINCED "THE MAYOR" THAT MORE CONSTRUCTION WILL DRAW MORE PEOPLE TO TOWN.
INCREASE THE POPULATION.
CAFÉS.
CLEAN THINGS UP.
SPENDING.
FIX THE "VAGRANCY PROBLEM"
"IMPROVEMENTS."
I MOSTLY STAY OUT OF THAT STUFF BUT IT'S GETTING HARD TO BRUSH IT OFF.
HE'S GONNA RUIN THE TOWN.

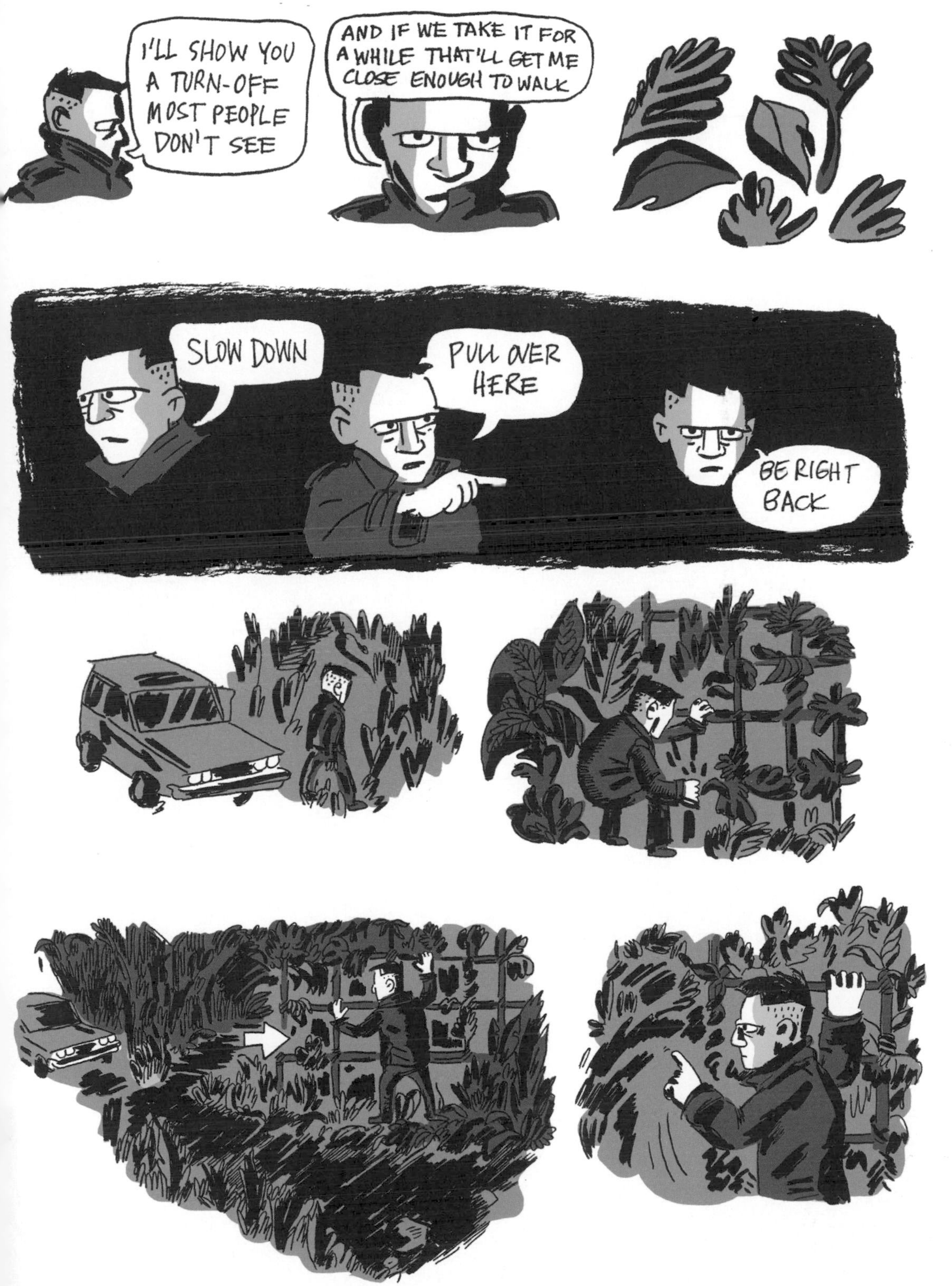
I'LL SHOW YOU A TURN-OFF MOST PEOPLE DON'T SEE
AND IF WE TAKE IT FOR A WHILE THAT'LL GET ME CLOSE ENOUGH TO WALK
SLOW DOWN
PULL OVER HERE
BE RIGHT BACK

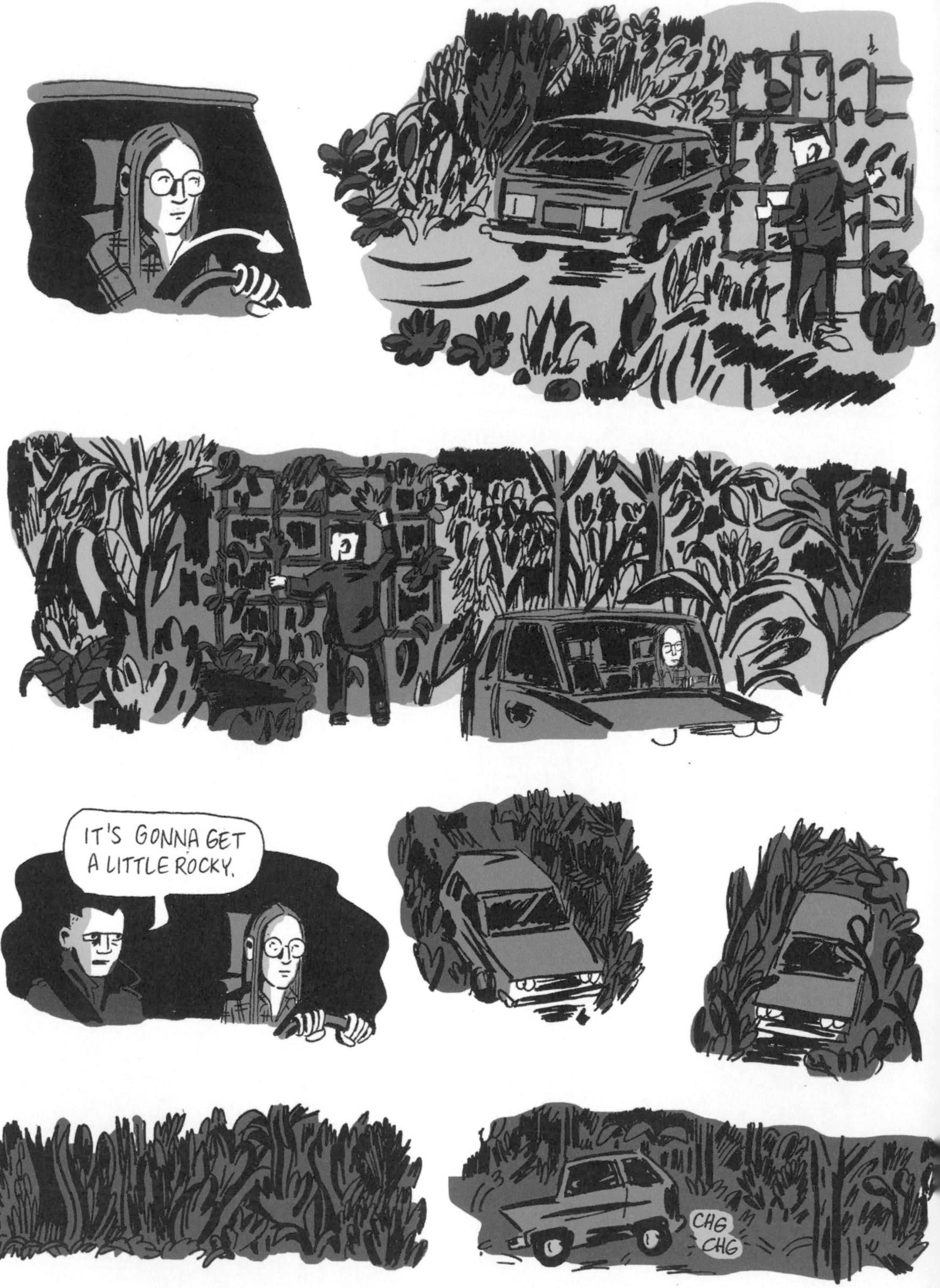
IT'S GONNA GET A LITTLE ROCKY.
CHG
CHG

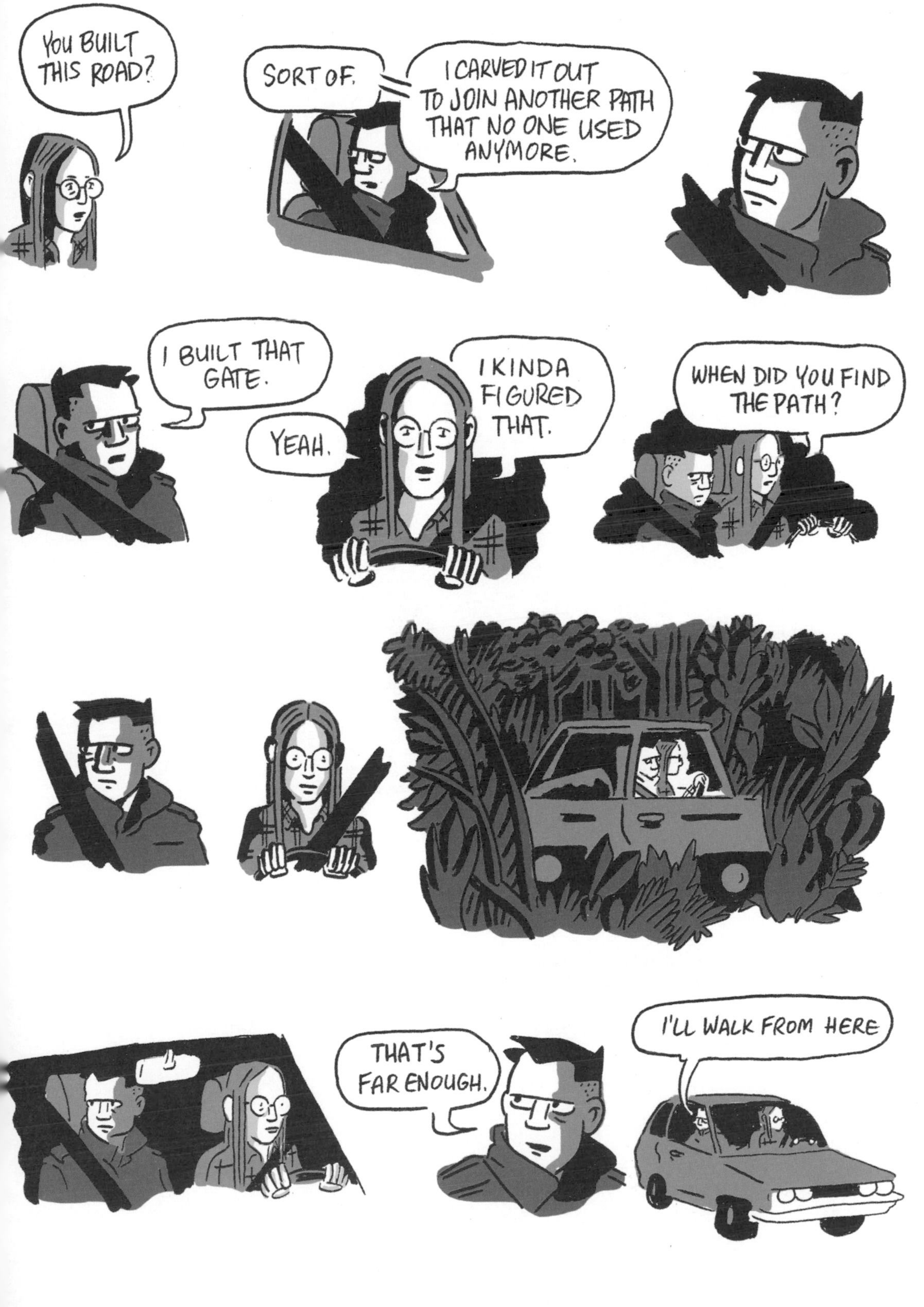

YOU BUILT THIS ROAD?
SORT OF.
I CARVED IT OUT TO JOIN ANOTHER PATH THAT NO ONE USED ANYMORE.
I BUILT THAT GATE.
YEAH.
I KINDA FIGURED THAT.
WHEN DID YOU FIND THE PATH?
THAT'S FAR ENOUGH.
I'LL WALK FROM HERE

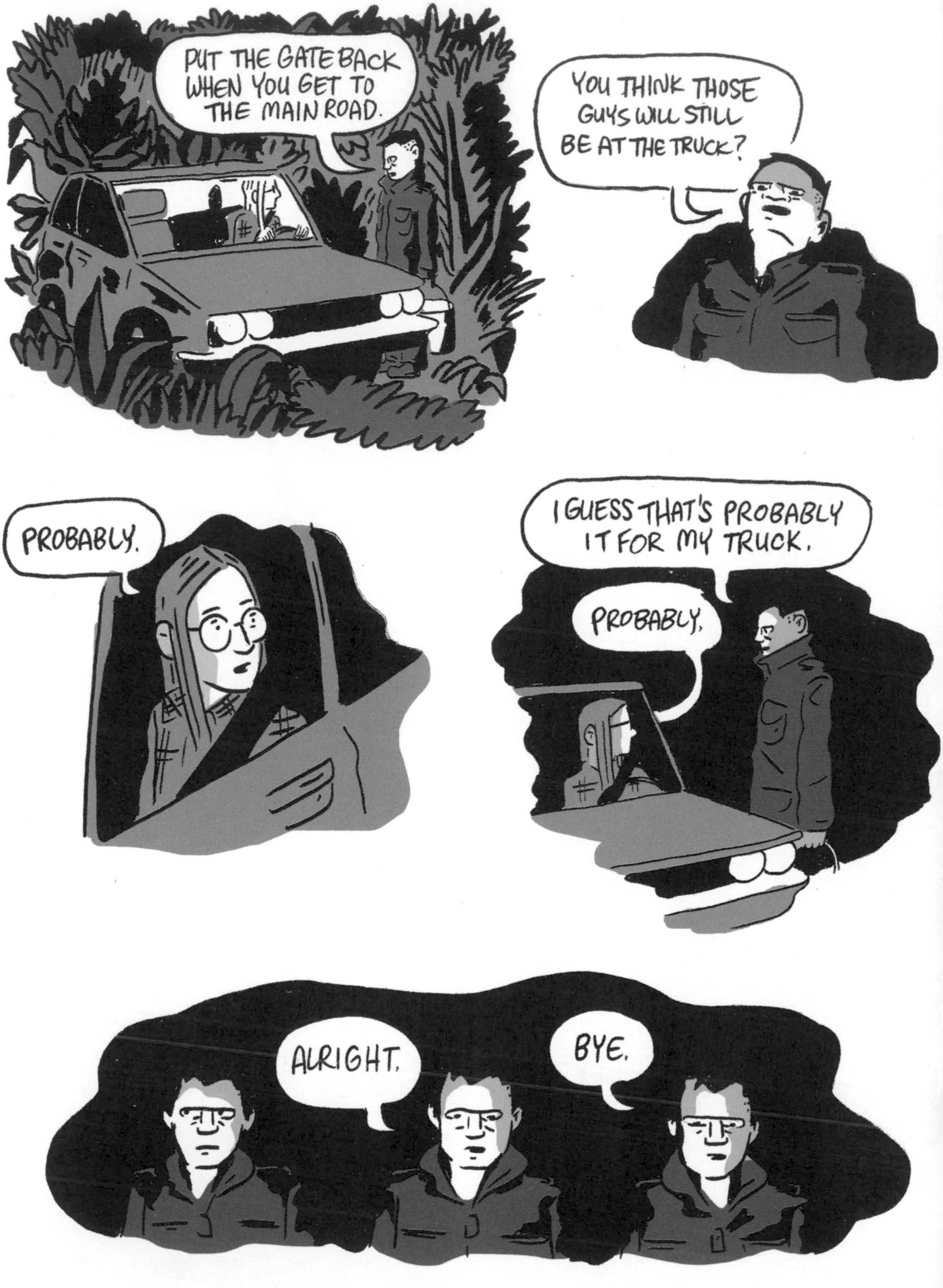
PUT THE GATE BACK WHEN YOU GET TO THE MAIN ROAD.
YOU THINK THOSE GUYS WILL STILL BE AT THE TRUCK?
PROBABLY.
I GUESS THAT'S PROBABLY IT FOR MY TRUCK.
PROBABLY.
ALRIGHT.
BYE.

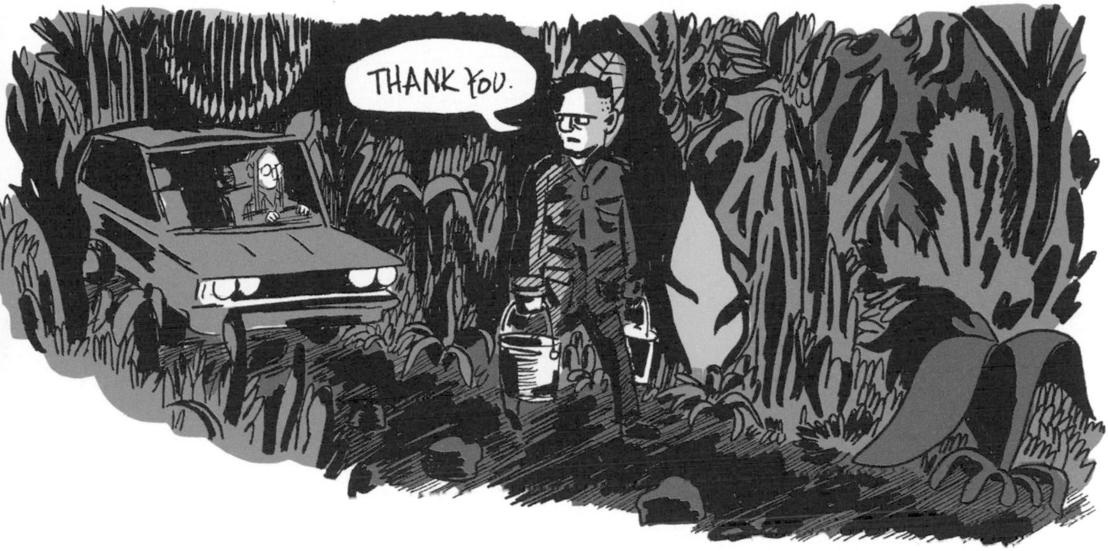
THANK YOU.

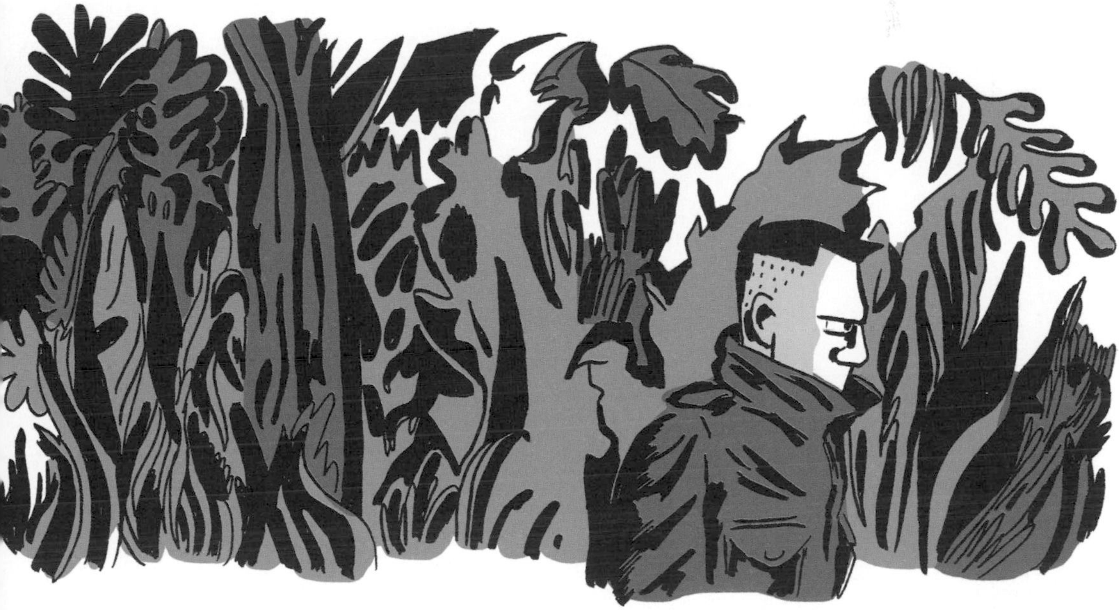

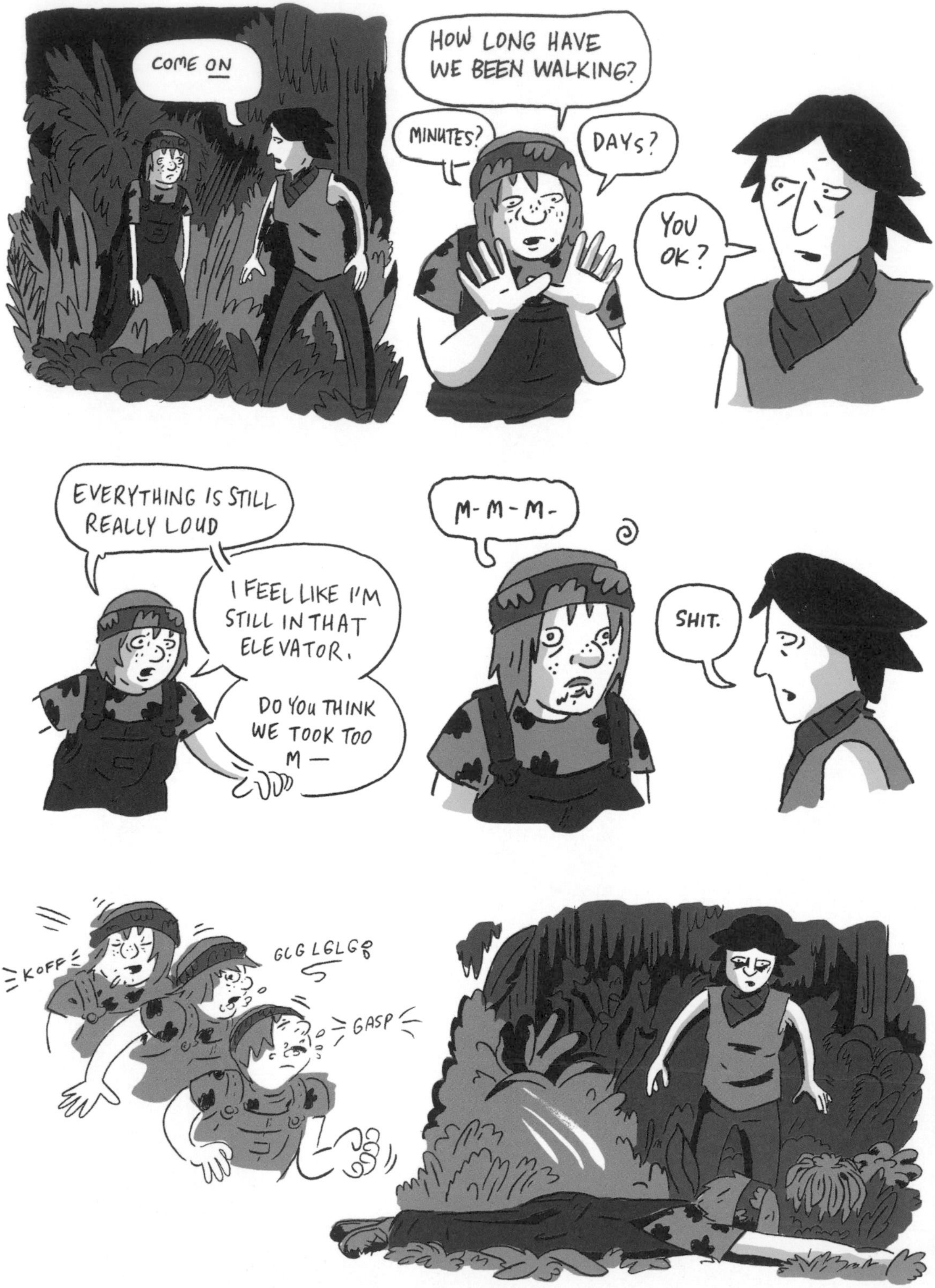
COME ON
HOW LONG HAVE WE BEEN WALKING?
MINUTES?
DAYS?
YOU OK?
EVERYTHING IS STILL REALLY LOUD
I FEEL LIKE I'M STILL IN THAT ELEVATOR.
DO YOU THINK WE TOOK TOO M—
M-M-M-
SHIT.
KOFF
GLG LGLG
GASP

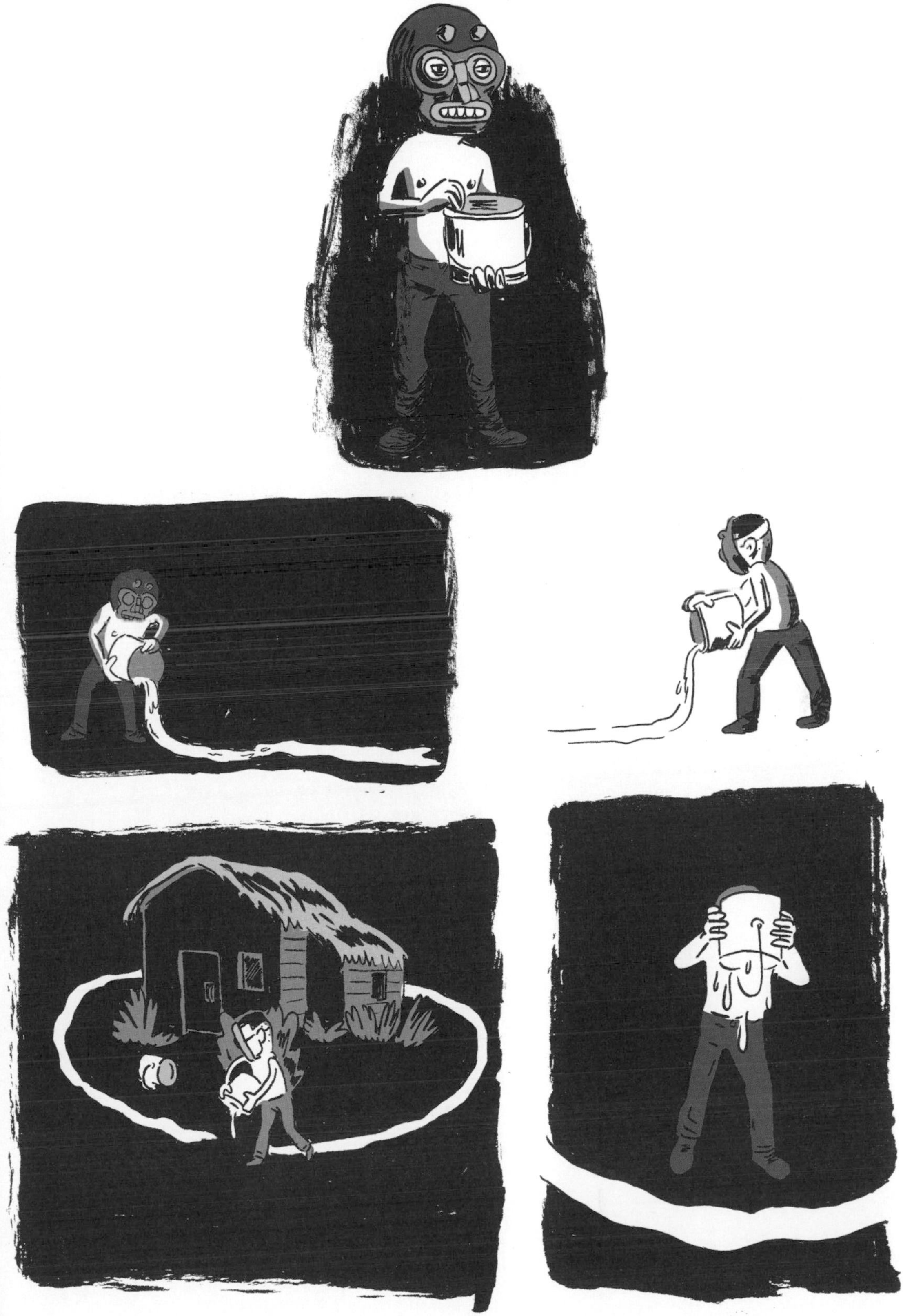

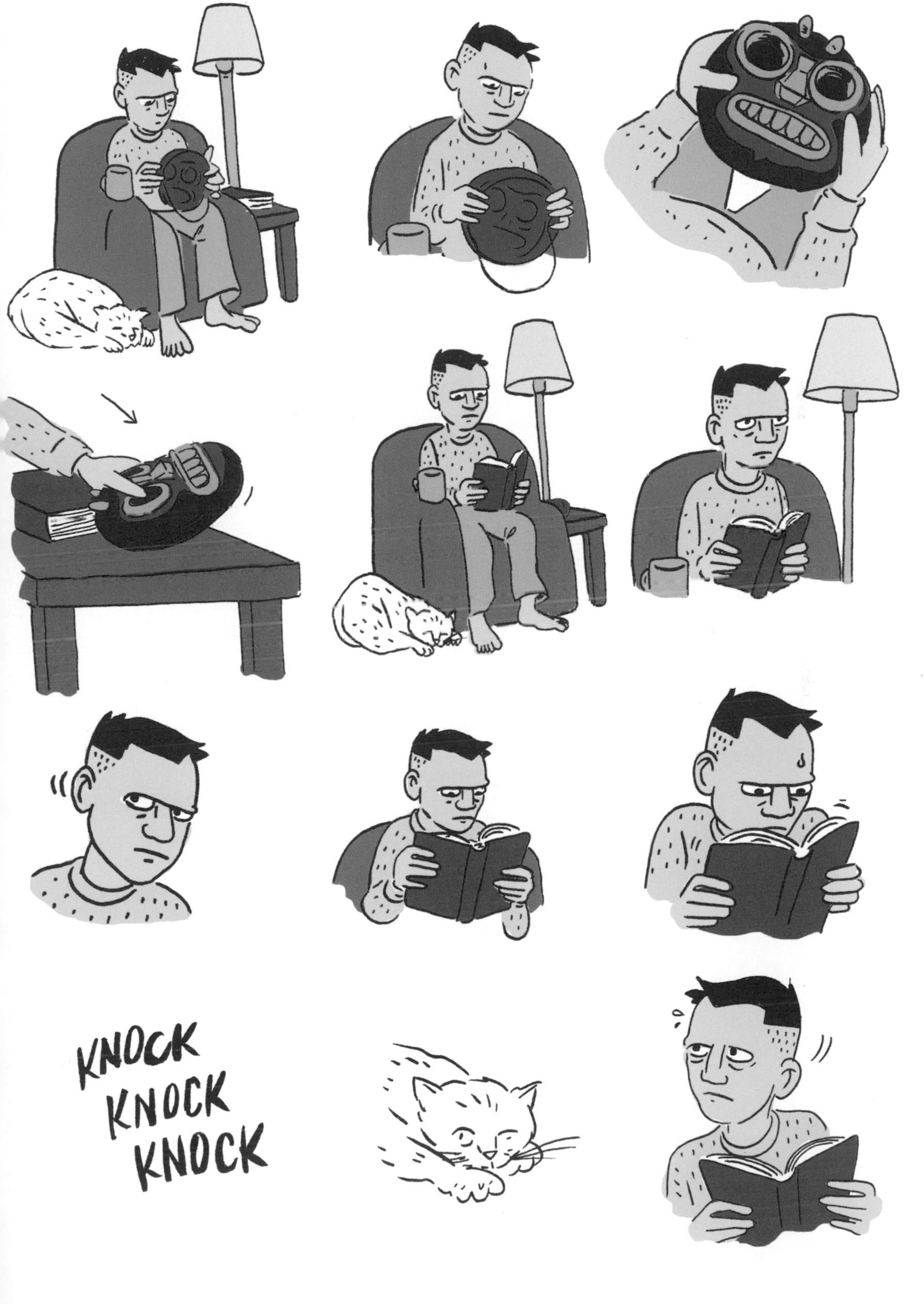
KNOCK
KNOCK
KNOCK

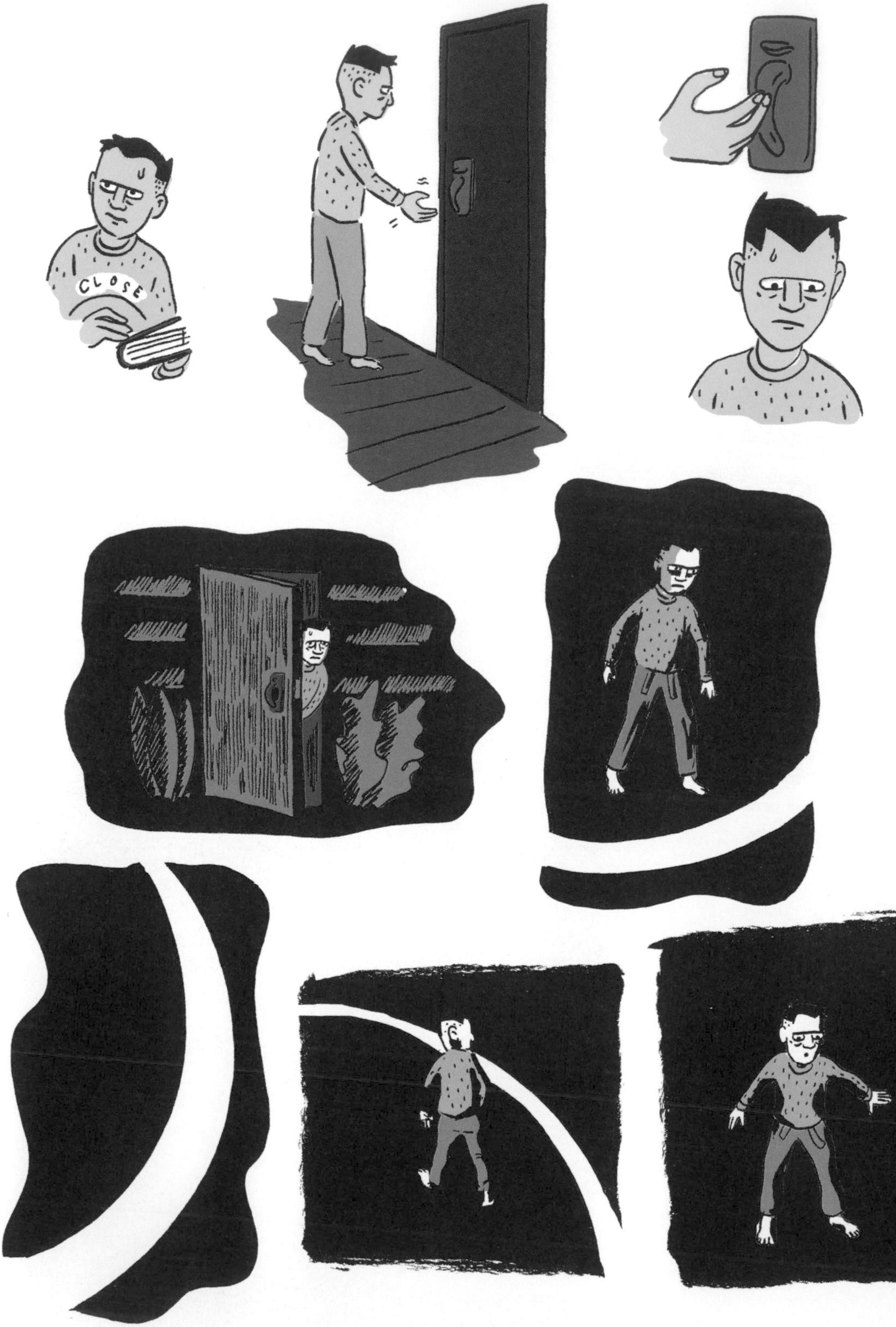
CLOSE

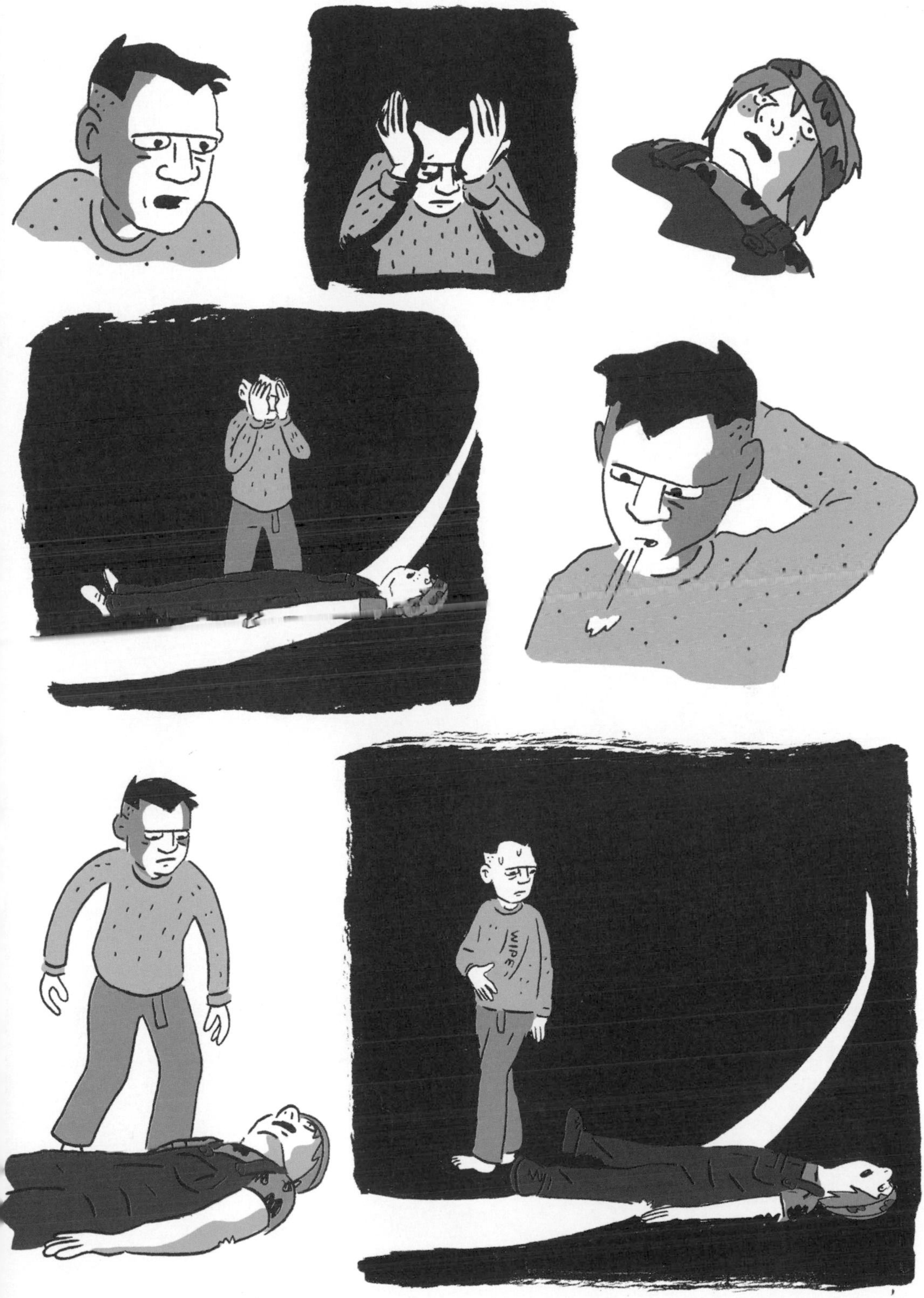
WIPE

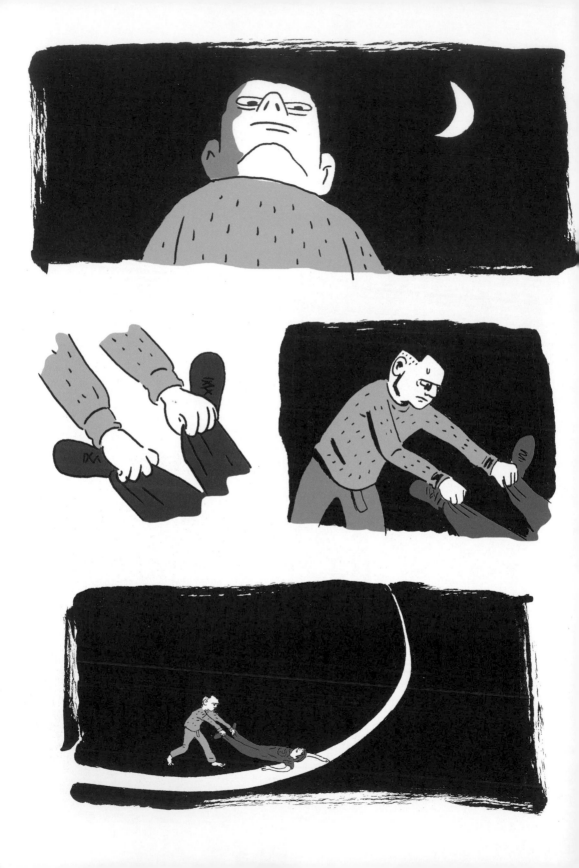

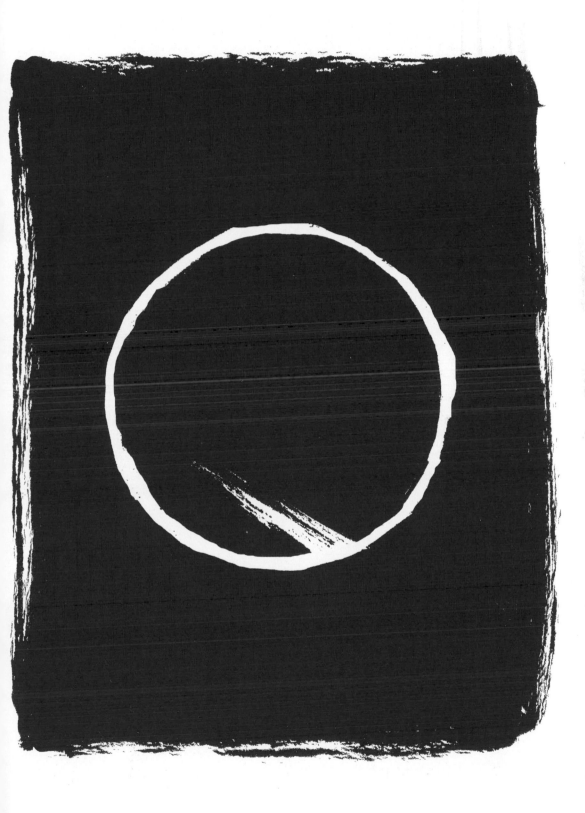

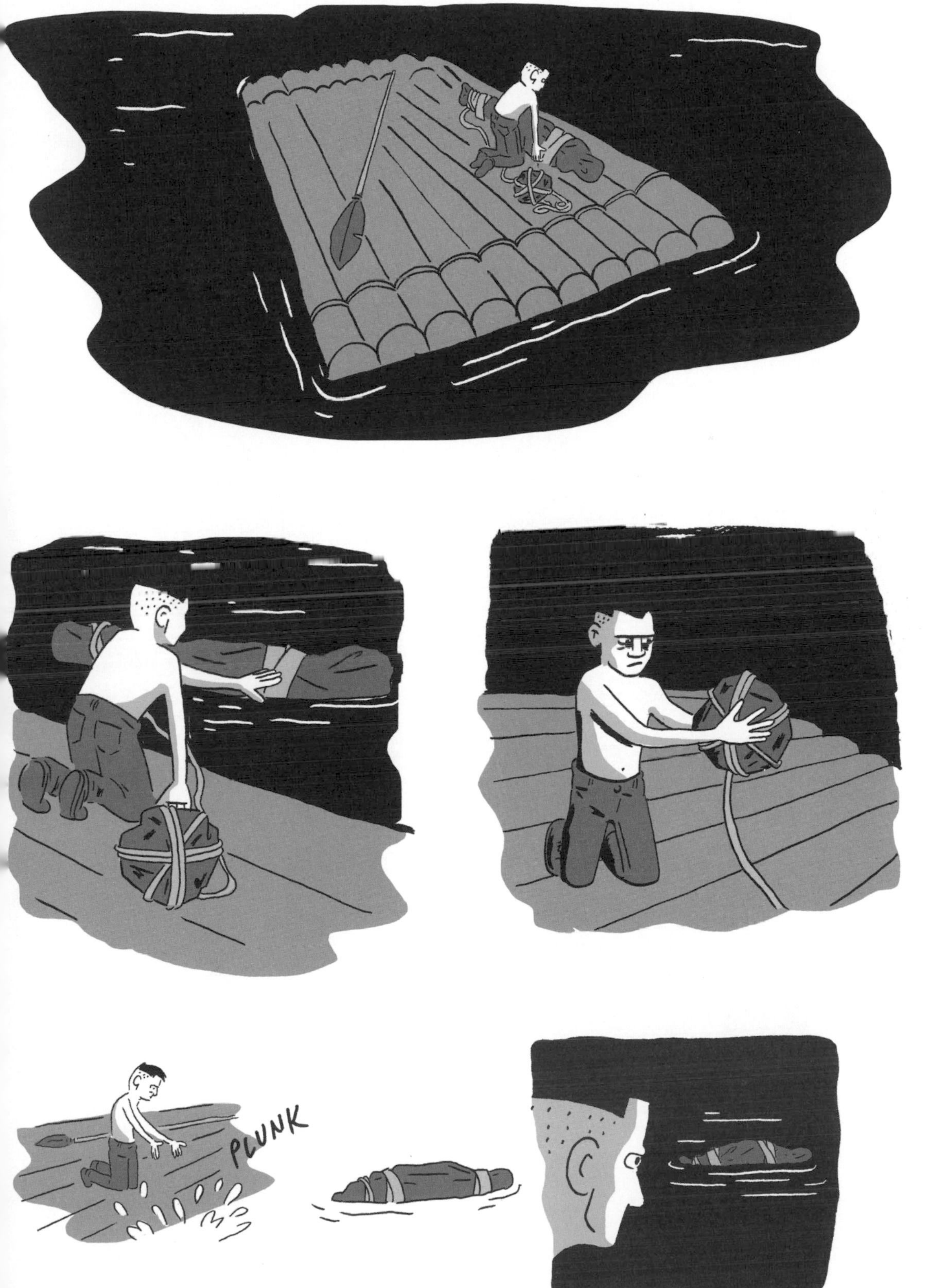
PLUNK

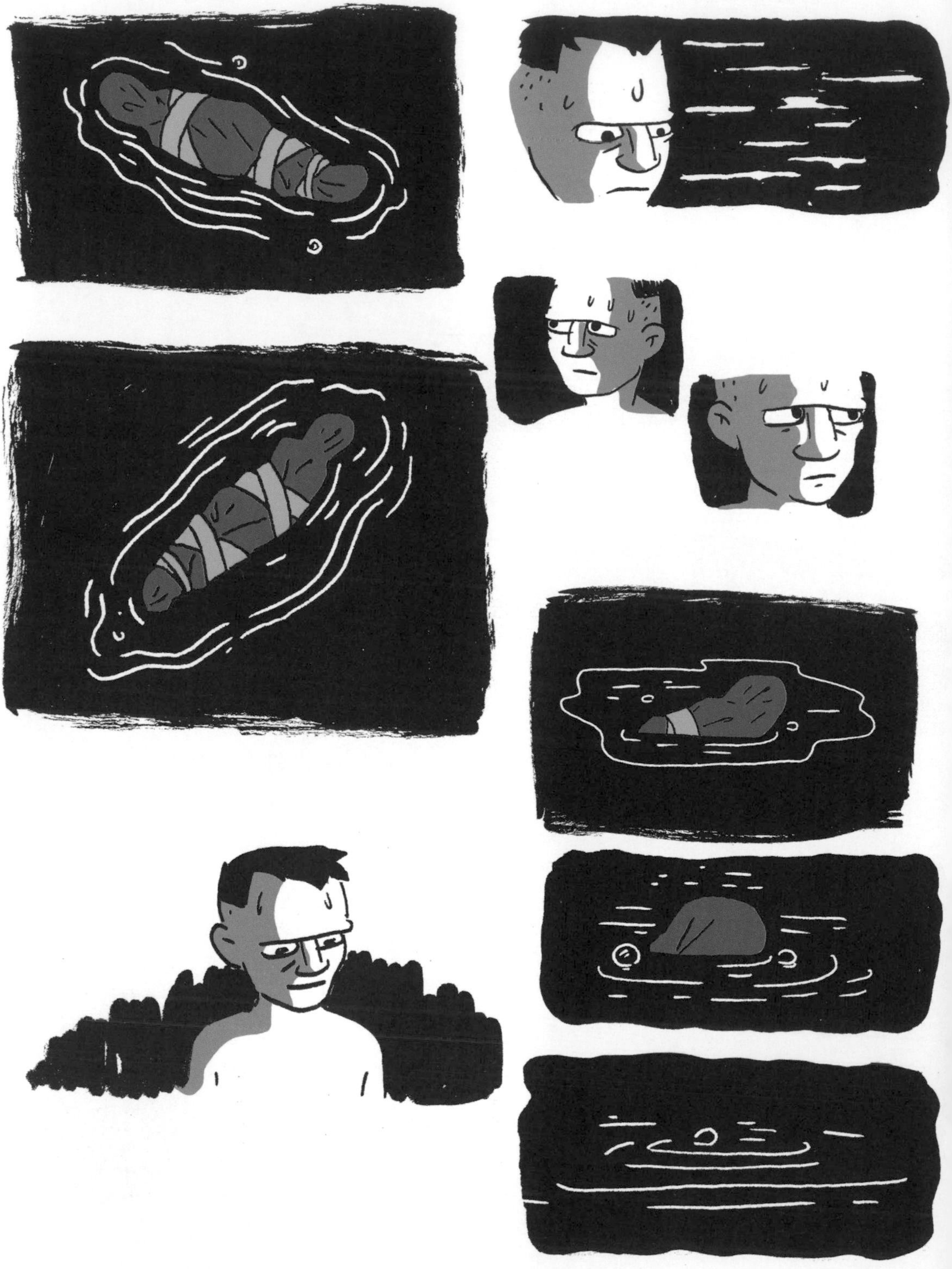

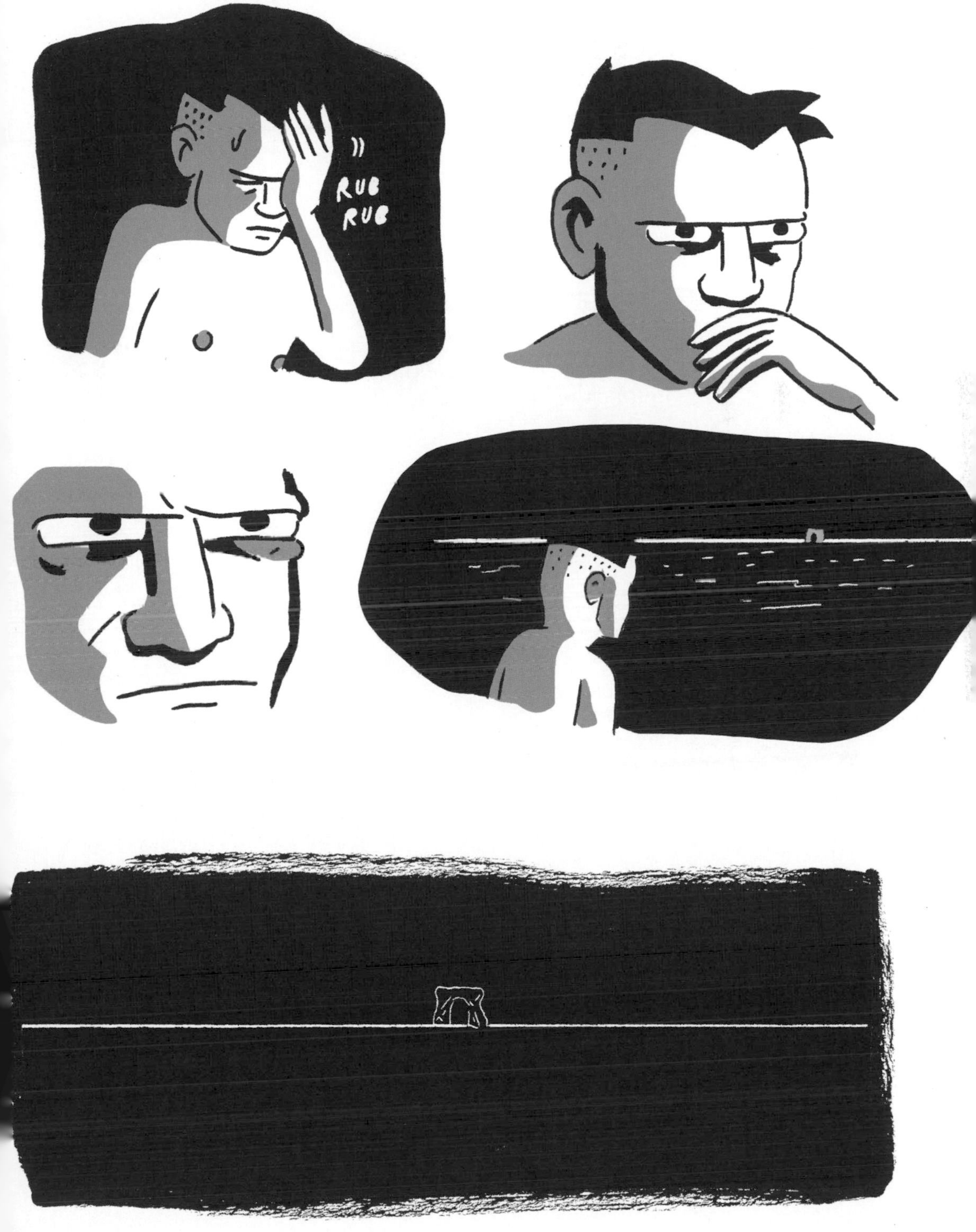
RUB
RUB

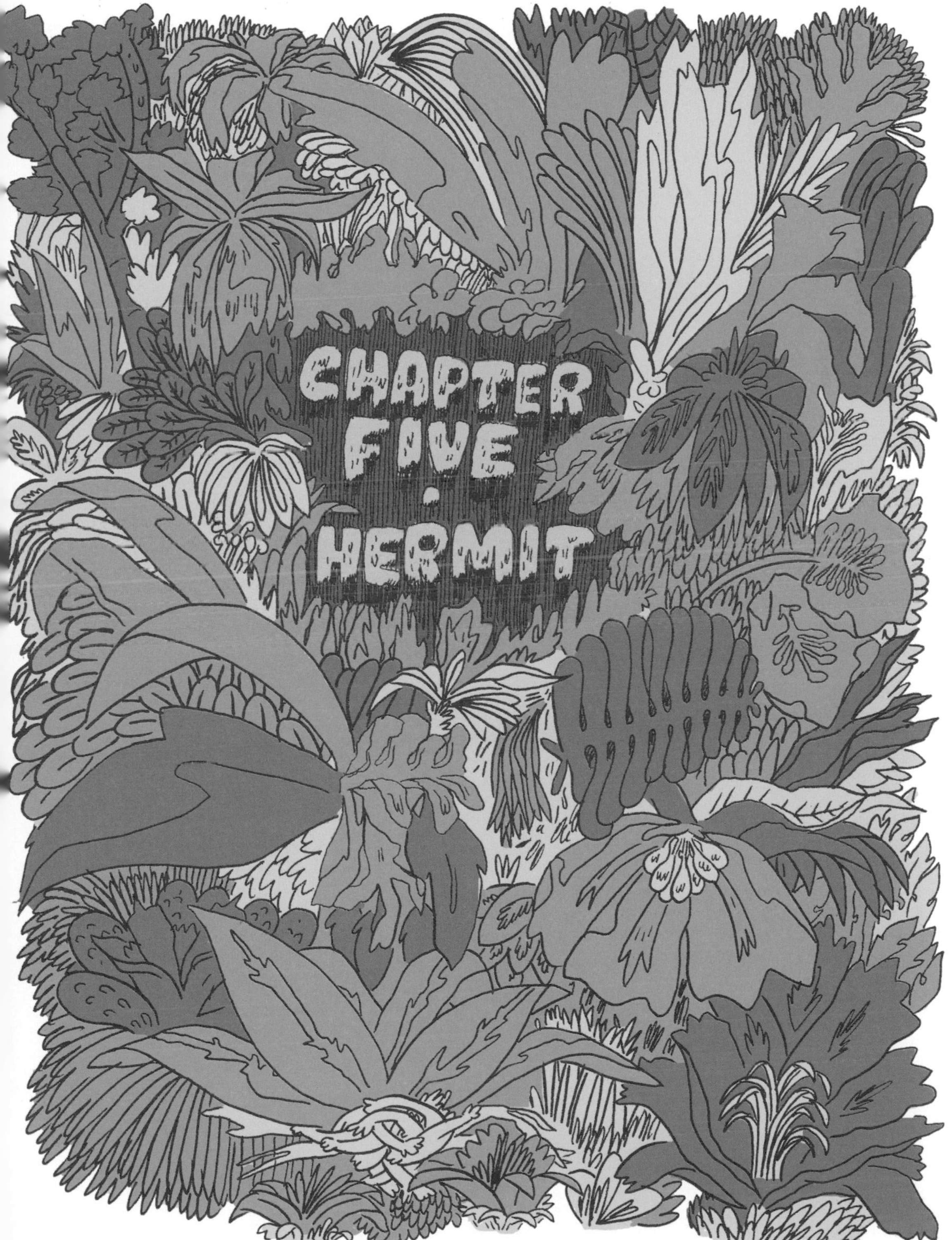
CHAPTER FIVE
HERMIT

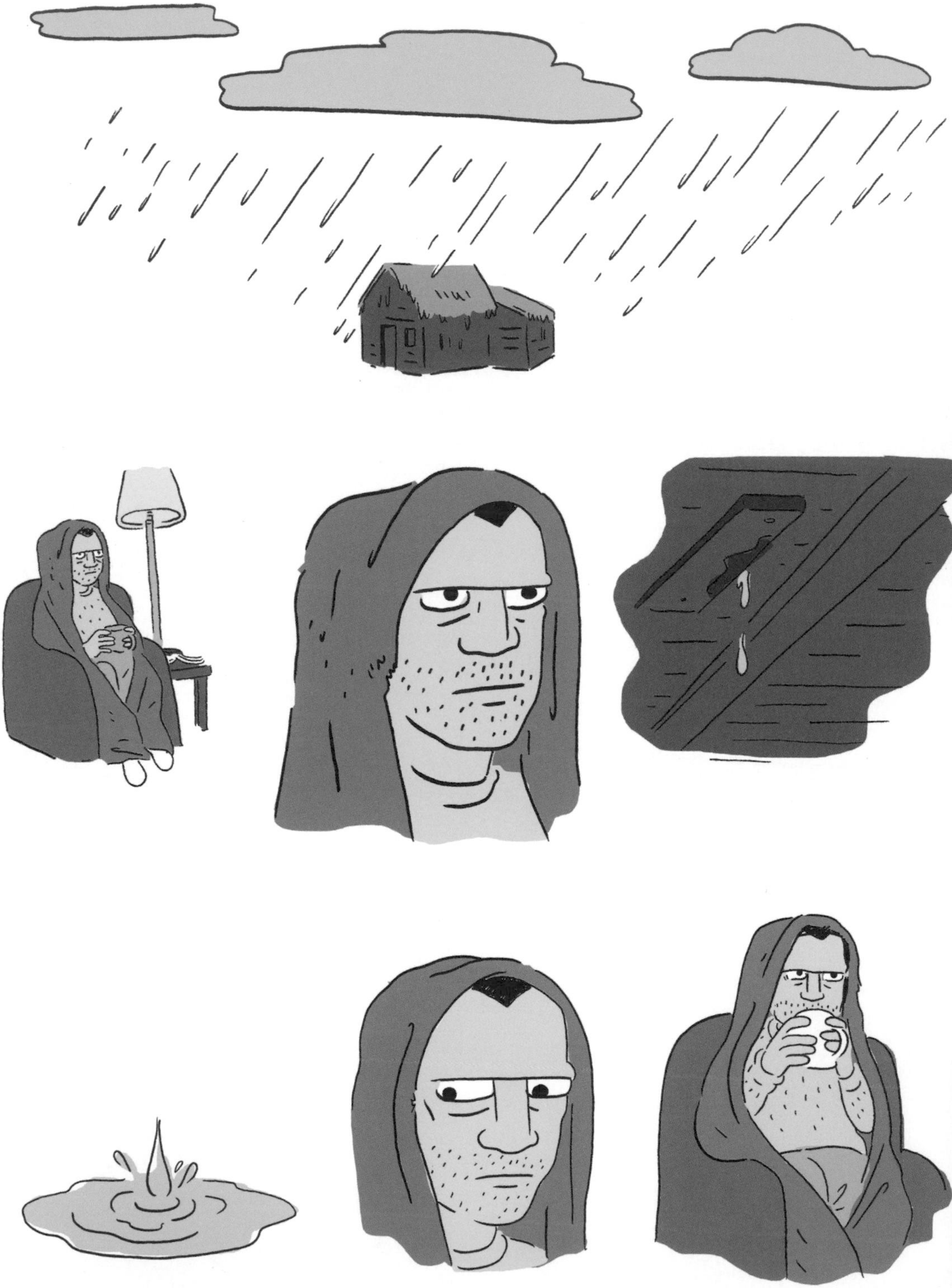

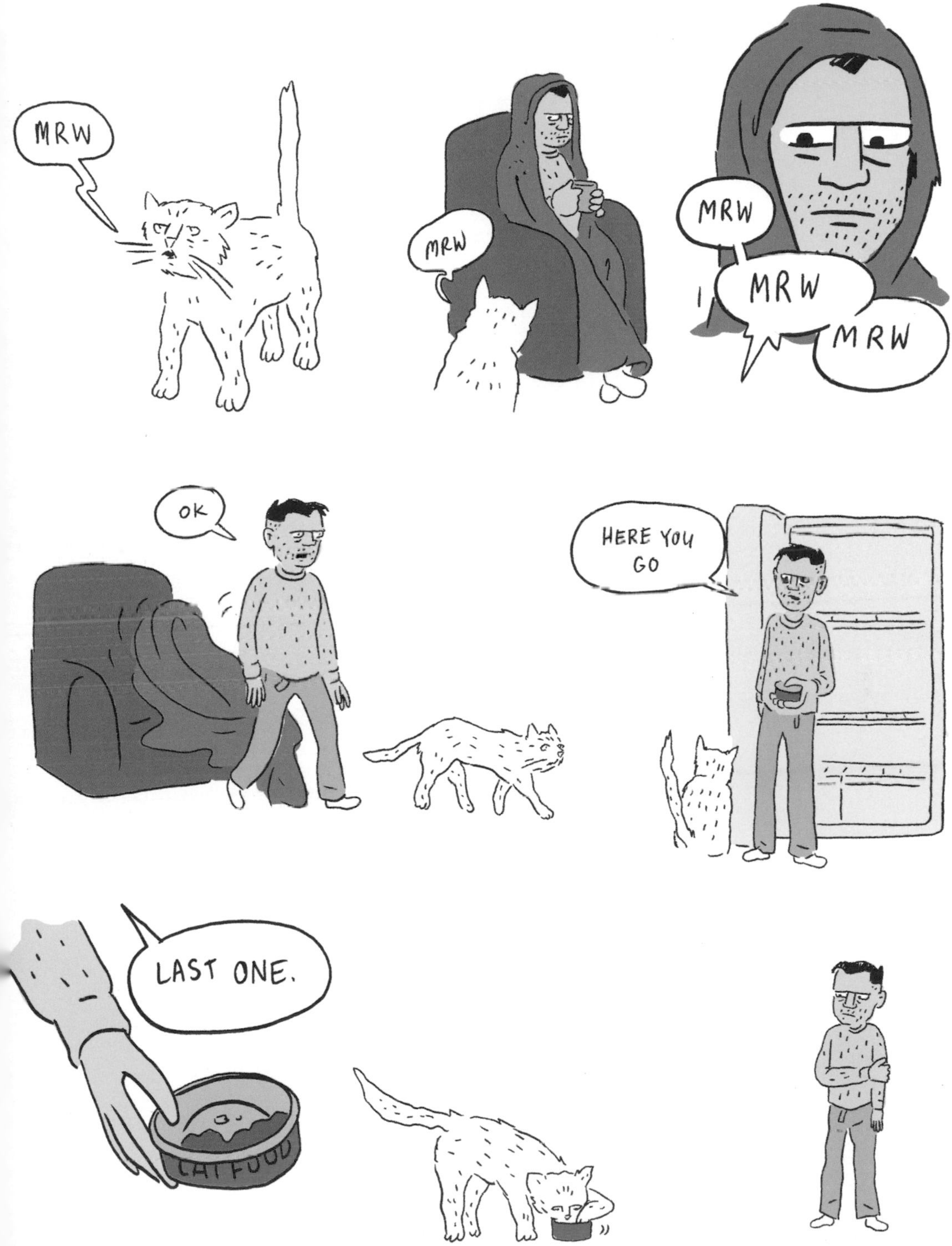
MRW
MRW
MRW
MRW
MRW
OK
HERE YOU GO
LAST ONE.
CAT FOOD

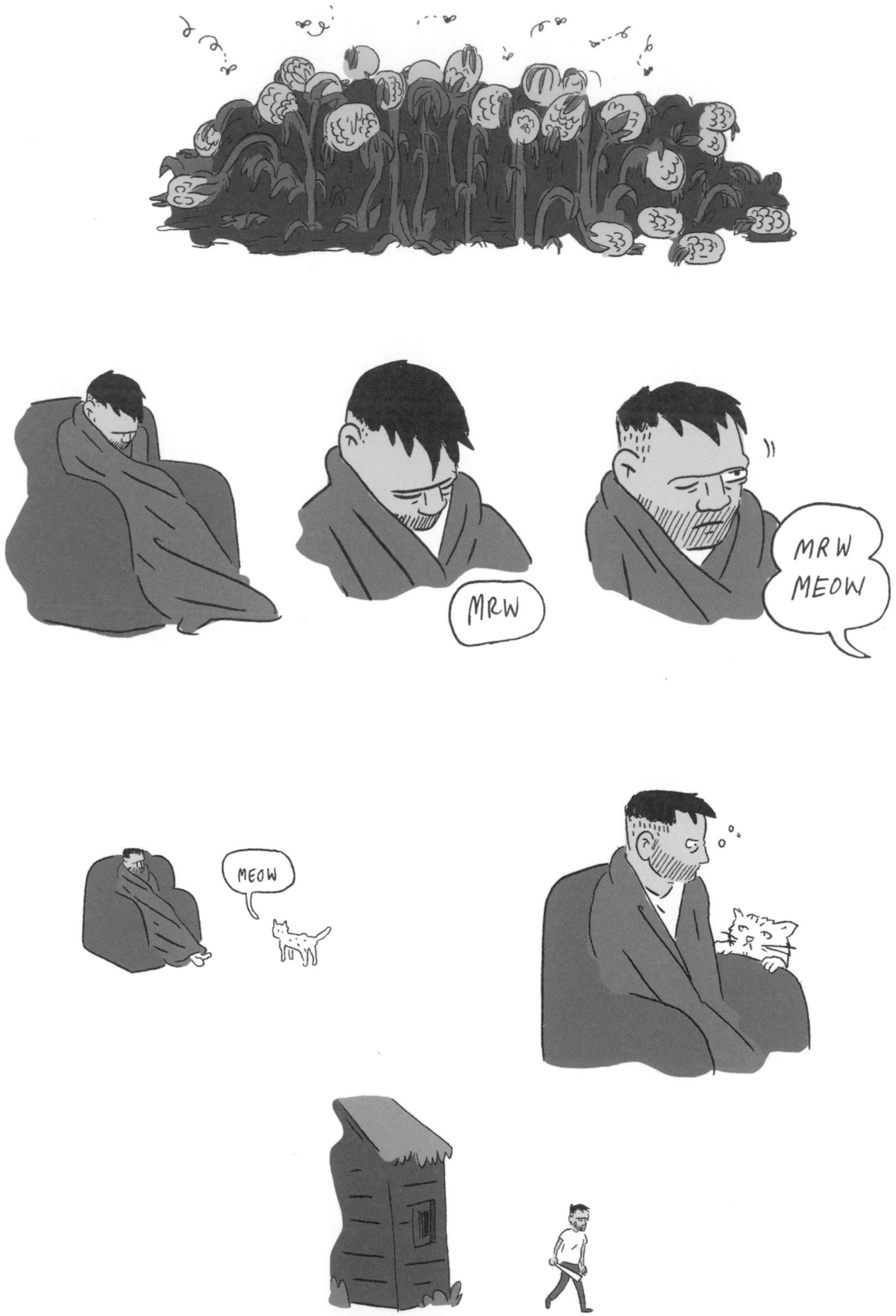
MRW
MRW MEOW
MEOW

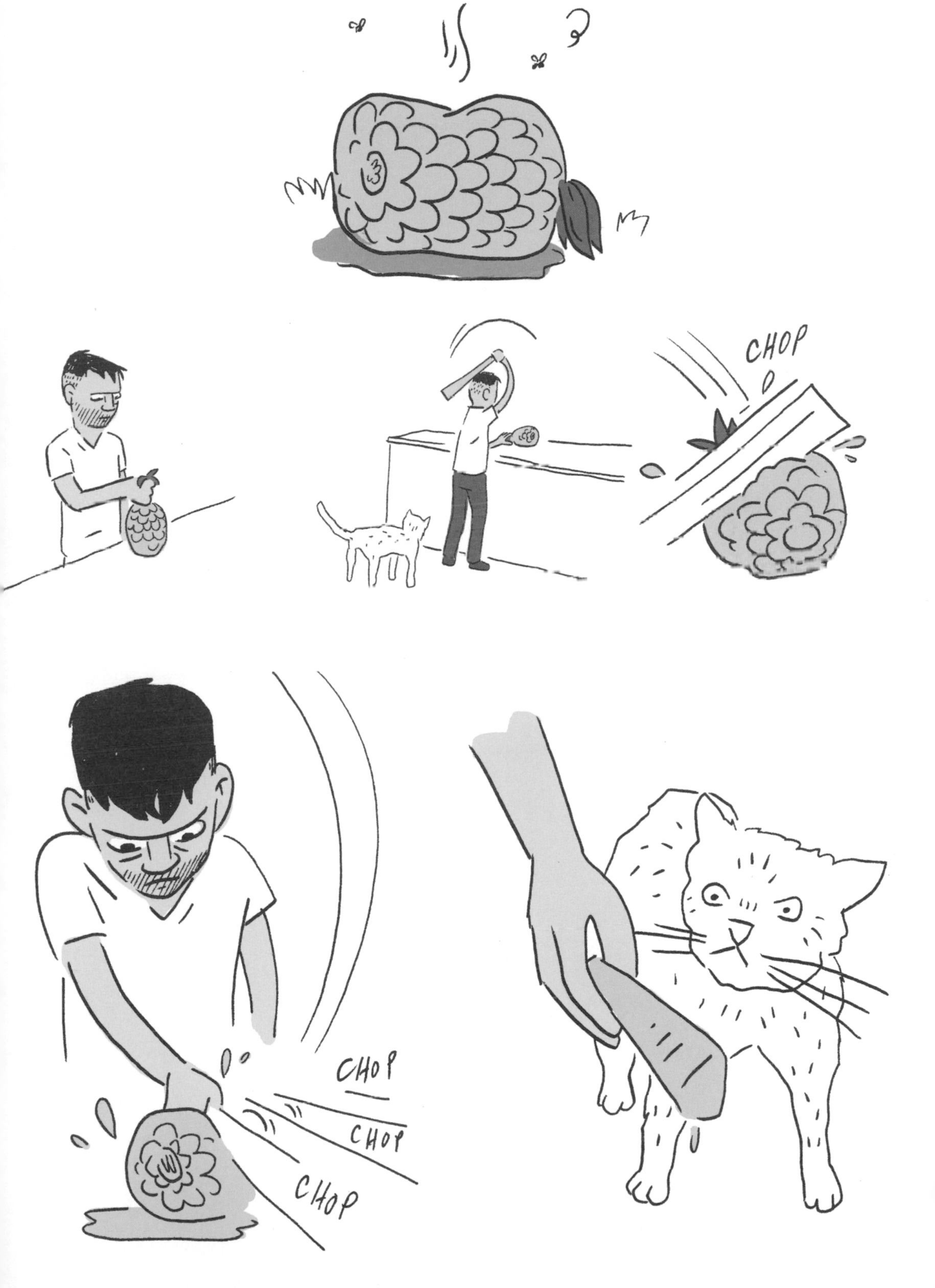
CHOP
CHOP
CHOP
CHOP

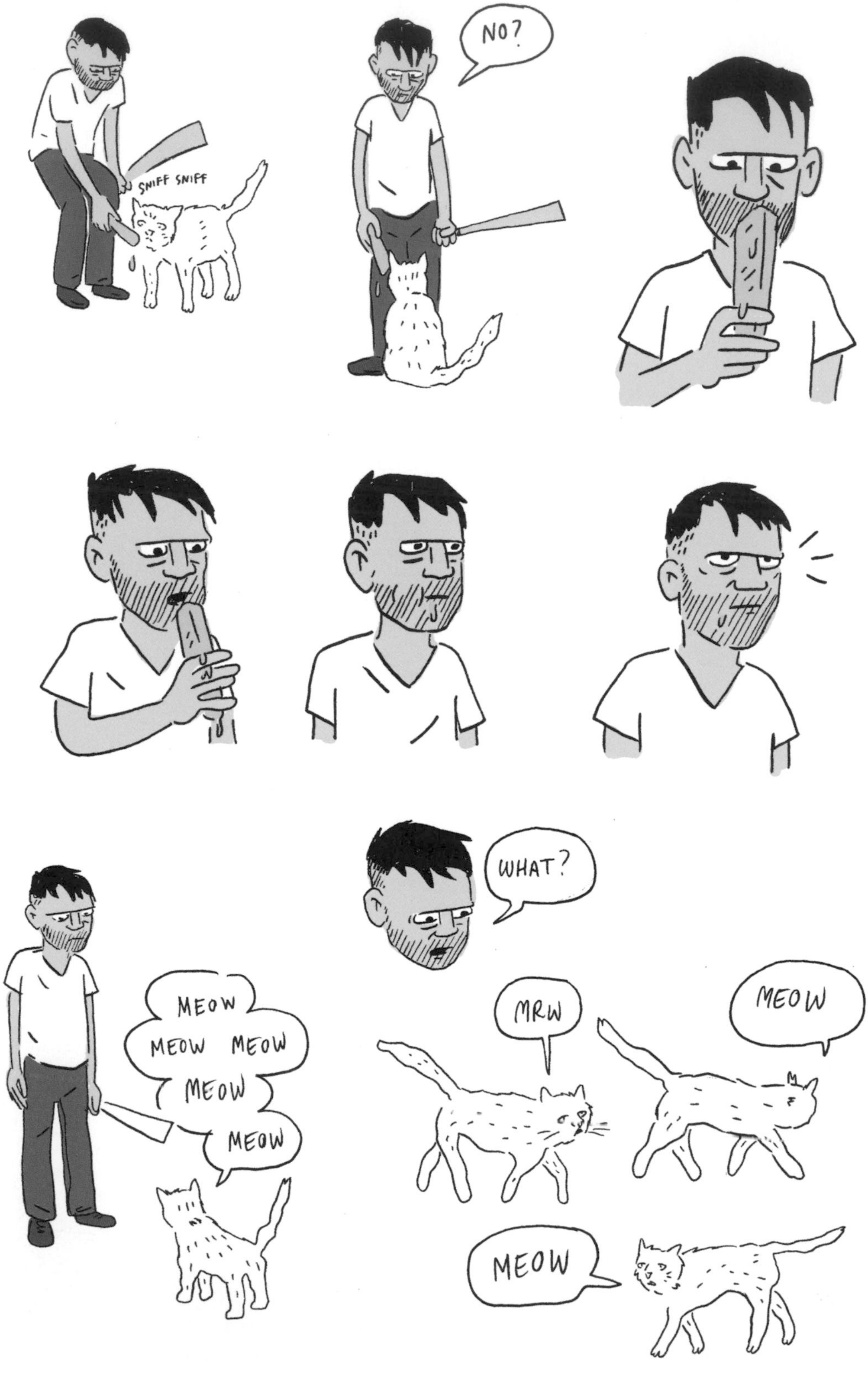

SNIFF SNIFF
NO?
WHAT?
MEOW
MEOW MEOW
MEOW
MEOW
MRW
MEOW
MEOW

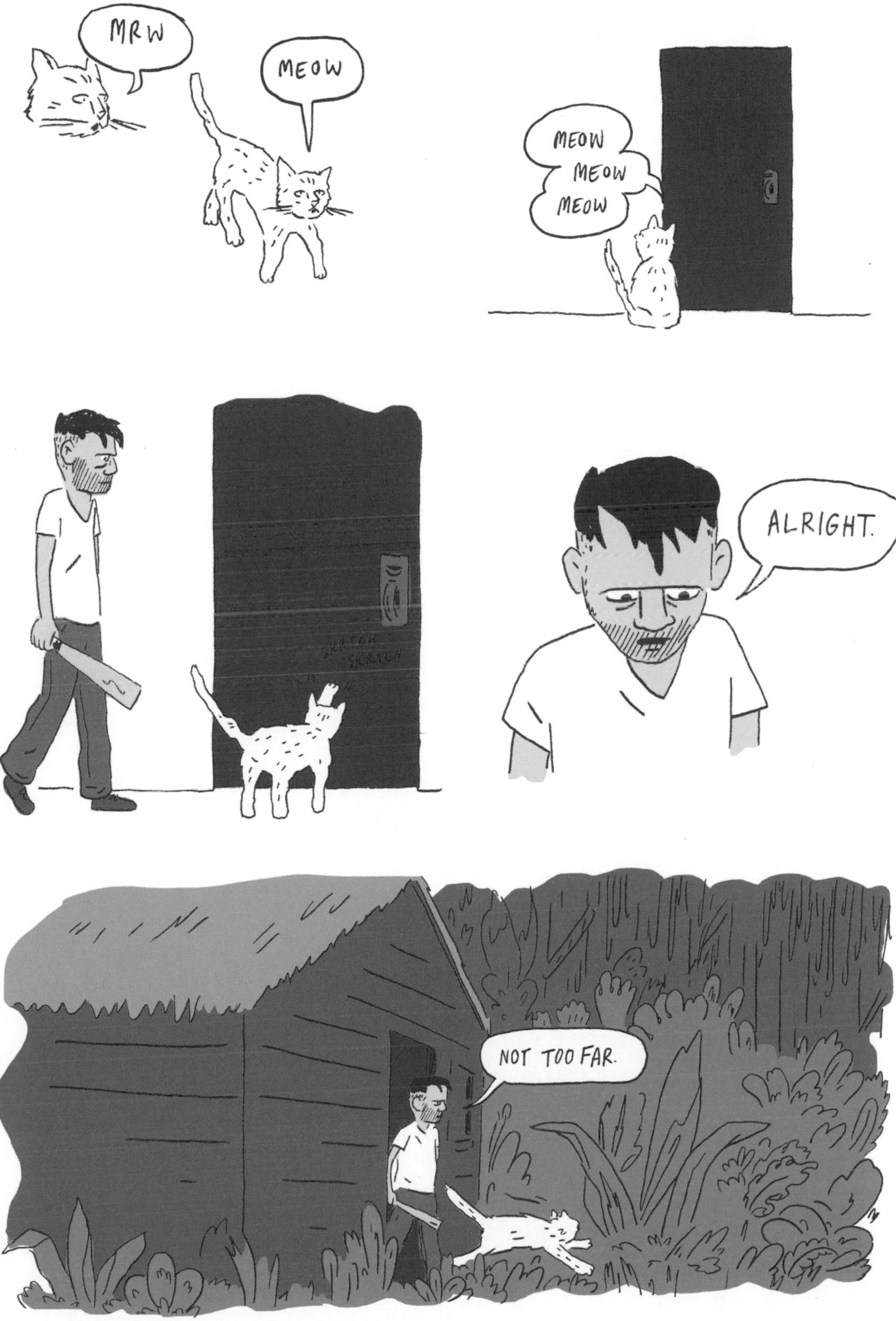
MRW
MEOW
MEOW
MEOW
MEOW
ALRIGHT.
NOT TOO FAR.

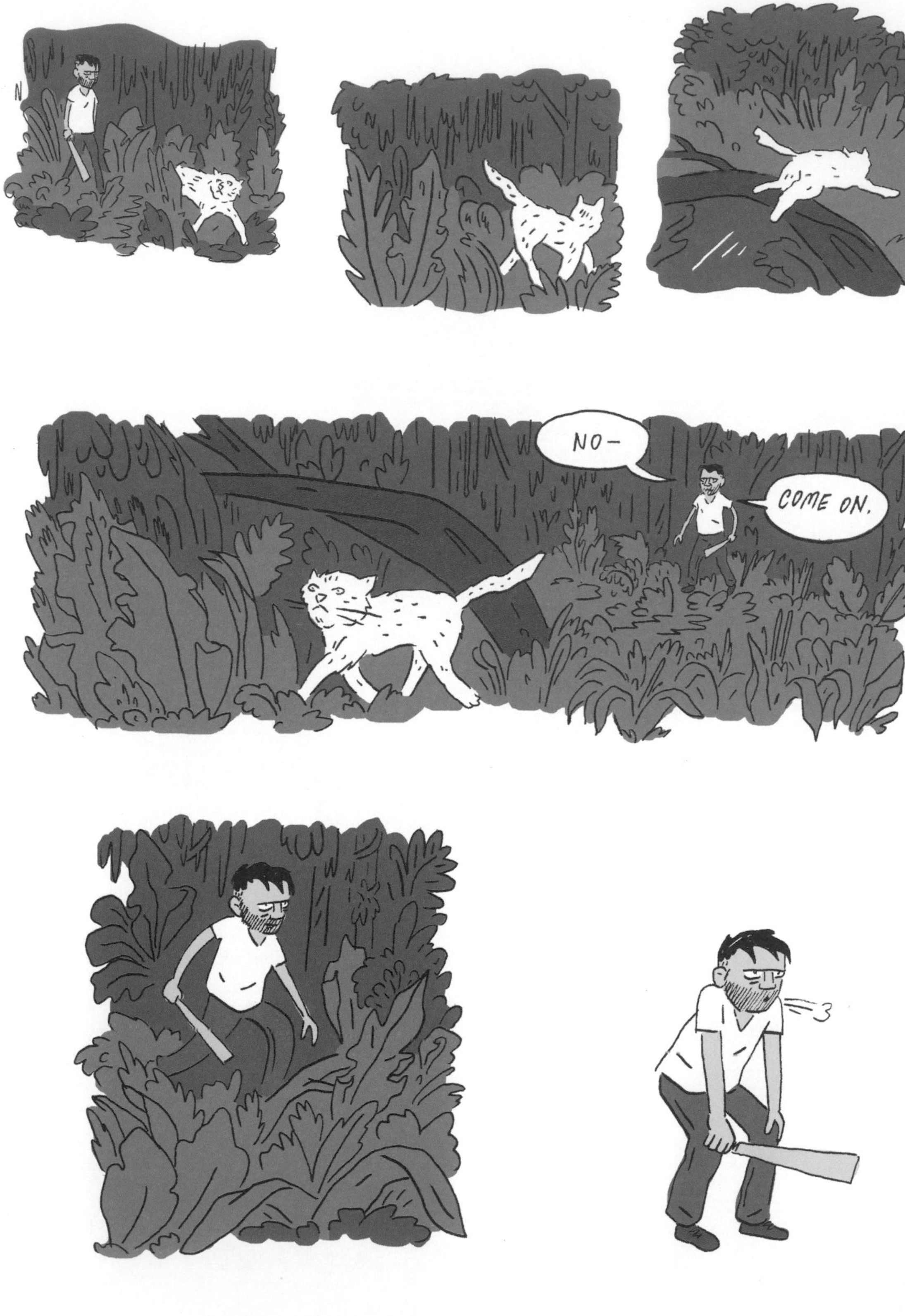
N
NO–
COME ON.

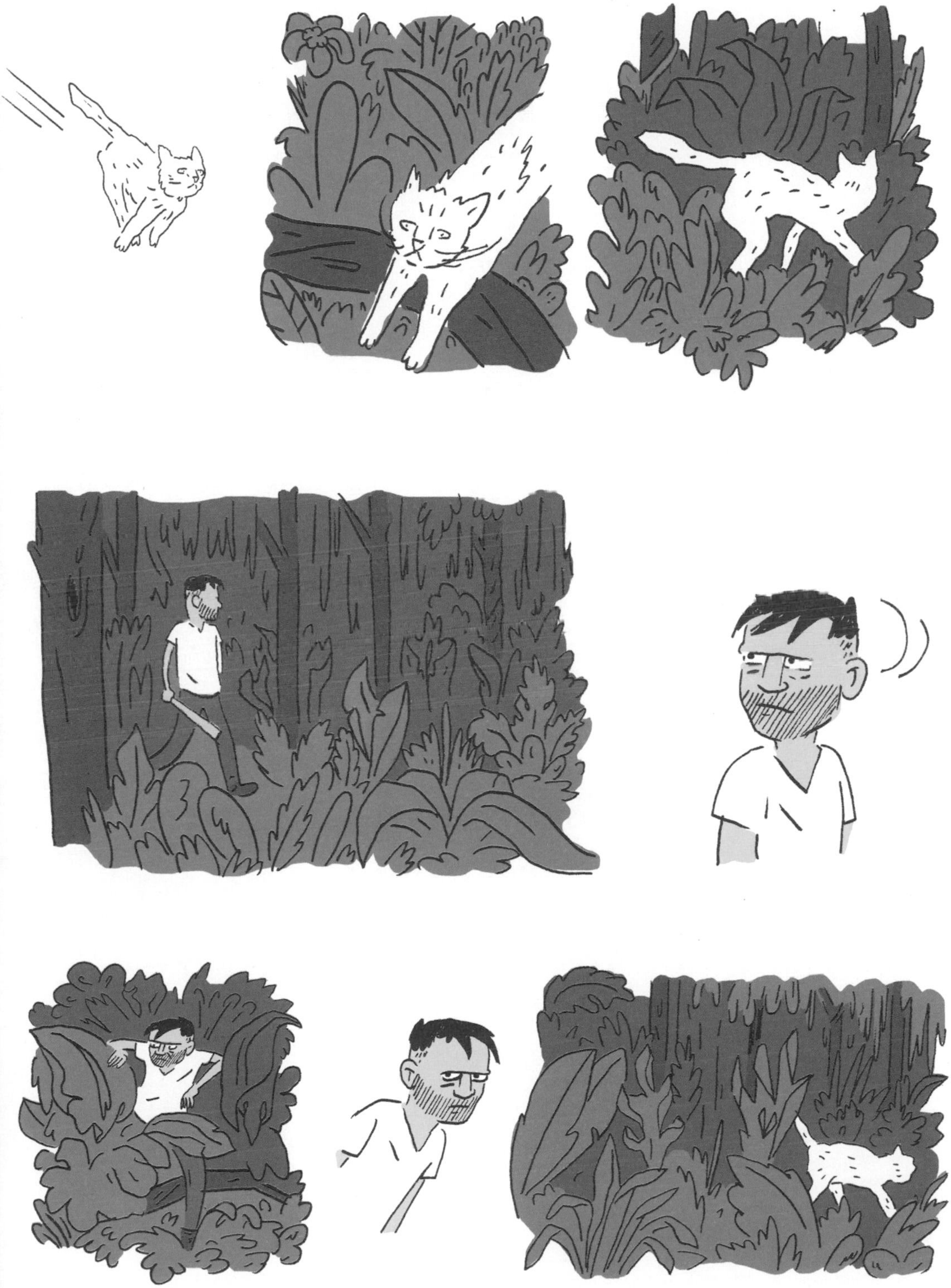

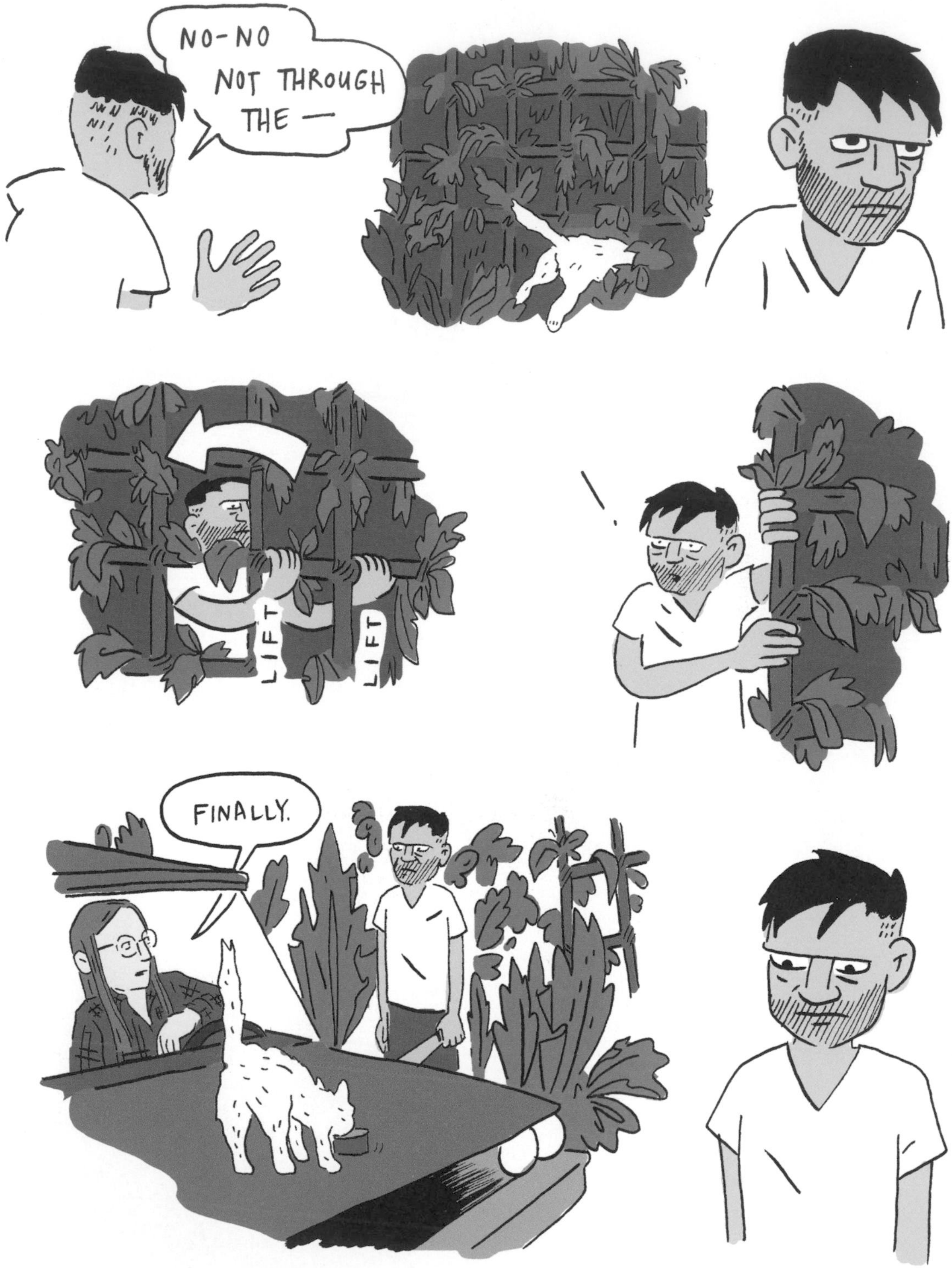
NO-NO NOT THROUGH THE —
LIFT
LIFT
FINALLY.

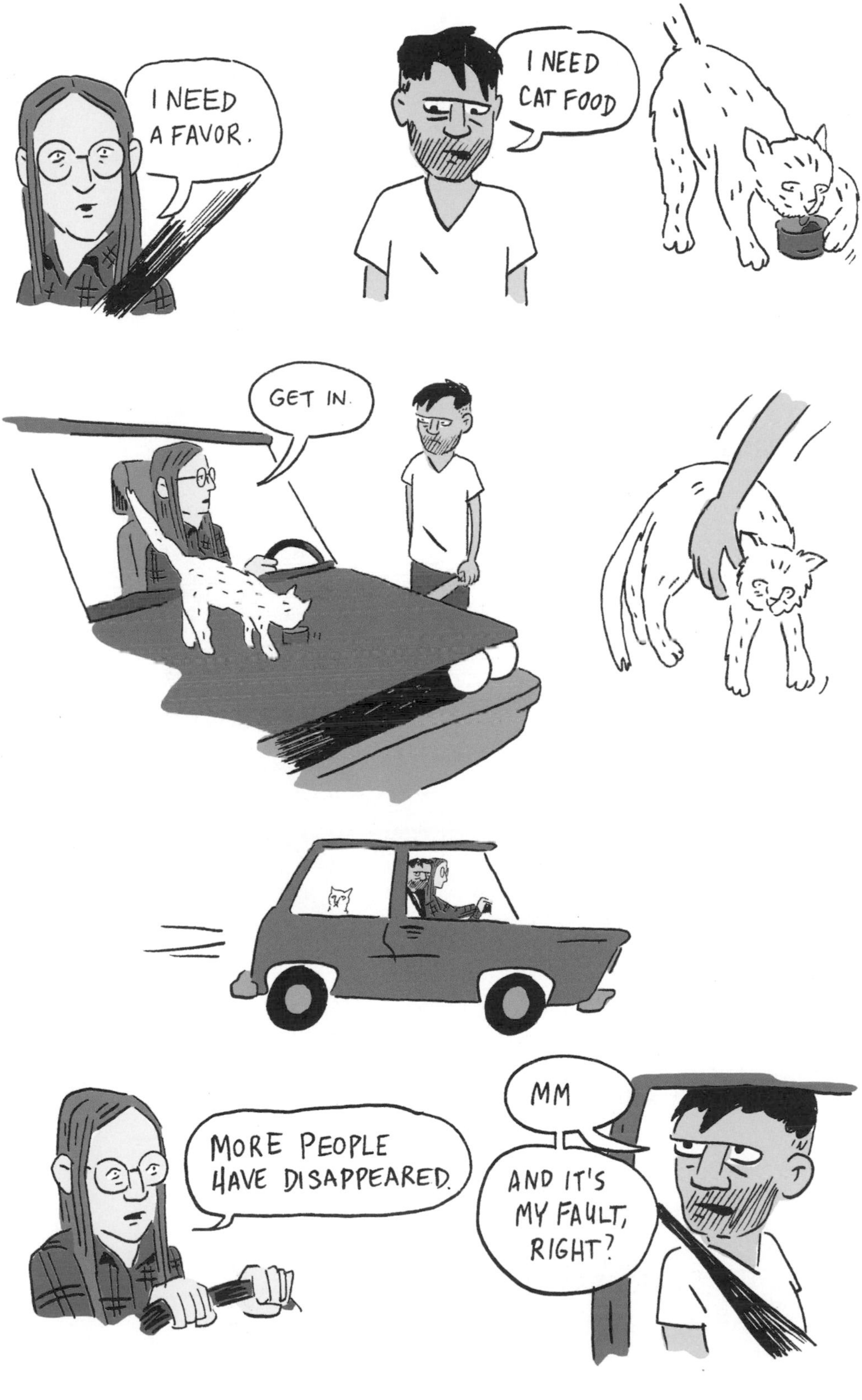
I NEED A FAVOR.
I NEED CAT FOOD
GET IN.
MORE PEOPLE HAVE DISAPPEARED.
MM
AND IT'S MY FAULT, RIGHT?

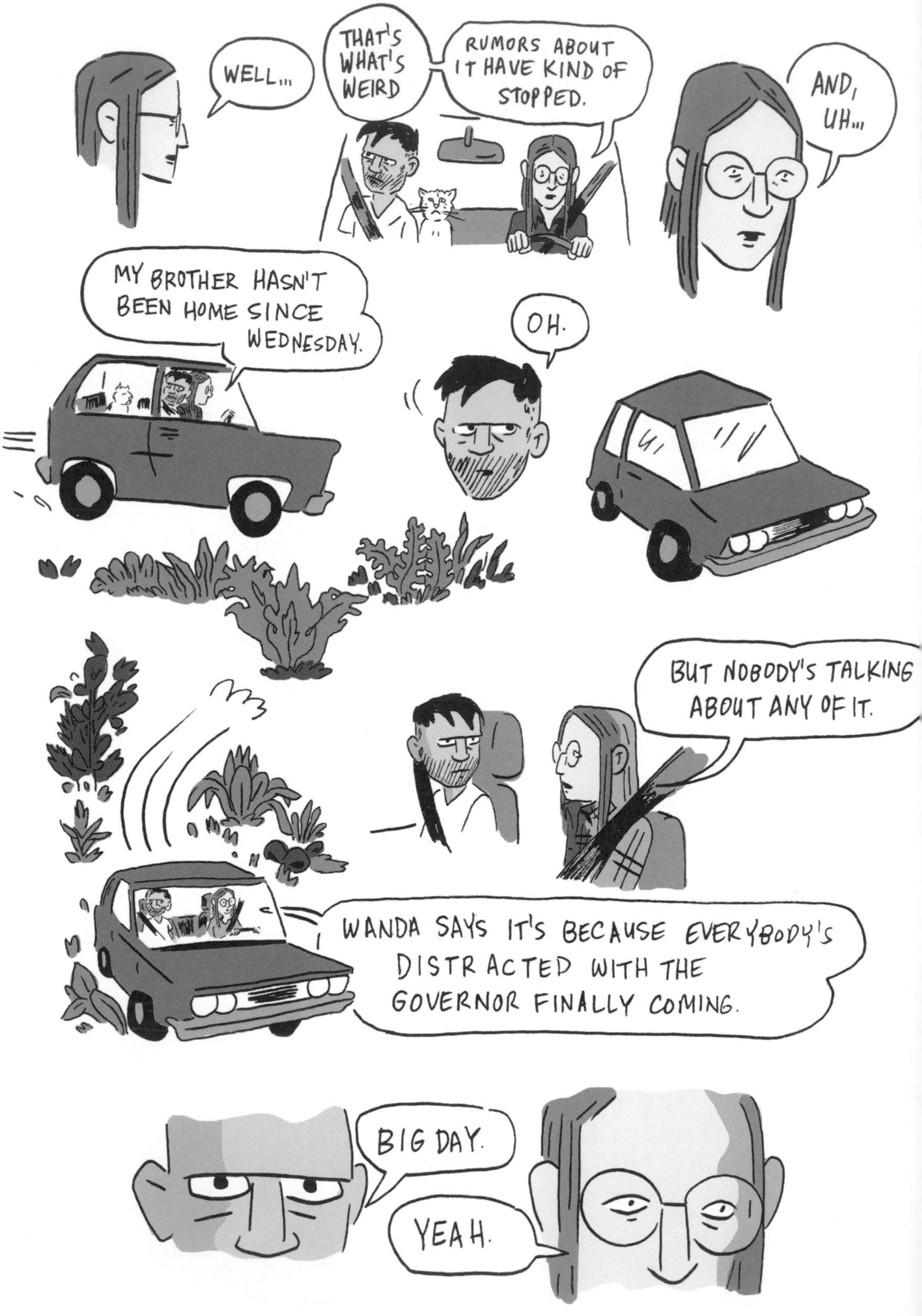
WELL...
THAT'S WHAT'S WEIRD
RUMORS ABOUT IT HAVE KIND OF STOPPED.
AND, UH...
MY BROTHER HASN'T BEEN HOME SINCE WEDNESDAY.
OH.
BUT NOBODY'S TALKING ABOUT ANY OF IT.
WANDA SAYS IT'S BECAUSE EVERYBODY'S DISTRACTED WITH THE GOVERNOR FINALLY COMING.
BIG DAY.
YEAH.

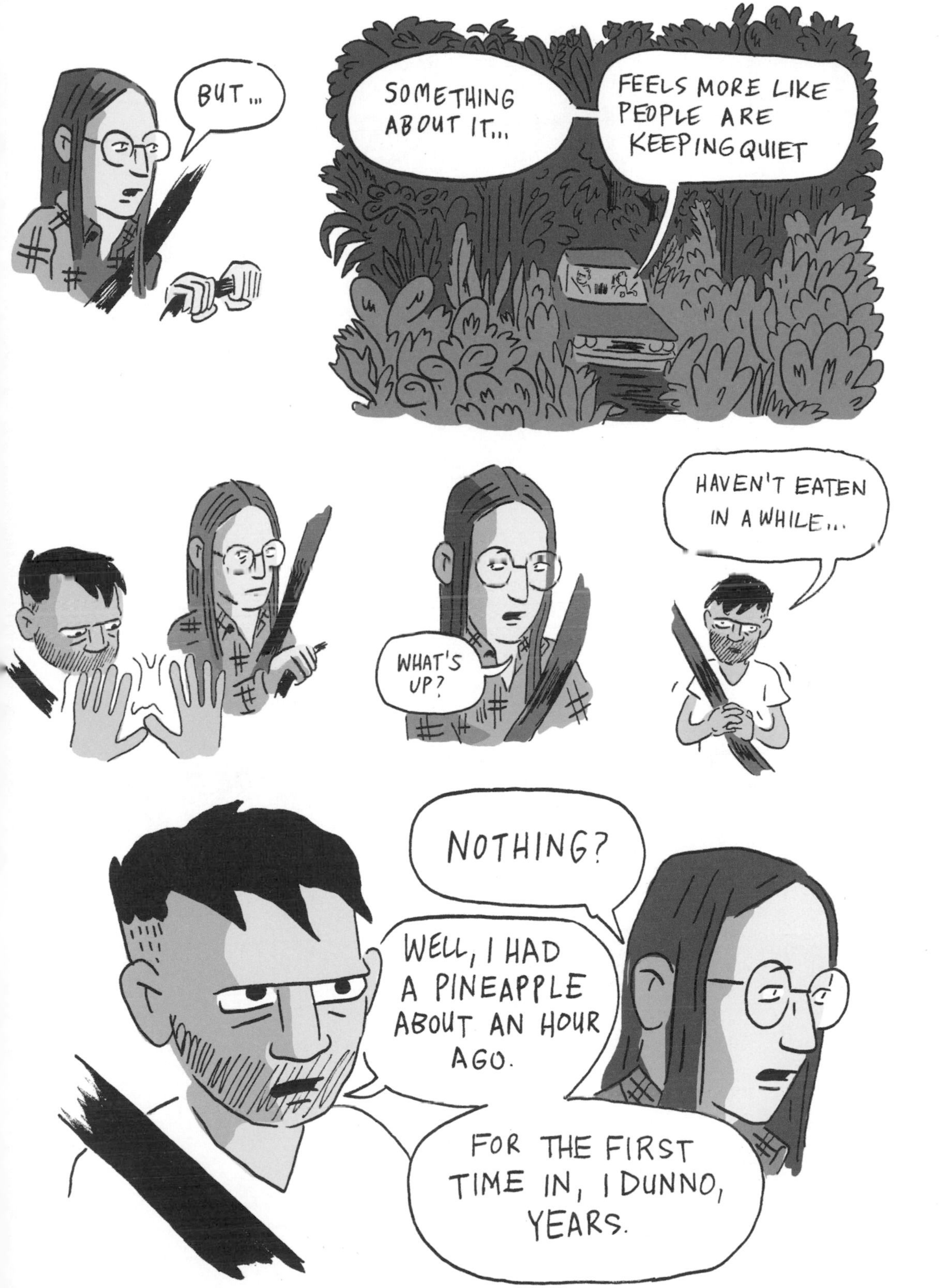
BUT...
SOMETHING ABOUT IT...
FEELS MORE LIKE PEOPLE ARE KEEPING QUIET
WHAT'S UP?
HAVEN'T EATEN IN A WHILE...
NOTHING?
WELL, I HAD A PINEAPPLE ABOUT AN HOUR AGO.
FOR THE FIRST TIME IN, I DUNNO, YEARS.

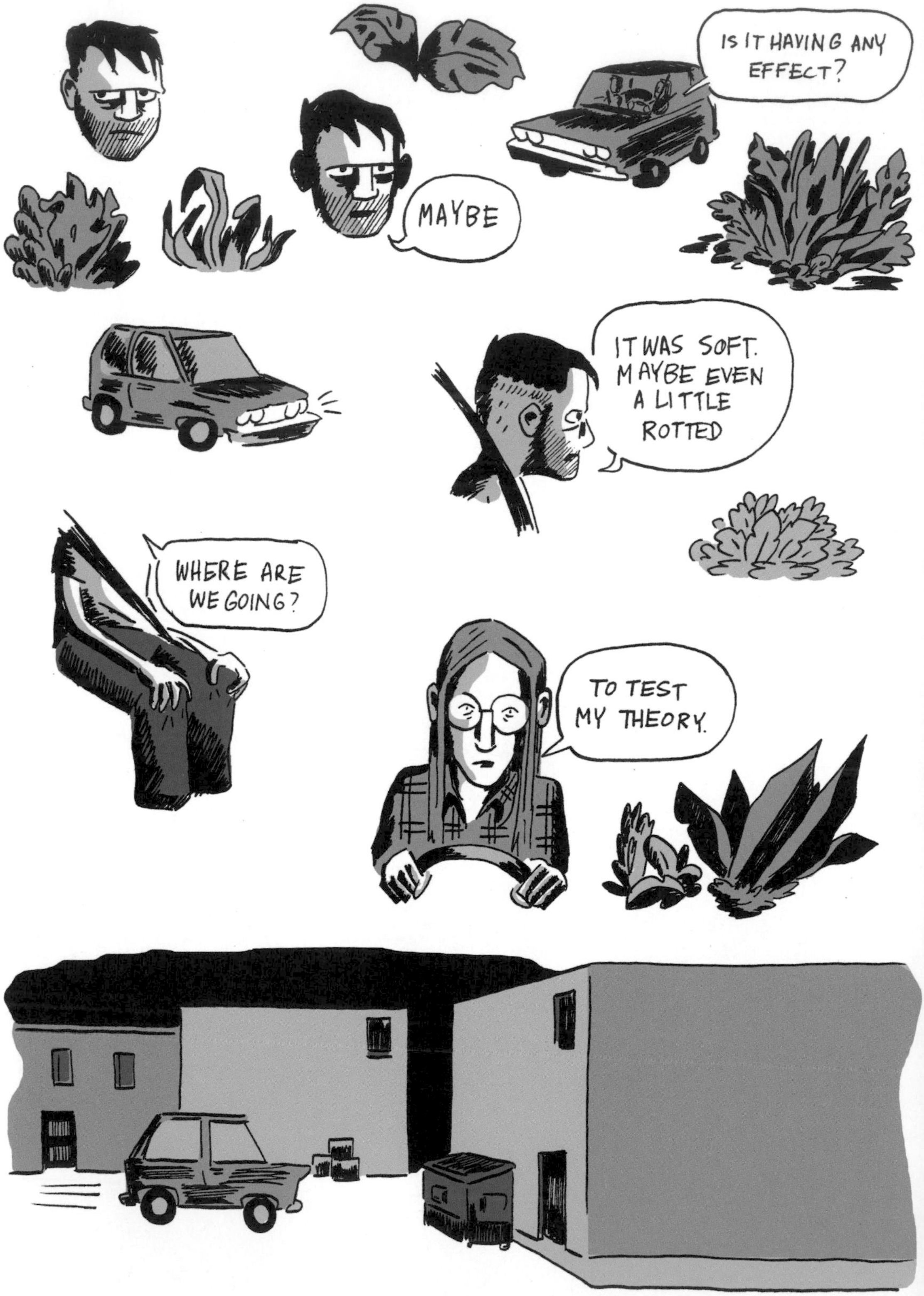
IS IT HAVING ANY EFFECT?
MAYBE
IT WAS SOFT. MAYBE EVEN A LITTLE ROTTED
WHERE ARE WE GOING?
TO TEST MY THEORY.

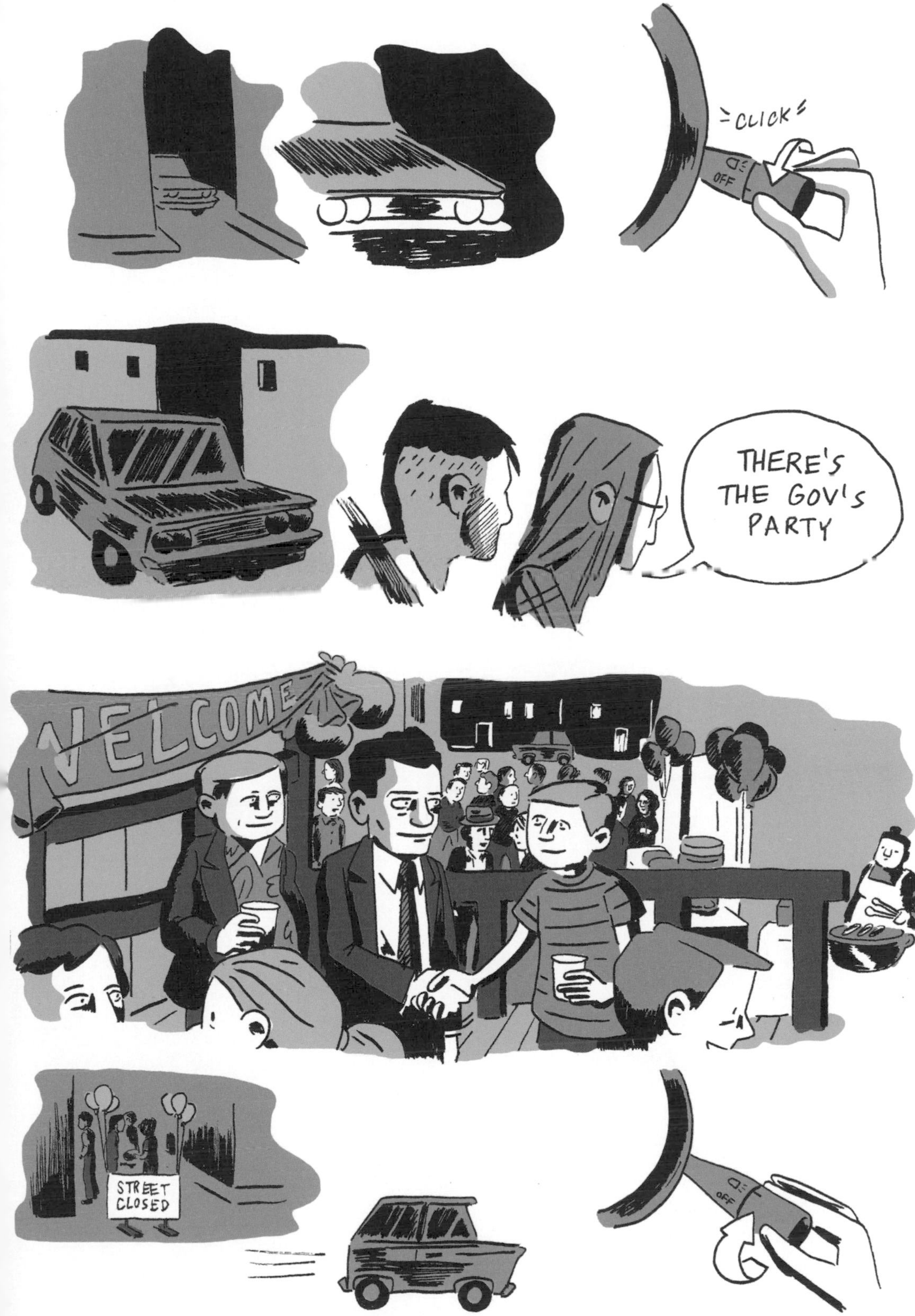
CLICK
OFF
THERE'S THE GOV'S PARTY
WELCOME
STREET CLOSED
OFF

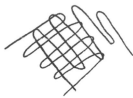

OK

HERE WE ARE.

THE DUMP

MAYBE BRING YOUR, UH...

OH

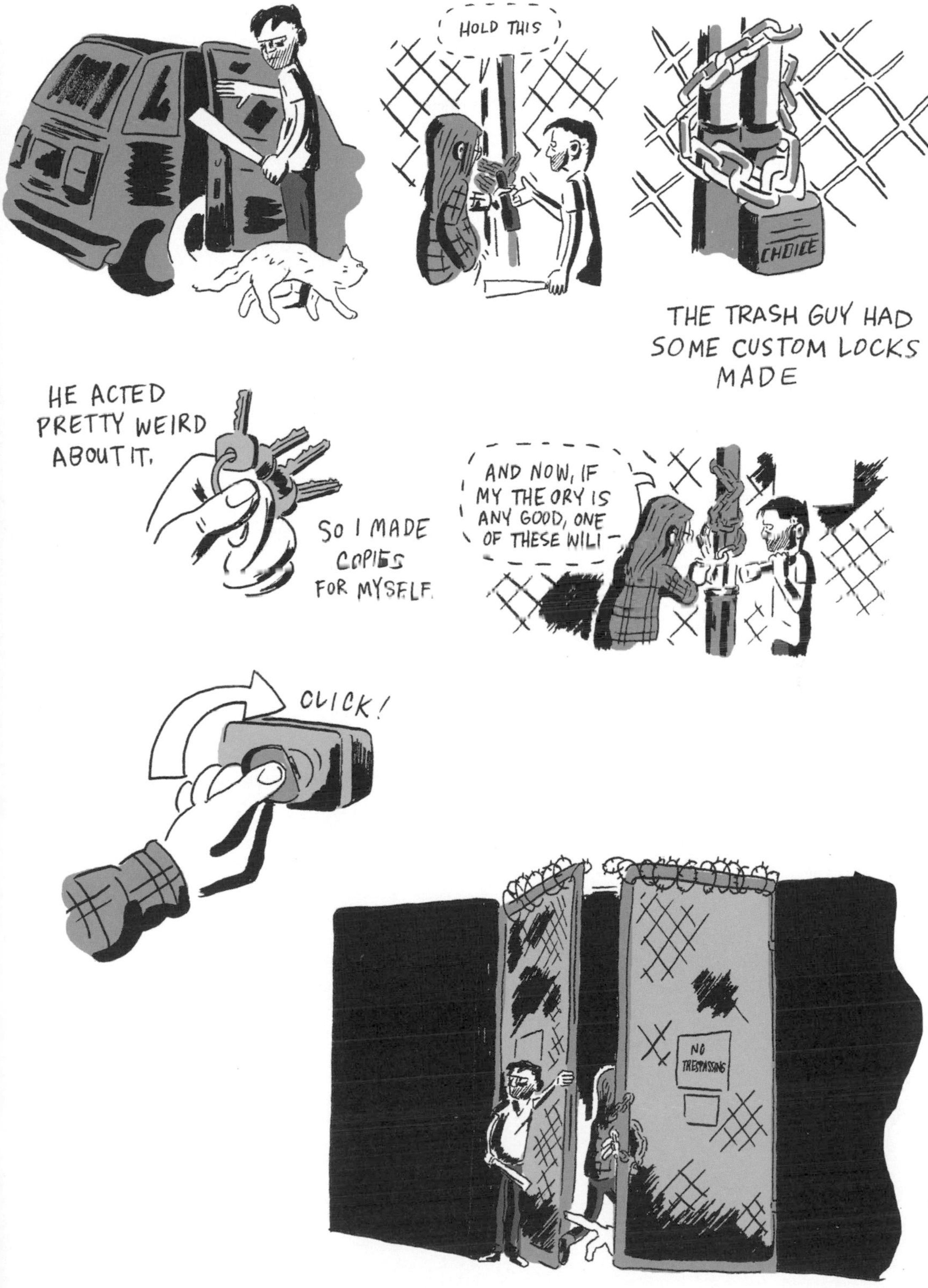
HOLD THIS
CHOICE
THE TRASH GUY HAD SOME CUSTOM LOCKS MADE
HE ACTED PRETTY WEIRD ABOUT IT.
SO I MADE COPIES FOR MYSELF.
AND NOW, IF MY THEORY IS ANY GOOD, ONE OF THESE WILL -
CLICK!
NO TRESPASSING

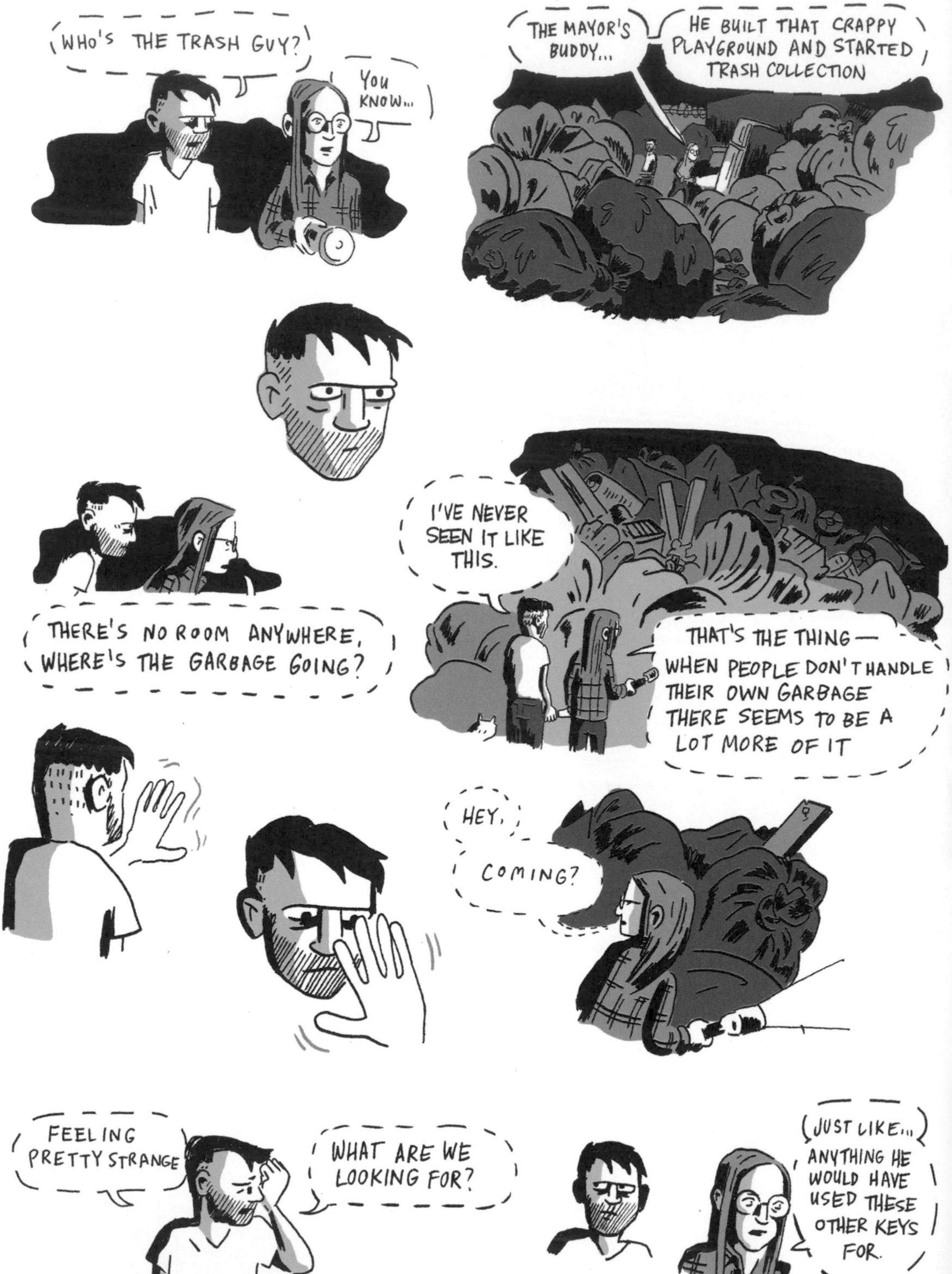
WHO'S THE TRASH GUY?
YOU KNOW...
THE MAYOR'S BUDDY...
HE BUILT THAT CRAPPY PLAYGROUND AND STARTED TRASH COLLECTION
I'VE NEVER SEEN IT LIKE THIS.
THERE'S NO ROOM ANYWHERE, WHERE'S THE GARBAGE GOING?
THAT'S THE THING— WHEN PEOPLE DON'T HANDLE THEIR OWN GARBAGE THERE SEEMS TO BE A LOT MORE OF IT
HEY,
COMING?
FEELING PRETTY STRANGE
WHAT ARE WE LOOKING FOR?
(JUST LIKE...)
ANYTHING HE WOULD HAVE USED THESE OTHER KEYS FOR.

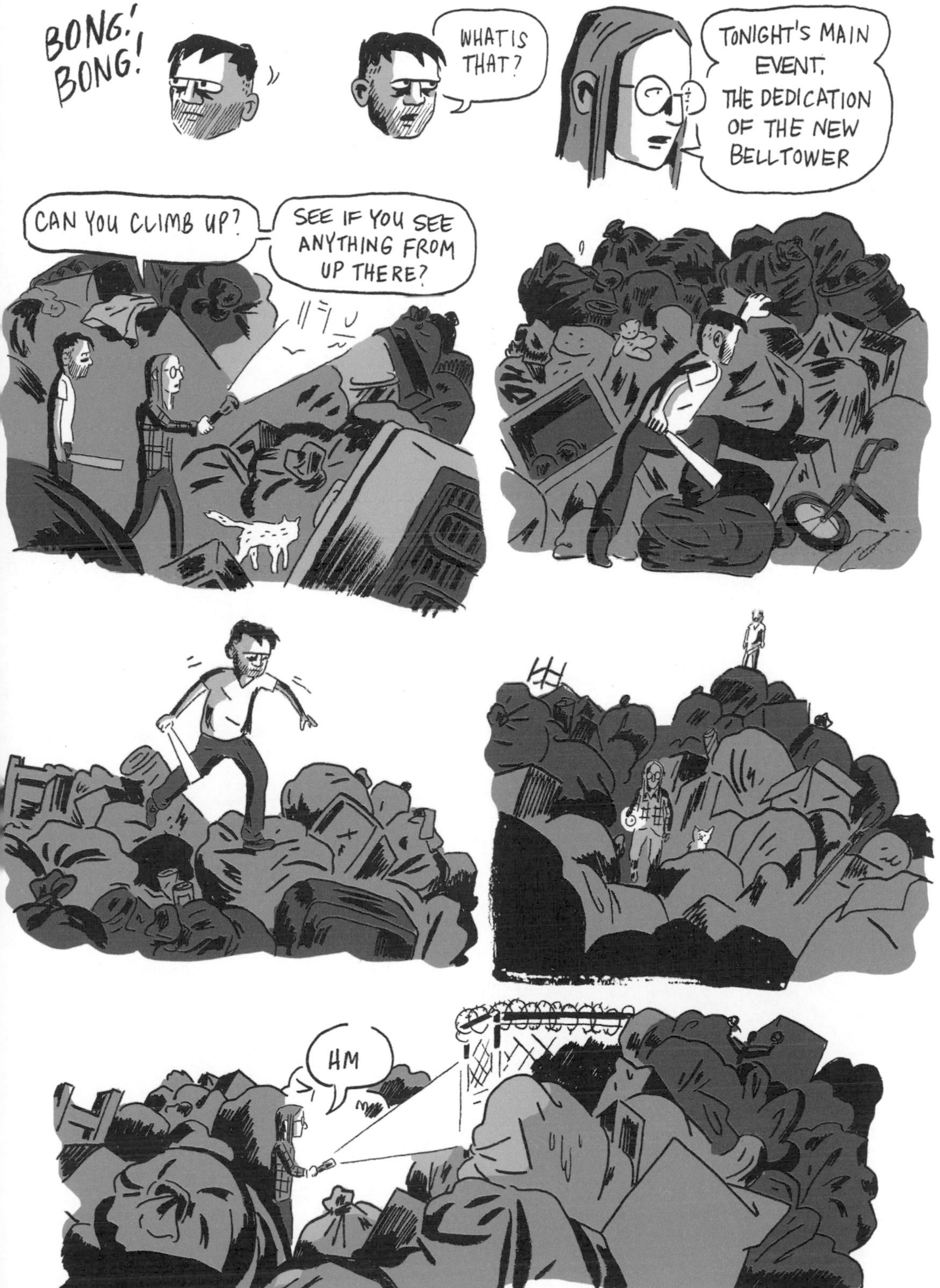

BONG! BONG!
WHAT IS THAT?
TONIGHT'S MAIN EVENT. THE DEDICATION OF THE NEW BELLTOWER
CAN YOU CLIMB UP?
SEE IF YOU SEE ANYTHING FROM UP THERE?
HM

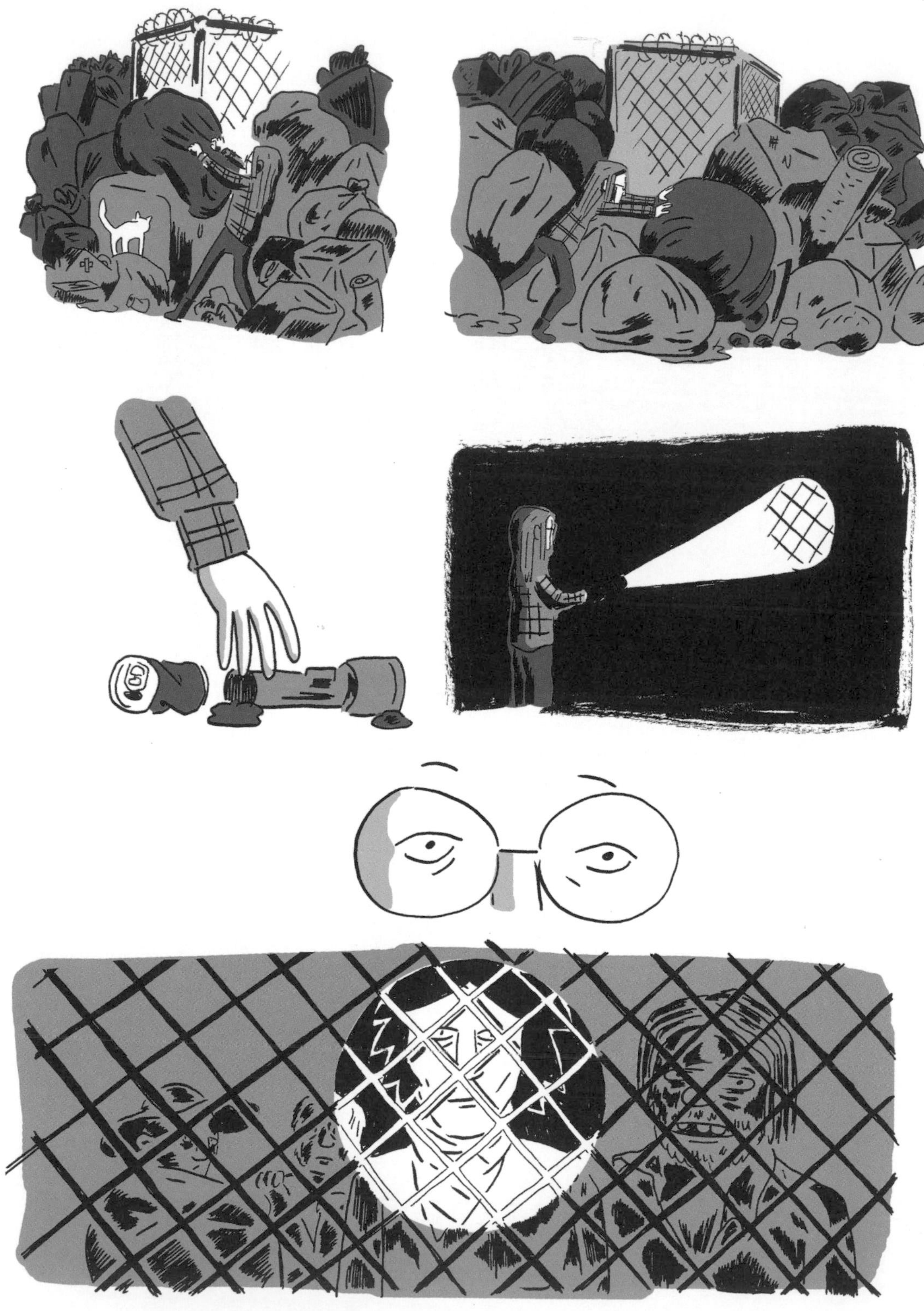

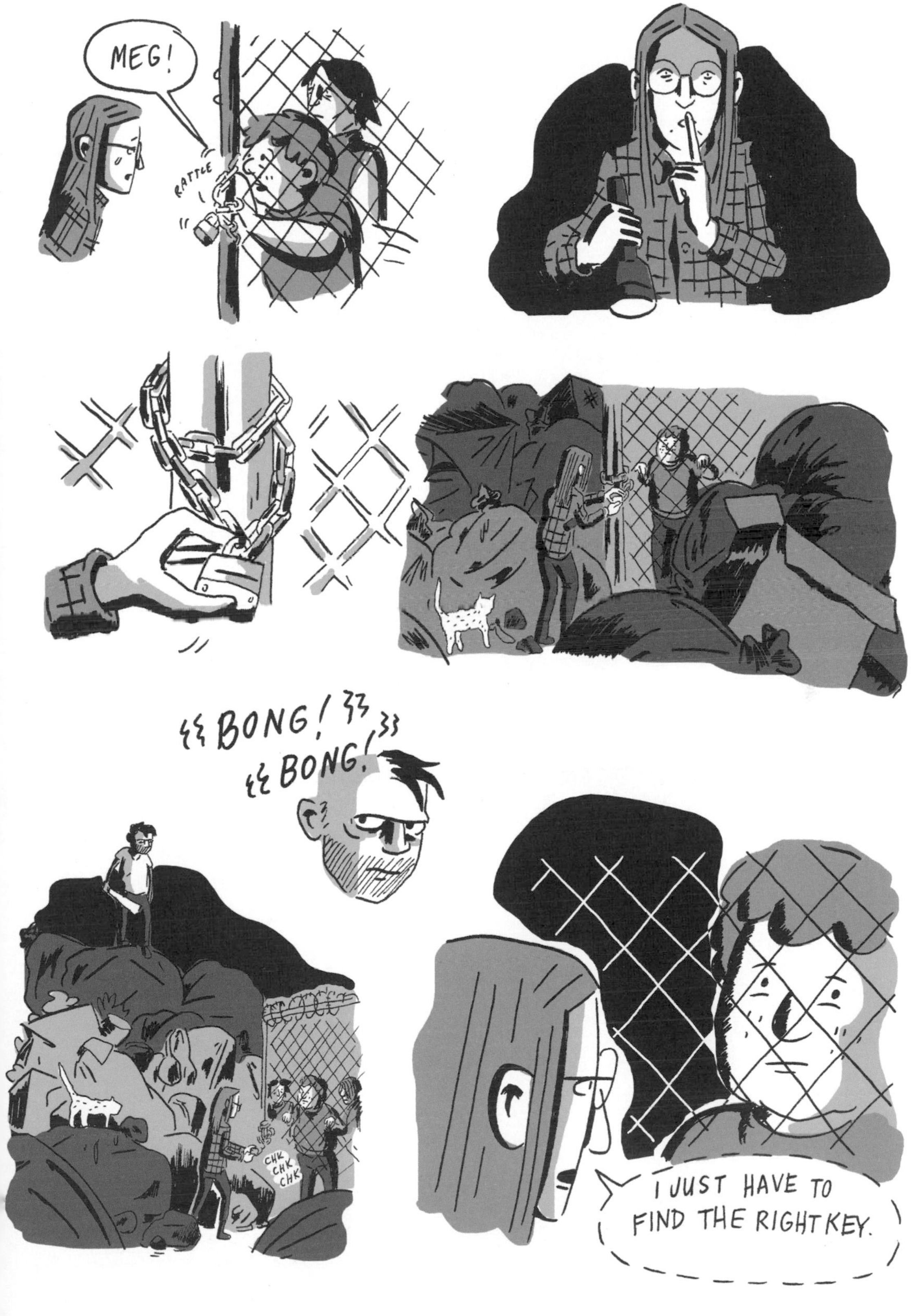
MEG!
RATTLE
BONG!
BONG!
CHK CHK CHK
I JUST HAVE TO FIND THE RIGHT KEY.

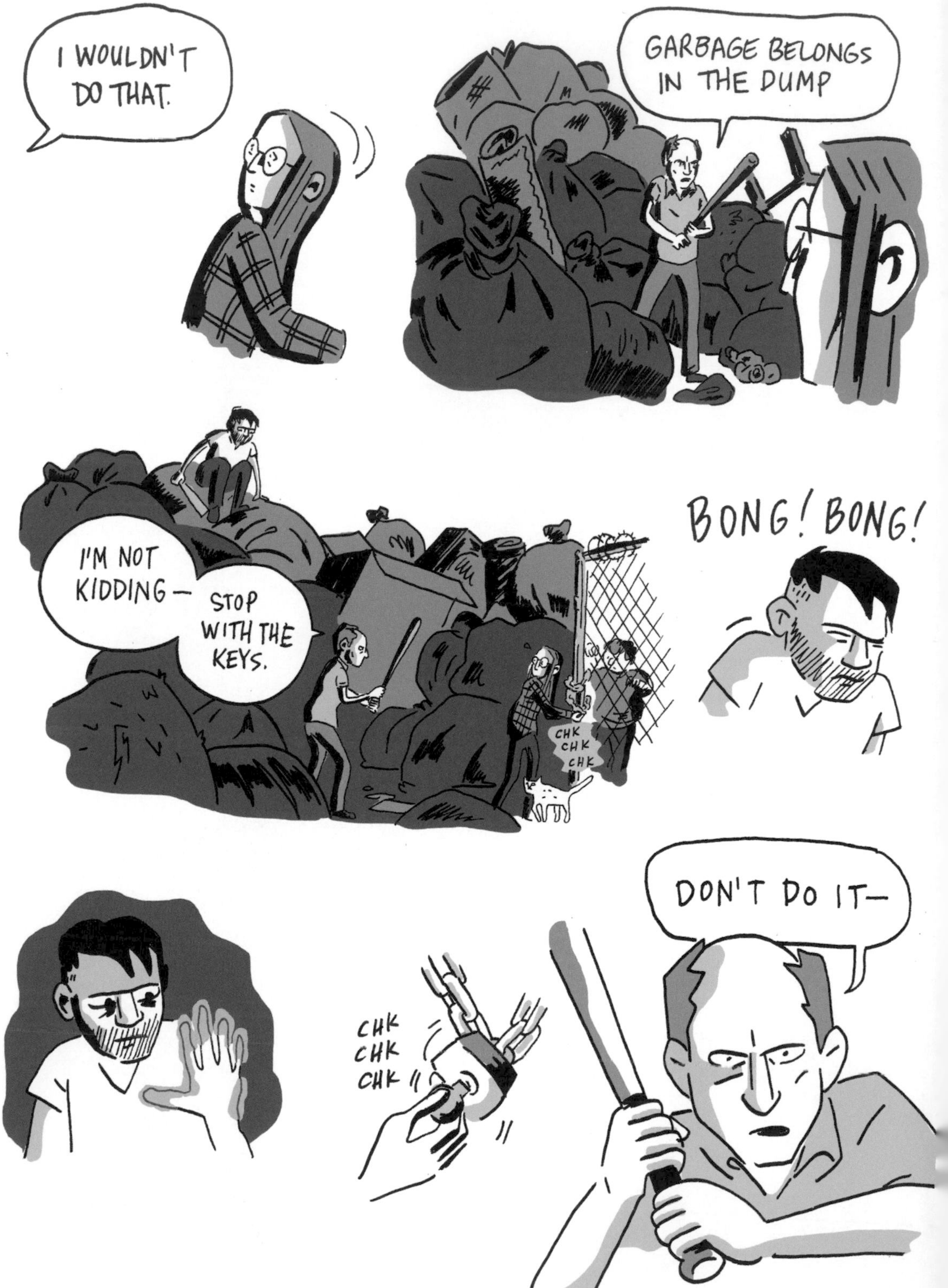

I WOULDN'T DO THAT.
GARBAGE BELONGS IN THE DUMP
I'M NOT KIDDING—
STOP WITH THE KEYS.
CHK CHK CHK
BONG! BONG!
DON'T DO IT—
CHK CHK CHK

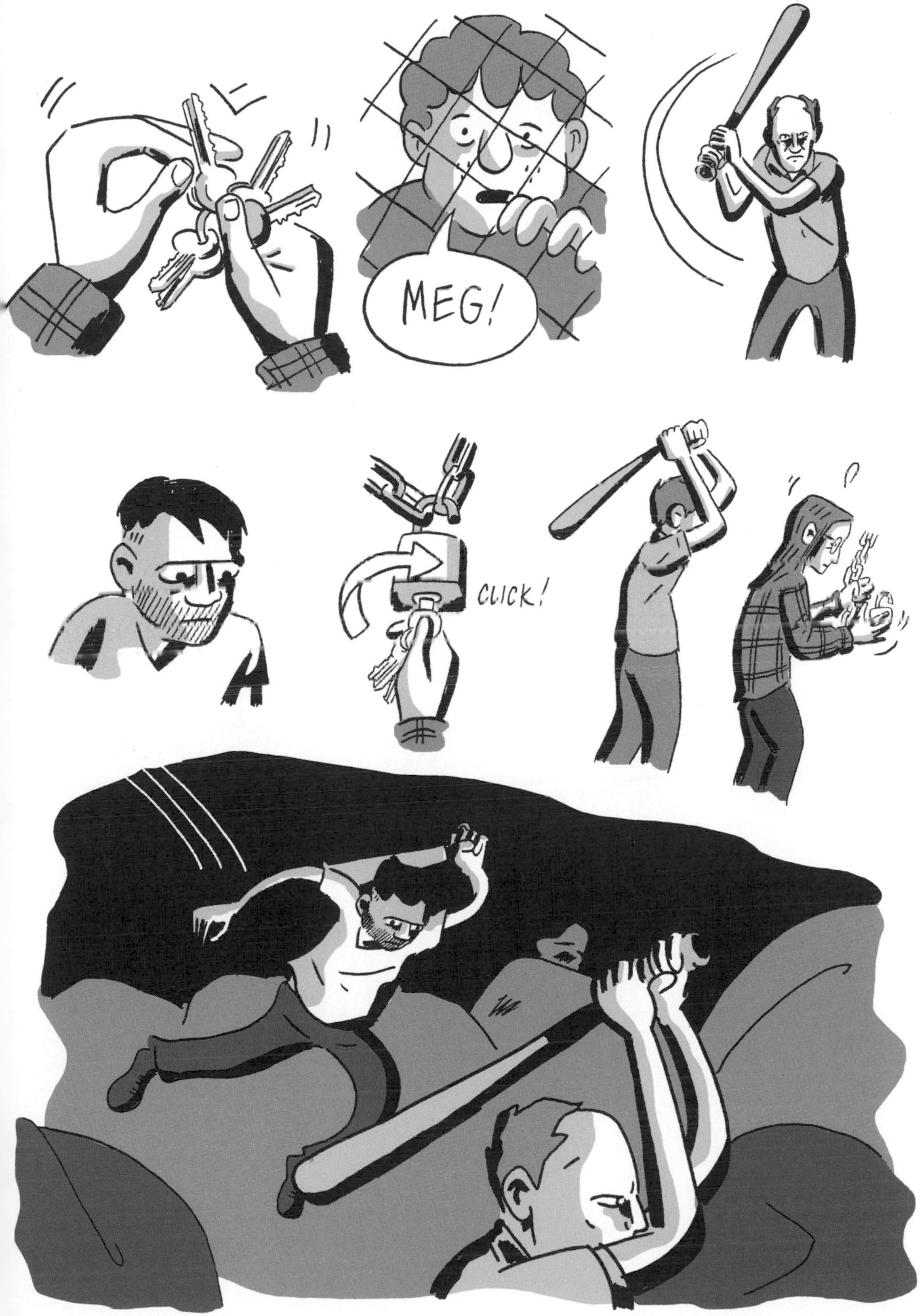
MEG!
CLICK!

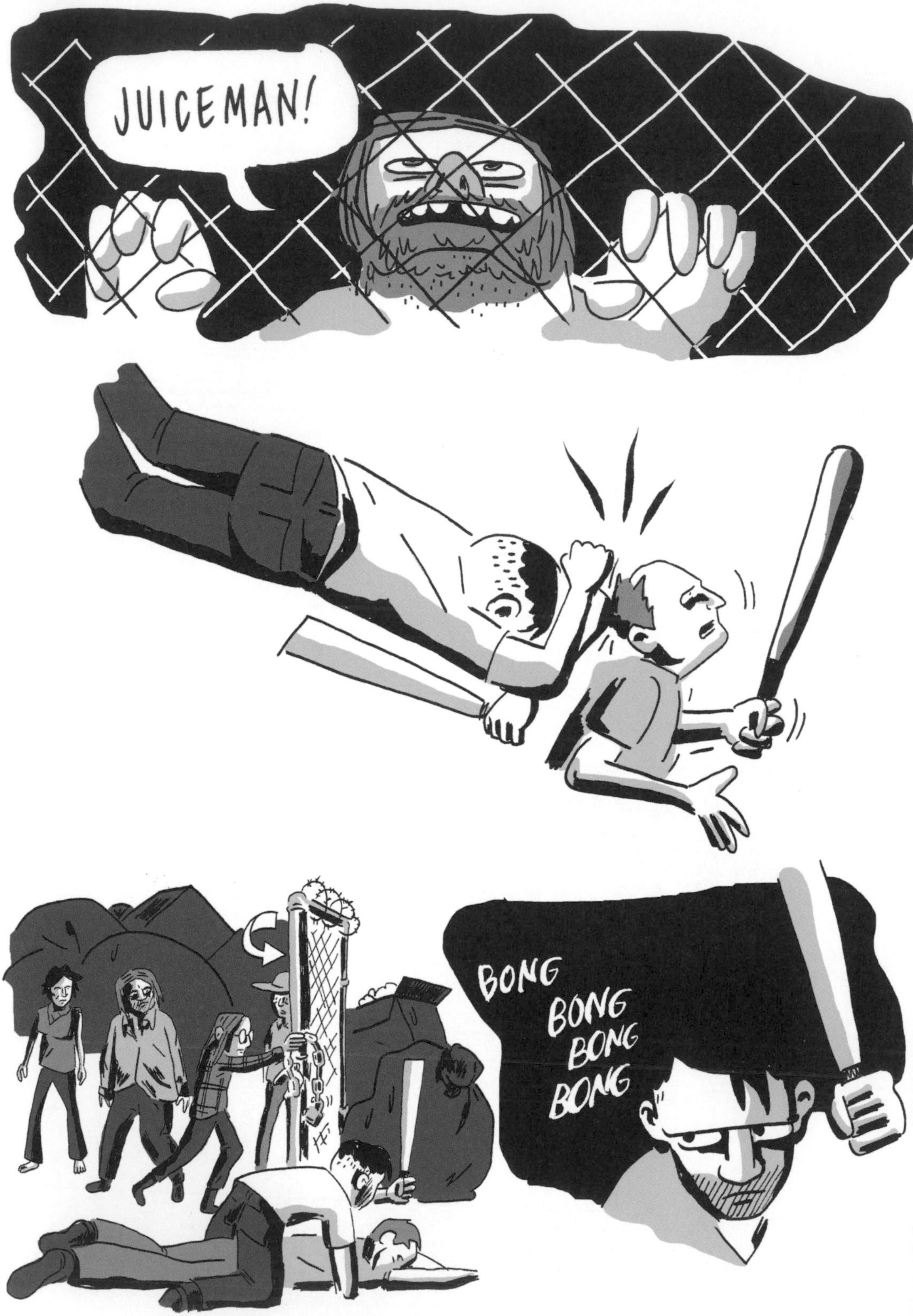
JUICEMAN!
BONG
BONG
BONG
BONG

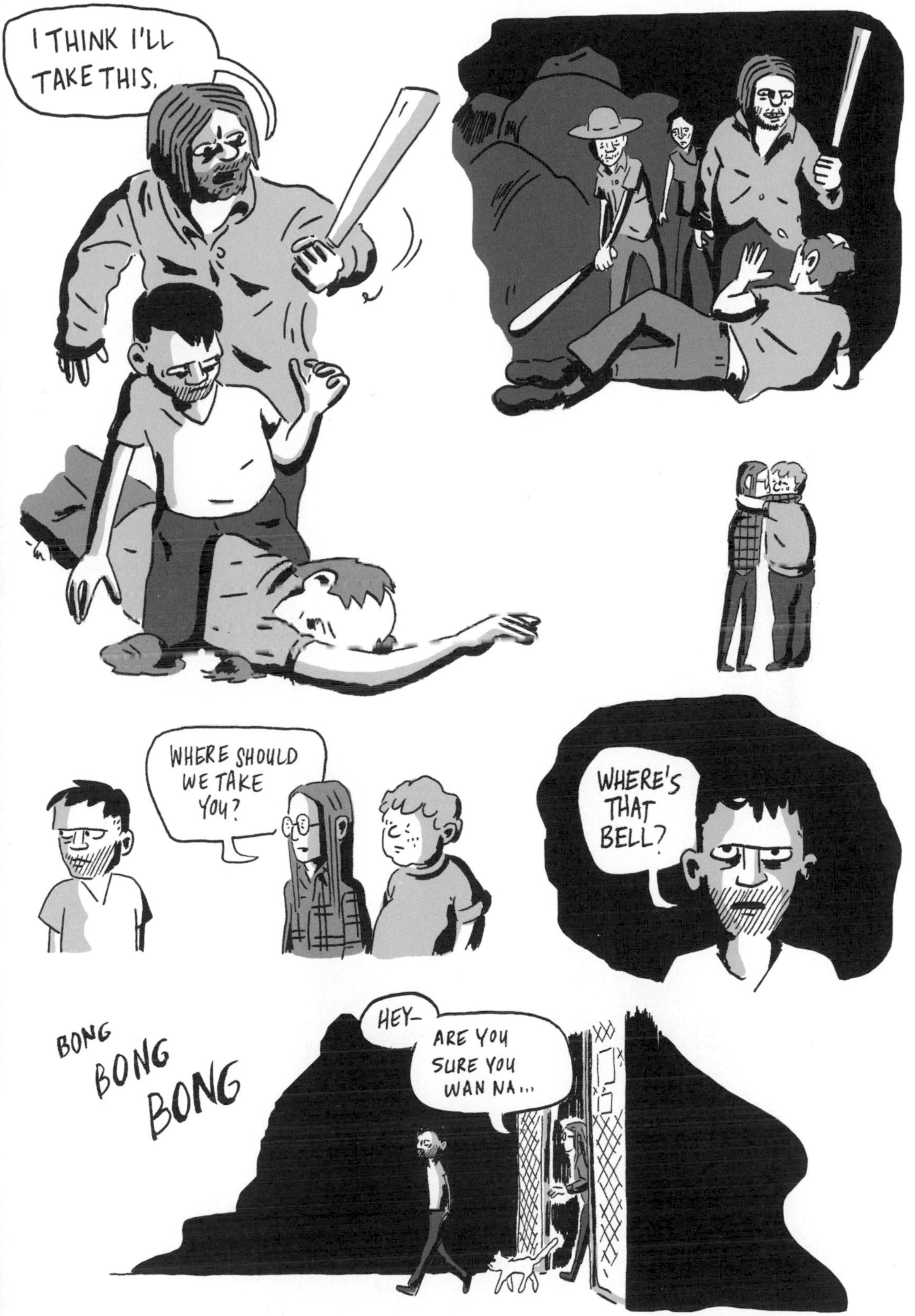

I THINK I'LL TAKE THIS.
WHERE SHOULD WE TAKE YOU?
WHERE'S THAT BELL?
BONG BONG BONG
HEY—
ARE YOU SURE YOU WAN NA...

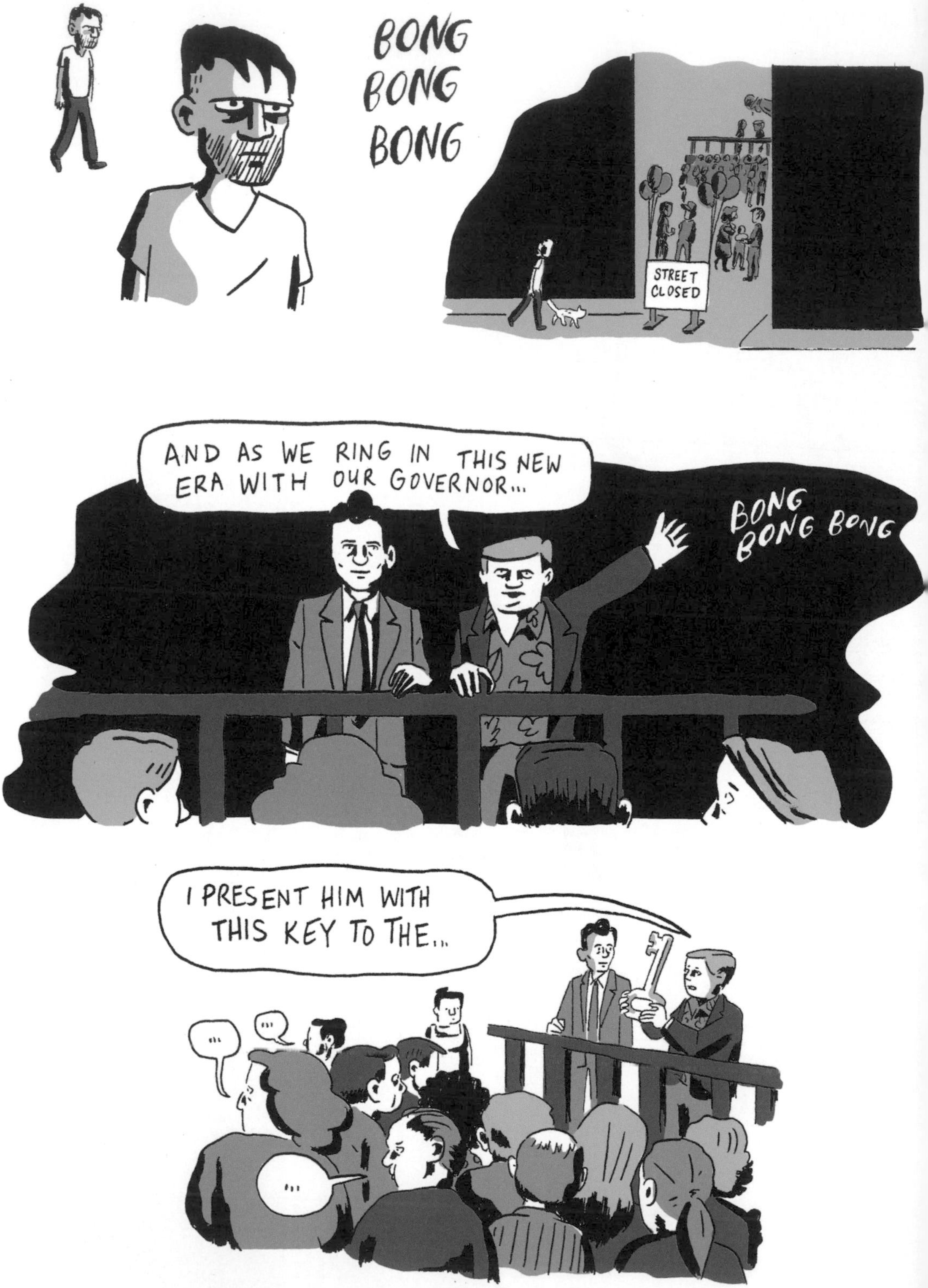
BONG BONG BONG
STREET CLOSED
AND AS WE RING IN THIS NEW ERA WITH OUR GOVERNOR...
BONG BONG BONG
I PRESENT HIM WITH THIS KEY TO THE...
...
...
...

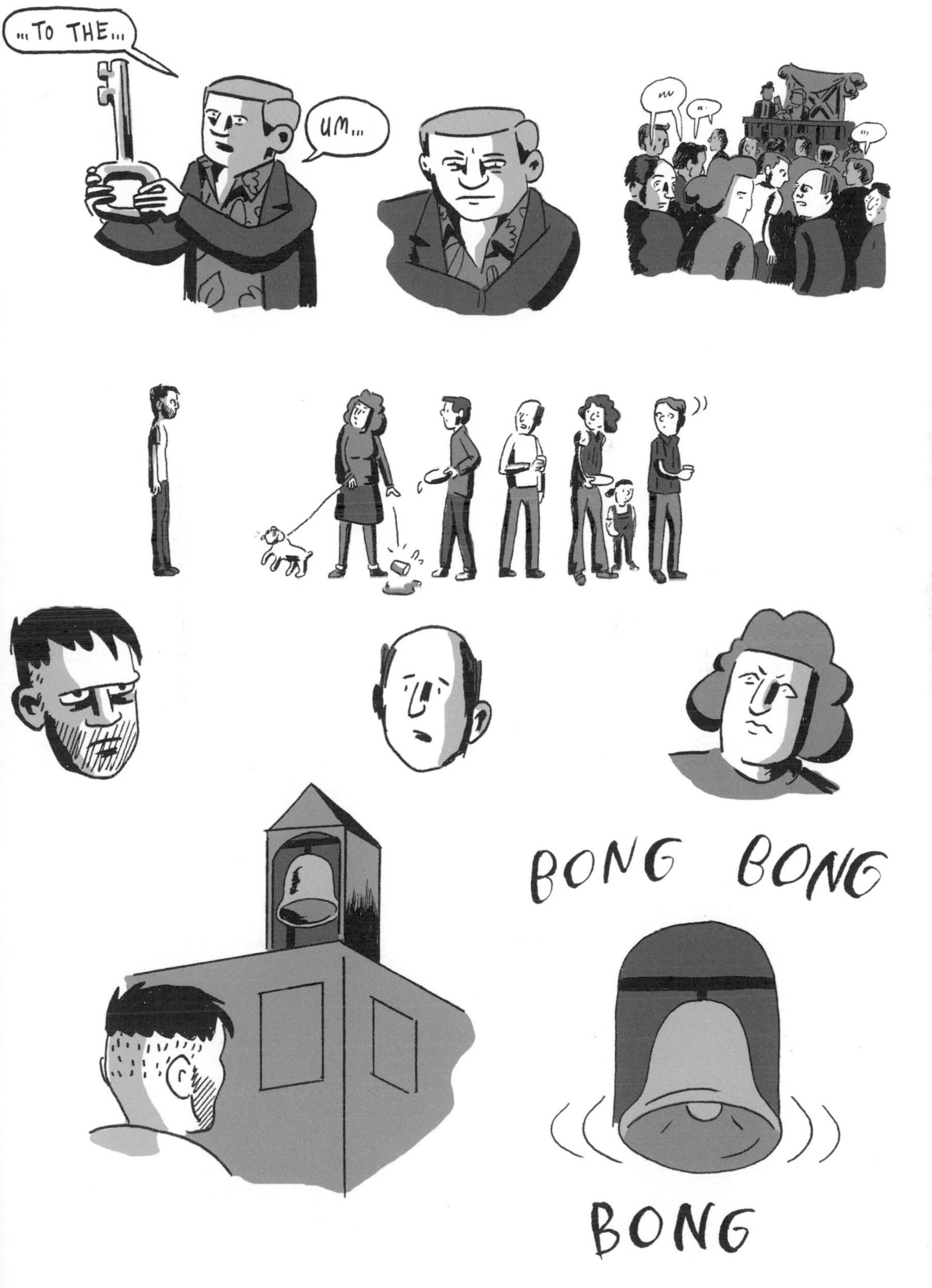
...TO THE...
UM...
BONG BONG
BONG

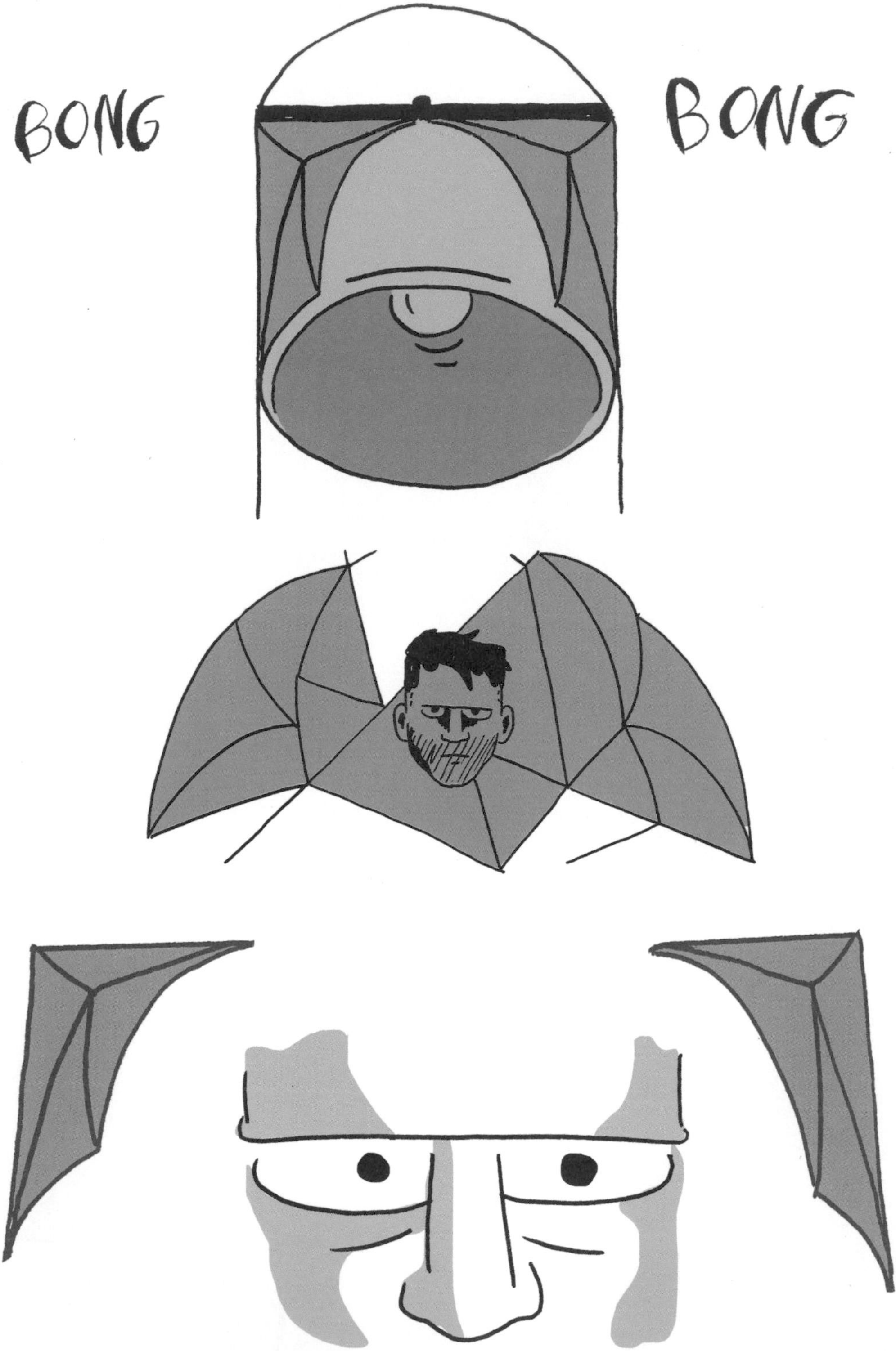
BONG
BONG

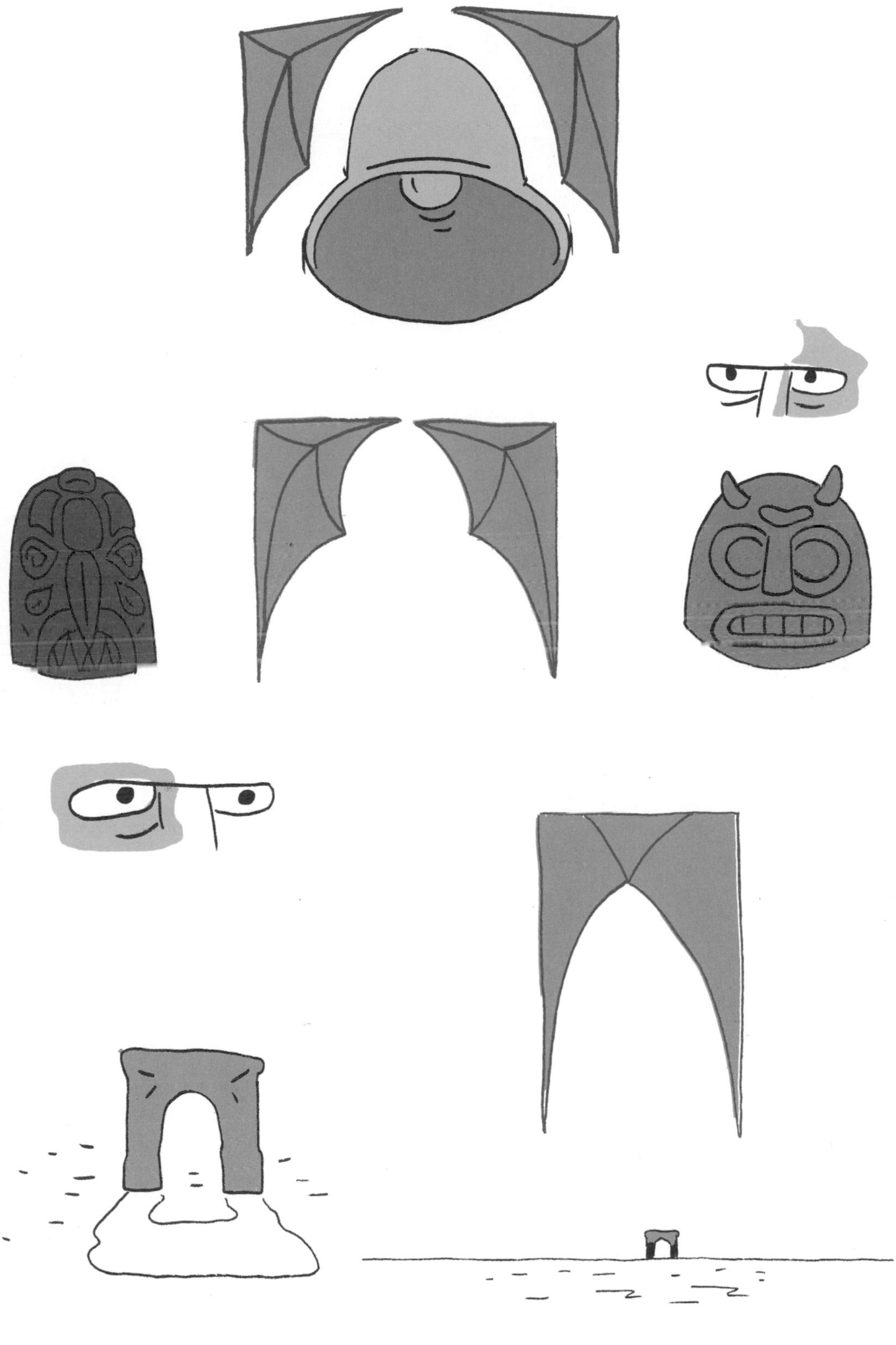

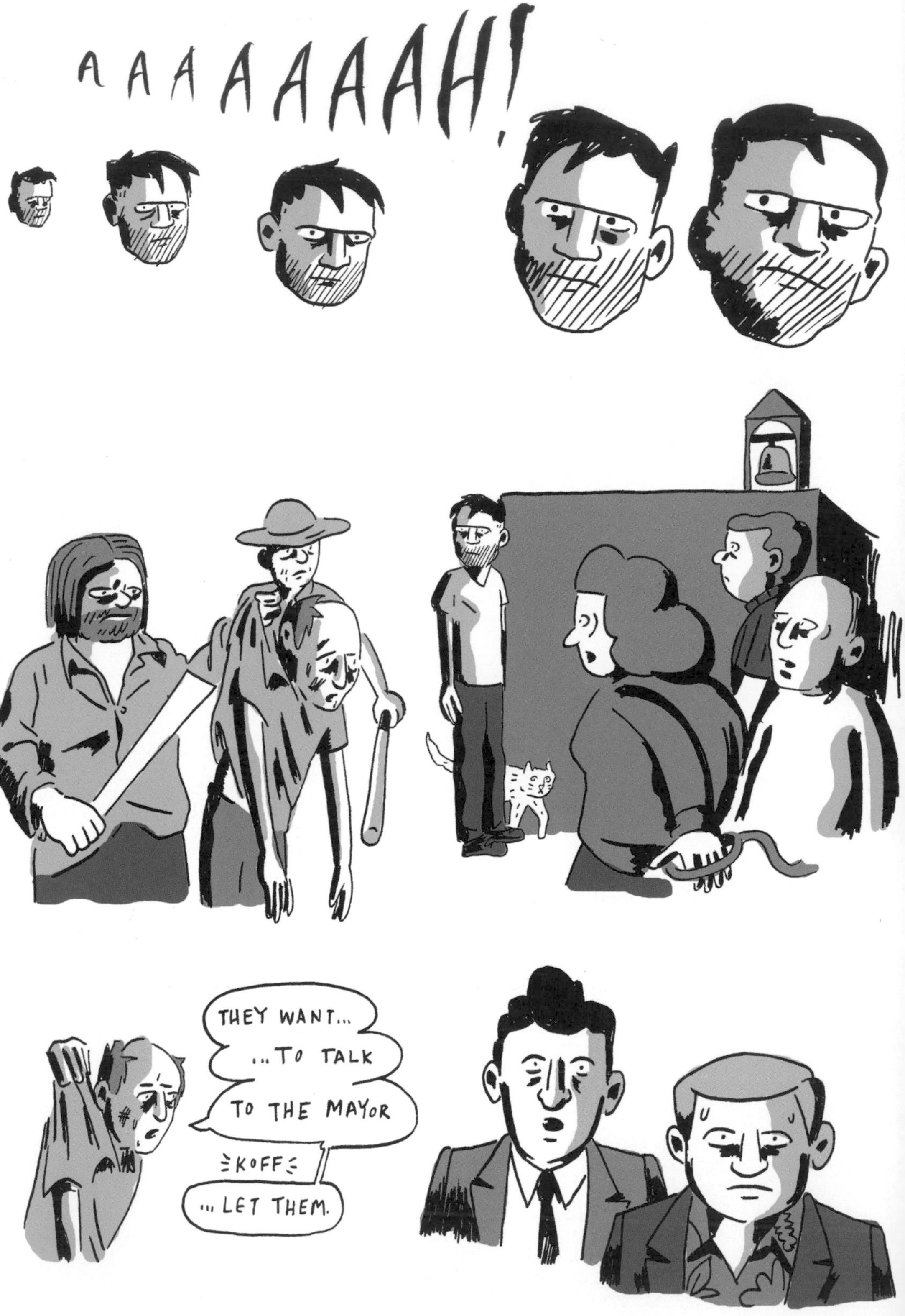
AAAAAAAH!
THEY WANT...
...TO TALK
TO THE MAYOR
KOFF
...LET THEM.

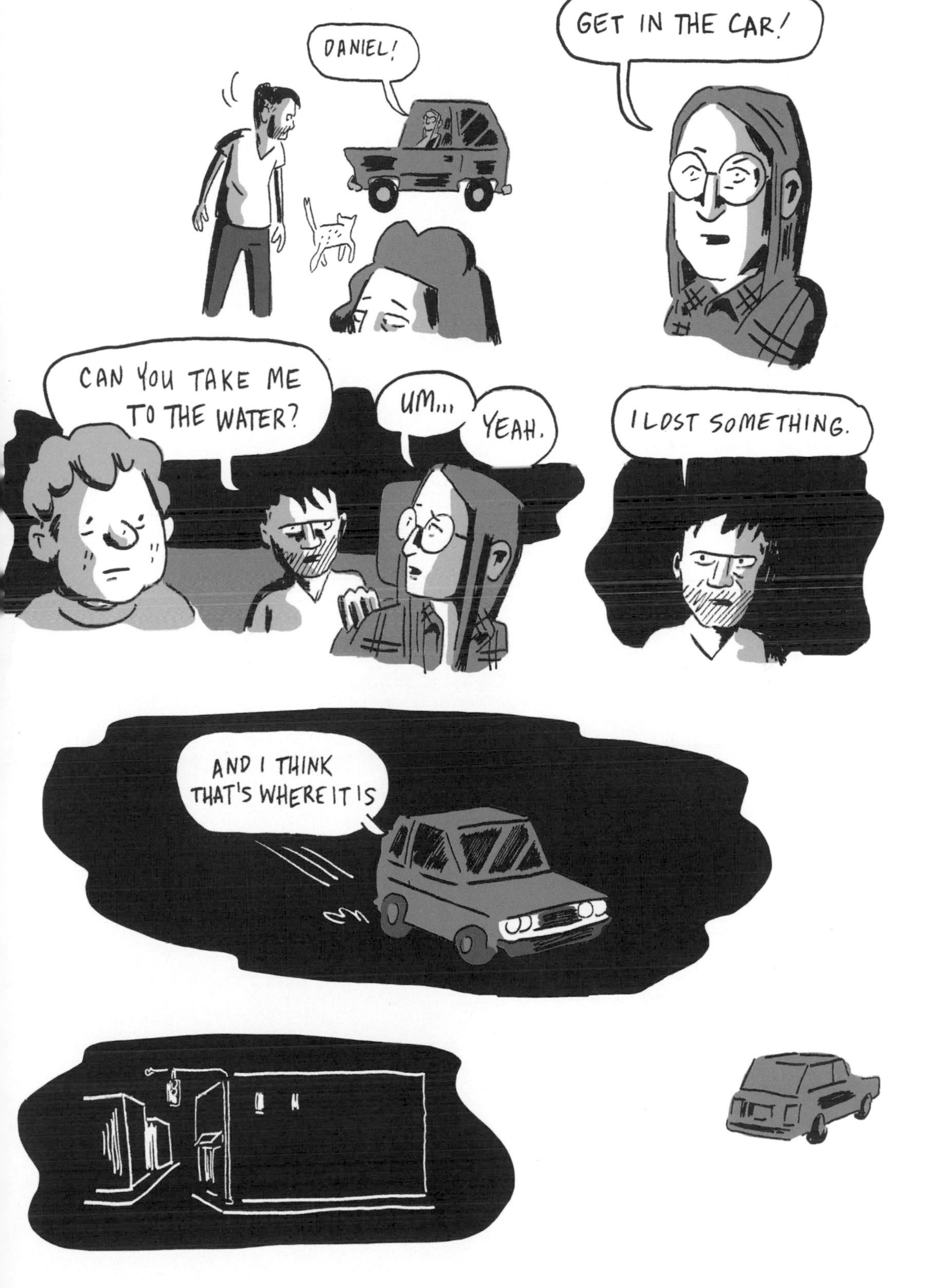
DANIEL!
GET IN THE CAR!
CAN YOU TAKE ME TO THE WATER?
UM...
YEAH.
I LOST SOMETHING.
AND I THINK THAT'S WHERE IT IS

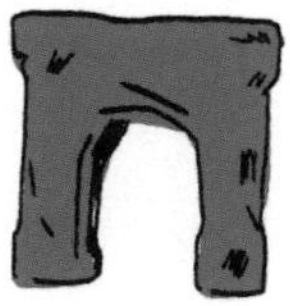

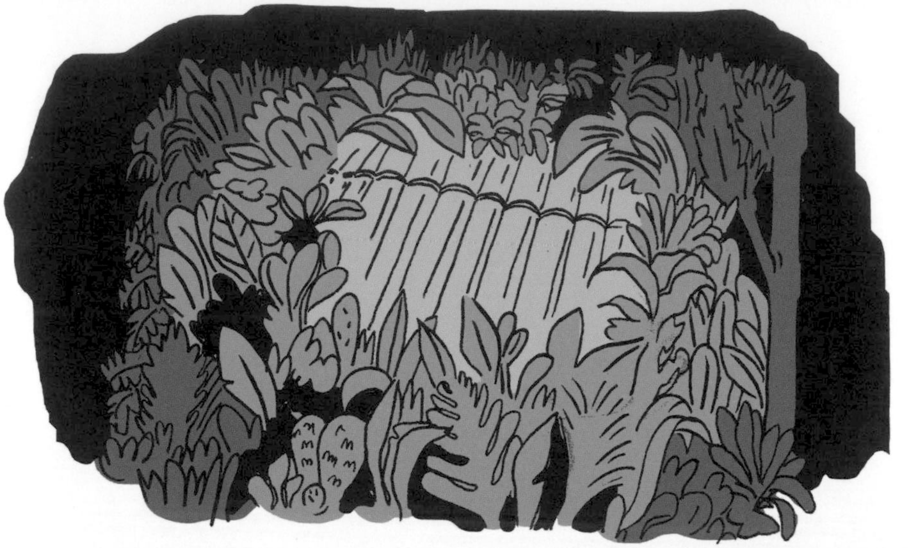

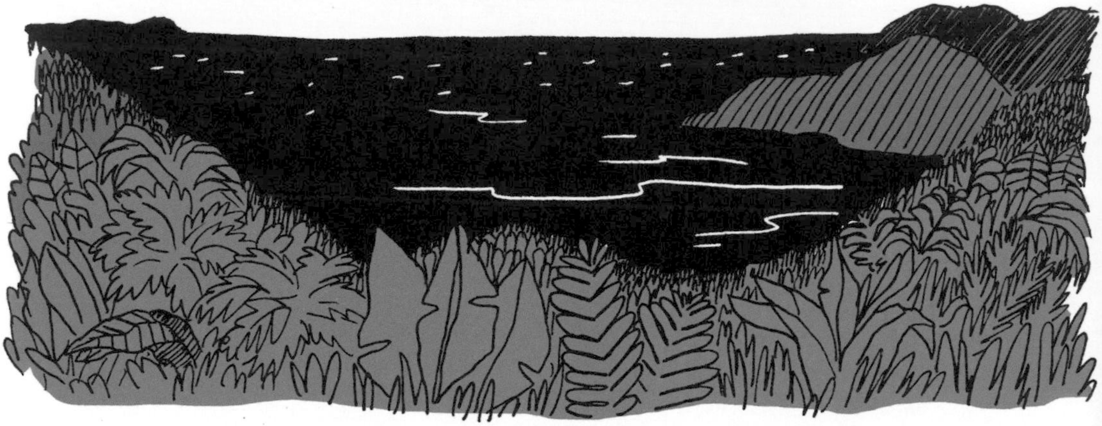

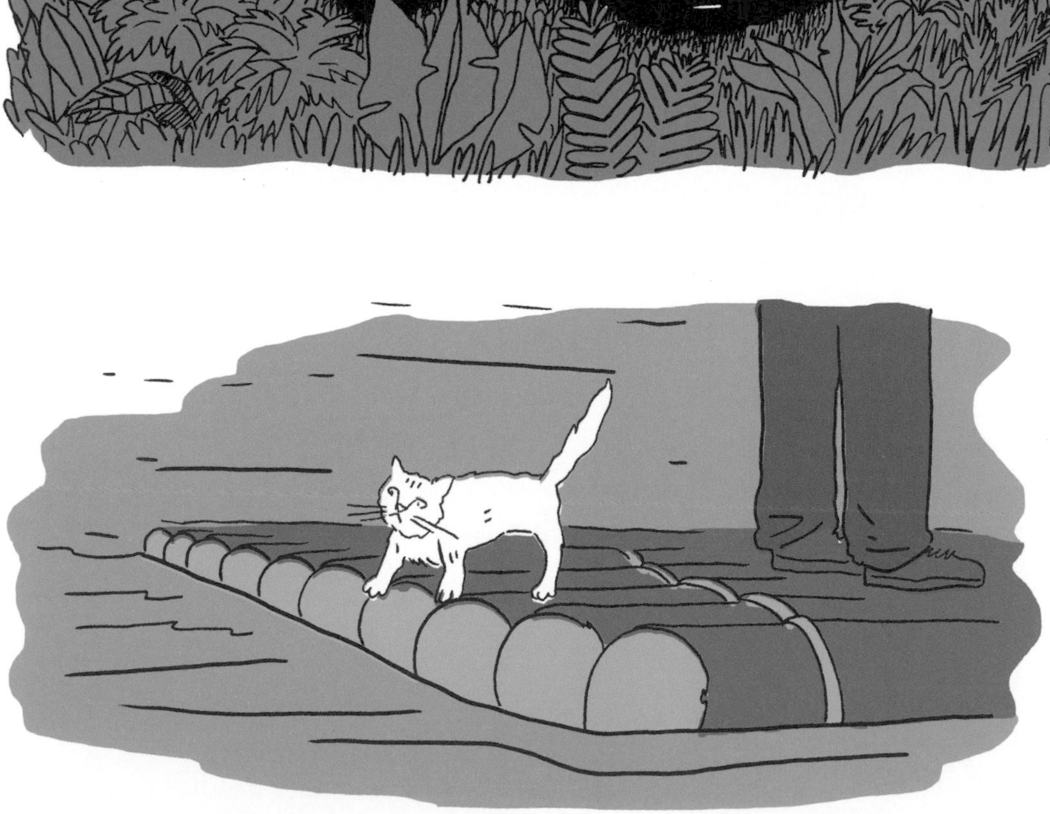

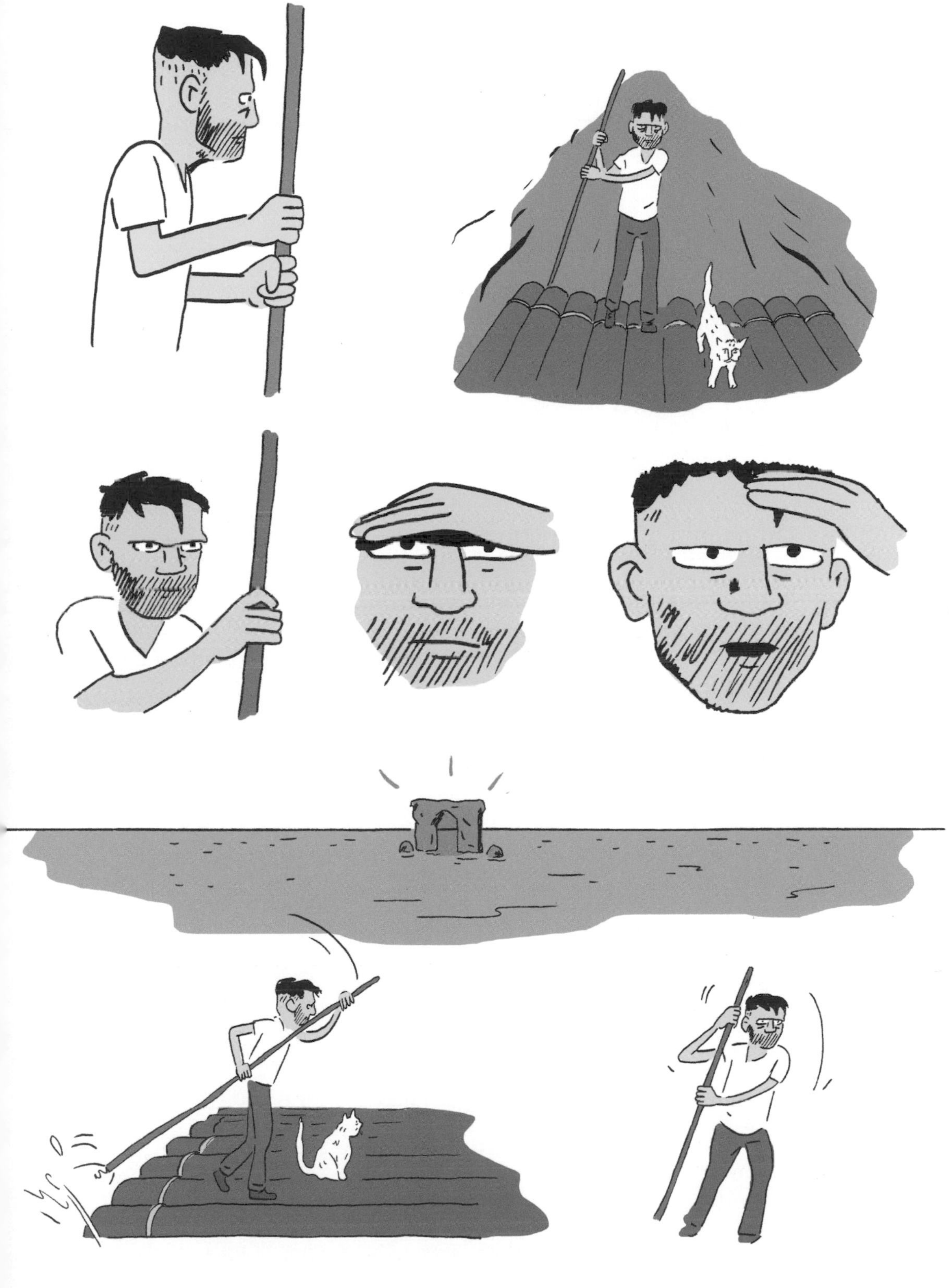

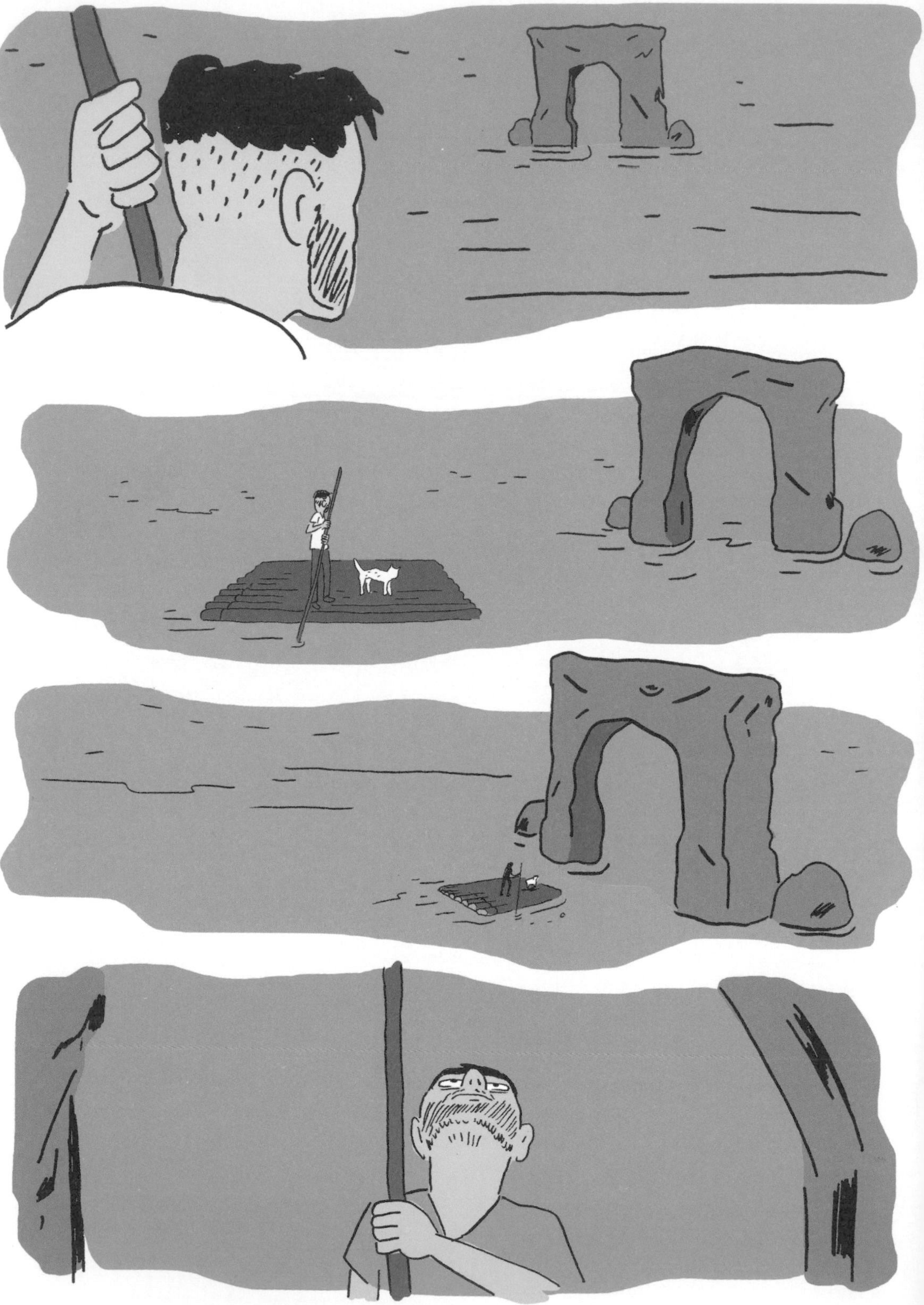

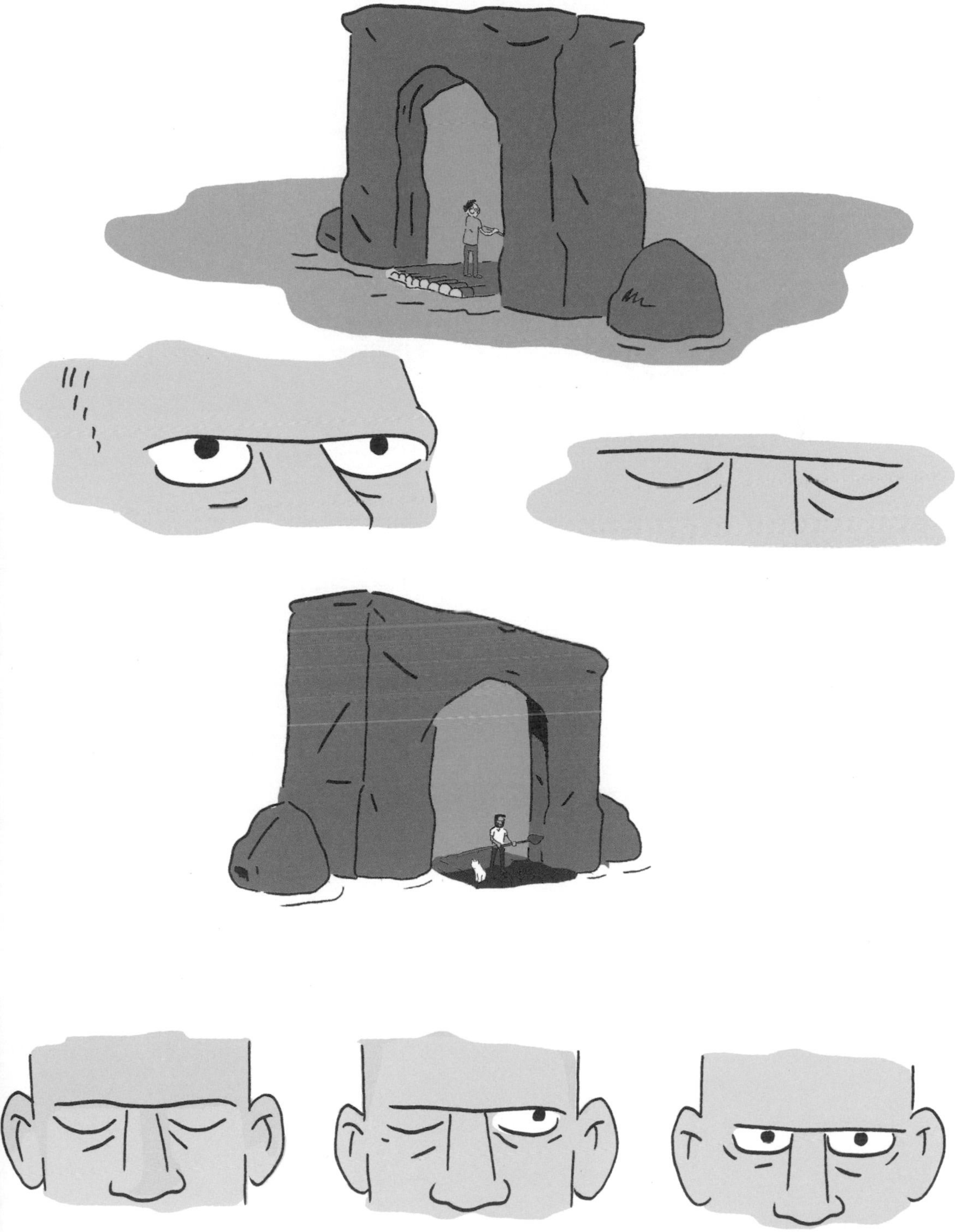

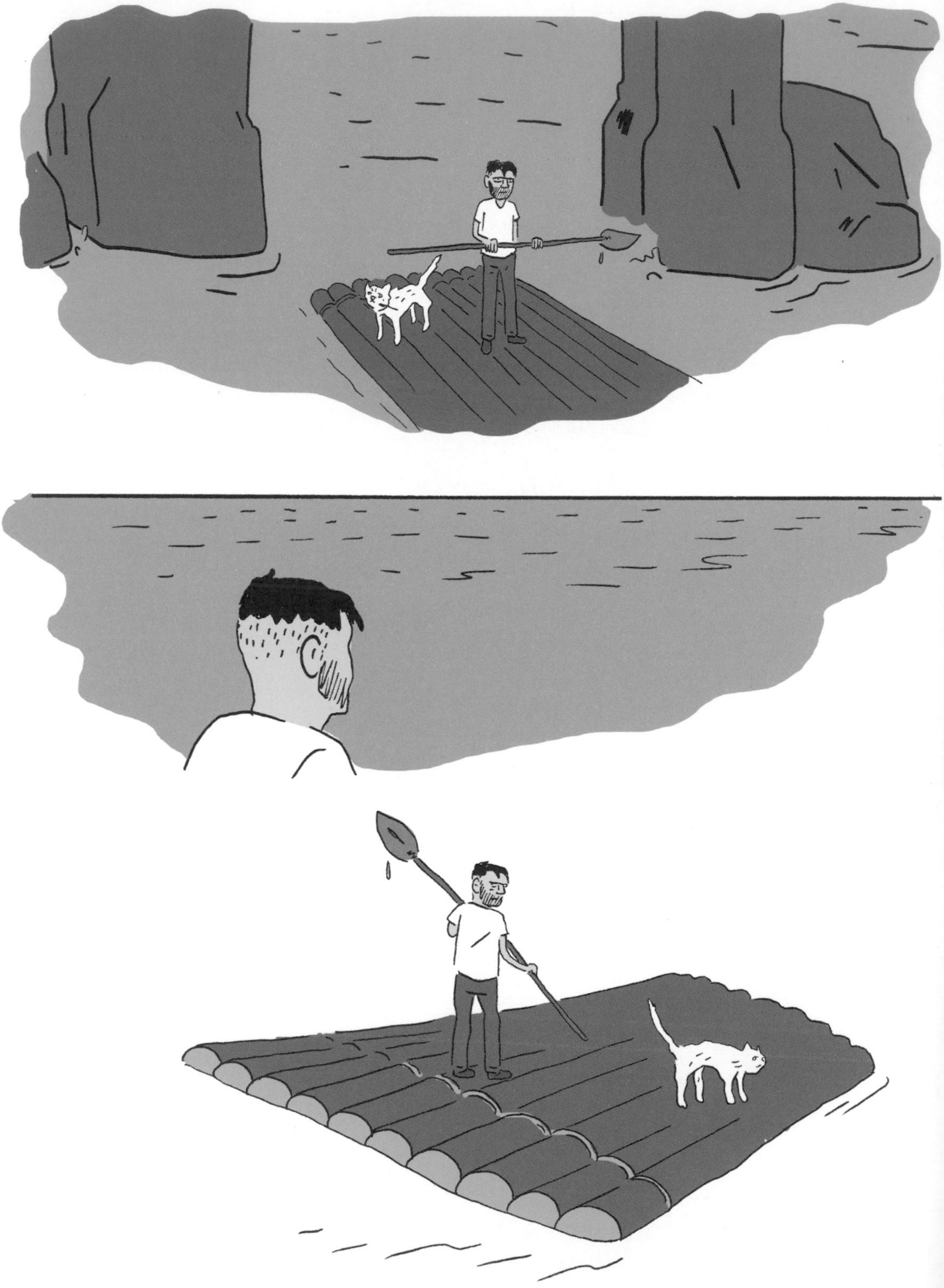

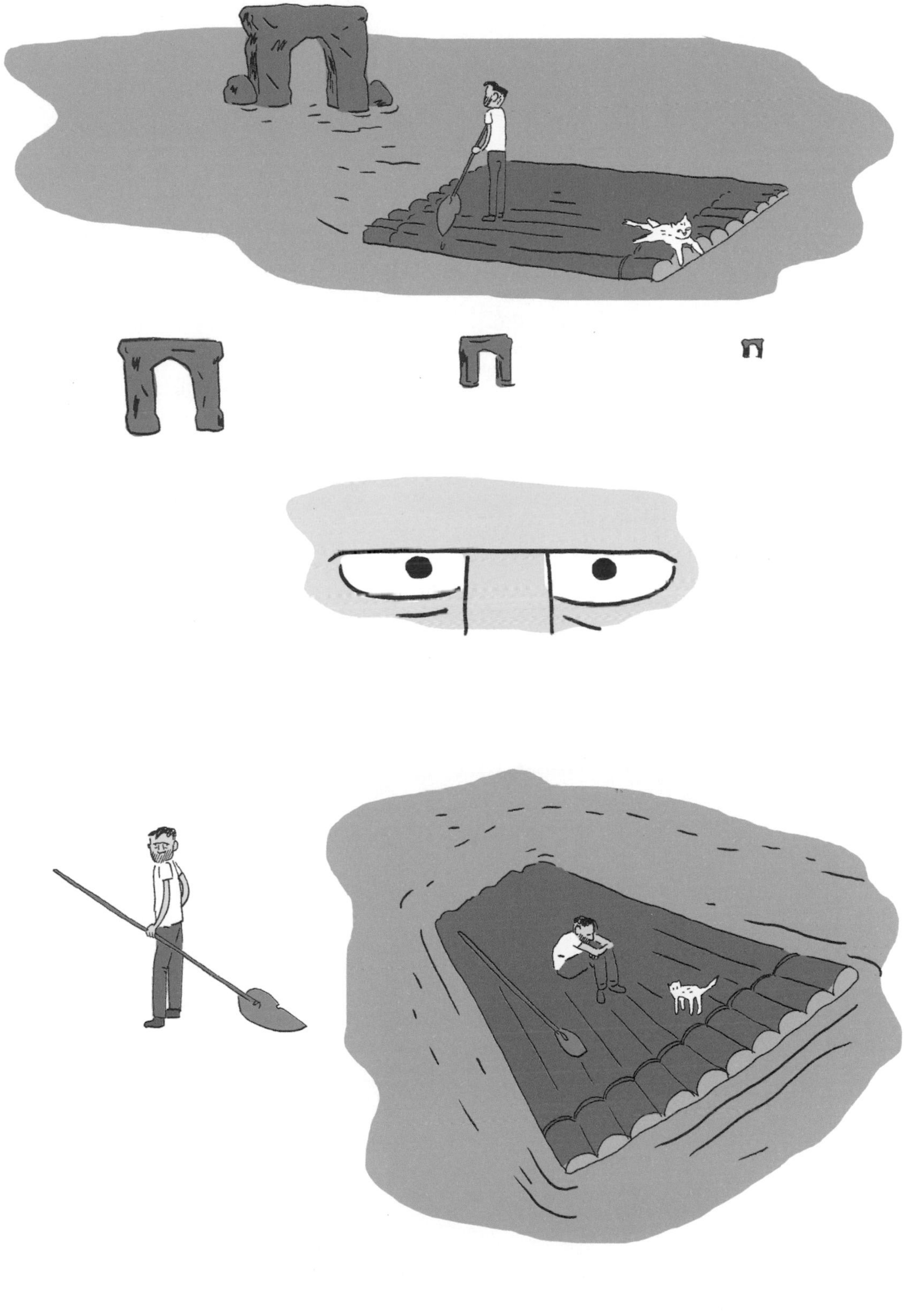

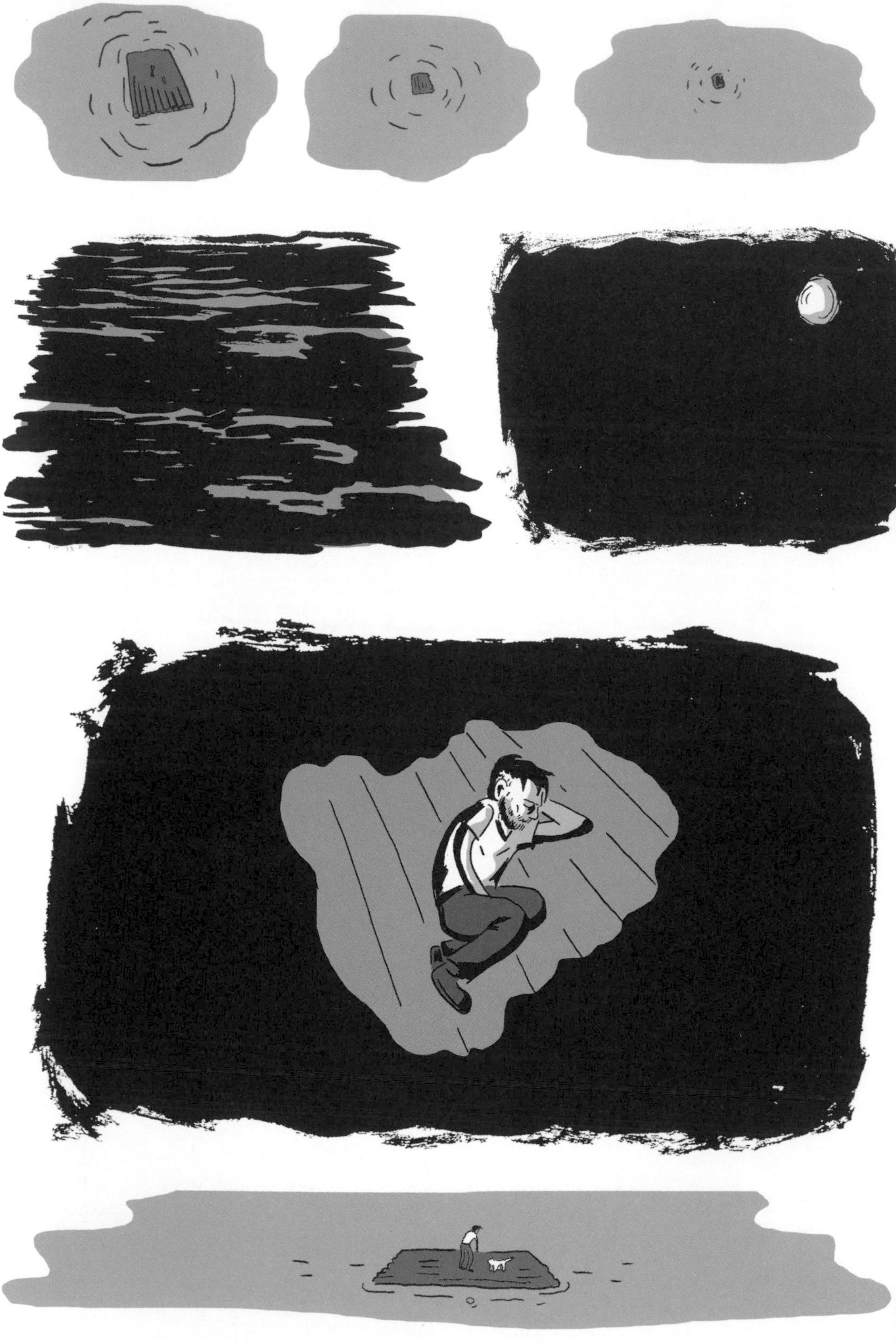

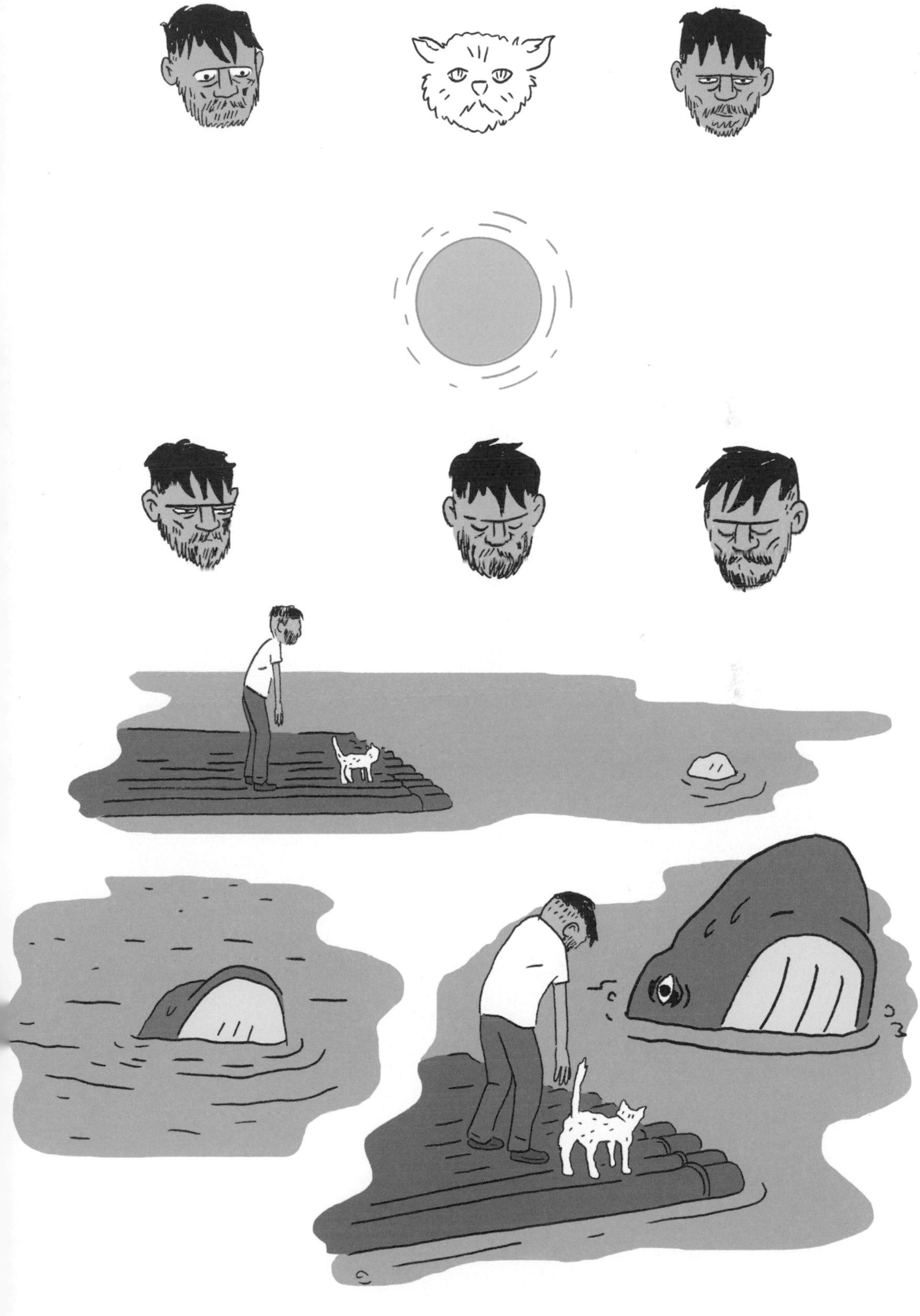

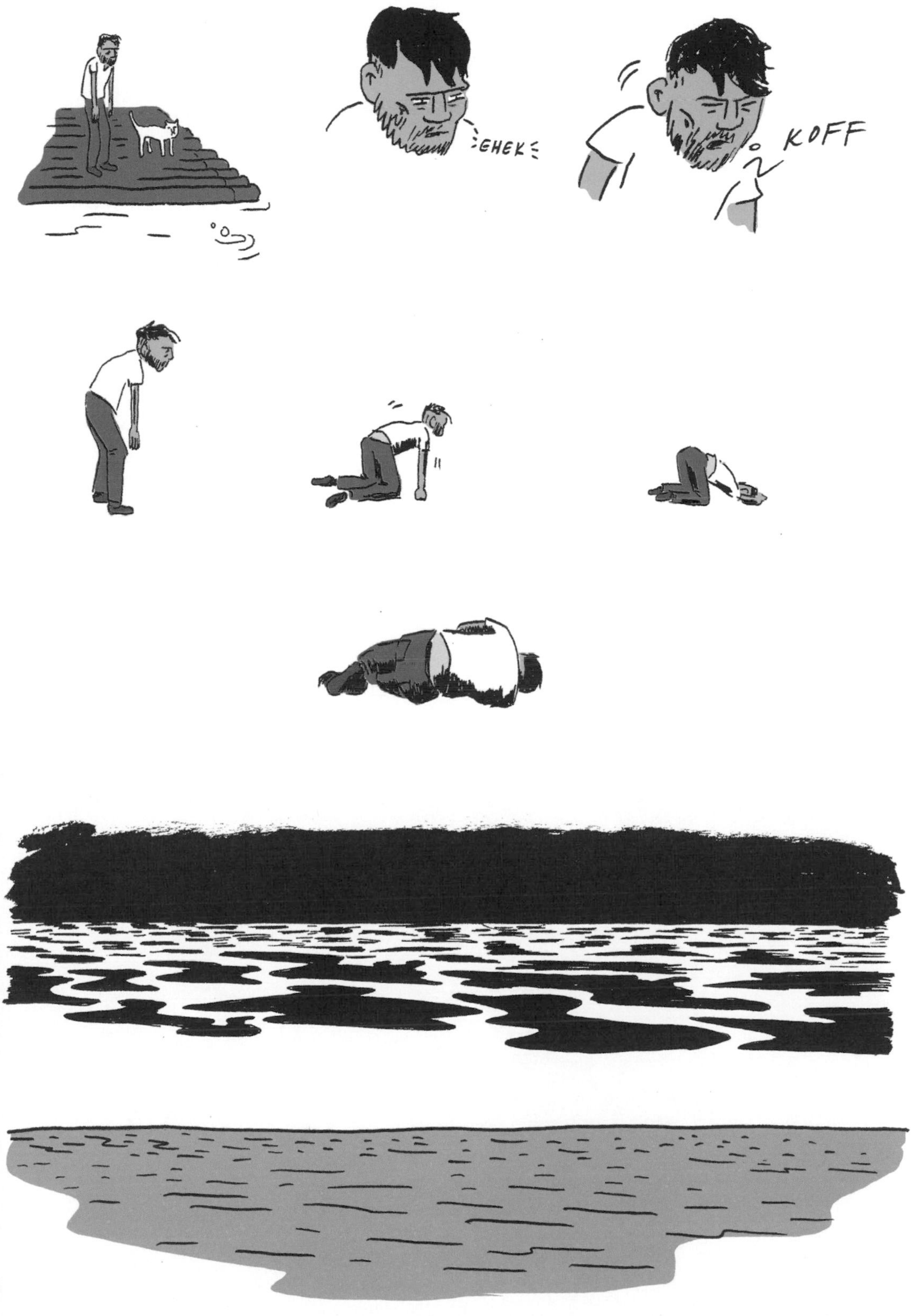
GHEK
KOFF

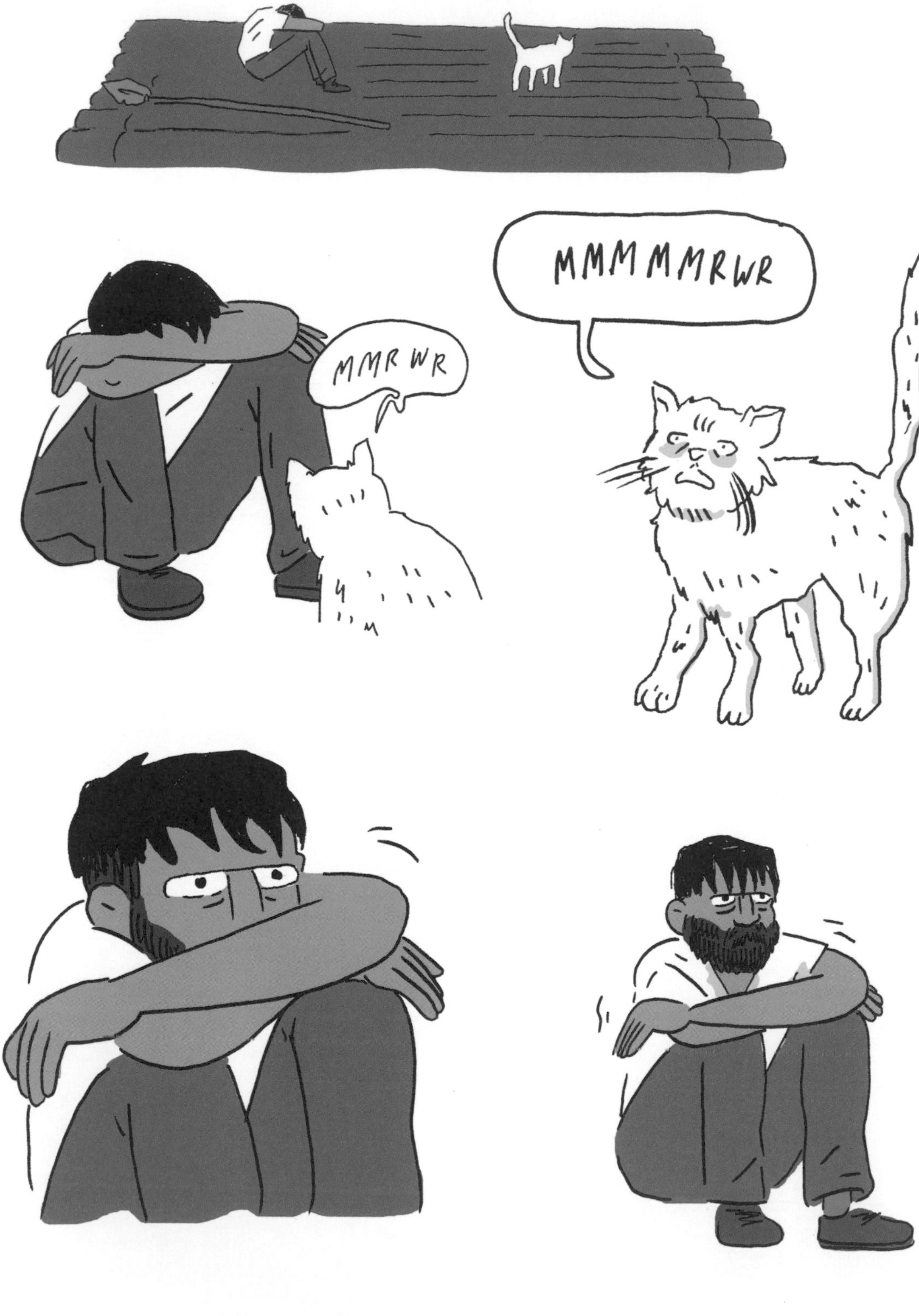
MMRWR
MMMMMRWR

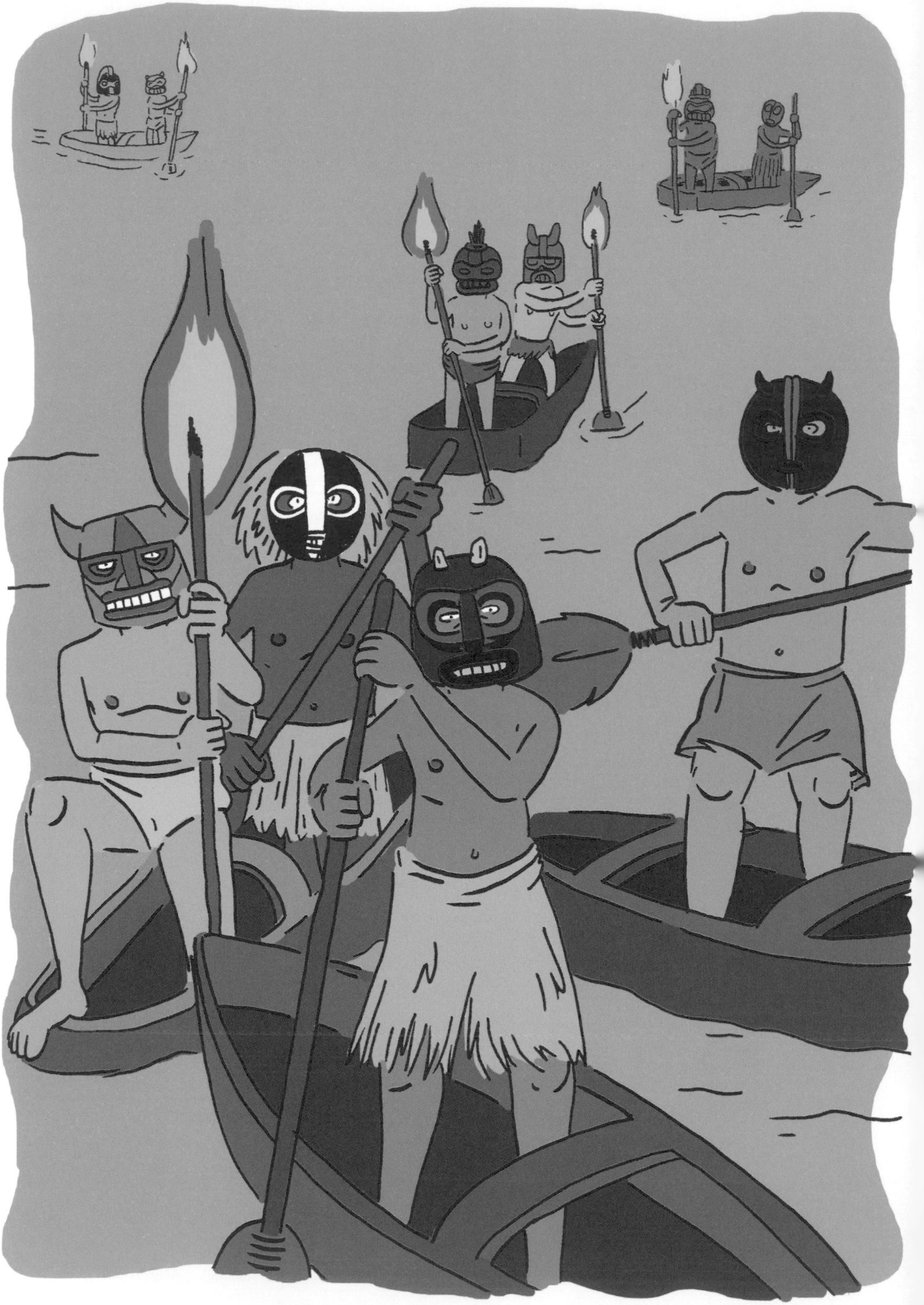

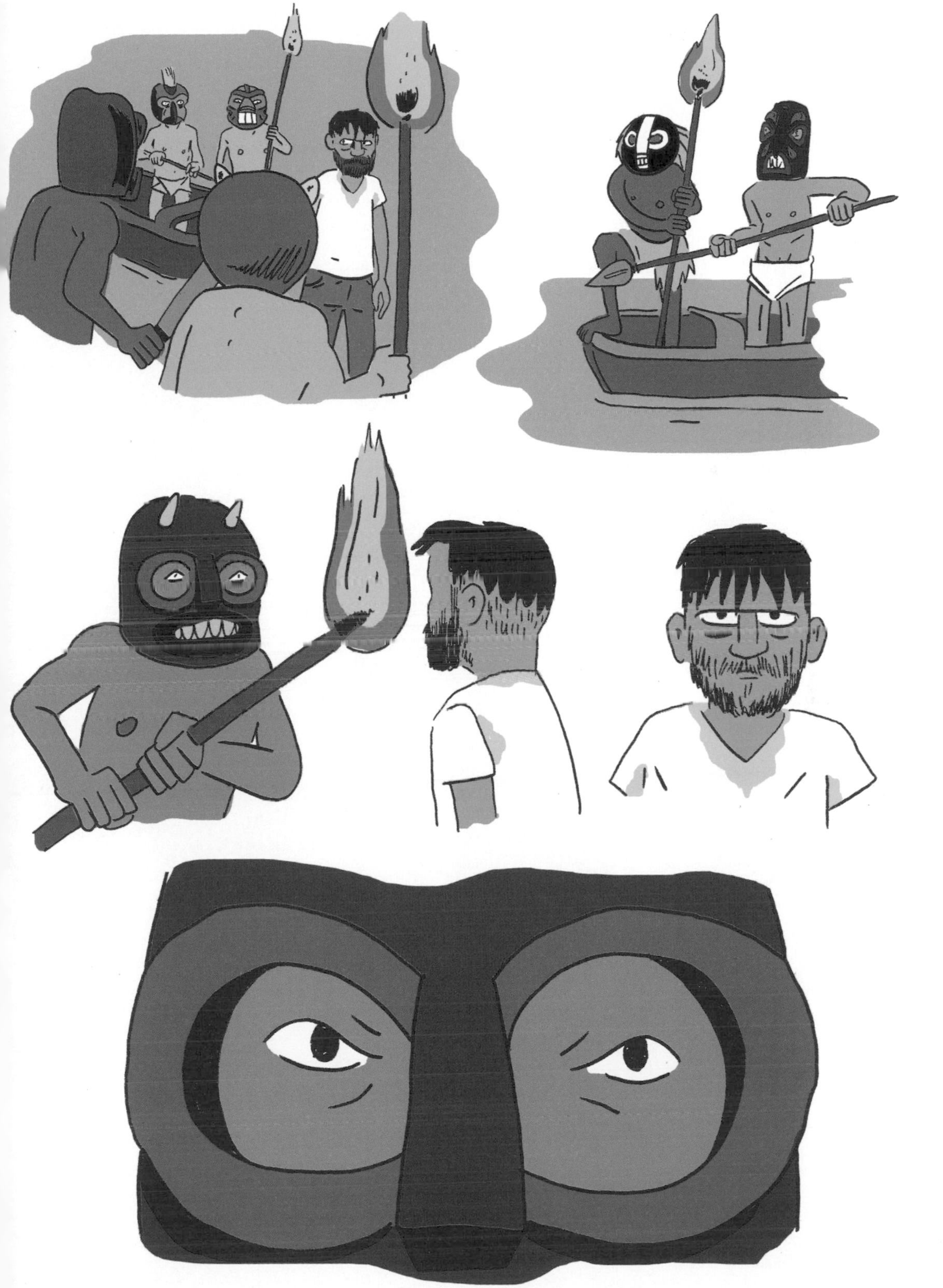

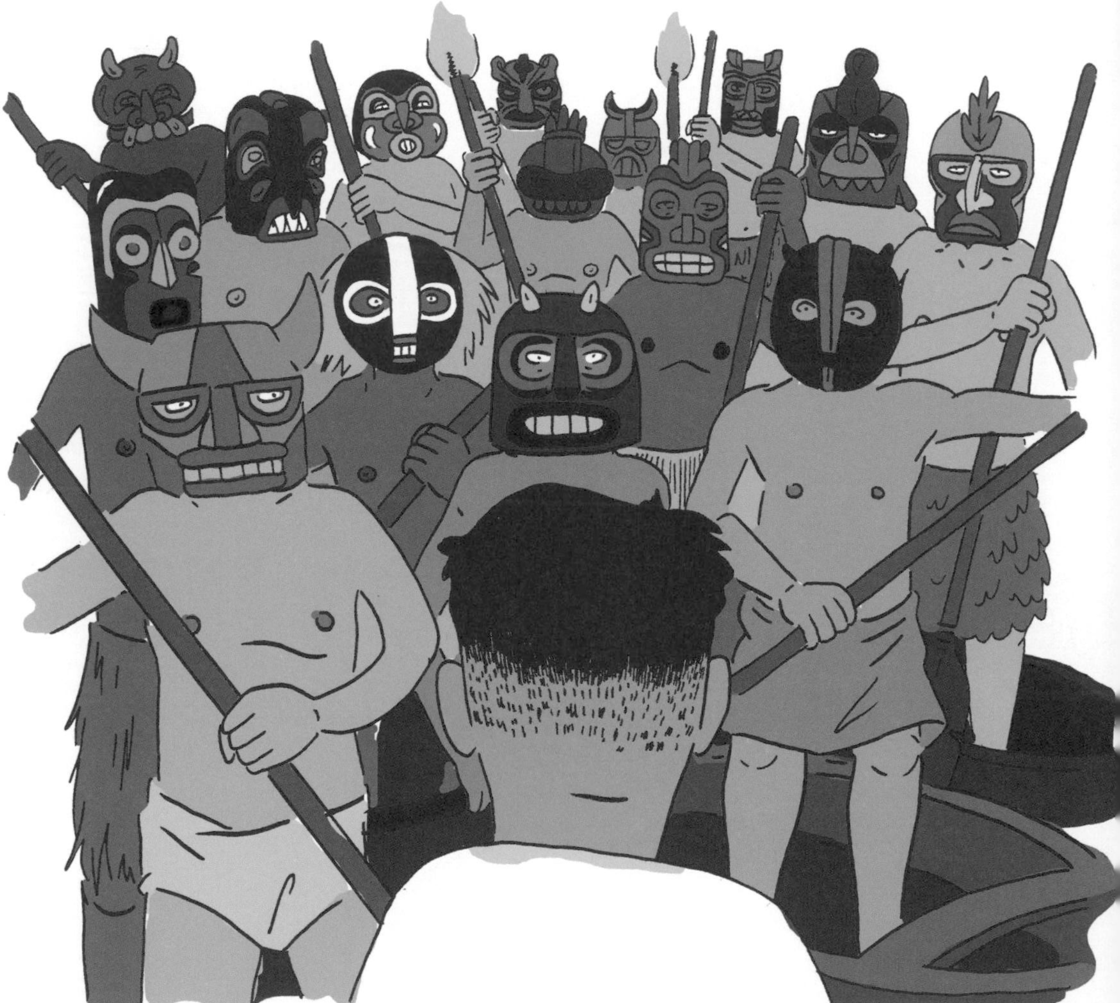

THANK YOU JOLIE MAYERS, CHRIS JACOBSON, VIOLAINE HUISMAN, DANTE HARPER, ANNA STEIN, DIANE BRESSLER, MATTHEW THURBER, GABRIELLE BELL, VANESSA DAVIS, CLAIRE FRISBIE, MOM AND DAD

EXTRA GRATITUDE TO ANYA DAVIDSON
FOR BELIEVING IN THIS BOOK
AND HELPING TO PUT IT IN THE WORLD